ISLAM

George W. Braswell, Jr.

ISLAM

Its Prophet, Peoples, Politics and Power

BROADMAN
& HOLMAN
PUBLISHERS

Nashville, Tennessee

4211-69
0-8054-1169-0

Dewey Decimal Classification: 297
Subject Heading: Islam
Library of Congress Card Catalog Number: 95-44451
Acquisitions and Development Editor: John Landers
Page Design and Typography: TF Designs, Mt. Juliet, Tennessee

Unless otherwise stated all Scripture citations are from the King James Version. Citations from the Qur'an are from *The Meaning of the Holy Qur'an: New Edition with Revised Translation and Commentary.* Brentwood, Md.: Amana Corporation, 1993, used by permission.

Library of Congress Cataloging-in-Publication Data

Braswell, George W.
    Islam: its prophet, peoples, politics, and power / George W. Braswell, Jr.
      p. cm.
    Includes bibliographical references and index
    ISBN 0-8054-1169-0
    1. Islam. 2. Islam—Relations—Christianity. 3. Christianity and other religions—Islam. I. Title.
    BP161.2.B731996
    297—dc20   95-44451
                                                          CIP

2 3 4 5 6 01 00 99 98 97 96

CONTENTS

Preface xi

1. **Understanding Islam** 1
   Stereotypes 1
   Another View 2
   Religion in Context 3
   Twenty Questions 4

2. **The Prophet Muhammad: The Man and His Mission** 7
   Mecca 8
   Muhammad: The Prophet of Islam 10
   The Hegira: Flight from Mecca to Medina 14
   Establishment of Theocracy in Mecca: Muhammad's Death . . 1
   The Legacy of Muhammad . . . .

3. **The Expansion of Islam** . . . .
   Four Caliphs (632–661) . . . .
   Umayyad Caliphate (661–750): Spain to India . . . .
   Abbasid Caliphate (750-1517) . . . .
      Renaissance of Islamic Art, Literature, Science, Medicine
      Fatimid Dynasty and Cairo and Other Rulers

Birth Control and Contraception 134
Abortion 136
Homosexuality 138
AIDS 139
Euthanasia and Suicide 141
War and Peace 142
The Role of Women 148
Human Rights 156
Islamic Fundamentalism 158

9   Global Islam 165
Muslim Regions, Peoples, Leaders

Middle East 168
    Saudi Arabia
    Jordan
    Iran
    Iraq
    Israel
    Lebanon
    Syria
    Turkey
    Palestine Liberation Organization (PLO)
North Africa and Sub-Sahara Africa 184
    Egypt
    Libya
    Morocco
    Tunisia
    Algeria
    Nigeria
    Sudan
Far East and South Asia 194
    Indonesia
    Malaysia
    Philippines
    Brunei (Brunei Darussalam)
    India
    Pakistan
    Afghanistan
    People's Republic of China
Russia and the Commonwealth of Independent States 201
    Azerbaijan
    Kazakhstan
    Kyrgyzstan
    Tajikistan
    Turkmenistan

Uzbekistan
Russia
Europe 204
Albania
Yugoslavia
France
Germany
England

10.   Muslims in America: A Growing Religion **207**
Introduction 207
Immigrant Muslims: Transitional Muslims and Citizens 210
Four Waves of Immigration
Muslim Organizations
Nativistic Islam I: Small Groups 214
Noble Drew Ali and the Moorish Science Temple of America
The Ahmadiyya Community of North America
Ansaru Allah
The Nubian Islamic Hebrews
The Hanafi
The Islamic Party of North America
United Submitters International
The American Druze Society
Nativistic Islam II. 219
Nation of Islam with Elijah Muhammad and Malcolm X 220
Origins
Elijah Muhammad
Malcolm X
The Nation of Islam
Elijah and Malcolm X at Odds
Death Takes Malcolm and Elijah
Rise of Wallace and Farrakhan
American Muslim Mission and Wallace Deen Muhammad 228
Wallace Deen Muhammad
Changes in the Nation of Islam
American Muslim Mission
Troubles in the American Muslim Mission
Demise of the American Muslim Mission
The Nation of Islam and Louis Farrakhan 235
Louis Farrakhan: Life with Elijah
Separation from Wallace
Farrakhan's Revival of the Nation of Islam
The Million Man March
Orthodox Islam in America 241
Peoples, Mosques, and Associations
Muslim Beliefs and Practices in America

11. **The Encounter between Islam and Christianity** 247
   Christianity and the Beginnings of Islam. 247
   The Qur'an and Christianity 248
   Christians as People of the Book and as Dhimmis 252
   Christianity Under Early Muslim Rule 253
   Early Muslim Polemics and Apologetics. 254
   Encounters in Medieval Europe and the Crusades. 256
   Toward the Modern Encounter between Islam and Christianity . .
      260
   Missionaries and Orientalists and Islam 262
   Islamic Revival and Resurgence 268
   Muslim-Christian Encounters 272
   Challenges of Islam for Christianity into the
      Twenty-First Century 276
      Christianity's Priority with Islam
      Qur'anic Islam and Christianity
      Jesus: Similarities and Differences in the Qur'an and the Bible
      Folk Islam and Christianity
      Christianity and Islam: Government and Religious Freedom
      Christianity and Islam: Encounters of Change, Conversion, Contextu-
         alization

12. **Islam: Review and Preview** 291
   Review 291
   Ten Major Patterns of Islam. 293
   Responding to the Twenty Questions 294
   Glossary 309
   Notes. 319
   Bibliography 329
   Index. 333

PREFACE

I taught at the Faculty of Islamic Theology of the University of Teheran from 1968 until 1974, preparing men and women as teachers and mosque functionaries. I also taught at Damavand College, a liberal arts college for women. I have been in a hundred mosques, heard thousands of Muslims pray, listened to many sermons by mullahs, visited countless families in their homes in both urban and rural settings, and engaged in hundreds of hours of conversation with Muslim neighbors, friends, and hosts.

Travels have taken me to Morocco, Egypt, Lebanon, Syria, Jordan, Israel, Turkey, Central Asia, and Iran. I have also observed European Islam. For over twenty years I have taken several thousand students to mosques in New York, Washington, Atlanta, and Raleigh for extended conversations with Muslims. Muslim leaders have lectured in my campus classes. In addition to my dissertation on religion and politics in Iran, I have written articles and a previous book on Islam.

Even so, writing a book on Islam is a challenge. Islam is a world religion with fourteen centuries of history and with a billion adherents. I do not write as an insider but as one informed by western civilization and experienced in the Protestant Christian tradition. Yet I write as one who strives for objectivity.

In writing this manuscript, I must express appreciation and gratitude to my wife, Joan, and to my family members. The Braswell family lived in Iran during the late sixties and early seventies. They traveled in the Middle East. The youngest was born in Teheran. They have been most supportive and understanding of the time and distance necessary in this writing project.

Generations of my students, for classroom assignments, have conversed with Muslims, have visited their mosques, and have studied their religion. In discussions they have shared their knowledge of the Islamic religion, their friendships with Muslims, and their encounters and sometimes confrontations with Muslims in theological and faith statements. To all of them I am grateful.

Dr. Braswell in conversation with the Director of the Islamic Center on Mass. Ave., Washington D.C. in front of the Mihrab (prayer niche) inside the Mosque. (A personal photo)

Some of my Muslim friends and acquaintances have furnished information for this writing. I thank them.

I have used the reflections and viewpoints of both Islamic and non-Islamic scholars. However, I must take full responsibility for both the form and the function of the manuscript. I have sought to provide the reader with enough information on the key ideas and behavioral patterns and institutions of Islam to ignite further interest to pursue them in the footnotes and bibliography.

I have attempted to be consistent in transliterating Islamic terms. Quotes from the Qur'an are taken from Abdullah Yusuf Ali's *The Holy Qur'an*, New Revised Edition, compliments of Al Rajhi Company for Commerce and Industry, and published by Amana Corporation.

1

UNDERSTANDING ISLAM

STEREOTYPES

Western mass media have presented Islam and Muslims in various images and stereotypes. As a result, the majority of people think that most Muslims live in the Middle East. Few know that the largest Muslim populated nation is Indonesia in Southeast Asia and that tens of millions of Muslims live in Central Asia, China, and India. Few know that there are more Muslims in Great Britain than Methodists; that France is ten percent Muslim; that there are more Muslims than Episcopalians in the United States.

Some may think that the Nation of Islam in the United States is representative of worldwide Islam, whereas the Nation of Islam is not acceptable among most orthodox Muslims. The casual observer does not know that Islam is an expanding world religion present on all continents and within many populations.

According to a stereotype, all Arabs are Muslims, but millions of Arabs are Christians. Iranian Muslims are from Indo-European stock while Arab Muslims and Jews are from Semitic stock. Iranian Shi'ite Muslims may have more in common with Iraqi Shi'ite Muslims than with Iraqi Sunni Muslims or Saudi Arabian Sunni Muslims.

According to popular conception, early Muslims have been presented as militant warriors from the hinterland of Arabia. Westerners know little of the excellence of medieval Islam's art, science, literature, medicine, architecture, and urban development. While Christian Europe languished in the dark ages, the Muslim Middle East excelled in the fineries of civilization.

There are searing memories among Muslims of the Western crusaders of the medieval ages who came from Christianized Europe to liberate Palestine from the Muslims. The holy wars of Christianity against the Muslims have been compared with the holy wars of Muslims against the West. Images of war, bloodletting, and vicious atrocities have been presented in the name of religion, both in Christianity and Islam.

Recent history brings up vivid images to westerners: the oil embargo, the Persian Gulf War, airline hijackers, militia groups such as Mujahidin and Hamas. The Ayatollah Khomeini of Iran became known as the archetypal Islamic fundamentalist as he hurled the term "Great Satan" against the United States. The bombers of the World Trade Center building in New York City were depicted as radical Islamic fundamentalists. Some Muslim groups blow up embassies, bomb mosques, explode car bombs in crowded streets, and murder diplomats, and those groups claim credit for the violence and brutality in which innocent women and children often are killed. What does all this mean for Islamic belief and practice?

Thus, images and stereotypes about Islam float around in the public domain, fueled by events and reported by the media. The reader needs to make sense of the realities behind and beyond these images.

ANOTHER VIEW

Other images should also inform us. Former President Sadat of Egypt, leader of a predominantly Muslim nation, made peace with his neighbor, Israel. King Hussein of Jordan signed a peace accord with Israel. During the Persian Gulf War Islamic nations such as Egypt, Syria, Saudi Arabia, and others joined with Western nations to fight against Iraq. President Saddam Hussein of Iraq had declared a Muslim holy war against the West as he invaded a neighboring Muslim nation, Kuwait.

Across the world, Muslims live beside non-Muslim neighbors. Their children attend school together. They work together. They share in community events together. Muslim medical doctors treat non-Muslim patients. Images of Muslims and non-Muslims living out their lives together seldom find a place in media presentations. There are about one billion Muslims. Most of them live peaceful lives, removed from the violent happenings of the headlines. What do they themselves think about and feel toward the reporting of their religion as it is so often depicted in extreme behavior? I hope these pages will give insights into the nature and function of the religion called Islam and the people called Muslims.

RELIGION IN CONTEXT

The study of Islam is the study of a religion. Religion means different things to people. Clifford Geertz has written seminal books on religion in general and on Islam in particular. He studies religion as a system of meanings embodied in symbols. These symbols compose the religion proper and are related to the socio-structural and psychological processes of a society. Symbols serve to synthesize a people's worldview and a people's ethos.

Geertz then sees religion as a socially available system of significance, including beliefs, rites, and meaningful objects, in terms of which subjective life is ordered and outward behavior guided. In *Islam Observed*, Geertz compares the Islam of Indonesia with that of Morocco. Orthodox and popular Islam are seen in their cultural diversities and myriad forms.[1]

William Cantwell Smith, a world-renowned specialist in Islamic studies, has written that the use of the word *religion* is a Western concept. He has attempted to replace it with the terms *faith* and *cumulative tradition*. By *cumulative tradition* Smith means the mass of overt historical data such as creeds, codes, and cults that have nourished and continue to influence the faith of individuals. By *faith* he means an inner religious experience or involvement of an individual; faith is what one feels and the way one lives when one encounters "transcendence."[2]

Several writers present their studies of religion in various categories or typologies. W. Richard Comstock writes of five methodological perspectives on religion: the psychological, the sociological, the historical, the phenomenological, and the hermeneutical. Ninian Smart describes six dimensions of religion: the experiential, the mythic, the doctrinal, the ethical, the ritual, and the social.

Robert S. Ellwood Jr. presents a schema of religion that includes the self, history, psychology, symbol and rite, sociology, and truth and conceptional expression. Gary L. Comstock presents seven features of religion: cultus, creed, the uncanny, community, code, course, and character.

These writers study Islam in the categories that they have discreetly singled out. Thus, in a scholarly pursuit religion becomes an observed entity with the study of words, beliefs, rituals, feelings, behavior, and community action. On the other hand, William Cantwell Smith draws attention to the personal, private, subjective side of religion that often is difficult to observe and to measure.

Webster's Third New International Dictionary defines religion as "the personal commitment to and serving of God or a god with worshipful devotion, conduct in accord with divine commands, esp. as found in accepted sacred writings or declared by authoritative teachers, a way of life recognized as incumbent on true believers, and typically the relating of oneself to an organized body of believers." A short, practical definition of religion is that religion is that part of some people's lives that involves rituals, beliefs, organizations, ethical values, historical traditions, and personal habits and choices, some of which refer to the transcendent.

The reader may use some if not all of the categories these writers have used to study religion in general and Islam in particular. Islam is a religion with a transcendent God, Allah, with stated beliefs and creeds, with various rituals and ceremonies, with a system of law for all of life, and with ethical norms for governing behavior. Islam also includes a personal and devotional side to religion within and beyond the rituals of prayer and pilgrimage. It is a religion of revelation, reason, faith, and faithfulness.

TWENTY QUESTIONS

The following questions and challenges are constantly voiced today about the religion Islam and the people called Muslims:

1. What was the relationship of the worldview of the prophet Muhammad to the Judaism and Christianity of his time?

2. Where did Muhammad gain his information about Abraham, Moses, Jesus, the Bible? Was it from Allah, angels, his travels, Jews and Christians of his time?

3. What are the grounds for the Muslim belief that Jesus did not die on a cross when history and historians confirm it?

4. In the one hundred years after the death of Muhammad, how did Islam advance so rapidly and so far into the Middle East, North Africa, Spain, Persia, and India? Was it by holy warfare *(jihad)*? Did people voluntarily accept Islam or were they coerced?

5. During the Dark Ages of Christianized Europe, what was the greatness of Islamic civilization and why? What were the advances in Islamic science, art, medicine, culture? Why were they more advanced than in Europe? What was the genius of Damascus and Baghdad and Cairo?

6. How have the Christian crusades influenced the Islamic world? What did Christians do to Muslims? What did Muslims do to Christians? Why have the Muslims never forgotten?

7. Why have the words *terrorist* and *militant* been associated with Muslims in the mass media? What kind of Muslim groups accept responsibility for violent acts? Do the teachings of the Qur'an and Islamic tradition justify these acts?

8. How does Islam perceive itself in relation to other religions? What is this perception when and where Islam is the dominant religion? What is this perception when and where it is one among other religions in a religiously pluralistic society? Does Islam allow freedom of religion and religious liberty? What does Islam mean when it says there is no compulsion in religion? Do Muslims believe Islam is the only true religion and all others are false? Can a Muslim become a Jew or Christian or Hindu without persecution from Islam?

9. What is the meaning of political Islam and religious Islam and what are differences between them, if any? Is Islam a theocratic religion? In Islamic political philosophy, is the Qur'an the constitution for law and order in the society?

10. Is one born a Muslim? How does this affect one's citizenship and one's religion? How does one become a Muslim: by birthright, by conversion, by adoption? Once a Muslim, is one always a Muslim? In a Muslim nation can a non-Muslim serve in the military or marry a Muslim or be a bonafide citizen?

11. When a spokesman for Hezbollah *(party of God)* speaks, what authority does he have in relation to Islam? Does he represent Allah? Islam? a few Muslims? an Islamic nation?

12. In a world of nation states, how does Islam address the issues of theocracy, separation of church and state, religion and politics, and freedom of religion? Why did Ayatollah Khomeini call for returning to the Constitution of Medina?

13. What religious, political, and cultural meanings does Islam attach to the city of Jerusalem and to the land of Palestine? Is Jerusalem an object of jihad *(holy war)*? What is the meaning of Jerusalem compared to Mecca and Medina? Why does Islam bar non-Muslims from the city of Mecca? If Muslims controlled Jerusalem, would they allow non-Muslims inside?

14. What is jihad *(holy war)* according to the teachings of the Qur'an and to Islamic tradition? Who can declare jihad officially? What are

the criteria for jihad? Why does one Muslim leader declare jihad against another Muslim leader?

15. What are Islamic views on sexuality, gender roles, and marriage and family life? Does Islam speak with one voice on these matters? Are there differences between Qur'anic Islam and Folk Islam on these subjects? Are Muslim women required to wear a veil? Can a Muslim have several wives? What does Islam teach about the role of women in family and in society, about divorce, homosexuality, abortion, contraception, polygamy, AIDS, and suicide?

16. What is appropriate and taboo in greeting Muslims? A handshake? Words? Why does Islam prohibit accepting interest on loans? Do Muslims use contracts in business deals or is their word enough?

17. What legitimizes a Muslim group among other Muslim groups? How do various groups of Muslims relate to each other? Can one group declare jihad against another? Why do Sunnis fight Shi'ites? Iraqis fight Iranians? Muslim nations fight Iraq? What are the similarities, differences, and relationships among these groups: Sunni, Shi'ite, Sufi, Ahmadiyya, Nation of Islam, Hamas, Hezbollah, Palestine Liberation Organization, Alawite, and Wahhabis.

18. Various leaders of Islamic nations or Muslim groups often speak in the name of Islam. Is one more legitimate or acceptable than the others? How have Islamic traditions related to the following: King Hussein of Jordan, President Saddam Hussein of Iraq, President Assad of Syria, President Mubarek of Egypt, King Fahd of Saudi Arabia, Ayatollah Khomeini of Iran, President Rafsanjani of Iran, Yasser Arafat, Wallace Deen Muhammad, and Louis Farrakhan?

19. Why did Muslims come to America? Who are "Black Muslims," about whom one reads in the press? What do Elijah Muhammad, Wallace D. Muhammad, Malcolm X, and Louis Farrakhan have in common and/or what are their differences? What is the meaning for American society and religions in America when scholars say Islam will be the second largest religion in America in the near future?

20. What—if any—challenges do Muslims face in the United States? What are Muslims' strengths and weaknesses? How is Islam in America related to worldwide Islam?

This book investigates these questions. A postscript after the last chapter returns to these twenty broad concerns and attempts to outline some of the findings.

2

THE PROPHET MUHAMMAD:
THE MAN AND HIS MISSION

I slam arose in the seventh century in and around the desert-oasis complex of Mecca and Medina in the Arabian peninsula. It began among the nomadic peoples of the plains, the agriculturalists in and around the oasis, and the merchants and traders of the towns. Mecca and Medina were characterized by patrilineal tribal alliances, by animistic and agricultural orientations, by social control, and by blood revenge.[1]

The Arabian peninsula was bordered on the east by the Sassanian Persian Empire and on the west by the Byzantine Empire. The Persians were officially Zoroastrians; the Byzantines were Eastern Orthodox Christians. The Byzantine Christians not only had territorial conflict with the Persians but also theological controversy and divisions with the Roman Catholic papacy in Rome. Heresies were declared, leaders were excommunicated, and there was division in the Church. A major controversy centered on Christology, teaching on the human and divine natures of Christ. Tribes of the Arabian peninsula were exposed to both Persians and Byzantines as their trading expeditions visited Damascus and other cities of the Levant and Mesopotamia.

Jewish and Christian populations in the peninsula were sparse. Because there were trade routes into Arabia as well as Arab traders

plying their wares beyond, there was opportunity for exchange of ideas and cultures. With land disputes between empires and with religious controversy within the Church, the Arabian peninsula around the year A.D. 625 appeared ready for transition and change.

W. Montgomery Watt identifies six factors that contributed to the emergence of Islam:

- social unrest in Mecca, Medina, and their environs
- an emerging movement toward monotheism
- a reaction against the Hellenism in Syria and Egypt
- decline of the Persian and Byzantine Empires
- opportunities for Arab nomads to plunder neighboring lands
- Muhammad: the prophet, reformer, administrator, and political strategist [2]

MECCA

The three cities of Mecca, Medina, and Jerusalem are crucial to the beliefs and practices of Muslims.[3] For Muslims worldwide, the city of Mecca is the central place of pilgrimage to the birthplace of their Prophet Muhammad and to the Ka'ba, which he transformed into the symbol of his monotheistic faith. Pious Muslims face the direction of Mecca five times daily in their prayers.

Medina is the city north of Mecca to which he emigrated in the year 622 and in which he first established his theocratic community. The Mosque of the Prophet and his tomb are located in Medina.

Jerusalem is the present location of the Dome of the Rock, where Muslims believe that Muhammad visited heaven during his lifetime and returned to describe its environs. Tradition also associates the Rock with Abraham and his son Ishmael.

Mecca at the time of Muhammad was the major trading town in the Hejaz region. Today it is about seventy-two kilometers from the Red Sea port of Jidda. It is the most sacred and remembered city of Islam. Not only is it the birthplace of Muhammad and the place where he received his visions, but it also contains the Masjid al-Haram *(the Great Mosque)* within which is the Ka'ba.

The Ka'ba, known as the bayt Allah *(house of God)*, is situated in the center of the Great Mosque. Several traditions are associated with it. A Black Stone is in its eastern corner and is connected to the supernatural

CHRONOLOGY OF ISLAM

0	500	750	1000	1250	1500	1750	2000

1. Environment of Pre-Islamic Arabian Peninsula
Tribalism, Animism, Polytheism
Byzantine and Persian Empires
Christian and Jewish
Influences in Peninsula

2. Muhammad the Prophet (570-632 A.D.)
Born in Mecca; Married Khadijah 595;
Revelations began 610;
Flight to Medina 622;
Mecca recaptured 629

3. Early Caliphs (632-661)
Abu Bakr, Omar, Uthman, Ali
Expansion into Palestine, North Africa, Persia

4. Umayyad Caliphate (661-750)
Damascus headquarters;
expansion into Spain and India
Husein son of Ali killed at Kabala 680; Sunni-Shi'ite split widened

5. Abbasid Caliphate (750-1258)
Baghdad; Islamic Renaissance in Literature, Art, Science, Medicine
European Crusades 11th through 13th Centuries;
Turkish invasions

6. Fragmentation of Islamic Lands (1258-1517)
Seljuk, Mamluk, Mongol Turk invasions;
Constantinople captured 1453
Muslims expelled from Spain 1492

7. Ottoman Empire (1517-1924)
Ottoman Turks headquartered in Constantinople
Persian with Safavid Dynasty of Shahs and Shi'ite Islam
Napoleon invades Egypt 1798;
European Colonization/Support of Rulers
World War I; End of Empire
Ataturk: Father of Modernization in Turkey; Secularism's influence over Islam

8. Islam In the 20th Century
Nationalism in Islamic Countries; Shah of Iran's Secularism of Islam
Islam and Zionism and Palestine and Jerusalem
Islam and Economics of Petroleum
Rise of "Islamic Fundamentalism" with Ayatollah Khomeini in Iran
Islamic Expansion and Revitalization in Europe, the Americas, Central Asia
Factionalism in Islam: Iran-Iraq War; Sunnis versus Shi'ites; Louis Farrakhan's Nation of Islam versus Orthodox Islam
Persian Gulf War with Muslims against Muslims
Islam's Influence in Geopolitics, International Economics and World Cultures

occurrence of a falling meteor. The Ka'ba also housed the spirits venerated by Arab tribes and visiting traders. Those spirits included al-Lat
(the Goddess), al-Uzza *(the Mighty One)*, and al-Manat, representing the
Sun, the planet Venus, and Fortune.

The Ka'ba, once cleansed from its animism, polytheism, and paganism by Muhammad, became the central focus for all Muslims, their
place of pilgrimage and the place toward which they pray. The Qur'an
reports that the foundations of the Ka'ba were built by Abraham and his
son Ishmael.

Today, Mecca has a population of more than 300,000. During the
time of the pilgrimage some two million Muslims visit and perform religious ceremonies there. Mecca is the center of the universe for the faithful. Only Muslims may inhabit and visit the city.

MUHAMMAD: THE PROPHET OF ISLAM

Millions of faithful Muslims repeat the name of Muhammad many
times each day as they recite the Shahada: " La Ilaha illa Allah, Muhammad rasul Allah." Its translation from Arabic is, "There is no deity
except God; Muhammad is the Messenger of God." Muhammad has a
unique role in Islam, for he is the last prophet.[4] Belief in his status as
prophet is second only to belief in the oneness of God. Orthodox Islam
insists, however, that Muhammad was human and had no supernatural
standing.

A Muslim scholar stated the consensus of Islamic opinion by saying
that:

- Muhammad had some extraordinary experiences during his childhood;

- he was exceptionally moral and religiously-inclined;

- he was sent to all humankind with essentially the same religious
  message which was given to earlier prophets;

- his total message is inclusive, complete and is basically good for
  all times and places;

- he was the last prophet sent by Allah.[5]

Three principal sources inform us of the life of Muhammad:

1. Ishaq wrote a eulogistic and reverential biography in Arabic in about
   775.

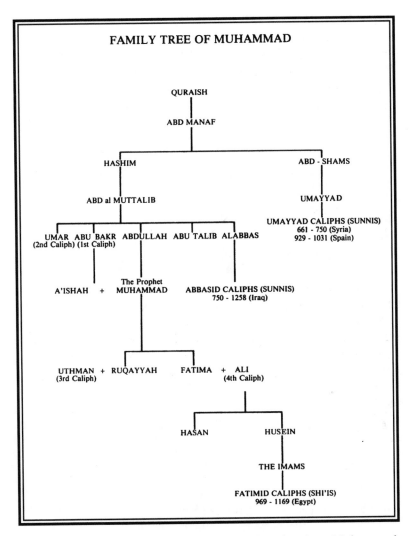

FAMILY TREE OF MUHAMMAD

2. The Hadith, a collection of sayings of and stories about Muhammad, must be evaluated upon the reputation and standing of those who reported the sayings and stories.

3. The Qur'an is not a life of the prophet but discloses a great deal about his thought and action.[6]

Muhammad was born in Mecca around A.D. 570, the year the Persians defeated the Abyssinian Christians and took the Arabian peninsula under their tutelage. Muhammad was the son of Abdullah, son of Abdul-

Muddalib of the clan Hashim of the tribe Quraysh, who were the keepers of the Ka'ba. His father died before his birth, and his mother, Amina, died when he was six. He was raised by his uncle Abu Talib, a traveling merchant. Muhammad often accompanied his uncle to Syria and very possibly to other regions.

Little is known of Muhammad's childhood, though certain stories have circulated. Prophecies indicating his future greatness came from Arab soothsayers, as well as from Jews and Christians. On a trip with his uncle Abu Talib to Syria, a Christian monk, Bohira, foresaw his potential and warned his uncle to protect Muhammad from the Jews.

One tradition says that he was illiterate. Another reports that he was a shepherd boy. Certainly he was without great wealth. About 590, Muhammad was present with his uncle and other tribesmen at the Wicked War, a tribal feud over the control of the Ukaz fair. He was present at the formation of the League of the Virtuous, a commercial alliance formed by the Meccans after the Wicked War.

At age 25 he married Khadija, a wealthy widow who was forty years old. He had worked as her caravan agent in trade with Syria. She provided him economic security and psychological support. They had two sons who died in infancy and four daughters. He supervised her trade caravans and gained new status among the tribal leaders in Mecca.

His increased economic security allowed him more time for leisure and visits to a popular cave at Mount Hira, three miles from Mecca. There he would spend one month each year. At the cave he would wrap himself in a garment, keep night vigils, and repeat the name Allah. Often his family would join him.

The years from 595 to 610 are known as his Silent Period. They are reflected in the Qur'an in dreams,[7] in his commission,[8] and in his calling to rise and warn.[9] In the year 610, at age forty, Muhammad received a vision during the month of Ramadan while at the cave. The angel Gabriel appeared to him and spoke the Arabic word *Iqra*, meaning "read" or "proclaim" or "recite." Muhammad responded that he could not read. Nevertheless, he recited the words of the angel: "Proclaim (or Read!) / In the name / Of thy Lord and Cherisher, / Who created— / Created man, out of / A (mere) clot / Of congealed blood: / Proclaim! And thy Lord / Is Most Bountiful— / He Who taught / (The use of) the Pen— / Taught man that / Which he knew not."[10]

Gabriel was to be the medium of communication between God and Muhammad. These communications or recitations over time were to become the sacred scriptures, the Qur'an. Muhammad questioned his experiences with the angel. He thought that either he was an illiterate poet or that he was under the influence of an evil spirit. Fear and despair came to him. He experienced doubts and contemplated suicide. Khadija reasoned with him that it was an angel, not a devil. Her Christian cousin, Waraqa, compared Muhammad's experience with that of Moses. Encouraged by Khadija and Waraqa, Muhammad accepted his experiences at Mount Hira as a message from God.

A tradition describes the counsel of Waraqah:

> Narrated Aisha: Khadija then accompanied Muhammad to her cousin Waraqa who, during the Pre-Islamic Period became a Christian and used to write with Hebrew letters. He would write from the gospel in Hebrew as much as Allah wished him to write. He was an old man and had lost his eyesight. Khadija said to Waraqa, "Listen to the story of your nephew, O my cousin!" Waraqa asked, "O my nephew! What have you seen?" Allah's Apostle described whatever he had seen. Waraqa said, "This is the same one who keeps the secrets (angel Gabriel) whom Allah had sent to Moses. I wish I were young and could live to the time when your people would turn you out." Allah's Apostle asked, "Will they drive me out?" Waraqa replied in the affirmative and said, "Anyone who came with something similar to what you have brought was treated with hostility; and if I should remain alive till the day when you will be turned out then I would support you strongly."

> But after a few days Waraqa died and the Divine Inspiration was also paused for a while.[11]

From 610 until 622, Muhammad lived in Mecca and continued to receive communications from Gabriel. For three years he was silent. Then, he launched his prophetic mission. He laid out the foundations for Islamic ritual and morality: prayer five times daily with the proper ritual of cleansing with water. He preached against theft and fornication.

His first converts were few: his wife Khadija, his adopted slave son Zayd, his cousin Ali the son of Abu Talib, and his companion Abu Bakr. Abu Bakr was a distinguished merchant and pillar of Mecca. As Muhammad preached his message, he gained other followers and many more detractors.

Muhammad's followers came from other clans. They were under forty years of age and from some of the best families of Mecca. They were impressed with his qualities, with the words of the emerging

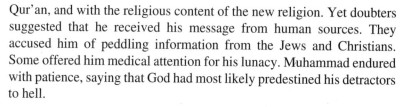

Qur'an, and with the religious content of the new religion. Yet doubters suggested that he received his message from human sources. They accused him of peddling information from the Jews and Christians. Some offered him medical attention for his lunacy. Muhammad endured with patience, saying that God had most likely predestined his detractors to hell.

Most Meccans rejected Muhammad's message when he attacked the idols housed in the Ka'ba. They considered his preachments an economic threat to the commercial traders who visited the Ka'ba and a cultural threat to their way of life.

Others offered to make him king when he later stated that he would allow the pagan deities al-Lat, al-Uzza, and al-Manat a place in his religion.[12] But Muhammad soon changed his mind and dispensed with the other deities, insisting that there is only one God. His insistence on monotheism resulted in his misery in Mecca.

Meccan tribal leaders and his own extended kin began to persecute him. As early as 615 some of his followers fled for refuge to the Christian king of Abyssinia. The last influential Meccan convert was Umar. In 619 Muhammad's wife and his uncle Abu Talib died. During these difficult days Muhammad's uncle Abu-Lahab became head of the clan and refused to protect him. Muhammad married Sawdah, a Muslim widow. He sought refuge in al-Taif but was refused.

At this time Muhammad had a supernatural experience.[13] He was taken by Gabriel to Jerusalem. He met Abraham, Moses, and Jesus and led them in prayer. Afterwards, he was taken to the seven heavens from the famous rock that has become the Dome of the Rock.

Upon his return to Mecca, he preached his message of Islam, or submission, more fervently. It was a call to become a Muslim, which meant one who submits.[14] It was the summons to turn to monotheism and the worship of one God that meant a threat to the polytheism of the Ka'ba.

THE HEGIRA: FLIGHT FROM MECCA TO MEDINA

Twelve men from Medina came to visit Muhammad in Mecca in the year 620. They sought his counsel about their local problems. They became Muslims and returned to Medina. In 622, seventy-three men and three women came to Mecca and met Muhammad at Aqabah. They took an oath to obey Muhammad and to fight for him. This was known as the "Pledge of War" or "The First Pledge of al-Aqabah." As relationships worsened between Muhammad and the leaders of Mecca, he sent most of his followers to Medina, where new Muslim converts provided them lodging. Muhammad, Abu Bakr, and Ali remained in Mecca.

The tribes of Mecca plotted against Muhammad, and each tribe sent a young man to kill him, thereby sharing the blood over the several tribes. A story emerged that Ali took the place of Muhammad in bed, and as the killers approached, he slipped out. All three fled to Medina to be with both the Meccan emigrants and the new Muslim converts.

The most famous date in Islam is the Hegira or Flight to Medina (July 16, 622). On this date, Muhammad fled from Mecca to Medina, some two hundred miles to the north. It is the beginning of the Islamic calendar, 1 A. H., the year of the Hegira or the Flight to Medina. Muhammad and Abu Bakr with the remaining Muslims escaped Mecca. They hid in caves for three nights along the way until they arrived in Medina.

Medina, also known as Yathrib, was very different from Mecca. It was a rich agricultural oasis. Its population included Jewish tribes who had settled among Arab tribes. Medina lacked a central authority, and there was strife among the tribes. Some of the community leaders encouraged Muhammad to come to Medina to settle disputes and establish unity. For Muhammad it was a place to establish his religion, and for the people of Medina it was an opportunity to have a reconciling leader.

Not only was there turmoil between Jewish and Arab tribes, but there also developed distrust between the emigrants *(Muhajirun)* from Mecca and the native helpers *(Ansar)* in Medina. Muhammad attempted to attract the Jews to his leadership. Some accepted him as prophet, but most became hostile to him.

In order to appease the Jews, Muhammad offered Friday as a beginning of the sabbath and the city of Jerusalem as the direction for prayer. When this effort failed, Muhammad selected Mecca toward which to pray and changed the Day of Atonement observance into the month-long fasting season of Ramadan. He adopted Abraham as the patriarch. (Abraham was considered the father of all Arabs, as father of Ishmael through whose lineage Muslims claim descent back to Adam, and as the first and most prominent *hanif*, the obedient one or Muslim).

Muhammad considered Abraham as neither a Jew nor a Christian nor an idolater, but as the model Muslim surrendered to Allah. Consequently, Jews were considered idolaters, were attacked by his warriors, subdued, and required to pay taxes. Muhammad profited from Jewish wealth captured or controlled.

Muhammad developed a document, the Constitution of Medina, which declared the existence of a community of people *(umma)* who looked to Allah and his prophet Muhammad.[15] The Constitution included stipulations about waging war, paying blood ransom, and ransoming captives. The document stated, "Whatever difference or dispute between the parties to this covenant remains unsolved shall be referred to God and to Muhammad, the Prophet of God—may God's peace and blessing be upon him. God is the guarantor of the piety and goodness that is embodied in this covenant."[16]

When the Jews turned against Muhammad, he recited Allah's judgment against them: "Those who conceal / The clear (Signs) We have / Sent down, and the Guidance, / After We have made it / Clear for the People / In the Book—on them / Shall be Allah's curse."[17] Jewish tribes were expelled from Medina. Wars ensued. Jews played little part in Muhammad's umma.

The city of Medina provided the milieu in which Muhammad established his rule over the young Muslim community, a rule based on the injunctions in the Qur'an. Grunebaum points out that Muhammad faced three new questions in founding the umma: how to live correctly; how to think correctly; how to organize correctly.[18]

The character of the umma was based on religious affiliation rather than on tribal blood kinship. The Constitution of Medina recognized God and Muhammad as the center and reference for the people. Muhammad received messages from God as directives for the people. Thus, the early Muslim community was founded on a theocratic polity.

Unbelievers and idolaters were enemies of the community. Muhammad made peace or war. He or his designates collected a tax *(zakat)* from Muslims and provided protection *(jizya)* for non-Muslims. In the raiding expeditions, a fifth of spoils *(khums)* went to Muhammad for public purposes; the rest was divided equally among the warriors.

In Medina, Muhammad built his mosque, formulated into clear principles the revelations given to him by Allah, administered the religio-political, economic, and legal affairs of the Medinians, and counseled the people. He became the prophet, statesman, warrior, and messenger of Allah. He continued to receive revelations, and by the time of his death the entire content of the Qur'an had been revealed. He established the basic rituals of prayer, almsgiving, fasting, and pilgrimage, and he formalized many other laws.

Muhammad has been considered a social reformer.[19] Before his establishment of Islam, the security of life and property was maintained by blood feud and by *lex talionis* of the tribes. He replaced the tribal concept with the umma. He taught that a believer who deliberately kills another believer will pay in hell.

Marriage and family were encouraged. Muhammad advocated a plurality of wives. Those men who had one or two wives were encouraged to marry up to four wives. He did not limit those who already had ten or twelve wives. However, he emphasized that a man must be able to treat all wives with equity. The husband provided his wife a dowry that remained her own. Inheritance was to be shared by both men and women, but males were favored with two shares to every one share of the female.

Muhammad accepted slavery as a fact of life. However, he gave admonitions for the kind treatment of slaves and the possible freeing of them. Usury, the taking of financial interest, was condemned. He had disliked the Jewish practice of lending money with interest. He taught that all believers were brothers and ought to help each other. He prohibited drinking wine. A calendar which regulated religious practice was instigated and was based on the lunar movements and seasons.

By 624 Muhammad had married his youngest wife, Aisha. She was six years old when they married, though he did not consummate the marriage until she was nine. Fatima, his daughter, had married his cousin Ali. An older daughter Ruqayyah had married Uthman, who later become the third caliph. Raids (*razzias*) had begun against Meccan caravans traveling through the area. In the Battle of Badr in 624, Muhammad's warriors defeated a Meccan caravan which ultimately set the stage for his conquest of Mecca. Muhammad saw God's vindication of his leadership in a revelation: "O Prophet! rouse the Believers / To the fight. If there are / Twenty amongst you, patient / And persevering, they will / Vanquish two hundred: if a hundred, / They will vanquish a thousand / Of the Unbelievers: for these / Are a people without understanding."[20] It was also revealed, "It is not ye who / Slew them; it was Allah."[21]

In the battle of Uhad in 625, Muhammad lost to the Meccans near Medina. After a siege of Medina, the Meccans withdrew. He attacked the last Jewish tribe. All men were put to death, and women and children were taken into slavery.

In 626 he married two additional wives who had been widowed by the deaths of their husbands in battle. In 627 he married Zaynab, his cousin, the former wife of Zayd, his adopted slave son.[22] The siege of Medina was begun in 627 by the Meccans, but it proved unsuccessful. The Jews of the Zurayzah were executed for treason. In 628 Muhammad made an abortive pilgrimage to Mecca, but he won concessions by the treaty of al-Hudaybiyah to make a pilgrimage the following year, and peace was instituted.

ESTABLISHMENT OF THEOCRACY IN MECCA: MUHAMMAD'S DEATH

By 630, Muslim armies had taken Mecca. The military and economic strength of Mecca had been in decline. Muhammad cleansed the Ka'ba of pagan deities. Afzal Iqbal reports that Muhammad returned home at the head of a victorious army. The Meccans feared revenge. Muhammad had many enemies. His chief commander said, "Today is the day of war. Sanctuary is no more!"

But Muhammad stood at the door of the Ka'ba and addressed the Meccans who had pleaded for his mercy: "There is no God but Allah alone; He has no associate. He has made good His promise and helped His servant. He has put to flight the confederates alone. Every claim of privilege or blood or property are abolished by me except the custody of the temple and the watering of the pilgrims. . . . O Quraysh, God has taken from you the haughtiness of paganism and its veneration of ancestors. Man springs from Adam and Adam sprang from dust." Then he recited to them, "O men, We created you from male and female and made you into peoples and tribes that you may know one another: of truth the most noble of you in God's sight is the most pious." Then Muhammad asked, "What do you think I am about to do with you?" Then he concluded, "Go! You are relieved; no more responsibility burdens you today; you are the freed ones."[23]

Iqbal writes that Muhammad thus restrained his army from shedding blood. He observes that in comparison with other conquerors Muhammad's treatment of the Meccans was unmatched by a similar act of clemency. "Has any conqueror in history behaved so gently or mercifully with the vanquished foe?"[24]

Muhammad gained the respect of the Meccans, and other tribes joined the community (umma) of Islam. Muslims won the Battle of Hunyan against the nomadic tribes. He led an army of 30,000 against Tabuk. He was bringing Arabia under his dominion at a time when warfare was most intense between the powers of Byzantium and Persia.

At this time his wife, Mariyah, the Copt, bore him a son, Ibrahim, who lived for only a brief time. Thus by the time of his death in 632, Muhammad had led a pilgrimage to Mecca, remembered as the Pilgrimage of Farewell, and thereby established the rites of pilgrimage (hajj).

On June 8, 632, after an illness Muhammad died in Medina. There he is buried in the "city" of the Prophet. He was succeeded by Abu Bakr, the first caliph. Muhammad left nine widows and an Egyptian concubine. Of his children four daughters survived. One daughter, Fatima, had

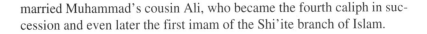

married Muhammad's cousin Ali, who became the fourth caliph in succession and even later the first imam of the Shi'ite branch of Islam.

THE LEGACY OF MUHAMMAD

By the end of his life, Muhammad had emerged as a religious and political leader without equal in the Arabian peninsula. He had founded a monotheistic and prophetic religion that included a basic and straightforward confessional statement, a worldview of one God who sent angels to prophets with a message embedded in a perfect scripture. Islam provided a specific and orderly lifestyle of prayer, fasting, and pilgrimage in the context of the mosque and under the guidance of religious and political authorities. A Muslim was taught to walk the straight path of Allah and thereby attain heaven and avoid hell.

During the last ten years of his life, Muhammad served the Muslim community as prophet, as political and economic leader, and as commander-in-chief of his warriors. He established the umma with such strength that shortly after his death Islam moved quickly beyond the peninsula to claim vast territories and peoples under its banner.

The crescent moon became the symbol on the minarets of mosques and on flags. The mission of Islam had been set. The world was divided into two domains: that world which was to exist under Allah, the teachings of the Qur'an, and the traditions of Muhammad; and that world which was still in ignorance and disobedience and which needed to be brought to submission under Islam. The destiny of Islam, which Muhammad had set, was to extend from Mecca to the moon.

As Islam developed and expanded and mixed with other cultures, views of others toward Muhammad were influenced by a variety of conditions. Unlike orthodox Islam, the emerging popular Islam attributed supernatural qualities to Muhammad. Orthodox Muslims held him to be the last of the prophets with special charisma and gifts but adamantly rejected the tendencies of popular Islam to treat him as divine, as a savior, or as a saint.

Islam, however, associates certain miracles with Muhammad. Ibn Ishaq writes of five of them.[25] The prophet's father was saved from being sacrificed by his own father by the alternate plan of sacrificing a hundred camels after an elaborate ritual of casting lots. The old Christian hermit, Bohira, recognized the prophet while he was still a young child traveling with his uncle on the caravan routes. The prophet overcame the strong man Rukana by supernatural force while a tree moved at his command. The miraculous night journey of the prophet occurred at Jerusalem, where he met with Jesus and Moses and viewed the seven heavens. The waters were restored from the rock at Wadi al-Mushaqqaq on the prophet's return from Labuk.

Islamic traditions have reported sayings about the Prophet's physique, his character, and his own words about his work. "Narrated Anas: Allah's Apostle was the most handsome, most generous, and the bravest of all the people."[26] One tradition describes him: "Narrated Rabi'a Abdur-Rahman: I heard Anas bin Malik describing the Prophet saying, 'He was a medium height amongst the people, neither tall nor short; he had a rose colour, neither absolutely white nor deep brown; his hair was neither completely curly nor quite lank. . . . When he expired, he had scarcely twenty white hairs in his head and beard.' Rabi'a said, 'I saw some of his hair and it was red. When I asked about that, I was told that it turned red because of scent.'"[27]

His lifestyle of scarcity and humility is described: "Narrated Amir bin al-Harith: Allah's Apostle did not leave a Dinar or a Dirham or a male or a female slave. He left only his white mule on which he used to ride, and his weapons, and a piece of land which he gave in charity for the needy travellers."[28]

One tradition gives the Prophet's own words about himself and his status among others:

> Narrated Jabir bin Abdullah: The Prophet said, "I have been given five things which were not given to any one else before me.
>
> 1. Allah made me victorious by awe, (by His frightening my enemies) for a distance of one month's journey.
> 2. The earth has been made for me (and for my followers) a place for praying and a thing to perform Tayammum, therefore anyone of my followers can pray wherever the time of a prayer is due.
> 3. The booty has been made halal (lawful) for me yet it was not lawful for anyone else before me.
> 4. I have been given the right of intercession (on the Day of Resurrection).
> 5. Every Prophet used to be sent to his nation only but I have been sent to all mankind."[29]

As Muhammad neared death, he is reported to have said, "Narrated Aisha: The Prophet said, 'O Allah! Wash away my sins with the water of snow and hail, and cleanse my heart from sins as a white garment is cleansed of filth, and let there be a far distance between me and my sins as You have set far away the East and the West from each other.'"[30]

Other hadiths suggest his concern with forgiveness, sin, and heaven. "Narrated Abu Huraira: I heard Allah's Apostle saying, 'By Allah! I ask for Allah's forgiveness and turn to Him in repentance more than seventy times a day.'"[31] "Narrated Um al-Ala: The Prophet said, "By Allah, though I am the Apostle of Allah, yet I do not know what Allah will do to me.'"[32]

Muhammad condemned the worship of the deceased at shrines. "Narrated Aisha: Um Salma and Um Habiba had been to Ethiopia, and both of them narrated the Church's beauty and the pictures it contained. The Prophet raised his head and said, 'Those are the people who, whenever a pious man dies amongst them, make a place of worship at his grave and then they place those pictures on it. They are the worst creatures in the sight of Allah.'"[33] This Hadith is of great interest in view of popular Islam and its saint worship at tombs and shrines.

Muhammad's death from illness occasioned a crisis in the fledgling Islamic umma. He had established a cohesive community in the ten years since the flight to Medina. Muhammad had become not only the messenger of God but the theocratic ruler. He had functioned as prophet, judge, ruler, counselor, prayer leader, and commander-in-chief of the nascent community.

He had built the mosque in Medina which became known as the Prophet's mosque, established the pilgrimage center in Mecca known as the Ka'ba, unified various tribes under the piety and practice of Islam, and assembled the strongest military force in Arabia, a force that would exert its influence far beyond the borders.

The crisis centered around the leadership of the Islamic community. There could be no other prophet, for Muhammad was the last. But the community needed a leader. The choice of the leader precipitated a division within Islam that continues to the present.

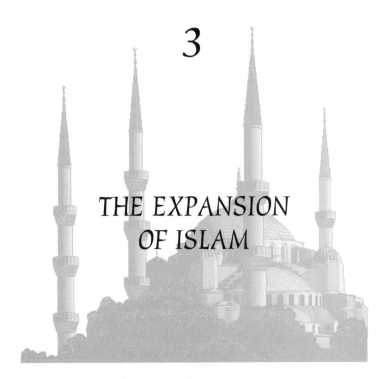

3

THE EXPANSION OF ISLAM

FOUR CALIPHS (632–661)

Caliph means the deputy of the Messenger of Allah. After the first four caliphs (Abu Bakr, Umar, Uthman, and Ali), the title passed to the Umayyads and then to the Abbasids.

Abu Bakr, Umar, Uthman, and Ali served as caliphs during the thirty years after the death of Muhammad. These were the years of the consolidation, growth, and expansion of Islam across North Africa and Persia. During these same years, dissension and conflict began within the Islamic community, including questions of successorship and the Sunni-Shi'ite division.

Abu Bakr, Muhammad's father-in-law, had been one of the first converts to Islam, an intimate friend and counselor of Muhammad. He was named the first caliph (632–634) by consensus of the community. He dealt with rebellious tribes by sending his armies to the east, west, and north of Mecca. He defended the law (*shari'a*) of Islam and organized holy war (*jihad*).

Before he died, Abu Bakr appointed Umar as his successor. The second caliph (634–644) expanded Islam into Syria and Iraq by 638. Muslim armies had taken Jerusalem and its environs and Egypt by 640

MUSLIM EXPANSION (632–711 A.D.)

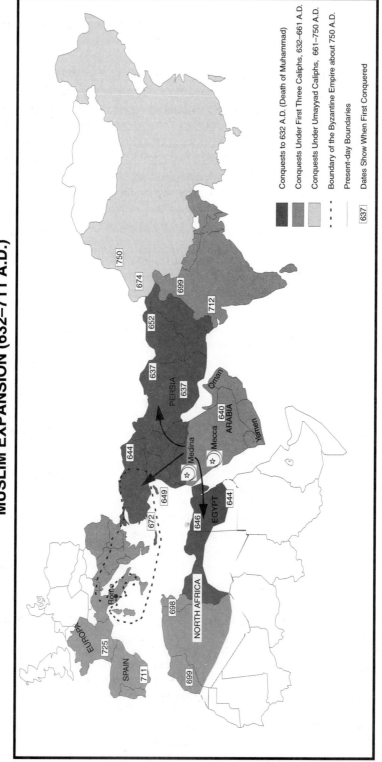

Conquests to 632 A.D. (Death of Muhammad)

Conquests Under First Three Caliphs, 632–661 A.D.

ConquestsU Under Umayyad Caliphs, 661–750 A.D.

Boundary of the Byzantine Empire about 750 A.D.

Present-day Boundaries

637   Dates Show When First Conquered

and parts of Persia by 642. Certain lands became state properties. Jews and Christians were placed under protection of the Islamic state and were required to pay taxes.

In 644 Umar was murdered by a Persian slave. Before his death he had appointed a council of six elders to name his successor. The council chose Uthman, a wealthy Meccan and son-in-law of the Prophet, over Ali. During the caliphate of Uthman (644-656), Islamic armies pushed across North Africa as far as Tunisia by 647, and Persia became a province of the caliphate by 651. Under his rule the Qur'an was codified. Intrigue and dissension revolved around the caliphate. Uthman was killed. His kin were later to establish the Umayyad caliphate.

Ali succeeded Uthman as caliph (656–661). Unrest had resided among the followers of Ali since Muhammad's death, for Ali was not immediately chosen to succeed his father-in-law. Divisions had begun in the *umma*. The Sunni branch (the orthodox or traditionalists) had determined that leadership after the prophet was to be a decision of the community. The Shi'ite branch (followers or partisans to Ali) had insisted that leadership after the prophet be entrusted to a member of the Prophet's family; thus, Ali should have been the successor. Ali was later to be named the first imam and to inaugurate the imamate. The Kharijites, another sect, said that true sovereignty must reside in the faithful umma.

Mu'awiya, the nephew of Uthman and his great general, challenged the legitimacy of Ali's caliphate. A battle ensued between his forces and those of Ali. Ali sought arbitration. The Kharijites seceded from the community, and one of them killed Ali. Schism had begun on a wider scale. Ali had designated his son Hasan to succeed him. However, Mu'awiya forced him out of the caliphate, and tradition reports that Mu'awiya had Hasan poisoned.

The Shi'ites were to grow and were to consider Ali as the first imam of the imamate, as opposed to the caliphate. Ali's two sons, Hasan and Husein, were to become more prominent in Shi'ite history and tradition. Hasan was to become the second imam, and Husein was to be the third imam.

UMAYYAD CALIPHATE (661–750): SPAIN TO INDIA

Mu'awiya became the first of fourteen caliphs of the Umayyad Caliphate. Damascus, Syria was their capital. The period became known for its external conquest. By 664, Islam had expanded from Khorasan to the Indus Valley to Lahore. By 715, it had extended to Chinese

Turkestan, to the Maghrib through Morocco, and to the Berbers in Spain.

Muslim armies had crossed over the Pyrenees from Spain into France. They were stopped by the Christian armies of Charles Martel between Tours and Poitiers in 732. During the first century of Islam, Muslims expanded from the Arabian hinterlands eastward to the edges of China and westward through the Middle East and North Africa into Spain.

The Umayyad rulers relied on their client states to administer their policies. The Umayyad reign was a period of conquest and expansion, a time of empire building, of great wealth, and of family feuding, and a period when worldliness entered official Islam.

Damascus has been described as the oldest continuing city in existence. Damascus under the Umayyads was blessed with beautiful gardens and orchards. From Damascus, Muslims ruled from the Bay of Biscay to the Indus River. Mu'awiya was a ruler of great personal character and ambition. He has been described as having the Arab virtue of Muru'ah or "manliness." He ruled for twenty years with competence and by his own sayings, "I apply not my sword where my lash suffices, nor my lash where my tongue is enough. . . . When men pull, I loosen, when they loosen, I pull."[1]

Two great Islamic structures were built during this period:

1. The Dome of the Rock in Jerusalem was erected by Abd al-Malik on the Temple Mount (about 691), and is considered the third holiest place in Islam, celebrating both the prophet Abraham and the Prophet Muhammad;[2]

2. The Great Mosque of Damascus, the fourth holiest edifice of Islam, built by Walid I (705–715), replaced the great Cathedral Church of St. John and required eighteen camels to carry the expenditure accounts for its construction. It is said that Caliph Walid refused to look at the accounts, saying, "Verily we have spent this for God and will have no accounting of it."

Life in Damascus presented the struggle between the piety of Islam and the extravagances of worldly living. Caliph Walid II (743–744), on the one hand, had the habit of swimming in a pool of wine from which he indulged. On the other hand, Caliph Umar II (717–720) donned old clothes and mixed with commoners as they prayed in the mosque.[3]

Damascus was divided between Arab and non-Arab followers of Islam. The local population had become Muslim with the Arab invasion and did not have equal status with Arabs. Umayyad society also

HOUSE OF GOD

The Muslim legend of the Ka'ba goes like this: When Adam gleaned the will of God, he fell from his place in paradise to a lofty mountain-top in India or Ceylon. Adam was very, very tall—larger than earthly things, and by standing silently on the mountain peak, he could still hear angels singing. The angels were moved by the sight of this sorrowing man and asked God to make him a size proper for his place on earth. God complied with their request and told Adam that it was his task to seek the Divine Throne on earth. Then Adam began his long migration. It took him from Asia Minor to the Hejaz. There he found a basin ringed by huge, black mountains. He recognized this as the navel of the earth, the axis of God's throne. In the middle of the basin stood a canopy supported by four emerald columns and roofed with a giant ruby. Under it lay a luminous white stone. Adam made this place God's temple, and when he died, one of his sons buried the stone with him. A thousand years later Ishmael, the son of Abraham, wandered to the Hejaz. Years afterward his father visited him, and the two decided to build a temple for God. They were directed to the site of Adam's temple, and the stone which had lain buried so long was miraculously brought to them. The temple they built there was the Ka'ba—the one, true House of God.

recruited many black, yellow, and white slaves from the conquered territories.

The first of the great Christian apologists, John of Damascus, was a product of the Umayyad administration. It is reported that John debated in the presence of the caliph. Mosque preaching developed and grew into an art form during this period. It fit with the functions of the great mosques being built.

Husein, the son of Ali and grandson of Muhammad, was killed in battle by the militia of the Umayyads in 680. The Shi'ites had begun their succession to Muhammad by naming Ali as the first imam and his first son, Hasan, the second imam. In fact, Hasan had been proclaimed caliph two days after the death of Ali. Mu'awiya had forced Hasan to abdicate. Hasan was not strong either in morals or in leadership qualities. He retired with his sixty wives to Medina and was later poisoned.

Hasan's brother Husein retired with him to Medina while Mu'awiya reigned. At the death of Hasan, Husein sent his son, Muslim, to Kufa in Iraq to test popular support for his leadership. His son was killed. Husein left for Kufa with his family of some eighty members. Near Kerbala, Iraq, a battle occurred in which the family was brutally slaughtered. The head of Husein was taken to Damascus and presented to Yazid, the son of Mu'awiya, who was reigning. Husein's body was trampled under foot by horses.

The tragedy at Kerbala happened on the tenth day of the month of Muharram. A shrine to Husein at Kerbala is a most important pilgrimage place for Shi'ites. It is said that a pilgrimage to Kerbala to Husein's shrine has the merit of a thousand pilgrimages to Mecca, of a thousand martyrdoms, and of a thousand days of fasting. Shi'ites have developed a passion play to commemorate the tragedy as well as a religious calendar of services especially during the first ten days of the month. The shedding of Husein's blood has become a symbol of his sacrifice and of his vicarious suffering for his people. Husein became the third imam in the Shi'ite chain of twelve imams.

Why was it possible within one hundred years of the Prophet's death for Islam to spread so widely and so quickly? Some have said that it was the fanaticism and brutality of Muslim armies. Holy war, in part, may promote fear and atrocity. Some of that occurred. But Islam also spread for other reasons.

The Byzantine and Persian empires had become exhausted in a long series of wars. Christianity was destabilized by schisms and heresies. Many who lived near the Arabian peninsula hoped the Arabs would bring them stability and peace.

The Islamic Arabs quickly conquered and integrated the new people into their culture. They considered Jews and Christians as People of the Book and granted them special protections and allowed them to maintain their own religious traditions as long as they were peaceable and paid their taxes.

By the end of the Umayyad caliphate, Islam had witnessed tremendous expansion and influence. Though it was to develop its philosophies, law schools, science, art, and architecture, it offered a simple belief system and religious practice. This simplicity may well have attracted many. Islam was now ready to turn its attention to its internal life of developing an Islamic civilization under the Abbasid Caliphs. The Umayyads continued their reign in places other than the heartland of Islam.

As the Abbasids conquered the Umayyads, an heir to the Umayyad dynasty, 'Abd al-Rahman, escaped and fled through North Africa to Spain. He established his rule in Cordoba in 756 with the support of the Umayyads in Spain. The heights of Cordoba and Iberian Islam under the Umayyads were reached under the third caliph, 'Abd al-Rahman (912–961).

The great mosque of Cordoba was erected with its forests of pillars and served as the focal point for the vitality of the Spanish Muslim capital. Cordoba had a population of half a million, 300 public baths, 70 libraries, and 700 mosques. There were religious animosities with the adjacent Christian powers of Castile, Aragon, and Leon in the Iberian peninsula. "Cordoba records some of history's most striking instances of Christian martyrdom by the sword of Islam and of the passions begotten of religious antipathy."[4]

Umayyad power ended in 1031, but during two centuries, Ibn Hazm (994–1064) and Ibn Rushd (1126-1198), made their contributions. Ibn Hazm was the grandson of a convert. He wrote on theology, philosophy, and tradition. His *On Sects, Heresies and Creeds* was a pioneering study of varieties of religious experience. Ibn Rushd, known as Averroes, was a judge, astronomer, physician, interpreter of the writings of Aristotle, and an influence on the later thought of Thomas Aquinas. He championed the role of reason and advocated two kinds of truth: one from human reason and the other from divine revelation. Both of these intellectuals were influential in their city as well as for generations of scholars to come.

ABBASID CALIPHATE (750-1517)

Renaissance of Islamic Art, Literature, Science, Medicine

The Abbasid Caliphate signaled an age of internal expansion with its capital in Baghdad (750–1258) and in Cairo (1261–1517). During much of these centuries, the geographical territory of Islam was little more than it was in A.D. 750, but Islam built up a great civilization. Islam became highly developed in this formative period of contact with Jews, Christians, Zoroastrians, Manichees, and Buddhists. By the time the Mongols sacked Baghdad in 1258 to end the Abbasid Caliphate there, Islamic civilization had been shaped in theology, law, and science; and Arabic was spoken from Spain to India.

The Abbasids defeated the Umayyads in A.D. 750. Under the second caliph al-Mansur (754–775) the city of Baghdad was built on the banks of the Tigris River. After al-Mansur, the greatest and most effective caliphs were al-Mahdi (775–785), Harun al-Rashid (786–809), and al-Ma'mun (813–833). "Under these sovereigns, Baghdad became a splendid metropolis, presiding with energy as well as with ruthless power over a vast dominion, enjoying a far-flung commerce and housing one of the greatest intercultural centers of intellectual exchange in the history of the world."[5]

The Tigris joined the Euphrates and had the Persian Gulf downstream to provide a gateway for commerce to India and the Far East. The rivers north and west linked Baghdad with Syria, "the Fertile Crescent," and beyond to Byzantium. The early Abbasid rulers battled Byzantium for years while receiving the Frankish emperor Charlemagne with lavish diplomacy.

Art in the Islamic world symbolized the indirect and the abstract. It pointed to the transcendent reality or "to the glory of God." Its patterns were found on ceramic tiles, lacquered boxes, carpets, vases, and friezes. Its abstract designs took three basic forms: geometrical, vegetal (Arabesque), and calligraphic. "Calligraphy of Qur'anic verses is a way of praising God without picturing God. It is really a form of communicating the Word of God as much as it is an art form. That is why so much of it appears on walls, facades, and domes of mosques."[6]

It is said that the "Muslim engineer's creative genius is expressed in the Red Fort in Delhi, the Alhambra in Grenada, and the Taj Mahal in Agra. But it is the mosque which remains the Muslim architect's lasting monument. As a tribute to Islamic architects, mosques have been called 'calligraphy in architectural form.' Others have called these sanctuaries and places of prayer 'theology in concrete.'" [7]

Muslims invented the clock pendulum, the magnetic compass, and the astrolabe. They created instruments to measure special weights and gravities of elements. Muhammad ibn Musa al-Khwarizmi (d. 850) invented algebra (al-jabr), which in Arabic means "to restore broken parts." After the zero was borrowed from India, al-Khwarizmi began a system of counting known as Arabic numerals.

Schools of law developed, five of which have continued: the Hanafi school (the largest), the Shafi'i school, the Maliki school, the Hanbali school, and the Ja'fari school. Judges and lawyers came from these schools. Islamic law, known as the Shari'a, was authored by these early schools; it has provided the foundation and the direction for Muslim life.

The Shari'a informs the religious, political, legal, economic, and health matters for all of Islamic civilization.

The Thousand and One Nights describes Harun al-Rashid's Baghdad. It presents characters and circumstances from Persia, India, Egypt, Syria, China, and Greece. It mirrors the escapades of caliphs, courtiers, artisans, and peasants of the Baghdad society. "The resourcefulness of Shahrazad in *The Thousand and One Nights* to sustain a nightly recital was no more than the resources of wealth, of intrigue, of magnificence, of curious lore, that lay at hand around the palaces and gardens or that belonged with the travelers, the slaves, the eunuchs, the judges *(qadis)*, the viziers, the merchants, and the knaves that haunted them."[8]

al-Ma'mun built the House of Wisdom that included a library second to none in medieval history. It became a center of Islamic scholarship. It gave translations of Greek and Syrian works into Arabic. Through this library, the writings of Aristotle, the medicine of Galen and Hippocrates, the geometry of Euclid, and the *Republic* of Plato came into Muslim culture and then back to the western world.

During the dark ages in Western Europe, culture and science illuminated the Islamic world of the Abbasid era. Scientific inquiry centered around the University of al-Azhar in Cairo. Paper was introduced. The pointed arch was invented (later utilized in the construction of European cathedrals). *Canon of Medicine* by Ibn Sina and *On Smallpox and Measles* by al Razi were the regular textbooks for the practice of medicine. Islam claimed several firsts in medicine:

- first use of anesthesia in surgery

- first cauterization of wounds

- first discovery that epidemics arise from contagion through touch and air

- first ambulatory hospital (carried on a camel's back)

- first prescription, and thus, the separation of pharmacology from medicine.[9]

About the year 1000, al Buruni discovered the earth's rotation on its axis and measured the earth's perimeter. Arabic numbers replaced Roman numerals.

Six crusades, beginning in 1099, occurred during this caliphate. Western Christendom made forays into Palestine to recapture the lands from the Muslims. The Muslim General Saladin became famous as the

Muslims retained hegemony over the Holy Land. The crusades have remained a dark memory for Muslims toward the Christian West.

From A.D. 1100 Sufism, a form of Islamic mysticism, gave vital spiritual energies and self-renewal to Islam. The Sufis wanted to experience God personally. Sufism became a pincer missionary force extending Islam to Africa, India, Indonesia, Turkestan, China, and southeastern Europe.

Mongol invaders from central Asia sacked Baghdad, ending the Abbasid Caliphate and the Arab Empire by 1258. A succession of caliphates and dynasties swept across the Muslim-dominated territories in the years from 1258 until 1517. The Mamluk Turks who ruled Egypt, Arabia, and Syria preserved Arab Muslim civilization. Turks captured Constantinople in 1453, ending the Byzantine Empire, and the city become the seat of the Ottoman Empire. By 1500, the Safavid dynasty ruled Persia and established Shi'ite Islam as the official religion.

Thus, during the Abbasid Caliphate, Islam flowered to a greatness unparalleled in its history in theology, law, literature, science, medicine, art, and architecture. The crusades caused an unforgettable scar in Islamic memory. Sufism renewed the spirit of Islam and became its major missionary movement. And the Turkish invaders fragmented the Islamic world with their occupations.

Fatimid Dynasty and Cairo and Other Rulers

Cairo was a provincial center during Umayyad times and the zenith of the Abbasid Empire. Already in 642, as Islam expanded from the Arabian peninsula, Muslims established their first place of prayer in Africa on the Nile near Cairo. As the Abbasids in Baghdad declined, Egypt began to flourish. Several Turkish dynasties broke from Baghdad and aided Egypt's growth. Then, al-Aziz (975–996) brought the Fatimid dynasty from Tunis and began a significant reign. al-Aziz claimed descent from Fatima, the prophet Muhammad's daughter. The Fatimids were Shi'ites.

The sixth caliph of the dynasty was al-Hakim (996–1021). He declared himself the incarnation of God. He persecuted his non-Muslim subjects *(dhimmi)*, both in Egypt and Syria. His armies destroyed the Church of the Holy Sepulchre in Jerusalem, and his actions contributed to the Christian crusades. In 1171, his dynasty and followers were overthrown by the Muslim general Saladin (Salah al-Din), who was to become the warrior against the crusaders and the liberator of Jerusalem for Islam.

al-Azhar, the great mosque-university, was built in Cairo in 972–973. Although it was inspired by Shi'ite influence, it became the most famous of Sunni Islamic centers of theology and law. "Its traditional pattern of Qur'anic exegesis, scholastic theology, logic, grammar, rhetoric, and jurisprudence established the classic form of orthodox education, by memorization, citation of authorities, and utter respect for the faithfully transmitted past, of which al-Azhar became the supreme example. Its great open court and pillared porticos and colonnades have housed generations of Muslim students from the whole world of Islam."[10]

The Mamluk Turks reigned from Cairo from 1250 until their overthrow by the Ottoman Turks in 1517. Mamluk rulers were former slaves who had gained prominence in both the government and military. Renowned writers of this later period in Cairo were Jalal al-Din al Suyuti (1445–1505), a scholar of wide range; Ibn al-Farid (d. 1235), a Sufi poet and contemporary of St. Francis of Assisi; and Ibn Khaldun, a historian and social analyst.

Transoxiana: Bukhara, Samarkand, Tashkent

During the Umayyad period a frontier of Islamic influence was established between the Oxus and the Jaxartes rivers known as Transoxiana. The area included the three cities of Bukhara, Samarkand, and Tashkent. Islam reached its height during the rule of the Samanids from 874 to the end of the tenth century. These rulers were virtually autonomous, giving only nominal allegiance to the Abbasids.

Bukhara served as the capital. It became known for the home of the eminent physician, al-Razi, who greatly influenced western medicine. Also, al-Bukhari (810-870), the renowned Hadith scholar, took his name from the city. His collections of the Hadith are the most widely cherished sources of Muslim piety. From this region, paper became available to the Islamic world. Schools of theology were plentiful. Ibn Sina was the most famous student of the Bukhara school.

Successive invaders from Central Asia affected Transoxiana. Jenghiz Khan crossed it on his way to the Middle East. Timur (Tamerlane) made his capital at Samarkand; he sacked Baghdad in 1393 and Damascus in 1401 before his death in Samarkand in 1404.

The area was also known for its itinerant Sufism. The Sufis operated out of the cities to carry their mystical and popular form of Islam to the tribes and wandering nomads. The Sufi dervishes were famous for their devotional meetings with chants and prayers.

These cities and their surrounding regions were on the frontiers of Islam, far removed from the Umayyad, Abbasid, and Ottoman rulers. In more modern times, reformers were evident in the area. They were informed by Jamal al-Din al-Afghani (1839–1897) who was a leader of pan-Islamic revival. These reformers, energized by socialist ideals wedded with Islam, directed their criticisms both against the Czars and the conservative Muslim scholars. The region became the center of Turkish and Islamic encounters with the Russian communist revolution.

From 1917 until after World War II, Muslims suffered anti-Islamic suppression. With the dismemberment of the USSR in the early 1990s, the new emerging republics, including Uzbekistan and Kazakhstan are struggling to define the role of Islam in their societies.

India: The Mughals and Delhi

The Umayyads took Islam to northwestern India by 712. Yet it was to be another three hundred years before Islam advanced. It was Muhammad of Ghor in 1191 who established the Turkish Sultanate of Delhi. He erected the Qutb Minar around 1200, a circular five-story tower built of red sandstone and marble with Arabic inscriptions. The Sultanate of Delhi lasted until 1398, serving as a buffer from the advances of Jenghiz Khan from Mongolia through Central Asia to Persia.

Timur sacked Delhi in 1398. From his descendants came Babul, the first ruler who established the Mughal Empire. Babul's successors pushed southward to dominate much of the Indian subcontinent. Among these was Akbar the Great, who came to power at age thirteen in 1556. He has been described as one of the most personally powerful figures in history.

Akbar began in orthodox Islam, but he intentionally married a Hindu princess to relate his religion and his rule to a predominant Hindu population. He avoided the methods of his predecessors by leaving intact the Hindu images of deities and refusing to suppress the peoples by taxation and military force. He assumed the role of Plato's philosopher-king. "He felt his way toward a concept of the royal supremacy in which the crown was considered to be a divine right, the sovereign being a part of the inalienable order of the universe as ordained by God its creator. A similar understanding of monarchy was central to the English Tudors and Queen Elizabeth (almost to a year his exact contemporary). This is an uncanny parallel in religious history."[11]

Akbar abolished the tax on non-Muslims. He included Hindi teachers in his court. In his closing years he required that prayers be directed to himself, the emperor, as the divine authority on earth. Orthodox Muslims condemned his rule and religion, but Hindus appreciated him.

Akbar attempted to relate to the widespread Hinduism of his land and to religious pluralism, but his program did not survive after his death.

Akbar's successors moved back toward orthodox Islam. Shah Jahan built the exquisite Taj Mahal at Agra and the Grand Mosque and Red Fort of Delhi. The last of the dominant Mughal rulers, Aurangzeb (1657–1707), brought orthodox Islam back. With the emergence of British India, fragmentation occurred across India in its rule and expressions of religion. The recent history of India has seen partitions of lands resulting in an Islamic state and also much internal conflict within India between religions.

OTTOMAN EMPIRE (1517–1924): CONSTANTINOPLE AND BEYOND

The Ottoman Turks ruled several provinces in Asia Minor before taking Constantinople in 1453. With Suleyman II, known as "the Magnificent," the Ottoman Empire began to flourish. It brought a powerful centralized state and Muslim orthodoxy and law to parts of Asia and North Africa.

During the 1500s the Ottomans ruled territories between the Austrian monarchy to the west and the Safavid Persians to the east. The 1600s saw the Ottomans at their zenith. The Muslim world reveled in its power, wealth, and splendor. The cities of Constantinople, Isfahan in Persia, and Agra in India rivaled the great European cities. The Sufi orders continued to carry Islam to Asia and Africa.

Yet Constantinople served as the Ottoman symbol and shrine for five hundred years. It became known as Istanbul. Its Christian rulers had held on for centuries against the attacks of the Umayyads and the Abbasids. With the taking of Istanbul, Islamic power resided across the bridge of Asia and Europe. Within a century it ruled from Muscat to the Danube.

Suleyman the Magnificent (1520–1566) was the Turkish Sultan, grand in rule and builder upon the foundations of others. Acclaimed as warrior, statesman, lawgiver, builder, and potentate, he appeared larger than life. He transformed the imposing Saint Sophia Cathedral of Constantinople into the Mosque of Islam. It had been the home of the Christian giants of the Church, John Chrysostom and Justinian. Suleyman built the Suleyman Mosque with a dome even larger than Saint Sophia. Istanbul became a city whose skyline reflected tens of mosques with their minarets reaching skyward.

Ottoman art, architecture, poetry, music, and crafts flourished. One of the most famous poets was Baqi (1526–1600). Intrigue also abounded.

According to custom, the Ottoman ruler precluded acts against his succession by killing all brothers and their pregnant wives or slave women, strangling them with a silk bowstring as a symbol of royalty dignity. This practice was discontinued after 1618, when princes were confined to the women's quarters to live with their mothers and sisters.

By 1799, the armies of Napoleon had invaded Egypt. This event signaled the beginning of the colonialization and the decline of the Ottoman Empire. The British came to India and the Middle East. The French came to North Africa. The Dutch came to Indonesia. The Russians asserted themselves in Central Asia. As the twentieth century approached, the Ottoman Empire was ripe for disintegration by decay from within and by international influences from beyond.

World War I hastened the collapse of the Ottoman Empire. Turkey, the heartland of the empire, entered the war on the side of Germany. During the war the Arabs revolted against the empire. By 1922, the Sultanate had been abolished in Istanbul and the secularizer Kemal Ataturk became the first president of the Turkish republic. He took power away from the Islamic leaders. Islamic law, education, and culture were modernized according to western institutions and values. Ataturk was called "The Father of Modernization." Soon, the empire was a thing of the past, and even orthodox Islam was threatened.

Persia: The Great Sophy and Isfahan

Within thirty years of Muhammad's death, Islam had advanced into Persia. Yet Persia, now known as Iran, imposed its own image on Islam. As some say, since Persians were not Arabs, they Persianized their invaders' religion, especially in the areas of mystical religion, art, and poetry. The poetry and prose of Hafez, Saa'di, and Omar Khayyam came from Persia. By the beginning of the sixteenth century, Iranian Muslims had made their Shi'ite brand of Islam official and have basically remained Shi'ite.

Shah Abbas of the Safavid dynasty built the Masjid-i-Shah or Royal Mosque in the city of Isfahan. Isfahan (*nesfe jehan*) means "half of the world." The great Maidan, a huge rectangular area, had the bazaars to the north, the Royal Mosque to the south, the smaller Lutfallah Mosque on the east, and on the west the Ali Qapu or royal "dais" with three stories from which the Shah could survey the entire area. Also to the west of the Maidan was the Four Gardens (*Chahar Bagh*) housing the various Islamic schools for which the city was renowned. Southward, three bridges led to the new city of Julfa where the Armenian Christians lived.

The Shah had brought them from Azerbaijan and settled them with special protections for their skills in trade and artisan works.

The grandeur and reputation of Isfahan brought large numbers of Shi'ite scholars and theologians to its mosques and schools. The city was also known for weaving and textiles and for metal works and the painting of miniatures. Other cities like Meshed and Qum became centers of Shi'ite scholarship. Meshed, with its tomb of one of the twelve Shi'ite imams, became a rival of Mecca for Muslim pilgrims. Meshed was so important to the Shah that he reportedly walked some eight hundred miles from Isfahan to the tomb for a pilgrimage.

The last of the Safavids fell in 1796. Nadir Shah of the Afshar dynasty took his armies as far away as Bukhara and Afghanistan to extend his empire, but he failed. Modern Iran has remained a strong Shi'ite nation, especially with the overthrow of the Pahlavi dynasty of Muhammad Reza Shah and the founding of the Islamic Republic of Iran under Ayatollah Khomeini in 1979.

Islam in Southeast Asia: Indonesia to Malaysia

More Muslims live in Indonesia than in any other country. Islam is strongest on the main islands of Sumatra and Java. After the year 1100, Muslim merchants and missionaries from South India came to the northern tip of Sumatra and planted Islam. From Sumatra it spread to the eastern tip of Java. Marco Polo, upon his visit to Sumatra in 1292, said that the island was very pagan but that the ports were so much frequented by the Saracen merchants that they have converted the natives to the law of Mahomet.

In the fourteenth century Muslims from the Delhi region of India implanted the Shafi'i school of Islamic law in Indonesia, where it remains. By the early 1400s Megat Iskander Shah was the Muslim ruler in Malacca and strengthened Islam's hold on the peninsula. Muslim leaders and merchants by the early 1500s began to have monopolies in trade and in the management of the ports and harbors.

> Throughout, Islam in the archipelago has shown strong Indian and animist influences. Native arts developed when, after the coming of the Dutch in the seventeenth century, long-distance trade passed out of the hands of the harbor towns, and local commerce turned more into the interior in a web of local marketing. Despite the steady influence of pilgrimage to Mecca in relating the faith to classical standards, and despite the vigor of puritan movements in the nineteenth century, Sumatran and

Javanese Islam has remained strongly syncretistic, inclined to theosophic, illuminationist mysticism and to popular mixture with animistic cults. By and large, it was also what has been called "an oppositional Islam," supplying the emotional resistance to European colonialism and fortifying itself in the process.[12]

Islam South of the Sahara

Islam penetrated Africa in three major geographical waves:

1. Muslims came up the Nile valley into eastern Sudan.

2. Muslims came from Arabia by the Red Sea into the Horn of Africa and southward down the coast of Kenya and inland to Tanzania, Uganda, and Mozambique.

3. Berbers from North Africa came across the Sahara around the western shore of Africa into Gambia and Senegal.

By about 1350, Islam dominated the Sudan and Sudanese Christianity faded. In the Horn of Africa Islam took root early in the Umayyad period, especially among the tribes of the coasts and islands. Ethiopia continued to preserve its Christianity. Harar was a strong Muslim center. It was not until the nineteenth century that Islam penetrated inland from the East African shore. Trade carried Muslims into Tanzania and Mozambique with the Yao peoples becoming the strongest Islamic presence. The Isma'ili branch of Shi'ite Islam came from India to plant large settlements of Muslims in Kenya, Uganda, and Tanzania and also in Durban in the Natal.

North African Muslims brought Islam into the Senegal region of West Africa by about 1050. Through trade Islam came by way of Marrakesh to the ancient empire of Ghana; or through Timbuktu and Gao; or through the central Sahara from Tunis and Kano; or from Tripoli to Kanem. The Almoravids of Morocco conquered the capital of Ghana in 1076. The empire of Mali, founded in the thirteenth century, ruled from Senegal to the Hausalands east of Niger. Timbuktu began around 1100 as a Tuareg trading center and became a major Islamic center for the Mali rulers.

Askia Muhammad (1494–1528) ruled over the Songhai region and brought conciliation among the tribes as Islam was further established. The Hausa kingdoms were Islamicized by the eighteenth century. The Fulani tribes were introduced to Islam and a Fulani empire under Muhammad Bello, the son of Uthman Dan Fodio, ruled from their headquarters at Sokoto. The Fulani practiced an Arabized Islam in their indigenous contexts and incorporated whole animistic-practicing regions.

Africa was also influenced by Sufi movements with their sheikhs and brotherhoods like the Qadiriyyah and Tijaniyyah Orders. Islam in Africa thus has its own particular history and development. African traditional culture and Islam have blended and interacted in various ways. Cragg has written, "African Muslims may not belong to Islam in the classical normative sense, but they know that they belong."[13]

Twentieth-century Islam

Islam declined in the first half of the twentieth century. Traditional Islamic cultures in Turkey and Iran underwent nationalization and secu-larization. Ataturk of Turkey and Reza Shah of Iran usurped political power from Muslim leaders, limited the expressions of Islam, and sub-ordinated law, education, and general cultural values and institutions to secular government. Thus, nationalism and secularism threatened Islamic societies.

Meanwhile, however, Muslim activists in Egypt and India were laying the groundwork for Islamic revivalism and resurgence. Hasan al-Banna (1904–1949) organized the Muslim brotherhood in 1929 in Egypt; his thought has inspired Islamic political and revolutionary movements to the present and well beyond Egypt. Sayid Qutb (1906–1966) followed al-Banna's ideology and launched the Muslim Brother-hood into confrontations with the Egyptian government over its lack of implementation of Islamic principles for governance. Both he and al-Banna were killed by the government. Charles Beckett recognizes the establishment of the Muslim Brotherhood (al-Ikhwan al-Muslimun) in Egypt in 1928 as a major contributor to the Muslim resurgence. He refers to scholars who claim that the Brotherhood is the "biggest and most influential revivalist Islamic movement of the twentieth century and that it has inspired Islamic fundamentalism in the Sudan, Syria, Pal-estine, Jordan, and other countries."[14]

Mawlana Sayyid Abu'l-a la Mawdudi (1903–1979) began the activist organization Jama 'at-i Islami in India in 1941. He advocated return to the Qur'an and the Hadith. Later, with the establishment of the nation of Pakistan, he opposed the nationalist and secularist trends of the govern-ment. His thought has remained influential in the sub-continent.

The establishment of the state of Israel in 1948 also presented a chal-lenge and a threat to Islam. Israel had the support of western nations, espe-cially Great Britain and the United States. Already after World War I, mandates over former territories of the Ottoman Empire had been given to western nations. The British exercised control over Palestine and beyond. The French had a mandate over Lebanon and Syria.

Thus, Islam viewed the creation of the Israeli state, as well as the earlier mandates, as a replay of the crusades and an extension of colonialism. Also, the holy places in Palestine, including the Dome of the Rock and al-Aqsa mosque, were placed under the jurisdiction of the Jews, especially after 1967. Arab lands and Muslim holy places became issues.

The interests of the United States in the Middle East increased dramatically after World War II. The heartland of Islam became a political and economic pawn between the Soviet Union and the United States. Both nations vied over influence in the region. The rich oil deposits of Saudi Arabia, Iraq, Iran, and other Persian Gulf states were needed increasingly to run the industrial complex of the United States and western nations. The Soviet Union also wanted to guarantee its oil resources for the future as well as curtail its use in the West.

The oil embargo against the West, led by the richest Islamic nations in the 1960s, demonstrated the power of the nation-states of the Middle East and signaled a resurgence of Islam. Both Saudi Arabia and Iran used oil wealth to fund the expansion of Islam to the West. However, in Iran the modernization by the Shah was to lead to a total failure of his policies and usher in the reign of Ayatollah Khomeini and Islamic fundamentalism.

Events in Iran by early 1979 led to the downfall of the Shah of Iran and the establishment of an Islamic republic in Iran based on the radical ideology of Ayatollah Khomeini. The United States was denounced as "the Great Satan" and its embassy was held in hostage. Iran set out on a course to exemplify and export Islamic fundamentalism. Iran waged a protracted war with its Muslim neighbor, Iraq, each calling for a holy war *(jihad)* against the other.

During the 1980s and 1990s, Islam has undergone a revival and revitalization of its beliefs and practices around the globe. In various events and at different times, Islam has been missionary and militant. Islamic organizations such as Hezbollah and Hamas have fought the "Zionist" state of Israel. Muslims have migrated to western Europe and to the United States, built mosques, and formed Islamic associations. With the breakup of the Soviet Union, the various independent republics with Muslim majorities have received funds and missionaries from nations such as Saudi Arabia and Iran.

Islam is divided politically and religiously. The Shi'ite regime of Iran has waged war against the Sunni regime of Iraq. During the Persian Gulf War, the Islamic nations of Saudi Arabia, Syria, Egypt, Morocco, and others sided with western nations in war against Iraq, which had invaded the Islamic nation of Kuwait. The traditional Muslim nations of Egypt and Jordan have made peace treaties with Israel, inviting the wrath of those Muslim nations that continue to defy Israel. And Yasser Arafat, the leader of the Palestine Liberation Organization, made peace with Israel in order to regain territories lost in the wars of 1948 and 1967.

Islamic power and prestige have advanced in the late twentieth century. Many Muslims believe that Islam is on the verge of emulating the accomplishments of the glorious Abbasid era. Islam is a global religion with a missionary mandate and about a billion adherents.

The Center of the Islamic World
(percent of population that is Muslim)

China 2.8%

India 10%

Former USSR 9%

Afghanistan 99%

Pakistan 96%

Iran 98%

Saudi Arabia 100%

Iraq 95%

Turkey 98%

Syria 87%

Jordan 95%

Lebanon 40%

Somalia

Djibouti

Egypt 92%

Sudan 70%

Libya 97%

Chad

Niger

Nigeria

Tunisia 95%

Algeria 99%

Mali

Morocco 95%

Mauritania

Spain

4

ISLAMIC THEOLOGY

I slam is a religion of unity, uniformity, and universalism in its expressions of faith and practice. Whether in Saudi Arabia or Singapore or South America, Muslims share very similar beliefs about God, angels, prophets, books, and judgment. Muslims agree about the ninety-nine specific names that signify the attributes of God. They agree that the angel Gabriel revealed God to Muhammad. They revere the same prophets: Adam, Abraham, Moses, Jesus, and Muhammad. They accept the sacred writings of the original revelations of the Jews and Christians and affirm the great judgment after the resurrection with consequences for heaven and hell. In these beliefs there is little deviation.[1]

Both Orthodox Islam and Folk Islam consider the following beliefs to be important:

- the nature and characteristics of God

- the role of angels

- the status of prophets

- the importance of sacred writings

- views of the resurrection and judgment and heaven and hell

The Qur'an states, "But it is righteousness— / To believe in Allah / And the Last Day, / And the Angels, / And the Book, / And the Messengers."[2]

ALLAH

Pre-Islamic Deities

Before Islam there was no highly organized religion among the Arabs.[3] Arabs recognized many gods and goddesses. Tribes had their own deities. There were astral deities. Arab Bedouins focused on the moon because it provided light during the night for their grazing flocks. Contemporary Islam also focuses on the moon, as indicated by a crescent atop the mosque, a lunar calendar, and with festivals like Ramadan regulated by the rising of the moon.

Pre-Islamic Arabia also had its stone deities. They were stone statues of shapeless volcanic or meteoric stones found in the deserts and believed to have been sent by astral deities. The most prominent deities were Hubal, the male god of the Ka'ba, and the three sister goddesses al-Lat, al-Manat, and al-Uzza; Muhammad's tribe, Quraysh, thought these three goddesses to be the daughters of Allah. Hubal was the chief god of the Ka'ba among 360 other deities. He was a man-like statue whose body was made of red precious stone and whose arms were of solid gold.

Allat (with the t added to Allah) is the feminine form of Allah. She was represented by a square stone, and her major sanctuary was in the city of Taif. Some thought of her as the female counterpart of Allah. Al-Manat was the goddess of fate whose major sanctuary consisted of a black stone in the town of Qudayd between Mecca and Medina.

al-Uzza was the goddess of east Mecca and was the most venerated deity of the Quraysh tribe. It is said that human sacrifices were made to her. Islamic tradition reports that Muhammad's grandfather almost sacrificed his son, the father of Muhammad, to al-Uzza in fulfillment of a vow. However, he was counseled by a fortune teller to ransom his son with one hundred camels. Muslims interpret this as the will of Allah to bring Muhammad into existence.[4]

Other deities in the Arabian peninsula included al-Rahman and al-Hajar al-Aswad. al-Rahman was the name of an ancient deity in southern Arabia. Muhammad used the name of this deity, which means "merciful," 169 times in the Qur'an. With the exception of Allah, it appears in the Qur'an more than any other descriptive term for Allah. al-Hajar al-Aswad is symbolized by the black stone in the southeast corner of the

Ka'ba. The stone was purportedly received by Ishmael from the angel Gabriel. Muhammad included it in the pilgrimage rituals in Mecca, and Muslims on the pilgrimage kiss the black stone in veneration.

There were nature deities, and there were intangible deities. The concept of a supreme god, al-Ilah *(the god)* was known among the tribes. The poets called him Allah. Muhammad thus came out of a context of various beliefs and practices associated with animism and polytheism.[5]

The Name of Allah

The Arabic name of God is Allah. The word *Allah*, which is derived from al (the) ilah (deity), literally means "the god." The major Islamic understanding of God is that God is one. This is the doctrine of singularity *(tawhid)*. There is only one true God; therefore, all pagan gods are false. And God is neither plural nor triune. God is seen as separate and independent of creation and has no associations with any human traits.

The opposite of *tawhid* is *shirk*. *Shirk* means to associate partners or companions to Allah. For example, the Qur'an accuses Christians of *shirk*, in that Christians believe that Jesus is eternal or that God is triune. The belief that God is one, singular, and separate from creation is central to the concept of Allah.

The troublesome *Satanic Verses* have their origins in the Qur'an.[6] Muhammad first said that al-Lat, al-Uzza, and al-Manat were deities. Later, he changed his teachings and indicated that his thinking had been corrupted by Satan. Thus, he re-established his teaching on monotheism.

Not only is God one, but God is transcendent. Allah is distant from creation and from human beings. Muslims believe that Allah did not reveal himself but revealed his will. His will is limited to Islamic law. It is a metaphysical impossibility to be in a personal relationship with Allah. He is distant and removed from creation and creatures and relates to them through his will and law.

One may have a knowledge about Allah concerning his nature and law, but one does not have experiential and personal knowledge of him. One Muslim viewpoint is that Allah is unique in all his powers and attributes. On occasion one may discover a resemblance between the attributes of a thing or person and some of the attributes of Allah, but the resemblance is only apparent and superficial. To look for God as immanent in all existence and in contact with it, rather than as absolutely separate from it, is a futile search leading to error rather than to truth, harming rather than blessing the investigator.

One Muslim observed that the Qur'an is no treatise about God and his nature: his existence, for the Qur'an, is strictly functional. He is the Cre-

THE NINETY-NINE NAMES OF ALLAH

Meaning	Pronounced	Meaning	Pronounced
Singular	al-Wahid	Knower	al-Álim
Alone	al-Ahad	Hearer	As-Samí
Eternal	As-Samad	Seer	al-Basir
Mighty	al-Qadir	Kind	al-Latif
Powerful	al-Muqtadir	Expert	al-Khabir
First	al-Awwal	Forbearing	al-Halim
Last	al-Akhir	Magnificent	al-Ázim
Manifest	Az-Zahir	Forgiving	al-Ghafur
Hidden	al-Batin	Thankful	Ash-Shakur
Governor	al-Wadi	Lofty	al-Áliyy
Exalted	al-Mutáale	Great	al-Kabir
Pious	al-Barr	Preserver	al-Hafiz
Forgiving	At-Tawwab	Omniscient	al-Állam
Pardoner	al-Áfuw	Omnipotent	al-Qahir
Compassionate	Ar-Ráuf	Forgiver	al-Ghafir
Gatherer	al-Jamé	Creator	al-Fatir
Self-Sufficient	al-Ghani	Sovereign	al-Makik
Light	An-Nur	Gracious	al-Hafiyy
Guide	al-Hadi	All-Prevading	al-Muhit
Innovator	al-Badí	Called for help	al-Mustáan
Lord	Rabb	Sublime	Ar-Rafí
Manifest	Mubin	Sufficient One	al-Kafi
Mighty	al-Qadir	Predominant	Ghalib
Protector	al-Hafiz	Gracious	al-Mannan
Surety	al-Kafil	Glorious	al-Jalil
Appreciative	Ash-Shakir	Giver of Life	al-Muhyi
Most Bounteous	al-Akram	Giver of Death	al-Mumit
Creative	al-Khallaq	Inheritor	al-Warith
Patron	al-Maula	Awakener	al-Báith
Helper	An-Nasir	Everlasting one	al-Baqi
God	al-Ilah	Truth	al-Haqq
God	Allah	Trustee	al-Wakil
Merciful	Ar-Rahman	Strong	al-Qawi
Clement	Ar-Rahim	Firm	al-Matin
Ruler	al-Malik	Guardian	al-Wali
Pure	al-Quddus	Praiseworthy	al-Hamid
Safe	As-Salam	Alive	al-Hayy
Secure	al-Mu'min	Self-Sustaining	al-Qayyum
Controller	al-Muhaimin	Amicable	al-Wadud
Honorable	al-Áziz	Glorious	al-Majid
Compellor	al-Jabbar	Witness	Ash-Shahid
Proud	al-Mutakabbir	Wise	al-Hakim
Creator	al-Khaliq	Nourisher	al-Muqit
Maker	al-Bari	Reckoner	al-Hasib
Fashioner	al-Musawwir	Generous One	al-Karim
Forgiver	al-Ghaffar	Watchful	Ar-Raqub
Dominant	al-Qahhar	Near	al-Qarib
Bestower	al-Wahhab	Responsive	al-Mujib
Provider	Ar-Razzaq	Vast	al-Wasí
Opener	al-Fattah		

ator and Sustainer of the universe and man, and particularly the giver of guidance for man and He who judges man, individually and collectively, and metes out to him merciful justice.[7] There is little Muslim scholarship on the subject of God's essence and character. The bottom line of the Muslim confession about God is absolute oneness and sovereignty.

Muslims believe that God created the universe and administers its affairs. He is all-seeing, all-hearing, almighty, forgiving, just, unique, and the first and the last. He has no son, no daughter, no parents, and is above having such a relationship. He cannot be called father.[8] The basic relationship between God and humankind is God as Lord *(al-Rabb)* and humankind as slave servants *(Abd)*. Human response to God must be total submission.

The Names of Allah

The Qur'an does command Muslims to call Allah by his beautiful names. However, it does not enumerate them. One tradition *(hadith)* reports that Muhammad said, "There are ninety-nine names of Allah; he who memorizes them and repeats them will get into paradise." The power of belief in the names or attributes of God gives the believer power and God-consciousness. But neither the Qur'an nor the hadith establish the ninety-nine names. Thus, the list of names has been compiled by scholars who referenced the greatest names referred to Allah in the Qur'an.

When asked, "Who is God?," Muslims point out Allah's "most beautiful names."[9] The Qur'an states,

> Allah is He, than Whom / There is no other god— / Who knows (all things) / Both secret and open; He, / Most Gracious, / Most Merciful. Allah is He, than Whom / There is no other god— / The Sovereign, the Holy One, / The Source of Peace (and Perfection), / The Guardian of Faith, / The Preserver of Safety, / The Exalted in Might, / The Irresistible, the Supreme: / Glory to Allah! (High is He) / Above the partners / They attribute to Him. He is Allah, the Creator, / The Evolver, / The Bestower of Forms (or Colours). / To Him belong / The Most Beautiful Names: / Whatever is in the heavens and on earth, / Doth declare / His Praises and Glory; / And He is the Exalted / In Might, the Wise.[10]

Muslim writers have grouped the beautiful names in several categories depicting Allah. They are categories signifying majesty, generosity, beauty, essence, action, power, wisdom, goodness, names of terror, and names of goodness. One approach divides the names into seven groups: life, knowledge, power, will, hearing, seeing, and speech. Kenneth Cragg notes that these names "are to be understood finally as characteristics of the Divine will rather than laws of His nature."[11] Each surah of the Qur'an begins, "In the name of Allah, Most Gracious, Most Merciful."

The concept of God is deep and complex in Islamic theology and philosophy. Muslims believe that God is one, sovereign, and ruler over all. He has no partners. God's many names do not describe his essence, only his will and law. God is independent of his creation. He revealed his will and law through the angel Gabriel to his prophet Muhammad as well as to other select prophets.

ANGELS: GABRIEL TO THE JINN

The Islamic creed affirms belief in the angels.[12] They are numerous invisible beings who execute the commands of God. Angels are not superior to humans, for humans are the highest form of creation and have been given the title *caliphate*, meaning trustee or vice-regent of God on earth. The most famous angel is the Archangel Gabriel. He has appeared to the prophets and has spoken to them in their own languages about the will and law of God.

The last revelation (*wahy*) was given by Gabriel to the Prophet Muhammad beginning in 610. Other prominent angels include Michael (angel of providence and guardian of the Jews), Israfil (the summoner to resurrection), and Izrail (angel of death). It is believed that two angels are assigned to each person for guidance and to record everything the person does in obedience or disobedience to God. Angels are not to be worshiped. They reside anywhere in the universe as assigned by God.

Besides the angels there are other spiritual beings. There are the *jinn* which God has created.[13] Muslims believe that the jinn are intelligent creatures, usually invisible, with freedom of choice for good or evil. Thus, there are Muslim jinn and non-Muslim jinn. The non-Muslim jinn are the enemies of the righteous and cause them to follow erroneous teachings.

Satan disobeyed God by refusing to bow down to Adam after his creation. He caused Adam and Eve to eat the forbidden fruit in paradise. Some Islamic scholars consider Satan as an angelic being, but others place him in the category of the jinn. Satan was created before humanity,

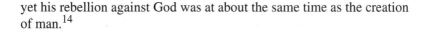

yet his rebellion against God was at about the same time as the creation of man.[14]

PROPHETS: ADAM TO MUHAMMAD

Islam holds that God has sent prophets to humanity with divine teachings.[15] The Qur'an states, "To every people (was sent) / A Messenger: when their Messenger / Comes (before them), the matter Will be judged between them / With justice, and they / Will not be wronged."[16]

The words *Nabi* and *Rasul* are used interchangeably to depict the prophets and messengers. The first prophet was Adam and the last one was Muhammad. Prophets were the model of good behavior and perfect character. They held to all virtues and were free from all vices. The traditional four virtues associated with the prophets are truth, honesty, conveying the message from God, and intelligence.

Muslims believe that God has sent a prophet to each people to warn them with the message. And the message of the prophets has been identical and universal. It has come from "The Mother of the Book."[17] The basic message is to acknowledge the oneness of God, to obey his laws, and to perform good works in light of the life to come. Muhammad is the last prophet and messenger ("prophet" and "messenger" are used synonymously) sent to humankind. Anyone claiming to be a prophet or messenger after Muhammad is an impostor and deceiver. (In this light the Ahmadiyya sect and the Nation of Islam are unacceptable to orthodox Islam.)

Muslim tradition indicates that there have been 124,000 prophets, since every people have been sent a prophet. The Qur'an mentions by name twenty-five prophets, and most of them are also found in the Bible. Five of the prophets are given high titles: Muhammad (the apostle of God), Noah (the preacher of God), Abraham (the friend of God), Moses (the speaker with God), and Jesus (the word of God). From Adam to Muhammad all prophets form an unbreakable chain.[18]

In the Qur'an, Abraham is considered the father of Muslims as he bowed his will to God's will and was true in faith. He is called the first *hanif* (monotheistic believer). It is Abraham's son, Ishmael, who is the direct progenitor of Muslims among the Arabs. However, Muhammad is the greatest of the prophets and the last one. It is his name which is recited daily in the Muslim confession.

Jesus is mentioned ninety-seven times in the Qur'an and seems to have a unique status as a prophet.[19] He is given such honorific titles as Messiah, Word of God, Spirit of God, and Speech of Truth. Jesus was

born of the Virgin Mary, performed miracles as a child, and appeared to
die on the cross.[20] God raised him up to heaven.[21] Muslims view Jesus
as human and in no way divine. The Qur'an indicates, "Christ, the son
of Mary, / Was no more than / A Messenger: many were / The Messengers that passed away / Before him."[22] Only his name alongside Abraham's appears in every list of the prophets.

The Muslim view is that the teachings of the prophets before Muhammad have been lost or corrupted. Although the message of each previous
prophet was the same as that of Muhammad, it was necessary for
Muhammad to correct and finalize the message which now is found in
the Qur'an. He is the last prophet.

THE QUR'AN AND OTHER SACRED BOOKS

Many of the messengers of God were sent with books which embodied God's teachings in the language of the people.[23] "People of the
Book" is a phrase Muslims use to refer especially to Jews, Christians,
and Muslims. Four books are well known to Muslims. The Torah was
revealed to Moses, the Psalms to David, and the Gospel to Jesus. The
most sacred book is the Qur'an.

According to Muslims, the Torah and the Gospel were genuine revelations of the "Mother of the Book," but they have been changed and
corrupted. Traditional Islam views the Qur'an as identical with the
"Mother of the Book" in heaven; the Qur'an contains the very words of
God himself.[24] Therefore, the Qur'an corrects the errors in the corrupted
books and finalizes the truth from God as transmitted from the Archangel Gabriel, recited by the Prophet Muhammad, and written down in the
Arabic language. The Qur'an records, "We have, without doubt, / Sent
down the Message; And We will assuredly / Guard it (from corruption)."[25]

Throughout history Islamic scholars have debated the nature of the
Qur'an. Some have argued that the Qur'an was created. Others have
believed that it is uncreated and is a quality of Allah like seeing, hearing,
and knowing. Orthodox Islam has generally affirmed that the Qur'an is
uncreated. Since Allah is preexistent to everything known and unknown,
they argue, his word is an integral part of his very nature. Thus, just as
Allah has not been created, so is the Qur'an not created.

In his famous discourses the Muslim scholar Jalal al-Din Rumi cited
Surah 53 for his understanding of the Qur'an. He set forth the concept of
a "celestial imparting of syntax, vocabulary and word sequence, so that
prophetic speech verbally iterates the divine speech and audition to

Shari'ah
law
(Islamic)

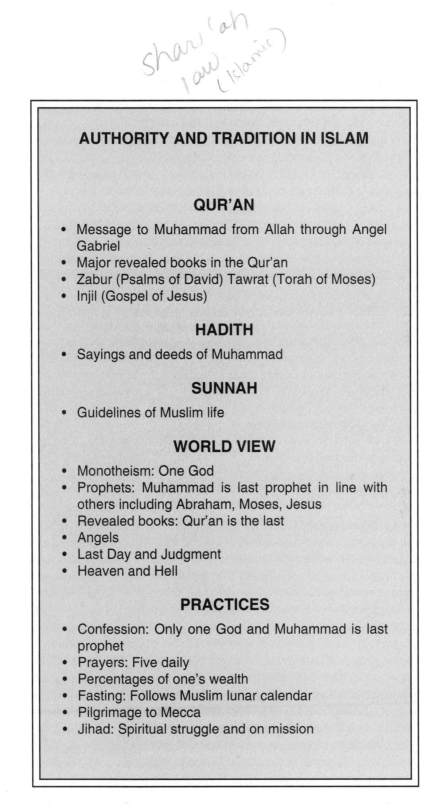

AUTHORITY AND TRADITION IN ISLAM

QUR'AN

- Message to Muhammad from Allah through Angel Gabriel
- Major revealed books in the Qur'an
- Zabur (Psalms of David) Tawrat (Torah of Moses)
- Injil (Gospel of Jesus)

HADITH

- Sayings and deeds of Muhammad

SUNNAH

- Guidelines of Muslim life

WORLD VIEW

- Monotheism: One God
- Prophets: Muhammad is last prophet in line with others including Abraham, Moses, Jesus
- Revealed books: Qur'an is the last
- Angels
- Last Day and Judgment
- Heaven and Hell

PRACTICES

- Confession: Only one God and Muhammad is last prophet
- Prayers: Five daily
- Percentages of one's wealth
- Fasting: Follows Muslim lunar calendar
- Pilgrimage to Mecca
- Jihad: Spiritual struggle and on mission

whom the Prophet dictates it thereby transcribing the sentences of a heavenly Book textually mediated to them, as to him."[26]

A tradition reports the angel Gabriel's approach to Muhammad:

> Narrated Aisha: Truth descended upon him (Muhammad) while he was in the cave of Hira. The angel came to him in it and asked him to read. The Prophet replied, "I do not know how to read." (The Prophet added), "The angel caught me (forcefully) and pressed me so hard that I could not bear it anymore. He then released me and again asked me to read, and I replied, "I do not know how to read," whereupon he caught me again and pressed me a second time till I could not bear it anymore. He then released me and asked me again to read, but again I replied, "I do not know how to read (or, what shall I read?)." Thereupon he caught me for the third time and pressed me and then released me and said, "Read: In the Name of your Lord, Who has created (all that exists). He has created man from a clot. Read and Your Lord is most Generous that which he knew not" (Qur'an 96:1–5). Then Allah's Apostle returned with the Inspiration, his neck muscles twitching with terror till he entered upon Khadija (Muhammad's first wife) and said, "Cover me!" They covered him till his fear was over and then he said, "Khadija, what is wrong with me?" Khadija said, "Never! but have glad tidings, for by Allah, Allah will never disgrace you."[27]

Inspiration of the Qur'an to Muhammad has been interpreted in various ways by students of Islam. It is evident that there was physical and psychological distress for Muhammad in receiving this revelation from the angel. Some have suggested hallucinations, epileptic seizures, and even demonic possession. However, one billion Muslims believe that Muhammad had an encounter with Allah through the angel.

The Qur'an contains 114 chapters *(surahs)*, and each chapter has a number of verses *(ayas)*. It was revealed to Muhammad during the period from A.D. 610 to 632. It serves as a roadmap for this life and the life to come. It provides guidance for worship, marriage and family, economics, politics, community affairs, hygiene, and all other affairs of humanity. Muslims memorize it, recite it, and create artistic expressions from it. As a literary piece of Arabic, it stands alone.

As stated, the Qur'an was revealed to Muhammad over a period of twenty-three years. It was compiled some twenty years after his death. This was quite an accomplishment: His followers carried portions on pieces of paper, stones, palm leaves, shoulder blades, bits of leather, and from the memories of men. Its compilation occurred under the third caliph, Uthman. Of the 114 surahs, eighty-six were revealed in Mecca and twenty-eight in Medina. The surahs are not in chronological order. Caliph Uthman is reported in a tradition: "Narrated Anas bin Malik: Uthman sent to every Muslim province one copy of what they had copied, and ordered that all the other Qur'anic materials, whether written in fragmentary manuscripts or whole copies, be burned."[28]

Muslims basically believe that there can be no good translation of the Qur'an since it was revealed in the "pure and godly" Arabic language. The Qur'an was not translated by Muslims during the first twelve centuries of Islam. The Qur'an was translated by Europeans in the early centuries but not by Muslims. Now there are many translations in many languages, including those by Muslim scholars. However, none can replace the Qur'an in the Arabic language as it was given to Muhammad. Muslims consider it the absolute perfection in language. It is the speech of God who spoke in the first person plural "We." Muslims believe it is inerrant.

Richard Martin has observed that the Islamic tradition offers the most vivid and convincing example of the active, oral-aural function of sacred scripture in the life of a religious community and culture. Islam's own view is that there are many scriptures of which the Qur'an is the final and most complete. The character of the Qur'an as verbatim speech of God sets it apart. "Whereas the divine presence for the Jew is in the Law and for the Christian is in the person of Christ, it is in the Qur'an for the Muslim as a direct encounter with God."[29]

Nasr wrote, "The soul of a Muslim is like a mosaic made up of formulae of the Qur'an in which he breathes and lives."[30] A Muslim who memorizes the Qur'an is called a Hafiz. A tradition praises the Muslim who accomplishes it. "Narrated Aisha: The Prophet said, 'Such a person as recites the Qur'an and masters it by heart, will be with the noble righteous scribes (in Heaven). And such a person as exerts himself to learn the Qur'an by heart, and recites it with great difficulty, will have a double reward.'"[31]

THE JUDGMENT: HEAVEN AND HELL

Muslims believe that as God created all, so God judges all.[32] Life is preparation for bliss in heaven or damnation in hell. There is an end to the world, a day of resurrection, a time of judgment, and an assignment of one's rewards.

Islam through its traditions alerts its people to the signs for the coming of the final day.

> Narrated Anas: I heard Allah's Apostle saying, "From among the portents of the Hour are (the following):
>
> 1. Religious knowledge will decrease (by the death of religious learned men).
> 2. Religious ignorance will prevail.
> 3. There will be prevalence of open illegal sexual intercourse.
> 4. Women will increase in number and men will decrease in number so much so that fifty women will be looked after by one man."[33]

The first three signs may be understandable, but the fourth one has its problems. A ratio of fifty women to one man in any circumstances is difficult to perceive. The final hour will come with suddenness although no specific time is given. For the unbelievers on the day of judgment and resurrection there will be great despair. A tradition reports: "Narrated Abu Huraira: Allah's Apostle said, 'The people will sweat so profusely on the Day of Resurrection that their sweat will sink seventy cubits deep into the earth, and it will rise up till it reaches the people's mouths and ears.'"[34]

The traditions do describe Muslims requesting an intercessor on the day of resurrection. They request Adam, Noah, Abraham, Moses, and Jesus to represent them before Allah. Each prophet in turn speaks of his inadequacy to mediate on their behalf and turns to the later prophet. Jesus also says he is unable and points Muslims to Muhammad. The intercession of Muhammad before Allah will be heard, and Allah will honor it. However, Muhammad's intercession cannot change the decrees of damnation on individuals as stated in the Qur'an.

The resurrection of the body is reported: "Narrated Abu Huraira: The Prophet said, 'Everything of the human body will decay except the coccyx bone (of the tail) and from that bone Allah will reconstruct the whole body.'"[35] Islam teaches that the decayed body will be resurrected from one bone. Muslims always bury the dead. Cremation is not allowed.

After everything on earth has perished, people will be revived or resurrected with the blast of a trumpet.[36] They will be gathered in one place. Their deeds will be weighed and assessed. All will be brought to account by God. The Book of Deeds is opened, and there is a scale of absolute justice. Fate rests on one's own neck.[37]

A Sunni tradition tells of the return of Jesus as messiah at which time he breaks the cross, kills pigs, dies, and is buried beside Muhammad. There is a popular tradition of an anti-Christ. A messiah is to come and destroy the anti-Christ.

Paradise

Muslims who follow the straight path of Islam look forward to paradise. The Qur'an and the Hadith present paradise as a place of extreme beauty, sinless, with no presence of pain or sorrow, and ample physical fulfillment. Satan is banished forever. Muslims will enjoy the eternal presence of Allah. Many graphic traditions focus on the sensual and sexual delights of paradise.

Thus, the righteous will receive their rewards in an eternal place called paradise. Those whose deeds are evil will receive their punishment in hell. Heaven has grades of felicity and is very delightful with its cool waters and delightful maidens. The Qur'an reports,

> And besides these two, / There are two other Gardens / Then which of the favours / Of your Lord will ye deny? /Dark green in colour / (From plentiful watering). / Then which of the favours / Of your Lord will ye deny? / In them (each) will be / Two Springs pouring forth water / In continuous abundance: / Then which of the favours / Of your Lord will ye deny? / In them will be Fruits / And dates and pomegranates: / Then which of the favours / Of your Lord will ye deny? / In them will be / Fair (Companions), good, beautiful— / Then which of the favours / Of your Lord will ye deny? / Companions restrained (as to / Their glances), in (goodly) pavilions / Then which of the favours / Of your Lord will ye deny? / Whom no man or Jinn / Before them has touched— / Then which of the favours / Of your Lord will ye deny? / Reclining on green Cushions / And rich Carpets of beauty. / Then which of the favours / Of your Lord will ye deny? / Blessed be the name / Of thy Lord, / Full of Majesty, / Bounty and Honour.[38]

Tradition observes that only Muslims will go to paradise. The People of the Book (Jews and Christians) are not admitted to heaven. "Narrated Abu Huraira: Then he (Muhammad) ordered Bilal to announce amongst the people: 'None will enter Paradise but a Muslim soul, and Allah may support this religion (i.e. Islam) even with an evil wicked man.'"

Soldiers and martyrs have a special place in heaven. "Narrated Abu Huraira: The Prophet said, 'Paradise has one hundred grades which Allah has reserved for the Mujahidun (men who fight in His Cause), and the distance between each of two grades is like the distance between the Heaven and the Earth.'"[39] Another tradition states, "Narrated Anas Bin Malik: The Prophet said, 'Nobody who dies and finds good from Allah (in the Here-after) would wish to come back to this world even if he were given the whole world and whatever is in it, except the martyr who, on seeing the superiority of martyrdom, would like to come back to the world and get killed again (in Allah's cause).'"[40]

In Muhammad's time martyrdom meant following his leadership, spreading Islam, and fighting Islam's enemies. In this way if one died, there was immediate entry into heaven with priority status. Heaven was so good that the martyr would be willing to do it all over again. During the Iran-Iraq war of the 1980s, Ayatollah Khomeini promised immediate entry to heaven for the tens of thousands of young men who would serve as martyrs on the frontlines of the Iranian forces.

Both in the Qur'an and in the Hadith are references to weddings in heaven. A tradition reports: "Narrated Qais: Allah's Apostle said, 'In Paradise there is a pavilion made of a single hollow pearl sixty miles wide, in each corner of which there are wives who will not see those in the other corners; and the believers will visit and enjoy them. And there are two gardens, the utensils and contents of which are made of silver; and two other gardens, the utensils and contents of which are made of so-and-so (i.e. gold) and nothing will prevent the people staying in the Garden of Eden from seeing their Lord except the curtain of majesty over His face.'"[41]

In this tradition wives are kept in separate quarters where their husbands discreetly visit them. Other traditions refer to married men being with new wives who are described as sensual, charming, and eternally youthful.

Hell

Hell is a burning and odorous place. The Qur'an graphically describes hell as boiling water and as pus and as a roasting place.[42]

Traditions compare the fires of hell to ordinary fire. One tradition reports more women in hell than men. "Narrated Usama: The Prophet said, 'I stood at the gate of the Fire and found that the majority of the people entering it were women.'"[43] Another tradition states, "Narrated Ibu Umar: The Prophet said, 'A woman entered the (Hell) Fire because of a cat which she had tied, neither giving it food nor setting it free to eat from the vermin of the earth.'"[44] In these two traditions inferences are

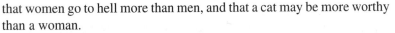
that women go to hell more than men, and that a cat may be more worthy than a woman.

The tortures in hell are descriptively vivid in the traditions. Boiling brains are mentioned in a number of Hadiths. Molten lead is poured into the ears of some. Hypocrites' intestines protrude outward as they go around hell telling of their double talk.

Muslim beliefs do not include the concept of original sin. Every person is responsible for one's own actions. No one can take away sin or die for another's sin. One must submit to God for all supplications, forgiveness of sins, and direction of life.

The ultimate goal and success in Islam is to be forgiven of all sins and to enter paradise. However, no one can depend upon his own good deeds. It is the mercy of God which allows one to enter paradise. There is no fallenness or depravity in human nature, only weakness and forgetfulness. Salvation is a future state experienced in the hereafter with pardon of one's sins and deliverance from hell and the gain of heaven.

Muslims believe in and do deeds of righteousness, saying their confession and believing in God's oneness, in his prophet Muhammad, and in the life after death. Also they practice the pillars of faith and rely on the mercy and forgiveness of God. al-Faruqi writes, "Religious justification is thus the Muslims' eternal hope, never their complacent certainty, not for even a fleeting moment."[45]

Islam holds to a predestination *(Qadar)*, which means that it believes in God's foreknowledge and decreeing all happenings in the world according to his will and wisdom. God is the creator of the cause-and-effect relationship. He has perfect knowledge of all that has happened in the past and all that will happen in the future. Good and evil are from God in the sense that God creates the laws that govern the cause and effect of good and evil.

Ali writes, "Sometimes we may not know the consequence of our action but God has the knowledge of the consequence of our action. It is, therefore, obvious that good works will lead to good results and evil works will lead to evil consequences. In this sense, all good and evil are from God because he is the Creator of Laws which govern the cause and effect relationship. It is simply called QADAR in Arabic; DESTINY is a poor translation of the term. There is no room for fatalism in Islam; God has NOT preordained for you everything that is happening to you. We, human beings, have freedom of action but no freedom of results which are controlled by the laws of God."[46]

As Muslims believe in the foreknowledge of God, so do they profess human freedom and the ability of the individual to determine the course of his voluntary acts. Muslims emphatically state there is no fatalism in Islam. Humans have freedom of action but do not have freedom of results which are controlled by the laws of God. Therefore, it is imperative to have proper knowledge before taking action to insure that the decision is good and will not cause evil consequences.

5

ISLAMIC DEVOTION

Muslim practices, like Muslim beliefs, are very similar. Regardless of their native tongue, Muslims must learn the Arabic language to say the formal prayers. Each orthodox Muslim must engage in at least six basic practices. Some writers refer to the first five of these as pillars of Islam: the confession, prayer, almsgiving, the fast of Ramadan, and the pilgrimage to Mecca. The confession must be said often—that there is only one God and that Muhammad is the Prophet of God. Prayers are said daily at stated times with specific rituals of purification and bodily motions and with focus toward Mecca. One gives specific monies and possessions for the upkeep and spread of Islam. A month of fasting is observed with rigorous ceremonies. One is required to make a pilgrimage in one's lifetime to Mecca. In addition to these five practices, every Muslim is to work purposefully to spread the religion.

THE GREAT CONFESSION

The confession *(shahada)* of Muslims is a simple statement but most comprehensive in nature and practice.[1] Seven Arabic words are whispered into a Muslim's ears at birth and death: "Ilaha illa Allah. Muhammad rasul Allah." Translated they are "There is no god but God. Muhammad is the messenger of God." Or another translation is "I testify that there is no deity except Allah, and I testify that Muhammad is His slave/servant and His messenger." The confession is uttered before prayers and on many other occasions. By daily uttering this confession Muslims are testifying about their monotheistic faith and that Muhammad is the final prophet.

This statement serves as the basis for the belief system. There are no other gods. Allah is the God. There are prophets, and Muhammad is the last. There are angels of God. There are sacred books, and the Qur'an is the complete and perfect one. There is a day of judgment and an afterlife.

In particular, the confession points to belief in God and accountability to God, who is the Creator, the Sustainer, and the Lord. It also points to Muhammad as the role model for the guidance that comes from God. Muhammad is a human being, not a deity and not to be worshiped.

A Muslim should know about the life of Muhammad, his character in public and in private, and his administration of social, economic, political, and military affairs. Knowing about the Prophet's sayings and actions found in the Hadith or sunnah provides a complementary source of knowledge to the Qur'an. The sources of law in Islam are found in the Qur'an and the Hadith.

The confession provides the basic roadmap for Muslim life. It contains the code words for daily living. Both belief *(iman)* and practice *(din)* fit together as one submits to God.

THE PRAYERS

One of the most vital and visible duties within Islam and for all Muslims is prayer.[2] Muslims should pray five times daily. They can pray in mosques and other places; they can pray individually but preferably with others. They should make themselves pure by ablution, face the direction of Mecca, and make the right intention.

Times of Prayer

The times of daily prayer are fastidiously followed. The Subh prayer may be from dawn to sunrise. The Zuhr prayer may be from noon to mid-afternoon. The Asr prayer may be from mid-afternoon to sunset. The Maghrib prayer may be from sunset to the disappearance of the evening twilight. And the Isha prayer may be from the evening twilight to the coming of dawn. In earlier times a prayer leader would ascend the roof of the mosque or climb the stairs of the minaret and call the people to prayer five times daily. He would utter the Adhan which included the

THE ISLAMIC PRAYER

Prayer is a very important part of life for the Muslim. He ceases his activities and prays toward the holy city of Mecca five times daily. In preparation for prayer time, he washes his face, hands, arms (to the elbow) three times; and his hair, ears and feet once. The following are the steps involved for a Muslin at prayer:

1. He raises his hands and says in Arabic, "God is great."
2. He folds his hands and quotes the opening of the Koran.
3. He bends over three times and says three times in Arabic, "Glorify the name of God most great."
4. He stands with hands to side and says once in Arabic, "Give thanks to God."
5. On his knees he touches the prayer rug while saying five times in Arabic, "Glorify the name of God most high."
6. He sits up.
7. Then he bows again and repeats step 5.
8. He stands and prepares to repeat the steps a second time.
9. He turns his head to the left and right. These steps end the series of prayers each time. The number of prayers varies: the first one is before sunrise; there are four at noon; four in the afternoon, three at sundown, and four in evening.

Adapted from Irma Duke, *Middle East Today* (Nashville: Convention Press), 1990. Used by permission.

words, "God is great. There is no god but God, and Muhammad is the messenger of God." The full call to prayer is:

God is most great. God is most great.
God is most great. God is most great.
I testify that there is no god except God.
I testify that there is no god except God.
I testify that Muhammad is the messenger of God.
I testify that Muhammad is the messenger of God.
Come to prayer! Come to prayer!
Come to success (in this life and the hereafter)!
Come to success!
God is most great. God is most great.
There is no god except God.

The call to prayer was begun by the Prophet Muhammad in Medina. A tradition describes the circumstances of its beginning.

Narrated Ibn Umar: "When the Muslims arrived at Medina, they used to assemble for prayer, and used to guess the time for it. During those days, the practice of Adhan (call to prayer) for the prayers had not yet been introduced. One time they discussed this problem regarding the call for prayer. Some people suggested the use of a bell like the Christians, others proposed a trumpet like the horn used by the Jews, but Umar was the first to suggest that a man should call (the people) for prayer; so Allah's Apostle ordered Bilal to get up and pronounce the Adhan for prayers."[3]

Rituals of Prayer

Each of the prayers may take from five to ten minutes. Before praying one must make ablution. At the mosque there is a source of water, often a pool or basin. The following functions of purification are:

- wash the hands up to the wrist three times

- rinse out the mouth three times

- clean the nostrils by sniffing water three times

- wash the face from forehead to chin and from ear to ear

- wash the forearms up to the elbows three times

- pass a wet hand over the whole of the head

- wash the feet up to the ankles three times, the right then the left.

Cleansing, prayer, and forgiveness are intertwined in Islam. A tradition reports, "Narrated Abu Huraira: I heard Allah's Apostle saying, 'If there was a river at the door of anyone of you and he took a bath in it five times a day would you notice any dirt on him?' They said, 'Not a trace of dirt would be left.' The Prophet added, 'That is the example of the five prayers with which Allah annuls evil deeds.'"[4] Another tradition reports the angels' assistance. "Narrated Abu Huraira: Allah's Apostle said, 'The angels keep on asking Allah's forgiveness for anyone of you, as long as he is at his Musalla (praying place) and he does not pass wind.'"[5] Angels have an intercessory role in prayer. Also, the phrase, "passing wind," shows the integration of the physical and spiritual aspects in Islam.

While praying one performs several actions called *rakahs*. A rakah includes standing, kneeling, standing, and prostrating two times. Various portions of the Qur'an are memorized and recited during the rakahs. The prayers should be stated in the Arabic language. A non-Arab should learn the prayers in Arabic. The words uttered are of praise, glorification of God, recitation of parts of the Qur'an, sending greetings and peace to prophets Abraham and Muhammad, and making supplications. Cragg has observed that Muslim prayer is a liturgy of adoration and submission, affirming the unity, sovereignty, and greatness of God.[6]

Prayer in the Mosque

A prayer leader in the mosque stands before rows of worshipers, facing Mecca, and leads them in the actions and words. Muslims are encouraged to perform their five daily prayers in a group or congregation or jama'a in the mosque. The mosque *(masjid)* is known as the place of prostration.

The architecture of the mosque is bare. It is not an auditorium for listeners nor a theatre. Calligraphy or script and some color are the basic decorations. The *mimbar* is the raised platform from which the speaker delivers the address. The *mihrab* is the niche showing the direction of Mecca.

Muslims may pray anywhere except in cemeteries or restrooms, but it is preferable to pray with the community in the mosque. A Hadith reports: "Narrated Abu Huraira: Allah's Apostle said, 'The reward of the prayer offered by a person in congregation is twenty-five times greater than that of the prayer offered in one's house or in the market (alone). And this is because if he performs ablution and does it perfectly and then

The Suleyman Mosque, known as the Blue Mosque, in Istanbul, Turkey (Author took photo)

proceeds to the mosque with the sole intention of praying, then for every step he takes towards the mosque, he is upgraded one degree in reward and one sin is taken off (crossed out) from his accounts (of deeds).'"[7]

Another Hadith emphasizes the importance of prayers said at the mosque: "Narrated Abu Huraira: The Prophet said, 'When it is a Friday, the angels stand at the gate of the mosque and keep on writing the names of the persons coming to the mosque in succession according to their arrivals. The example of the one who enters the mosque in the earliest hour is that of one offering a camel (in sacrifice). The one coming next is like one offering a cow and then a ram and then a chicken and then an egg respectively. When the Imam comes out (for Jumu'a prayer) they (i.e., angels) fold their papers and listen to the Khutba (sermon).'"[8]

Friday is a special day in Islam. It means the day of congregation. Muslims take baths, don clean clothing, and go to the mosque for prayers. The mosque leader delivers an address, khutba, in the early afternoon, followed by prayer. In many Muslim societies Friday is a holiday. Muslims are to cease work for the Friday address and prayer. Then they may return to their work or have a day of recreation.

During the five stated prayers individuals address God directly without an intercessor or mediator. Since there is no ordination in Islam, prayer leaders are selected often for their knowledge of Islam and for their ability to be an orator and for the beauty of their recitation of the call to worship and the prayers in Arabic.

Informal prayers (Do'a) may be voiced individually in one's native tongue. They may be extemporaneous petitions, pleas, praises, and statements to God. These informal prayers also have been associated with Folk Islam. Prayers are often voiced near the tombs and special mosques dedicated to Muslim hero types or saints. Perhaps because of their spontaneous and personal origins, Do'a prayers express the more emotional and heartfelt side of Islam.[9]

THE ALMSGIVING

Possessions and Percentages

The giving of alms *(zakat)* is required by the Qur'an; it is referred to as "poor due" or charity.[10] Zakat is a system established for equitable distribution of wealth in a Muslim society. It reminds Muslims that what they own belongs to God and that they are trustees of God on behalf of their wealth and goods.

Zakat is 2.5 percent of one's wealth. In certain cases such as farming and industry, it could be up to 20 percent of assets which one has held for a year. zakat is not an income tax.

There are two words in Arabic which have to do with almsgiving. zakat comes from a root word meaning "to grow" or "to be pure." Giving is a means of purifying one's soul. Sadaqat comes from a word meaning "true" or "sincere." Giving is a means of service to God. Some find in these two words a difference between obligatory and voluntary giving.

An Hadith reports the Prophet Muhammad's view of work and giving. "Narrated Abu Huraira: The Prophet said, 'No doubt, it is better for a person to take a rope and proceed in the morning to the mountains and cut the wood and then sell it, and eat from this income and give alms from it than to ask others for something.'"[11] The Prophet affirms the dignity of work in contrast to begging, and he teaches that the worker is to give alms to the less fortunate and needy.

In some Muslim nations zakat is required giving, and zakat stamps may be purchased from post offices. In other countries giving to mosques or Islamic endowments or to the poor is voluntary. An endowment *(Waqf)* is money or possessions left for a specific purpose: to build a shrine to a Muslim dignitary, a library, a hospital, a school, or a mosque. In the mosque there is usually a metal zakat box near the entrance. Muslims place their monies in the box as they leave.

Zakat in the Qur'an is associated with practicing regular charity and the gaining of paradise. Muslims view zakat as developing a sense of social responsibility as well as a duty which God requires of those who submit.

Cragg has written that almsgiving is a means to repentance, divine forgiveness, and practical reconciliation within the *umma*. It symbolizes voluntary acts of generosity. Islamic tradition observes that a camel loaned out for milk and a smile given to a neighbor are alms. These good deeds are called sadaqat and should be distinguished from the legal alms of zakat.[12]

Tradition gives the following sayings of Muhammad on almsgiving: "The Prophet said, 'Charity is a necessity for every Muslim.' He was asked: 'What if a person has nothing?' The Prophet replied: 'He should work with his own hands for his benefit and then give something out of such earnings in charity.' The Companions asked: 'What if he is not able to work?' The Prophet said: 'He should help poor and needy persons.' The Companions further asked: 'What if he cannot do even that?' The Prophet said: 'He should urge others to do good.' The Companions said: 'What if he lacks that also?' The Prophet said: 'He should check himself from doing evil. That is also charity.'"[13]

Phil Parshall has observed that Muslim peoples have challenges working out the practical dimensions of finances within the theocratic understanding that God is the ruler of all areas of life. A small wealthy class rules many Muslim nations while the masses are extremely poor. In some countries the government collects zakat; many people resent the zakat and question how the money is used. Islam prohibits usury, yet this prohibition is seldom followed either on an individual or national level.[14]

A Hadith reports of the angels and their relationship to giving and not giving: "Narrated Abu Huraira: The Prophet said, "Every day two angels come down from Heaven and one of them says, "O Allah! Compensate every person who spends in Your cause", and the other (angel) says, "O Allah! Destroy every miser"."" [15]

FASTING AND RAMADAN MONTH

The Arabic word for fasting *(sawm)* means abstinence. Fasting is observed during Ramadan, the ninth month of the Islamic lunar calendar.[16] Ramadan is the time when Muhammad received the revelation of the Qur'an from the angel Gabriel. The Qur'an asserts, "O ye who believe! / Fasting is prescribed to you."[17]

Fasting means to abstain from drinking, eating, and certain other sensual pleasures during the daylight hours of the month. Among the acts that violate the fast, the sexual act is the most serious. If it occurs during the fasting period, it means one must fast sixty consecutive days. If one is unable to do so, one has to pay sixty needy people the cost of one day's food. Thus, throughout the Hadith, there are strict prohibitions against having sexual intercourse while fasting. However, there is one tradition reported by Muhammad's favorite wife, Aisha: "Narrated Aisha: 'The Prophet used to kiss and embrace (his wives) while he was fasting, and he had more power to control his desires than any of you.'"[18] The Qur'an forbids touching one's wives while fasting. However, in this tradition the Prophet kisses and touches his wives. Apparently he stopped short of intercourse. The Prophet is reported in a tradition to say: "Narrated Alqama: The Prophet said, 'He who can afford to marry should marry, because it will help him refrain from looking at other women, and save his private parts from committing illegal sexual relation; and he who cannot afford to marry is advised to fast, as fasting will diminish his sexual power.'"[19] Cragg writes that "the withholding (imsak), as the term goes, of the body from its natural satisfactions from dawn till dusk reminds it, compellingly, of a divine claim and imposes a pattern of discipline that educates and habituates it for other tasks."[20]

In some of the Hadith, fasting is associated with deprivation, rewards, and joy. "Narrated Abu Huraira: The Prophet said, 'Allah said, The Fast is for Me and I will give a reward for it, as he (the one who observes the fast) leaves his sexual desire, food, and drink for My sake. Fasting is a screen (from Hell) and there are two joys for a fasting person, one at the time of breaking his fast, and the second at the time when he will meet his Lord.'"[21]

Some Muslims may be exempted from fasting, including aged adults, young children before puberty, and pregnant women. However, there are provisions to make it up at other times or to give food to the poor. Missing a day of fasting is taken seriously. "Narrated Abu Huraira from the Prophet: 'Whoever did not fast for one day of Ramadan without a genuine excuse or a disease, then even if he fasted for a complete year, it would not compensate for that day.'"[22] Muslims are encouraged to eat a meal just before dawn of the fasting day and another meal soon after sunset. It is a time to be more generous to the poor, to avoid harsh speech, and to give more time to prayer.

At the end of Ramadan there is a special festival, Id Fetr, when the fast is concluded with celebrations and a return to normal routines. On the special day of the festival Muslims don new clothes and proceed to the mosque for prayer. After the Id Fetr prayer, there is visitation in homes with feasts and celebrations. The poor are provided with either money or food.

The Muslim calendar is based on the lunar year and the phases of the moon. The lunar year is 354 or 355 days, some 10 or 11 days shorter than the solar year. It takes some thirty-three years for a month to pass around the calendar. Thus, the fasting season falls in both cool months and hot months. When Ramadan is in summer, the heat may cause hardships for workers who must refrain from drinking water.

Fasting is especially difficult during the hot season, when one must rinse one's mouth in preparation for prayers. A true believer and practitioner will not swallow one drop of water. All in all Ramadan tests endurance and self-denial. Upon its successful completion, one may feel that not only has one's moral duties been observed but also that paradise has come closer.

THE PILGRIMAGE

Pilgrimage *(Hajj)* is a visit to Mecca during a special annual season to perform certain rituals in and around Mecca.[23] The season includes the tenth and eleventh months and the first ten days of the twelfth month. The Qur'an places an obligation upon all Muslim men and women who are capable of making the journey both physically and financially at least once in a lifetime. The Qur'an states, "And complete / The *Hajj* or *Umrah* / In the service of Allah."[24]

Phil Parshall has raised an interesting question about the pilgrimage in light of Islam's strong opposition to any form of idolatry. The Ka'ba, a cubical building housing a holy black stone, has become the focal point of all Muslims. Muslims circumambulate the Ka'ba and kiss the covered stone which has been worn down by human touch.[25]

Why is the kissing of the black stone so central in the pilgrimage rites? A tradition reports: "Narrated Abis bin Rabi'a: Umar came near the Black Stone and kissed it and said, 'No doubt, I know that you are a stone and can neither benefit anyone or harm anyone. Had I not seen Allah's Apostle kissing you I would not have kissed you.'"[26] Umar thus cites Muhammad's example of kissing the stone as sufficient reason to do so. The stone appears neutral.

The Prophet Muhammad had a burning desire to return to Mecca after he was forced to flee the city to Medina in 622 (1 A.H., the first year of the hegira or flight). Shortly before his death, ten years later, he returned to Mecca with his triumphant militia. There he had his farewell pilgrimage speech at the Ka'ba.

Muslims associate the prophet Abraham with Mecca and the pilgrimage. Abraham had a son, Ishmael, by a concubine, Hagar. Hagar and her son were confined in a desert place. In their need of water she discovered a well which came to be known as Zamzam. Around the well the town of Mecca began to grow. Later, Abraham had a dream to offer his son as a sacrifice to God. But the son was saved and a ram was offered in his stead. Abraham on the command of God built a house of worship and invited the people to make a yearly pilgrimage (Hajj) there. This place became known as the Ka'ba.

The Arabs corrupted the religion of Abraham with their idolatry at the Ka'ba. However, Islam removed the idolatry from the Ka'ba and continued the practice of the Hajj, making it an obligation upon all Muslims with few exceptions. Both Zamzam and the Ka'ba are central places in the pilgrimage.

Upon arriving in Mecca, the pilgrims dress in two pieces of unsewn white material. The simple dress of pilgrims is to point to their egalitarianism. There are to be no differences between the rich and the poor during the Hajj. It is a symbol of unity. For a brief time there are no kings and no paupers behind the white coverings. They say prayers, refrain from sensual pleasures, and concentrate on the rites of the pilgrimage. They circumambulate the Ka'ba seven times, and if possible, kiss or touch the Black Stone in one of its corners. They remain in Mecca about seven days, all the while praying in the surroundings of the mosque and the Ka'ba and tasting of the water of the well of Zamzam in the mosque.

On the eighth day the pilgrims proceed to Mina and Mount Arafat for prayer and contemplation, far from all worldly temptations. In the following days they throw stones at a shrine named Aqaba, symbolizing their condemnation of the devil and all evil ways. They offer a lamb in sacrifice; the ceremony is known as *Id-e-Adha*. They cut their hair, and then they resume their ordinary clothes as they return to Mecca. Again, they circumambulate the Ka'ba and say prayers. Walking around the Ka'ba, known as *tawaf*, is considered the highest form of worship of God. All Muslims face toward the Ka'ba for the five daily prayers. All mosques around the world are built to face towards the Ka'ba. But the Hajj offers the worshipper the supreme experience of seeing and touching the Ka'ba. Within about two weeks the pilgrimage has been completed.

Before leaving Saudi Arabia some pilgrims visit the city of Medina some 250 miles north of Mecca. They see the sites of the Prophet Muhammad, especially the mosque he built and his grave. It is of particular importance to pray at the Prophet's mosque. Also, they may visit the graves of Abu Bakr, Umar, and Fatima. The Pilgrims return to their homelands with gifts for family and friends. They share their story. They are looked upon with great respect, for they have made the required journey of a lifetime.

Some two million Muslims make the Hajj to Mecca each year.[27] Millions more around the globe celebrate the Id-e-Adha on the tenth day of the twelfth month of the Islamic calendar. On this day Muslims attend the community prayer and afterwards sacrifice an animal as their compatriots do on the Hajj. The meat is divided into three parts, that for the family, that distributed to the needy, and the third part given to friends. There is a lesser pilgrimage or *umrah* which is different from the great Hajj. It may be performed anytime and does not include the journey to Arafat. Pilgrims may go to Medina to honor the Prophet at his mosque and gravesite. They usually take home with them water from the well of Zamzam, the holy spring in Mecca where Hagar saved her life and the life of her son Ishmael when they were sent into the desert by Abraham.

Muslims who make the pilgrimage experience a deep religious transformation. Their encounter with history and with the world community of which they are a part returns with them to their homelands and local communities. One of the best-known American Muslims, Malcolm X, wrote of his life-changing experience on his pilgrimage to Mecca: "There were tens of thousands of pilgrims, from all over the world. They were of all colors, from blue-eyed blondes to black-skinned Africans. But we were all participating in the same ritual, displaying a spirit of unity and brotherhood that my experience in America had led me to believe never could exist between the white and the non-white . . . on this pilgrimage, what I have seen and experienced, has forced me to re-arrange much of my thought-patterns previously held, and to toss aside some of my previously held conclusions."[28]

Haram is an inviolable place. It is a place for protection and sanctity. Islam has three prominent protected or haram places: the Ka'ba or House of God in Mecca, the Mosque of the Prophet in Medina, and the Mosque of Aqsa adjacent to the Dome of the Rock in Jerusalem.

An Hadith about Mecca states, "Narrated Ibn Abbas: The Prophet said, 'Allah has made this place (Mecca) a sanctuary since the creation of the heavens and the earth and will remain a sanctuary until the Day of Resurrection as Allah has ordained its sanctity (sacredness).'"[29] Other traditions report that the Prophet said there was to be no fighting and bloodshed in the Ka'ba. In recent times, however, a gun battle was initiated by Iranian pilgrims within the sacred Ka'ba and deaths occurred in a shoot-out with Saudi Arabian forces.

JIHAD: MISSION AND WARFARE

Some Muslims include holy efforts in the cause of God *(jihad)* as the sixth pillar of Islam. Jihad is seen as a personal commitment by the Muslim to spread the faith. Jihad is also viewed as war on behalf of God. Basically the word means struggling or striving. Both Muslim and non-Muslim writers have used the phrase "holy war" with reference to jihad. However, Muslim scholars point out that Islam teaches that it is unholy to start war, though some wars are inevitable and justifiable.

Thus, within Islam there is the "greater jihad" and the "lesser jihad." Greater jihad is the warfare against sin and all that is against Allah and his teachings. It is a personal battle that each Muslim wages within for righteousness. Lesser jihad is the traditional holy war associated with the will of Allah and launched in the name of Allah against the enemies of Islam.

According to Islamic teaching, humans have two choices: (1) the way of heedlessness or ignorance *(al-Jahiliyya),* and (2) the way of submission to God *(al-Islam)*. The ways of submission and heedlessness are viewed as institutionalized in Islamic and non-Islamic political entities. Submission to God means the territory of Islam *(dar al-Islam);* heedlessness means the territory of war *(dar al-harb)*. The struggle and the program of action to extend the territory of Islam over against that of the territory of war is jihad.

Muhammad is instructed in the Qur'an, "Then fight in the cause / Of Allah,"[30] and "then fight and slay / The Pagans wherever ye find them."[31] The Qur'an also states, "when ye meet / The Unbelievers (in fight), / Smite at their necks,"[32] and "Fight those who believe not / In Allah nor the Last Day."[33]

E. Van Donzel writes,

> Holy War (A. jihad): the Arabic word, which signifies an effort directed towards a determined objective, is used for military action with the object of the expansion of Islam and, if need be, of its defense. The notion stems from the fundamental principle of the universality of Islam, according to which this religion, along with the temporal power which it implies, ought to embrace the whole universe, if necessary by force. This principle, however, must be partially combined with another which tolerates the existence, within the Islamic community itself, of the adherents of "the religions with holy books," i.e. Christians, Jews and Zoroastrians. For them Holy War ceases as soon as

they agree to submit to the political authority of Islam and pay the poll tax (A. jizya) and the land tax (A. Kharaj). At present times there is a thesis according to which Islam relies for its expansion exclusively upon persuasion and other peaceful means.[34]

A Muslim writer who resides in the United States has written:

> Muslims have a duty to establish an environment of freedom of expression to enable them to convey the message of Islam. If there is a tyrannical government which does not allow the freedom of presenting Islam to the people, then the Muslims have a duty to obtain a free environment by the best possible means of the time . . . It is the hardest of the struggles (jihad), that is, to implement the rule of God on earth. In a given geographical territory a system already exists, therefore it is not easy to tell the followers of that system that there are flaws in their system and you would like to offer an alternative; people do not look at such ideas sympathetically. Nevertheless, it is the duty of every Muslim to convince the majority that Islam is a God-given system of life and it is far, far superior to any man-made system.[35]

The Qur'an also states that one should stay on the straight path, "And strive in His cause / As ye ought to strive, / (With sincerity and discipline)."[36] Also it counsels one to carry the message of Islam: "Only those are Believers / Who have believed in Allah / And His Messenger, and have / Never since doubted, but / Have striven with their / Belongings and their persons / In the Cause of Allah."[37]

Jihad, then, has several meanings. Muhammad is reported to have said, "It is the duty of every Muslim to command the good and forbid evil in the heart, the tongue, and the hand (or sword)." Although war and force were a part of jihad, some say that the "greater jihad" is the struggle in one's own heart to follow the will of God. Struggle with the tongue implies missionary work. To move from the tongue to the hand (pen) stresses the propagation of Islam to persuade others to come to the only God and to the only true religion.

The Hadith of Islam give approval for violence against both infidels and those who leave Islam as their native or chosen religion. The importance of jihad in the traditions is clear. Muhammad stated the purpose of jihad: "Narrated Abdullah: I asked the Prophet, 'Which deed is the dearest to Allah?' He replied, 'To offer prayers at their fixed times.' I asked,

'What is the next (in goodness)?' He replied, 'To be good and dutiful to your parents.' I again asked: 'What is the next (in goodness)?' He replied, 'To participate in jihad (religious fighting) in Allah's cause.'"[38]

A tradition reports Muhammad's concern and commitment to the cause of Allah. "Narrated Abu Musa: A man came to the Prophet and asked, 'A man fights for war booty; another fights for fame and a third fights for showing off; which of them fights in Allah's Cause?' The Prophet said, 'He who fights so that Allah's Word (i.e., Islam) should be superior, fights in Allah's Cause.'"[39]

Another tradition states the teaching of Muhammad about using force against nonbelievers. "Narrated Abu Huraira: Allah's Apostle said, 'I have been ordered (by Allah) to fight the people till they say: "None has the right to be worshiped but Allah," and whoever said it then he will save his life and property.'"[40] A tradition reports: "Narrated Hisham: My father informed me that Aisha said, 'Sa'd said, "O Allah! You know that there is nothing more beloved to me than to fight in Your Cause against those who disbelieved Your Apostle and turned him out (of Mecca)".'"[41] Here fighting and killing are described as a beloved activity.

As Islam spread from Arabia to the Middle East and North Africa, Muslim scholars have written that peoples were tired of the Byzantine rulers and many were waiting for other religious and political choices. That may be true. Certain Hadith, however, portray other reasons.

> Narrated Jubair bin Haiya: Umar sent the Muslims to the great countries to fight the pagans. . . . (The people under siege asked the Muslims who they are.) al-Mughira replied, "We are some people from the Arabs; we led a hard, miserable, disastrous life; we used to suck the hides and the date stones from hunger; we used to wear clothes made up of fur of camels and hair of goats, and to worship trees and stones. While we were in this state, the Lord of the Heavens and the Earths, Elevated is His Remembrance and Majestic is His Highness, sent to us from among ourselves a Prophet, the Messenger of our Lord, has ordered us to fight you until you worship Allah Alone or give Jizya (i.e. tribute)."[42]

Thus, those who were colonized by the Muslims had to choose whether to become Muslims or to pay a tax. Tradition speaks to one who forsakes Islam or is an apostate. "Narrated Ikrima: The statement of

Allah's Apostle, 'Whoever changed his Islamic religion, then kill him.'"[43] In other traditions apostasy is also punishable by instant death.

The Hadith describes different rewards for jihad. They include rewards for punishing non-Muslims and for being a martyr. "Narrated Abu Qatada: Allah's Apostle said, 'Whoever had killed an infidel and has a proof or a witness for it, then the salb (arms and belongings of that deceased) will be for him.'"[44] Martyrdom guarantees entry into paradise as well as an honorable name bestowed on one's family. "Narrated Abu Huraira: Allah's Apostle said, 'Five are regarded as martyrs: They are those who die because of plague, abdominal disease, drowning or a falling building, etc., and the martyrs in Allah's Cause.'"[45] Paradise is reached or booty is earned in following Allah's Cause. "Narrated Abu Huraira: Allah's Apostle said, 'To the person who carries out jihad for His Cause and nothing compelled him to go out but the jihad in His Cause, and belief in His Words, Allah guarantees that He will either admit him into Paradise or return him with the reward or the booty he has earned to his residence from where he went out.'"[46]

The Qur'an and the Hadith present jihad in a coercive and violent manner. Although Muslims understand it as an effort or struggle to bring righteousness and peace upon the earth, the history of jihad has also revealed it to be warfare against all whom Islam considers to be its enemies. In contemporary history Iran and Iraq waged a vicious war against each other, each declaring a jihad against the other. Hundreds of thousands were killed, and many others were maimed. Fighters were promised paradise in their martyrdom. Both sides waged jihad in the name of Allah. Both sides were Islamic countries. In another incident Salman Rushdie, author of *Satanic Verses*, was (and continues to be) subjected to a jihad by Ayatollah Khomeini for slandering the Prophet in a novel. Millions of dollars have been offered to the one who will kill Rushdie.

Islamic scholars and leaders, politicians and theologians can render a service to the non-Muslim world with clarity of what jihad means for them in the Qur'an, in the Hadith, in its historical development, and in its contemporary meaning in a religiously pluralistic world.

FOLK ISLAM

The unorthodox and informal ways of religion are sometimes called popular or folk expressions. Folk religion often assumes some of the orthodox ways and adds to them or changes them. People may practice both orthodox and folk ways but give major attention and time to the folk religion. While the orthodox expressions of religion may be historically primary in the development of the religion and may be more urban and professional, folk religion may be a deviant, emphasizing local expressions and heartfelt needs over intellectual interests.[47]

Islam began with its creed of the oneness of God and its final prophet Muhammad. The creed is still central in faith. However, the God of Islam is by definition a distant God, far removed from humanity and dis-associated from human nature. Sufism, the mystical wing of Islam, attempts to overcome this distance by emphasizing that God is closer than one's jugular vein. It talks of the love and closeness and presence of God. Sufis through their dancing (swirling dervishes) and music show the intense emotional side of religion and the nearness of God to the human condition.

According to orthodox Islam, Muhammad is a human being who accepted his appointment to be a prophet from God. But in popular Islam, Muhammad becomes a venerated figure whose image appears on the dashboards of taxis. Popular Islam names mosques and shrines after certain men and women. Often these figures become the mediators for the supplications and prayers offered to them and through them to God. They are prophets, saints, and figures of piety and wisdom. One shrine near Jericho is dedicated to the prophet Moses *(Musa)*. Hundreds of saints' shrines dot the landscape of North Africa and the Middle East.

Shi'ite Islam has an institution of veneration to the family of Ali, the prophet's son-in-law, including his wife Fatima and their two sons, Hasan and Husein. During the month of Muharram there are passion plays telling the narrative of the death of Husein and his vicarious suf-fering for his followers. Shi'ites march in the streets beating themselves with chains and drawing blood that reddens their white outer garments. At shrines dedicated to Ali and Husein, the faithful gather to utter prayers and to seek their advice and assistance. Shi'ite Islam in Iran especially holds the twelve imams in high esteem by naming shrines after them and by calling on their names in prayers.[48]

Popular Islam also changes the form and function of prayer. Ortho-dox Islam requires Muslims to memorize enough Arabic to voice formal prayers five times daily to Allah, preferably in a mosque with a group. But Folk Islam urges people to say their prayers in their own vernacular language at times of the day when they have specific needs. These prayers are addressed to Ali or Husein or others. They are heart prayers, more informal and personal, and often spoken at the tomb of a saint like Husein. A formal prayer in Arabic in the mosque may acknowledge the mercy of God. An informal prayer at the tomb of the saint may ask the saint to intervene to help a wife have her first child to be a son.

The author accompanied one of his students, Ferideh, to a shrine in Iran.

> The shrine entrance was engulfed with silver mirrored material, on both sides were situated the shoe-keeper and his shoe racks. Now, barefooted, we proceeded into the gate entrance which was heavily decorated with mirror or silver plates. The gates were made of beautiful inlaid work. The hallways of the shrine represented the best of all Iranian handicraft and art skills. The shrine itself was made of silver globes in the shape of a small room. Over the entrance each pilgrim gazed at the inscription and recited it as a permission request to enter the "holy of holies." It read, "In the name of the almighty Allah, And in the name of Mohammed, And in the name of Ali, And in the name of Fatemeh [Fatima], And in the name of Hasan, And in the name of Husain, And in the name of the descendants of Ali and Fatemeh, I seek the permission of entering the shrine of Abdol Abbas." Ferideh paused to murmur the request as I looked at the tomb, remembering the shoe-keeper's words of counsel as I tipped him ten rials (fifteen cents), "Whatever you request from the saint (Imam), you will receive it."[49]

Folk Islam has also established other pilgrimage centers in addition to Mecca. Shi'ites go to Mecca but also go to Kufa and Kerbala in Iraq and to Meshad in Iran. Why? Kufa and Kerbala are associated with the places where Husein died with his family members, where his blood was spilt for his followers, and where his name is called upon. Meshad in eastern Iran holds the shrine tomb with its golden dome of the eighth imam of the Shi'ite branch. Millions of pilgrims also plan a lifetime to go to Kerbala and to Meshad, not only to honor Husein and the eighth imam but also to seek their mediation in many of life's dilemmas and challenges. Pilgrims are honored upon their return. Men don a turban, and women wear special clothing. All achieve a special status in the community as persons of wisdom and experience.

Folk Islam has erected many mosques and shrines named after prophets and holy persons of the Islamic tradition. Donors receive special prestige and power among their family and friends. Often, when large sums are involved, government sets up an organization of endowments to handle the administration of the properties and personnel. Visitors and pilgrims attend the shrines. Often, there is a picture and/or a tomb of the individual. Pilgrims toss money within the gates of the tomb. A large

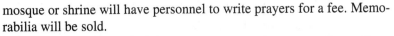

mosque or shrine will have personnel to write prayers for a fee. Memorabilia will be sold.

Thus, folk religion in Islam may assume giant proportions. From fetishes and amulets to saints' tombs, from pictures to relics, it is a large and widespread expression. The leaders of orthodox Islam disparage folk religion and preach against it. Movements like Wahhabism in Saudi Arabia try to eliminate it. Yet, it speaks to the heart and from the heart of Muslims. It is tangible and down to earth. It is a feeling religion. It honors personalities; it places hope in wise and pious deceased sages to help people meet the everyday challenge of life. In many ways folk religion is a challenge to and a critique of orthodox Islam.

A CALENDAR FOR ALL SEASONS

Day one of the Islamic calendar is the Hegira, the emigration of Muhammad with his followers from Mecca to Medina. Muslims date everything from that event. On the Christian calendar, the Hegira occurred in September 622. On the Muslim calendar, it is day one in the year 1 A.H. (After the Hegira).

The calendar follows the lunar year rather than the solar year used in the West.[50] In accordance with Surah 10:5, the new moon *(hilal)* determines the first of the month. Since the average interval between consecutive new moons is 29 days, 12 hours, 44 minutes, and 3 seconds, the lunar months alternate between 29 and 30 days in length. A given month may have 29 days in some years and 30 days in others. There are 12 months in the Muslim lunar year, or 354 days on average.

The Months

The Qur'an forbids the intercalation of a thirteenth month periodically to keep it in line with the solar year.[51] Hence, the Islamic calendar travels backward through the solar calendar about eleven days each year, returning to the same solar time in about thirty-three lunar years; thus thirty-three lunar years equal thirty-two solar years. The day, that is the period of twenty-four hours, begins in the evening. For example, the "night" of the 27th of Ramadan begins at nightfall on the 26th.

The names of the months in the Islamic calendar are:

1st Muharram	5th Jamadi I	9th Ramadan
2nd Safar	6th Jamadi II	10th Shawwal
3rd Rabi' I	7th Rajab	11th Dhul-Qu'da
4th Rabi'II	8th Sha'ban	12th Dhul-Hijja

Muslim holidays and religious observances follow the lunar calendar. Some are obligatory, but others are not. Some are occasions of joy and feasting, but others are more somber and serious. Some are universal throughout Islam, but others are special to a particular branch of Islam or to a region.

Holy Days

Friday (al-Jama'a) is the day of obligatory community worship. Muslims come together for the noon prayer, usually at a mosque. After a sermon, men form lines to pray. Women are segregated from men in the mosque. Unlike the Jewish Sabbath and Christian Sunday, Friday is not considered a holy day. Muslims may engage in business as usual before and after the corporate worship. In recent times some Muslim countries have adopted the western practice of closing businesses on weekends, and Friday has become the day off instead of Sunday.

The following occasions are listed, including the months in which they occur:

1st of Muharram. Ras al-Sana is the Muslim New Year; it is the first day of the first month. It commemorates the Hegira. It is not obligatory. It may be a day of exchanging greetings but not necessarily a vacation day in all Muslim countries.

10th of Muharram. Ashura means "the tenth." It is a day when Muslims may voluntarily fast from dawn to sunset, though it is not obligatory. For Shi'ite Muslims it is a day of sorrow commemorating the assassination of Husein, the son of Ali and grandson of Prophet Muhammad. The celebration for Shi'ites begins on the first of Muharram and culminates on the tenth with passion plays and parades which often include rituals of self-flagellation in sorrow and sympathy for Husein.

12th of Rabi' I. Maulid al-Nabi means "the birthday of the Prophet." It is not an obligatory holiday but is nevertheless widely observed. Often, it is an occasion for excessive veneration of the Prophet. There are meetings where addresses are given and poems read eulogizing the birth, life, and sufferings of Muhammad. In some countries, Saudi Arabia for example, the popular celebration of his birthday is discouraged. Sufis may have torch-light processions at night. Often it is a time of festivities and the exchange of gifts, with children receiving candy and toys.

27th of Rajab. Lailat al-Isra wa al-Mi'raj means "night of the journey and the ascension." This celebration remembers the night according to Muslim belief when Muhammad was taken on a winged animal from

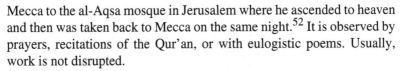

Mecca to the al-Aqsa mosque in Jerusalem where he ascended to heaven and then was taken back to Mecca on the same night.[52] It is observed by prayers, recitations of the Qur'an, or with eulogistic poems. Usually, work is not disrupted.

14th of Sha'ban. Lailat al-Bara'a means "night of repentance." According to Muslim tradition, God descends to the lowest heaven on this night to call to man and to grant forgiveness for his sins. In some countries, India and Malaysia for example, it is a night when prayers are said for the dead, food is given to the poor and sweets are eaten. In some areas of the Muslim world, it is treated like a new year's celebration.

Ramadan. Muslims are required to fast during the ninth month of the Muslim year. Fasting is one of the pillars of Islam as stated in the Qur'an. Each day from dawn to dusk there is to be no eating, no drinking, and no sexual intercourse. Normal daily and business activities continue; however, in some countries business hours are shortened to allow for more rest and religious observance. After sunset and prayers, a meal is taken. Also, before sunrise there may be a small meal. It is inappropriate for tourists and non-Muslims to eat and drink openly during Ramadan among Muslims who are observing the fast.

27th of Ramadan. Lailat al-Qadr is the next to the last night of the month of fasting. "The night of power and greatness" is a sacred time for Muslims. It commemorates the time when the first revelation was received by Prophet Muhammad. Pious Muslims may pray the entire evening in expectation that their prayers will be answered during this season.

1st of Shawwal. Id al-Fitr is "the feast of breaking the fasting month" and begins immediately after Ramadan. It is an obligatory feast day. It is a happy time when Muslims conclude their abstinence and purifying observances. Families and friends visit, have festive meals, exchange presents, and give pastries and sweets. The celebration may continue for several days. Often, business and government offices close for a portion of the time.

Dhu al Hijjah 1-10. The Qur'an requires Muslims to make a pilgrimage to the city of Mecca at least once in their lifetime. It is called the Hajj. It should occur in the last month of the Muslim calendar, Dhu al-Hijjah. Pilgrims come to Mecca from all over the world to perform the rituals during these ten days. Tradition reports that Abraham offered to sacrifice his son Ishmael, son of Hagar, to God at the place of pilgrimage in Mecca. This tradition is in contrast to the Jewish and Christian story of the intended sacrifice of Isaac, son of Sarah.

10th of Dhu al-Hijja. Id al-Adha is "the feast of sacrifice" or "the great feast." It is obligatory upon all Muslims whether they are in Mecca on the pilgrimage or at home. It marks the end of the pilgrimage or Hajj. A sheep, cow, or camel is slaughtered, and the meat is shared by family and friends. Sometimes the slaughter of the animals is held in a public place, and the meat is distributed to the poor as well as to others gathered. It also commemorates the sacrificing of an animal in the place of Abraham's son, Ishmael. It is a festive time with much visitation, eating, exchanging of gifts, and buying of new clothes. Often, businesses and offices close for some of the celebrations.

Prayers are an important part of Muslim life and are regulated by the calendar. The required five daily prayers, as already noted, are observed at stated times from about sunrise to bedtime. The religious observances and festivities occur both in the mosques and in homes. Often, mosques and homes are decorated with lights. On special occasions, the *ulama* (Muslim clerics) not only speak in mosques but also come to homes for special Qur'anic recitations for family and friends.[53]

6

ISLAMIC INSTITUTIONS, RELIGIOUS AUTHORITY, SECTARIANISM

FROM AYATOLLAHS TO LAW COURTS TO SHI'ITES

I slam is a religion based on monotheism, morals, mandates, and manners. It is comprehensive in its worldview and highly particular in its morals and conduct. It leaves little in private life and in public life for speculation and uncertainty in providing answers and directions for Muslims. Islam provides a roadmap for life on a daily, monthly, and yearly calendar.

Sources of Islamic authority include the Qur'an, Hadith, Sunnah, Shari'a, schools of law, the ulama, and mosques and Qur'anic schools. These institutions govern and administer Muslims and their communities.

Although Islam is monolithic in its beliefs and practices, history and tradition have brought fragmentation and sectarianism among its peoples. The division between Sunnis and Shi'ites arose early in Islamic history. Other divisions occurred as Islam expanded and other cultures assimilated it with their own beliefs and practices.

Various groupings of Muslims include Sunni, Shi'ite, Sufi, Ahmadiyya, and the Nation of Islam. Also, certain theologians have attracted adherents by their scholarship. This chapter considers Islamic institutions, religious authority, and sectarianism.

SOURCES OF RELIGIOUS AUTHORITY

The Qur'an, the Law, the Tradition, Schools of Law

The Qur'an states, "There hath come to you / From Allah a (new) light / and a perspicuous Book— / Wherewith Allah guideth all / Who seek His good pleasure / To ways of peace and safety, / And leadeth them out / Of darkness, by His Will, / Unto the light—guideth them / To a Path that is Straight."[1] The light which serves as the umbrella for guidance of Islamic faith and practice is Shari'a.

Shari'a is the sum of Islamic guidance revealed to Muhammad and transmitted by him to humanity. Its sources are the Qur'an and the authentic Hadith and Sunnah of Muhammad. The word *Shari'a* originally meant "a stream of water." Just as water is the necessity of life, so is the Shari'a of Islam for the order and harmony of private and public life.

The four sources of authority for the Shari'a or law of Islam are the Qur'an, the Hadith, the Ijma, and the Qiyas. The Qur'an is the primary source. The Hadith or sayings and traditions of Muhammad must never contradict the Qur'an and are complementary to it. And the ijma and qiyas are complementary to both the Qur'an and the Hadith.

The Qur'an is the primary and final authority of all law and life. Through the centuries there have been systematic studies and collections of commentaries on the Qur'an. The first was done by al-Tabari about A.D. 900. Perhaps the most authoritative and helpful for modern scholars is the commentary of al-Badawi, written about 922.

The Hadith are narratives, statements, or stories of what Muhammad said or did. It is the actual tradition or custom practiced by the prophet. The Hadith have been preserved in written form. The Hadith then provided the base for the developing customs and traditions of Islamic life and culture which became known as the Sunnah. Out of hundreds of thousands of Hadith, a system was developed to determine the genuine sayings and traditions of the Prophet. An early collection of Hadith by al-Bukari from about A.D. 870 is a popular collection.

Seyyed Hossein Nasr has written concerning the Hadith, "Scholars sifted the vast body of sayings attributed to the Prophet and classified them according to those that were certain, doubtful, and spurious. Gradually this process produced the six major canonical collections which came to be accepted by the Sunni community. . . . These works, all compiled in the third/ninth century, received the seal of approval of the ulama and the community in the form of ijma, or consensus. They came to form an indispensable source upon which Sunni Islam has relied for over a millennium."[2]

Muslims for some fourteen hundred years have looked to Prophet Muhammad for direction in the personal and community life. Ram Swarup writes of the importance of the Hadith and the life of Muhammad to Muslims worldwide:

> The Prophet is caught as it were in the ordinary acts of his life—sleeping, eating, mating, praying, hating, dispensing justice, planning expeditions and revenge against his enemies. The picture that emerges is hardly flattering, and one is left wondering why in the first instance it was reported at all and whether it was done by his admirers or enemies. One is also left to wonder how the believers, generation after generation, could have found this story so inspiring.
>
> The answer is that the believers are conditioned to look at the whole thing through the eyes of faith. An infidel in his fundamental misguidance may find the Prophet rather sensual and cruel—and certainly many of the things he did do not conform to ordinary ideas of morality—but the believers look at the whole thing differently. To them morality derives from the Prophet's actions; the moral is whatever he did. Morality does not determine the Prophet's actions, but his actions determine and define morality. Muhammad's acts were not ordinary acts; they were Allah's own acts.
>
> It was in this way and by this logic that Muhammad's opinions became the dogmas of Islam and his personal habits and idiosyncrasies became moral imperatives: Allah's commands for all believers in all ages and climes to follow.[3]

Phil Parshall, a non-Muslim scholar who has studied the Hadith in detail, has written that the Hadith texts are highly readable. "At places the reader will break into laughter, as when reading about Moses, naked, running after a rock that is stealing his clothes. Perplexity will come when pondering Muhammad's marital and sex life. Horror may be the reaction when jihad is described in gruesome form. But the result will be a dramatic new understanding of why Muslims think and act as they do."[4]

Ijma is the consensus of the Muslim community or of its leading scholars, the ulama. Ijma must be based on the Qur'an and the Hadith.

Qiyas is the fourth source. It is analogical reasoning and deduction based on the other three sources.

Four schools of law or jurisprudence *(fiqh)* developed. The Shafite school was founded by al-Shafi who died in 820. He is known for his classical theory of Islamic law based on proper prophetic tradition with the use of analogical reasoning for applications to new circumstances. The Hanafite school arose in Iran in the eighth century and was founded by Abu Hanafah. It allows more freedom in personal interpretation and is considered one of the more liberal schools.

The Malikite school was founded in Medina by Malik ibn Anas, who died in 795. He relied on the living tradition of Medina as supported by Hadith. The latest school is the Hanbalite begun by Ahmad ibn Hanbal, who died in 855. It is out of favor with the other three schools because its interpretations of the Qur'an are very literalistic and legalistic. It is the dominant school in Saudi Arabia.[5]

The Ulama: Religious Leaders

One of the most striking features inside the mosque is the mimbar, an elevated platform or pulpit, often with several steps ascending to it.[6] The mimbar is the place from which members of the ulama speak the Qur'an, the Shari'a, and the knowledge of Islam. The mimbar symbolizes a formidable institution, the ulama. Although Islam has no ordained clergy or priesthood in the western sense, the ulama are a sort of clergy or religious scholar/practitioner class.

The ulama "constitute a social organization with 'rites of passage,' a pattern of hierarchy, and a multiplicity of functions; and they are also vitally related to other social structures that encompass religion, economics, law, and government. The ulama have been the center of traditionalism and reaction, but they have also experienced intellectual ferment and social change. In modernizing societies the ulama have become the foci for conflicts between the rulers and the ruled. They have become politicized and de-politicized."[7] Islam has always had strong religious leaders. Muhammad was prophet, preacher, prayer-leader, legal adviser, interpreter of the Qur'an, and the religio-political leader of the community, the *umma*. Classical Islamic theory included no provision for a clergy, but the ulama arose in early Islamic societies with broad responsibilities: to study, interpret, and administer Islamic law; to preside over the rituals at the mosque; and to administer the Qur'anic schools.

The ulama were also specialists in the Arabic language, the language of the Qur'an, the Shari'a, the Hadith, and of many rituals.

Today young men attend Qur'anic schools at early ages. Some decide to devote a career to the study of Islamic law and philosophy. They continue their studies at seminaries or schools founded and administered by noted religious scholars. Upon completion of their formal studies, they become teachers of religion in the public school system or leaders of Qur'anic schools and mosques.

These religious leaders assume various titles like *sheikh* or *imam* or *ayatollah*. Members achieve increasing authority within the ulama by spending years in study, writing manuscripts on Islamic subjects that are widely read and considered authoritative, and by becoming a noted speaker/preacher of a mosque. A leader may found his own Islamic school, teach his own disciples, send them out to lead various schools and mosques, and expect them to revere him and look to him for counsel and guidance. He then may become the leading ayatollah or sheikh of the society.

Ayatollah Khomeini was a famous member of the ulama. He studied under noted Islamic teachers. He published writings on Islam which received a wide following. He established schools in Qum, Iran, to which students came to study under him. His influence widened. His interpretation of Islam and its political and social emphases differed from the views of the ruler of his country, Muhammad Reza Shah Pahlavi. He was exiled. In 1979, after his teachings and influence had inspired a revolution in Iran to topple the Shah, he returned to establish the Islamic Republic of Iran. His example has inspired Islamic leaders and their followers in other countries.[8]

Mosques and Shrines

A major institution in Islam for religious and social life is the mosque. The word mosque *(Masjid)* means "a place of prostration" or "a place of prayer." According to Islamic theory, a Muslim can pray anywhere when the time of prayer arrives. In practice, however, a Muslim attempts to find a mosque at prayer time to observe the rituals alone or in a group.

The center of the mosque is the prayer room, usually located under the dome. One or more minarets, outside spiraling columns, contain stairways for the prayer leader to ascend to call the people to prayer. Inside the prayer room there is the *mihrab,* a niche in the wall to remind worshipers to line up to face Mecca as they pray. The mimbar is a raised platform, sometimes of several steps, upon which the religious leader sits to address the worshipers, especially with the Friday sermon.

Mosques are found in all shapes, sizes, and places, but they can be broadly divided into five categories.[9]

1. The *street mosque* is usually a small, simple building composed of a prayer room. It may have been endowed by a wealthy donor in memory of a deceased relative or an organization of concerned Muslims. Its basic purpose is to provide a convenient place for individual or group prayer for workers or passers-by along the street. Worshipers who frequent this mosque may also be affiliated with other mosques. The street mosque also provides a place off the street for rest and recreation, informal business activities, and individual and group counsel with itinerant members of the ulama.

2. The *district mosque,* or quarter mosque, is larger than the street mosque, and may be composed of a prayer room, classrooms, a salon, and an office area. Districts or quarters within countries or provinces house the local political, economic, legal, social, and religious organizations. Formerly one mosque might be located in the district. However, several mosques may have been built in the district and may compete with each other for the attention and participation of the neighborhoods.

   The district mosque may have a full-time member of the ulama together with a board of directors who supervise and administer its many activities. These may include prayer rituals, Qur'anic study meetings, seasonal (following the Islamic calendar) festivities and rituals such as Ramadan, birthday of the Prophet Muhammad, pilgrimage celebrations, and burial functions. The district mosque attempts to oversee the religious needs of the community.

3. The *congregational mosque* of the village or city is usually called the Friday mosque *(masjid-i-Jama'a).* Often, the religious leader of this mosque is appointed by the political authority. The people of the city gather on Friday at noon to pray behind the religious leader and to hear the Friday sermon. From early Islamic times this kind of mosque and leader was traditional. Through the mosque the political leadership could voice its ideas and plans to the people. The prestige of the Friday mosque has declined in many places. Today the leaders of other mosques may be more prominent and powerful in Islamic and sometimes political matters.

4. The *national mosque* is a large structure with significant Islamic history and prestige. It may serve as a daily place of prayer, but it is also similar to a museum or a large shrine, attracting tourists and pilgrims. Examples include the Prophet's Mosque in Damascus, the Dome of the Rock and the al-Aqsa mosques in Jerusalem, and the

Imam Reza Shrine Mosque in Meshad, Iran. Most Muslim countries have a mosque in this category, often the mosque of the king or president.

5. The *shrine* is the last category of mosques. There are literally thousands of these mosques scattered throughout Muslim lands. A shrine is constructed by wealthy donors or by groups of devotees to honor a particular Islamic figure. Many are named after members of the family of the Prophet, of his close associates, or of the imams. Muslims may conduct pilgrimages to the various shrines to pray, to make vows, and sometimes to request miracles. In some well-endowed mosques, a religious leader is present to aid worshipers, but most mosques are small and isolated, known only to the local people.

In summary, the power, prestige, influence, and status of a mosque rest upon its history, location, financial resources, its ideological perspectives, the fame and gifts of its religious leadership, and the attachment of its community and followers. A Muslim may frequent all five types of mosques over a given time. However, the Muslim may say prayers and observe community on a regular basis in one particular mosque in the neighborhood.

At the mosque, the community gathers to say the daily prayers and to hear the Friday sermon. Men and women separate in the mosque. Separately they gather to socialize, to exchange news and gossip, to seek counsel from the religious leader, and to find marriage mates for their children. The mosque may have an attached library and a Qur'anic school. A mosque may have a distinguished religious leader in residence, a published scholar in Islamic theology, philosophy, and law who attracts students. Therefore, there are classrooms and dormitories associated with the mosque complex.

Most mosques have simple architectural and structural features. Besides those features already mentioned, there is a courtyard with water facilities for prayer rituals. Inside, the floor may be covered with carpets. Islam permits no pictures or portraits on the walls. There are no benches or chairs. There may be small wooden stands to hold Qur'ans. Arabic calligraphy with Qur'anic verses may adorn the walls and columns.

People come inside the mosque at stated prayer times to line up in rows and emulate the prayer leader in the prayer ritual. They also come inside to sit on the floors to pray, to reflect, and to read the Qur'an.

During the Friday prayers, the worshipers may overflow into the court-yard where they hear the sermon over the public address system.

AWQAF: RELIGIOUS ENDOWMENTS

Pious Muslims make contributions of either money or land and possessions to an institution called *Awqaf* or religious endowments.[10] Often, Muslims leave in their wills these inheritances to the Awqaf institution. These endowments are administered by either certain ulama, or boards of directors of mosques, or by government agencies.

Income from endowments is used to build mosques, restore mosques, support Islamic education and schools, print literature, extend Islam through mission and educational efforts, and in other ways. Historically, the Awqaf has been a religious and political issue as to who should administer the programs, especially to honor the wishes and arrangements as intended by the donors.

The Shah of Iran clashed with the religious establishment over governance of Awqaf. The Shah was accused of mismanaging and corrupting religious endowments in violation of Islamic principles and practices. This dispute contributed to the overthrow of the Shah and his government and the formation of the Islamic Republic of Iran by Ayatollah Khomeini.[11]

SECTARIANISM AND DIVERSE THEOLOGIES

Despite the high unity among Muslims in the essentials of faith and practice in the major doctrines and six practices already presented, there are differences and divisions which emerged at the time of the death of Muhammad and have hounded Islam ever since. The great division occurred about the time of the death of Muhammad and revolved around the issue of successorship to his leadership. The result was the Sunni and the Shi'ite split. There have been other splinter groups based on various interpretations of the Qur'an, the Hadith, the schools of law, and historical and cultural considerations.

Sunni

The Sunni represent orthodoxy in Islam. They teach that the successor to the Prophet Muhammad should be a male from the Quraysh tribe to which he belonged. By a process of consensus *(ijma)* the community should select the leader. He should be a caliph *(khalifa)* with responsibility to administer the affairs of the community according to the Qur'an and prophetic tradition. However, no one can assume the place of

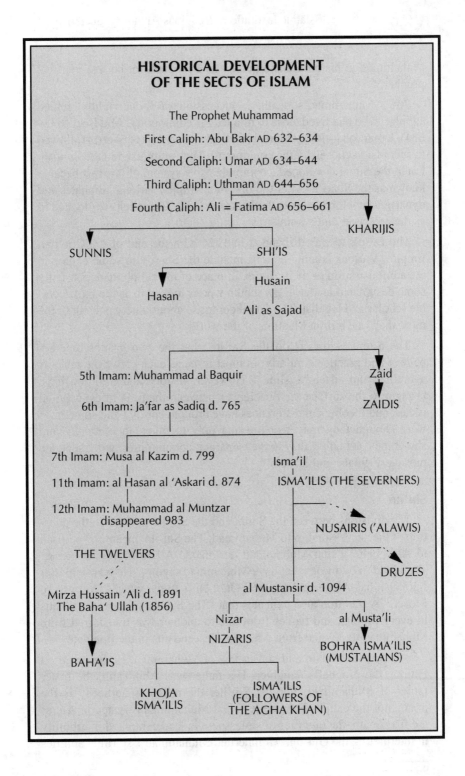

HISTORICAL DEVELOPMENT OF THE SECTS OF ISLAM

The Prophet Muhammad

First Caliph: Abu Bakr AD 632–634

Second Caliph: Umar AD 634–644

Third Caliph: Uthman AD 644–656

Fourth Caliph: Ali = Fatima AD 656–661

KHARIJIS

SUNNIS

SHI'IS

Hasan

Husain

Ali as Sajad

5th Imam: Muhammad al Baquir

Zaid

6th Imam: Ja'far as Sadiq d. 765

ZAIDIS

7th Imam: Musa al Kazim d. 799

Isma'il

11th Imam: al Hasan al 'Askari d. 874

ISMA'ILIS (THE SEVERNERS)

12th Imam: Muhammad al Muntzar
disappeared 983

NUSAIRIS ('ALAWIS)

THE TWELVERS

DRUZES

Mirza Hussain 'Ali d. 1891
The Baha' Ullah (1856)

al Mustansir d. 1094

Nizar

al Musta'li

NIZARIS

BAHA'IS

BOHRA ISMA'ILIS
(MUSTALIANS)

KHOJA
ISMA'ILIS

ISMA'ILIS
(FOLLOWERS OF
THE AGHA KHAN)

Muhammad in his nature and quality as a prophet, for he was the final prophet.

After Muhammad's death, a succession of "four rightly guided caliphs" who had lived close to him led the community. Abu Bakr (632–634), Umar (634–644), Uthman (644–656), and Ali (656–661) followed in succession chosen by the community. They administered the Sunnah. Later, the Sunni developed a comprehensive system of law that became known as the Shari'a. After the first four caliphs, various caliphates and dynasties developed across the Islamic world. The caliph was looked to as the preserver and administrator of the Shari'a.

The caliphate was disbanded in 1924 with the end of the Ottoman Empire. Various Islamic nations include the Shari'a to some degree in the administration of their affairs. In place of the caliph there is usually some designated leader like a sheikh who is looked to as the most notable scholar and legalist. The Sunni comprise about ninety percent of the more than one billion Muslims of the world.

The Sunni claim, as do the Shi'ite, that the two groups together believe and practice similarly. In most respects each views the other as a brother and sister Muslim.[12] However, history and tradition have brought to the surface the differences between them. Politics, national issues, and theological differences have brought conflict and sometimes war. Though they may worship and pray together, theoretically and sometimes actually, they have separate communities with separate mosques, rituals, and leaders.

Shi'ite

The divisions between the Sunni and the Shi'ite go back to the question of the successorship to Muhammad. The Shi'ite, meaning "partisan to Ali," believe that Muhammad designated Ali to be his successor. They hold to traditions that have Muhammad saying, "He whose master I am also has Ali for his master." Or, "Ali is to me what Aaron was to Moses." A tradition also indicates that "The Divine spirit which dwells in every prophet and passes from one to another was transferred from Muhammad to Ali and from Ali to his descendants in the Imamate."[13]

Ali was the cousin and son-in-law of Muhammad. He had married Fatima, the prophet's daughter. His father was Abu Talib, the foster father of Muhammad. For the Shi'ite, the religious authority is the imam, not the caliph. They believe that Muhammad invested in Ali, as the first imam, the qualities of sinlessness in leadership and infallibility in interpreting the Qur'an. Ali inherited Muhammad's spiritual abilities (*wilaya*). Ali, then, established the imamate of the Shi'ites as opposed to the caliphate of the Sunni.

The Shi'ite believe in the doctrine of the imamate. Ali, being the first imam, passed these spiritual qualities to his sons, Hasan and Husein, and they to their descendants in the line of the imams. The cycle of the imamate will be completed with the messianic return of the twelfth imam. The twelfth imam is believed to be in hiding or occultation since the ninth century. This imam supernaturally gives guidance to the community through designated leaders of whom the major members are the ayatollahs. The ayatollahs interpret the Shari'a and state the correct rulings for society.

Immediately after the death of Muhammad, Ali was denied the status of first imam. The community elected the four caliphs in succession, and Ali was the fourth caliph. He was 33 years old when Muhammad died, a rather young man to assume leadership in a tribal context. During his caliphate (according to the Shi'ite, Ali was the first imam of the imamate), he attempted to place his relatives in administrative posts. Conflict ensued. Ali himself was murdered. He was buried at Najaf, near Kufa, Iraq. A shrine covers his tomb, the shrine of Ali. Shi'ites believe that a pilgrimage to the tomb merits the worth of 100,000 martyrdoms and the forgiveness of sins of the past and the present.

Ali's first son, Hasan, was proclaimed caliph (second imam) two days after the death of his father. Muslims were divided. There had been rival caliphs with Ali vying with Mu'awiya. Mu'awiya forced Hasan to abdicate. Hasan with his sixty wives retired to Medina, where subsequently he was poisoned.

Husein, Ali's second son, retired with his brother Hasan in Medina while Mu'awiya reigned in Damascus. After the death of Hasan, Husein sent some of his followers to Kufa to learn whether he had support to be caliph (he would be considered the third Imam after Ali and Hasan). They were killed by dissidents. Husein then left with his family and followers for Kufa. On the way he was surrounded by Sunni forces, and his gathering was slaughtered at Kerbala, Iraq. His head was taken to Yezid ibn (*son of*) Mu'awiya in Damascus, and his body was trampled under the feet of horses.

Husein was killed at Kerbala, Iraq in the year 680 on the tenth day of the Muslim month of Muharram. That day has gone down in infamy, as the Shi'ites have held the Sunni responsible for the slaughter. The shrine of Husein was built at Kerbala. A pilgrimage to the shrine tomb merits the value of a thousand pilgrimages to Mecca, a thousand martyrdoms, and a thousand days of fasting, according to Shi'ite tradition. In this sense Shi'ite Islam could be considered a part of folk or popular Islam in direct competition with the orthodoxy of Sunni Islam.

The murder of Husein has become a distinct feature of Shi'ite faith and practice. He is considered a martyr. The shedding of his blood has sacrificial value for Shi'ites. He is the idea of martyrdom and suffering of the just at the hands of the evil ones. He is a model of sacrificial service to God. Each year his death is commemorated on the tenth day of Muharram. The first ten days of the month are given to sermons in mosques by members of the ulama, to storytelling by special narrators of the intricate and gruesome details of the brutal murders of Husein and his family, and to prayer meetings in the name of Husein at shrines and in homes.

On the tenth day, there are passion plays (*taziyahs*) dramatizing the battle and the deaths at Kerbala. Parades and processions in the streets demonstrate the details. Men don white cloth and beat their chests with chains, often drawing blood and reddening the cloth. They identify with the persecution and suffering of Husein and his family. These enactments demonstrate mourning, purging of the soul, identification with his cause against evil, and solace in the guidance and power that he may give to individuals and the community.

Thus, the Shi'ite differ from the Sunni concerning the imamate, concerning the elevation of the family of the Prophet Muhammad to leadership, concerning the spiritual qualities of its leaders, and concerning certain practices and rituals. The imamate is so important to the Shi'ite that they add to the confession *(shahada)* a phrase that declares Ali the commander of true believers and the "friend of God."

The Shi'ite also embrace the doctrine of light (*nur*), which teaches that a divine light is passed down from prophet to prophet. This divine illumination gives the imam the status of sinlessness and infallibility. Shi'ites often depict their prophets/imams with divine halos surrounding their heads.

Shi'ite Islam in Iran: A Noted Example

The Shi'ite represent about ten percent of the Islamic world, and Iran is the major Shi'ite nation.[14] Iranian Shi'ite Muslims profess the six basic norms which all Muslims must observe. A pious Iranian Shi'ite (1) professes that Allah is the God of the universe and Muhammad is his Prophet; (2) prays five times daily; (3) gives alms; (4) fasts during the month of Ramadan; (5) goes on pilgrimage to Mecca at least once in a lifetime; and (6) practices jihad.

One of the central clues in understanding Shi'ite Islam in Iran is the meanings surrounding Imam Husein. It has been mentioned that Husein is a legitimate descendant of the Prophet's family, namely the son of Ali and grandson of Muhammad. In one sense Husein may serve as a prototype of all the other imams in his identification with and suffering for the minority Shi'ite sect. Whereas other imams including Ali, have faced violent death, none has given up in death so many family members as Husein.

The drama of the Husein narrative is poised in historical consciousness and raw emotions. It traces the history of the Shi'ite community back to the battleground at Kerbala where Husein was slain in 681 by the Sunni forces. Husein was decapitated in front of his family, and they were in turn killed. "Not even a cup of water was given to Husein before his death when his lips were so parched."

The religious calendar of Iranian Shi'ite Muslims centers around the death of Husein. Throughout the year in religious gatherings and rituals (*Sofrehs* and *Rowzehs*)[15] and during the month of Muharram, narratives and dramas of the battle and death of Husein are recited and enacted in mosques, homes, and streets. Crying, wailing, beating of chests, and cutting oneself to draw blood are expressions elicited when the narrative is chanted and the play presented.

Listening to the narrative and participating in the drama in the presence of others help Shi'ites form their own self-perception. They see themselves as noble and courageous followers of Imam Husein, whom the majority denied; tenacious and faithful people who await the time of the coming of another like Husein; a people who have been persecuted but who nevertheless have always been correct in their iman (belief) and din (practice) because they are participants in an infallible tradition, which is the charisma and the light passed from the Prophet through his family to the Imamate.[16]

Although the Husein story and drama serve as a central focus for the Shi'ite worldview and ethos, there are other bases. Along with the six basic norms presented, a good Iranian Shi'ite Muslim claims at least five others.[17]

1. A good Shi'ite is a loyal family member, honoring his or her place within the family structure. In that structure, the father is the authority; the mother is child-bearer and nurturer; the child is obedient and respectful. Shi'ite families attempt to trace their lineage to the Prophet through genealogical ties or through various associations with the descendants of the Prophet. Members of the family may

wear a green-colored headdress or may display green colors around the house, acknowledging that they are *seyyids* (descendants of the Prophet). Ali, Hasan, Husein, Mohammad, and Reza are common first names among males; Fatima, the daughter of the Prophet and wife of Ali, is a familiar name among females. Shi'ites consider themselves a "family" in distinction particularly to Sunni Muslims, who killed many of the imams.

2. A good Shi'ite calls on the names of the imams, especially on the name of Husein, with whose suffering and death he identifies. He also calls on the Twelfth Imam and awaits his return to validate the just and righteous ways of Islam. Although all imams serve as patron saints for Iranian Shi'ites and all are called upon for various kinds of intercessions, Husein's is the premier name. In the formal prayer (*salat*) at the mosque, the name of Allah will be spoken, but in the informal prayer (*do'a*) petitions will be made to Husein and to other imams.

3. A good Shi'ite can afford to make the pilgrimage to Mecca. After completing the pilgrimage, one assumes the title Hajji. A Hajji is a religious elite in experience and authority within the community. Many Iranian Shi'ites are unable financially to go on the Hajj. Therefore, it has become acceptable and prestigious to go on Hajj to the several Shi'ite shrines in Iran, to Meshed, to Qum, and to various shrines (*Imamzadehs*) of lesser-known religious figures throughout Iran. Also, the Shi'ite shrines in Kerbala and Nejaf are pilgrim sites for Iranians. These saints are related to the Prophet's family. It is common to hear someone called Hajji who has made the pilgrimage to Meshed. Thus, one who becomes a Hajji gains authority, power, and charisma.

4. A good Shi'ite relies on his own knowledge of Islam for guidance in religious practice. If there is lack of sufficient knowledge, he selects members of the ulama to counsel and lead him.[18] Most Shi'ites rely on specialists among the ulama to interpret Islamic law in areas such as marriage and economics. Shi'ites also follow the advice of the ulama in political matters, prayer rituals, preparations and actual participation in the Hajj. Since the Qur'an, the Shari'a, and the Hadith are in the Arabic sources, most Iranian Shi'ites are unable to read them. They must turn to these religious scholars who are experts in Islam and in the Arabic language. Their reliance upon a member of the ulama in effect places great responsibility upon the religious leader,

who receives much respect and obedience from the Shi'ite. An example is the rise of Ayatollah Khomeini to be the imam or *Marje' Taqlid* (source of imitation) for millions of Iranian Shi'ites.

5. A good Shi'ite protects himself from overcommitment to the ruling political order in anticipation of the coming reign of the Twelfth Imam. He should be constantly aware lest he or his family be co-opted by the ruling powers. He should rely on his religious leader for counsel and direction in the interim period from the time of the disappearance of the Twelfth Imam until his return.

Shi'ite Subsects

The Shi'ites, too, have had their splits.[19] Most Shi'ites are of a group known as the Ithna Ashariya, or the Twelvers. They accept the line of twelve imams from Ali to Muhammad al-Muntazzar. Muhammad al-Muntazzar, the Twelfth Imam, was born in Samarra in 878. His father announced that his son was the *mahdi,* the expected messiah. At nine years of age Muhammad disappeared. The doctrine of the hidden imam developed. It was to be a time of concealment (*ghaiba*) until his return. While the imam is in hiding or occultation, he guides his followers through an agency known as a living imam or ayatollah. The Shi'ites of Iran compose ninety percent of this sect, and the Shi'ites of Iraq are more than fifty percent of the Twelvers.

Another group is the Isma'ilis, called the Seveners. They accept the first seven imams in the lineage of Ali, ending with Ismail ibn Jafar. The Isma'ilis have radical views and activities. They form secret societies with esoteric teachings. They enabled the Fatimid Dynasty (A.D 969–1174) of Egypt to gain power through revolutionary activities. During this time modern Cairo and the great Islamic al-Azhar University were founded. The Isma'ilis split into two groups. The Nazaris look to the modern day Aga Khan as their imam. The Mustalis, also known as the Bohoro Muslims, believe in a hidden imam who is not descended from Hasan or Husein.

The Ahmadiyya sect was founded in India in the early part of the twentieth century. The founder was Ahmad, who declared himself as the imam of Islam. The sect is strongly missionary and is considered heretical by other Islamic groups.

Other Theological Influences

The Kharijites, known as the "Seceders," first favored Ali to be successor to Muhammad, and then withdrew their support. They stressed moralism and purity.[20] Not only was the caliph to be absolutely pure in the faith, but also all Muslims were to be pure. Equality among believers was stressed. They showed little mercy toward their opponents. Kharijites are present in some communities of North Africa.

The Murjiites, known as the "Postponers," were less rigid than the Kharijites. According to them, those who adhered to Islam, practiced its creed, and observed its laws should be considered Muslims. They emphasized the forgiveness of God, insisting that judgment must be left to God at the last day. The Murjiites are now extinct as a community.

As schisms and theological variations continued, the Mutazilites arose in the eighth century, partly in opposition to the fanaticism of the Kharijites and the liberalism of the Murjiites. They defended freedom of the will to validate genuine moral responsibility but denied the possibility of forgiveness for sinners.

The Mutazilites buttressed their theology with Greek metaphysics. They opposed any efforts to attribute human characteristics to God, insisting on the unity of God. They disagreed with the thought of the uncreated Qur'an, saying it placed another god beside God. In their rationalistic metaphysics and abstract doctrines they were construed by the orthodox community as ignoring the personal and absolute unity of God. The Mutazilites provoked theological and philosophical discussions that have influenced Islamic scholarship through the centuries.

al-Ashari (d. 935) was a seminal and influential thinker who began as a Mutazilite but moved to orthodoxy. Because he taught that revelation is primary and superior to reason, he opposed the Mutazilitie emphasis on rationality. Later, al-Ashari came to use reason to support revelation.

al-Ashari's orthodoxy included four major ideas:

1. He taught that the Qur'an is the actual speech of God. In this point he agreed with Sunni orthodoxy, but he insisted that the Quar'an is distinct from God's essence.

2. He accepted the anthropomorphisms of the Qur'an such as references to the hand of God; but he said that they must not be completely interpreted as metaphors.

3. He accepted the eschatology of the Qur'an and insisted that it not be dismissed as only metaphor.

4. He opposed the Mutazilite understanding of free will. He said the human will has only the power to accept what God does through it.

al-Ashari gave the foundation for Islamic theology which came to be known as kalam.

Sufism

Islam is a religion of law, ritual, and duty. Sufism brought mysticism to Islam.[21] It stresses emotions, feelings, the personal attributes of God, personal relations with God, love, and heartfelt religion. The word *Sufi* can be traced to two meanings, "purity" and "wool." Sufism thus has roots in a theme of asceticism. Early ascetics wore garments of white wool and withdrew from society. They protested the worldliness of the Umayyad princes in Damascus and sought a direct experience of God apart from the rituals and duties of the formal religion.

The Sufis sought direction both in the Qur'an and in the life of their prophet Muhammad. The Qur'an states, "Send not away those / Who call on their Lord / Morning and evening, / Seeking His face."[22] It asserts, "For We Are nearer to him / Than (his) jugular vein."[23] Also the Qur'an describes light: "Allah is the Light / Of the heavens and the earth. / The parable of His Light / Is as if there were a Niche / And within it a Lamp: / The Lamp enclosed in Glass; / The glass as it were / A brilliant star: / Lit from a blessed Tree, / An Olive, neither of the East / Nor of the West, / Whose Oil is well-nigh / Luminous, / Though fire scarce touched it: / Light upon Light!"[24]

Sufis believed they could find God through introspection and inward experiences. They saw God as a light shining and burning within man who is the lamp. Sufi literature describes their religious experience as an intense light and a burning fire. The characteristics of prayer, fasting, self-denial, and discipline in the life of Muhammad found appreciation.[25]

The story of Muhammad's miraculous night journey from Jerusalem to the seven heavens to meet face to face with God at his throne became a treasure. Sufis interpreted this journey as the capacity of the soul to rise through prayer and discipline to the very presence of God and to be united with him. For some Sufis, the Qur'an was seen as an allegory of the quest of the soul for union with God.

By A.D. 800, a female Sufi saint, Rabia-al-Adawiya, said, "O God! If I worship thee in fear of Hell, burn me in Hell; and if I worship Thee in hope of Paradise, exclude me from Paradise; but if I worship Thee for Thine own sake, withhold not Thine everlasting Beauty." As Sufism grew, it tended to become unorthodox both in its theology of God and in its religious practices. It promoted a mystical way to truth and loving union with God. Mansur al-Hallaj exemplified the extreme form of mysticism when he said, "I am the Reality." As this was interpreted as his identifying himself with God, he was executed by crucifixion in 922.

Sufism popularized Islam and reacted against overly formalistic rituals. Orthodoxy was losing Muslims to the fervency of Sufi religious devotion. The scholar al-Ghazali (d. 1111) sought to reconcile orthodoxy and mysticism. He has been called the St. Thomas Aquinas of Muslim theology, and his theology and ethics have been the standards for Islamic scholarship.

As a successful and popular professor at a Muslim school in Baghdad during the Abbasid era, al-Ghazali experienced doubts about his faith. Introduced to Sufism, he had a personal encounter with God. After making the pilgrimage to Mecca, he basically retired from teaching and began a writing career. A major writing was *The Revivification of the Religious Sciences*.

al-Ghazali believed that religious certainty could be found only in religious experience. He taught that the love of God, rather than union with God, is central to religion. He wrote, "Whoever loves another than God for other than God's sake does so from ignorance . . . (though to love the Messenger of God is praiseworthy, for it is really loving God) . . . for among men of insight there is no true beloved except God most High, and none deserving of love save Him."[26]

Thus, al-Ghazali moderated Sufi mysticism. He not only stressed a return to the Qur'an and the traditions, but he also practiced the kind of mysticism which could include the idea of God who "knows the very thread of the blackbird in the dark night on the hard stone."

Orders or brotherhoods are famous among the Sufis. Jalal ad-Din Rumi (1207–1273) founded the order known as the "whirling dervishes." The dervishes or devotees whirl and dance as they repeat the name of God. The leader of the brotherhood, called *sheikh*, leads the followers in a discipline of spiritual exercises.

Often shrines were built in honor of the sheikh, and these served as centers for the activities of the brotherhood members. Thus the sheikh became a saint, and Sufis believed they could have communion with the saint because of his holiness and closeness to God. Ceremonies developed like *dhikr*, a remembrance of the saint by repetition of his sayings. Music also accompanied Sufi worship. One of the best-known brotherhoods is the Quadiriya.

Wahhabism

Wahhabism is a Muslim puritan movement founded by Abd al-Wahhab in eighteenth-century Saudi Arabia. Its members refer to themselves as unitarians because they emphasize the absolute oneness of God *(tawhid)*. They are Sunni and follow the legal school of Hanbali.

Wahhabi doctrine and practice seek a return to the golden age of Islam, a return to the time of the four rightly guided caliphs. Wahhabis are literalists and believe just what the Qur'an says. If it says God has hands and feet, then it is true. They condemn idols and saint worship that have crept into Islam. They despise Sufism. They say prayers daily in the mosque, using only the words of the Qur'an.

The Wahhabis collect alms as the Qur'an specifies, build schools, and trust their judges to enforce the Qur'anic penal law of beheading and the severing of hands for the appropriate crimes. They identify Islam with Arabia. The movement has been associated with the Saud ruling family of Saudi Arabia.

Through the years it has declared jihad against its enemies, including so-called Muslims. By the nineteenth century Wahhabism had been introduced into India, where its converts fought the Sikhs. In 1870 both the Sunni and Shi'ite communities of India condemned the Wahhabi doctrine of holy war. The government of Saudi Arabia has moderated the Wahhabi influence in contemporary times.

Nation of Islam

The Nation of Islam arose among Blacks in the United States.[27] Elijah Poole left his Baptist roots in the deep South for Detroit in the 1930s. He was introduced to a syncretistic Islam that combined racist teachings with Islamic vocabulary and occult mysticism. His name was changed to Elijah Muhammad; his movement became the Nation of Islam; and several million American Blacks joined. The Nation of Islam has never been accepted by orthodox Islamic leaders around the world and is considered a heretical movement.

At his death in 1975, his son Wallace Muhammad succeeded him as leader. Wallace launched a program to bring the movement into the mainstream of orthodox Islam. Because of some dissent and much financial difficulty, Wallace dissolved his organization, which had been named the American Muslim Mission. Louis Farrakhan, who had been a close associate of Elijah, refused to follow Wallace in his orthodoxy and continued as leader of the Nation of Islam.

America has several Islamic movements. Some are orthodox and acceptable to worldwide Islam. Others are highly unorthodox and rejected as heresies by the orthodox. An entire chapter will be devoted to Islam in America.

7

MUSLIM MORALS AND MANNERS

PERSONAL, FAMILY, SOCIAL, BUSINESS, POLITICAL

The good life based on morals and manners of proper conduct is addressed both in the Qur'an and in the Hadith and traditions of the prophet Muhammad. The Muslim community, known as the *umma*, seeks and expresses this good life from its religious authorities and in its daily life. These morals and manners include purity and cleanliness, clothing and adornment, diet, family, marriage and divorce, husband and wife and parent and child, status of women, economic life and the conduct of business, and political life.

Islam provides an all-embracing view and expression of life. Life is lived under the rule and order of God as given in the Qur'an and through the prophet Muhammad's teachings and life. Beliefs and rules of social behavior are specific and comprehensive. Islam teaches that God praises the good and condemns the evil and that He provides rewards and sanctions that are both spiritual and material.

There are instructions for personal life, family life, social life, economic life, and political life.[1] One is given guidance for the straight path in cleaning oneself before prayers; what food not to eat; what clothes to wear; marriage and family and roles of men and women; treatment of one's neighbors and other religions; good commerce and prohibition of usury; standards for governing society; and the conditions of waging war.

Descriptions in this chapter are based primarily on Islamic Arab culture. The Qur'an was given in the Arabic language, and Arab culture was the first to become Islamicized. The Prophet Muhammad reformed the Arab culture of his time with his Islamic teachings and practices. He also accommodated parts of Arab culture within the comprehensive system of Islam. Thus, general values and behavioral patterns shall be presented based on foundations in Islam and Arab culture. In other cultures where Islam is dominant, there may be variations and differences in some of the cultural expressions. However, where the Qur'an and traditions speak specifically to values and behavior, Muslims everywhere are to adhere to their counsel and guidance.

PERSONAL LIFE

Purity and Cleanliness

The Muslim must perform an ablution before each of the five daily prayers. Definite regulations govern these ablutions. Prayer must be offered with a pure heart and mind, with clean body and clothes, with pure intentions and on pure ground.[2] Islam, then, requires specificity of form and function in purity and cleanliness. There must be a concentration of time and energy many times daily in these matters.

Diet

Diet is important in keeping a pure heart, a sound mind, a healthy body, and a soul bound for eternity. The general principle of Islam is that all foods which are pure and good for humanity are allowed for eating in moderate amounts; all foods considered impure and bad are prohibited.

Islam teaches that God forbids certain foods and drinks. Forbidden foods include meat of dead animals and birds, flesh of swine, and anything slaughtered with the invocation of any name other than that of God.[3] Drinks which are harmful to morality and to morale and the body are intoxicants, including alcoholic beverages and certain drugs.[4] Muslims are invited by God, after refraining from these prohibited dietary items, to enjoy His gracious provisions and to experience gratitude to the Merciful Provider.[5]

Clothing and Adornment

The principles of decency, modesty, and chastity govern Islamic dress. Arrogance and false pride must not be stimulated nor should morality be called into question or weakened. One's character must be upheld in clothing and in adorning one's body.

Men are warned not to wear pure silk, gold, and certain precious stones; these are better suited for women. Women are to wear clothing which retains and develops their dignity and chastity. They must not be the subjects of idle gossip or suspicions or rumors.

The Qur'an teaches, "Say to the believing men / That they should lower their gaze and guard / Their modesty: that will make / For greater purity for them: / And Allah is well acquainted / With all that they do. / And say to the believing women / That they should lower / Their gaze and guard / Their modesty; that they / Should not display their / Beauty and ornaments except / What (must ordinarily) appear / Thereof; that they should / Draw their veils over / Their bosoms and not display / Their beauty except / To their husbands, their fathers, / Their husbands' fathers, their sons, / Their husbands' sons, / Their brothers or their brothers' sons."[6]

Both men and women are to dress with respect to their natures and natural instincts given them by God. God condemns men who behave in a woman's fashion and women who behave in a man's fashion. However, harmless items of clothing and adornments are considered beautiful gifts of God.[7]

Entertainment and Sports

It is said that Muhammad encouraged sports and entertainment that strengthened morals and spiritual and physical well-being. Most Muslim forms of worship, including daily prayers, the fasting season, and the pilgrimage rituals, use good exercise techniques and nurture the body.

Islam prohibits gambling because it subjects life to luck and mere chance. It is considered a frivolous and dangerous threat to mental and emotional stability and upsetting to normal patterns of life and work.

Alcohol consumption is unlawful because it destroys health, depresses the mind, dulls the soul, absorbs wealth, destroys families, abuses human dignity, and violates morality. Islam does not associate gambling and drinking with good entertainment and sports. It does not tolerate them. It bans them totally from individual and community life.

Perhaps the most popular form of recreation in the Muslim Arab world is visiting family and friends for meals or for going on picnics. If visiting is not done regularly, it is considered improper social behavior and is insulting to the person not visited. Visiting cafes and coffee and tea houses with friends is very popular, but is usually only for men.

Personal Relations and Honor

Arab Muslims value personal relations. An Arab will do almost anything for someone he likes. Honor, too, is held highly. If an individual becomes dishonored through ridicule, criticism, or any other offensive act or word, not only he but his family may become dishonored. Dishonor may bring ostracism upon him and/or his family, or may ostracize him from his family and others in his network of relationships upon which he depends. Therefore, it is important to unhold one's honor and, if it is threatened, to preserve it or regain it through retribution.[8]

Revenge and the blood feud may still be a part of sustaining honor for the person and the family. Arab Muslims are very proud people who look to their religion and their culture as superior to all others. Because of this pride, they may at times be easily insulted and offended.

Status and Public Appearance

For the Arab, status comes with the territory, with birth, with religion, with the family, and with one's inheritance. Respect, authority, and power are not necessarily gained from one's actions or from earning them, but they come from who one is. If Allah did not want a person to be born into a certain family or position, it would be different for that person. But since one is born with a status, one must protect it from the challenges around it.

"Face" is important to the Arab. Status rests upon the face presented to the public and upon appearances from personal dress to personal dignity. A street sweeper may do his work wearing a sports jacket, and at noon lay it down on the side of the street to bend over to say his noon prayers. An affluent Arab would not sweep his driveway or wash his car, for that would be the job of someone else. He might think less of an affluent foreigner who was living in his country and did those menial tasks.

Decision Making and Responsibility

Arab Muslims generally will accept shared responsibility but are not eager to accept total responsibility. If responsibility is accepted and something goes wrong, then the Arab will be blamed and dishonored. Also, his family may share in the dishonor. Consensus is preferred in making decisions because if something goes wrong, the blame is shared and diffused among others. Thus, the possibility of dishonor is lessened.

Indirectness may be a way for the Arab Muslim to maintain honor and save face. To admit that one does not know is to lose face and even status. If a professor were to admit that he did not know something, he would lose credibility with the students. It might be better for him to give false information or to act as if he knew. If one asks an Arab for directions, the Arab may give them even though he does not know them in order not to lose face.

FAMILY LIFE

Marriage

Marriage and the family are central in Islamic life and community. Both the Qur'an and the prophet say that when a Muslim marries, he has already perfected half his religion; therefore he must be careful and God-fearing with the other half. There is no asceticism in Islam. God created humankind out of one living soul, and created of that soul a spouse so that he might find comfort and rest in her.[9]

Muhammad is reported to have said that a woman is sought as a wife for her wealth, for her beauty, for the nobility of her stock, or for her religious qualities; but most fortunate is he who chooses his mate for piety above all else. The Qur'an commands marriage to the spouseless and the pious although they may be poor and slaves.[10] Whatever dowry a man gives his prospective wife and whatever she acquires before and after marriage belong to her alone. The husband is responsible for the economic security of the family.

Marriage is intended and expected to be permanent. Trial marriages or term marriages are forbidden. Muhammad said that men and women are condemned who frequently change marriage partners. Marriage, then, is taken as a serious and permanent bond. However, if it does not work out for some valid reason it may be terminated in honor and kindness and peace.

Husband-Wife Relationship

Marriage creates new roles for the man and woman. A man is to treat his wife with kindness, honor, and patience, and to keep her honorably or free her from the marriage honorably. Women have rights as well as duties, but men have a degree over them.[11] Men are trustees, guardians, and protectors of women because God has made some to excel over others and because men expend of their means.[12] Muslim scholars interpret this excelling of men in terms of a division of labor and role differentiation. It does not mean a discrimination or superiority of one gender over the other in Islamic understanding.

The wife has certain specific obligations. She must not deceive her husband in avoiding conception to deprive him of legitimate progeny.

She must have sexual intimacy only with her husband. She cannot entertain strange males without the consent of her husband. She is to make herself desirable, attractive, and responsive to her husband in sexual intercourse and may not deny herself to him.

Divorce

Islam purposes that marriage be a happy and lasting companionship in harmony and peace. However, if marriage does not serve its purpose, it may be terminated by divorce with the rights of husband and wife preserved. Divorce is the last resort. Muhammad described divorce as the most detestable of all lawful things in the sight of God.

Attempts are encouraged to prevent divorce. Husband and wife must attempt to settle their dispute between themselves. If this fails, two arbitrators, one from each party, try to bring reconciliation. Divorce is the final course of action. Once the divorce is granted, there is a waiting period of three to twelve months. The wife is supported by the husband during this period. They may reunite during or after this time. However, at the end of the period they no longer have obligations to each other and may remarry.

The Status of Women

The Qur'an defines the status of women as follows: "Men are the protectors / And maintainers of women, / Because Allah has given / The one more (strength) / Than the other, and because / They support them / From their means. / Therefore the righteous women / Are devoutly obedient, and guard / In (the husband's) absence / What Allah would have them guard. / As to those women / On whose part ye fear / Disloyalty and ill-conduct, / Admonish them (first,) / (Next), refuse to share their beds, / (And last) beat them (lightly;) / But if they return to obedience, / Seek not against them / Means of annoyance."[13]

Also, the Qur'an says to men, "Your wives are / As a tilth [or tillage] unto you; / So approach your tilth / When or how you will."[14] Wives are seen as subject to the control of their husbands.

Generally, Islamic interpretations hold that the rights and responsibilities of a woman are equal to those of a man, but they are not necessarily identical with them. From the Islamic perspective, women and men are created equal but not identical. In the story of creation both Adam and Eve were tempted; both sinned; God's pardon was granted to both after repentance; and God addressed them jointly.[15]

Dr. Hammudah Abdalati, a leading Islamic scholar, writes about various Islamic attitudes with regard to women.

1. Women are full and equal partners with men in the procreation of humanity.

2. Women are equal to men in bearing responsibilities and in receiving rewards for their deeds.

3. They may pursue education equal with men.

4. They have freedom of expression as men do. Both the Qur'an and history demonstrate that women argued and discussed with the prophet and with other Muslim leaders.[16]

5. Islam gives women equal rights to contract, to enterprise, and to earnings.[17]

6. The Qur'an reproaches the thought that women are inferior to men.[18]

7. Women receive a share of inheritance. In some cases men may receive more shares basically because they assume all financial responsibilities for the family and women have little if any responsibilities for the family.

8. Women have certain privileges unavailable to men. They are exempt from prayers and fasting during their menstruation periods, from attendance at the obligatory Friday services and from all financial liabilities. As mothers they have highest recognition in the sight of God. They have a dowry from their husband.

9. Women and men pray in separate places in the mosque, but this is not because of inferiority. Muslim prayers necessitate actions, motions, bowings, and prostrations. Men are not allowed to touch women during times of prayer. There could be distractions if they mixed.

10. The veil has been associated with Muslim women. The Islamic woman should stir the passions only of her husband. She should not expose her physical attractions before strangers. The veil is a matter of honor, dignity, purity, and chastity.

In drawing from the Qur'an and the Sunnah, Ibrahim al-Kayasis writes that a woman's dress must conform to several requirements simultaneously:

   a. It must cover and conceal the whole of her body except the face and hands.

b. The garments should not be so thin or transparent as to reveal her body.

c. The main garment must be a "flowing" one, that is, the woman must avoid tight or clinging clothes which exaggerate or show her figure.

d. Muslim women, in order to safeguard their cultural identity, are discouraged from imitating the dress of non-Muslim women.

e. It is necessary to avoid clothes that attract the attention of others.

f. Wearing perfume on clothes either outdoors or when meeting strangers indoors should be avoided.[19]

According to al-Kayasis, the veil is a covering to protect and conceal the woman's head and neck.

Ira Zepp, in *A Muslim Primer,* writes, "In the traditional societies of the Middle East, women are not socially independent. They need men to act on their behalf. They ask men's permission to leave home; and they are often secluded from male visitors to the home. Women cannot be imams, although they can lead prayer services for women in their homes. On the other hand, Sufi societies allow women to be religious leaders and are generally more positive about all aspects of womanhood."[20]

Zepp adds that "veiling" or *purdah* (words for seclusion) among women varies across cultures:

It is most prevalent in Saudi Arabia, Afghanistan, and post-revolutionary Iran, but to some degree it is present in most Muslim societies. Actually, purdah and complete veiling are Persian and Indian customs which, in time, many neighboring countries adopted. There is one verse in the Qur'an which mentions veiling: "Prophet, enjoin your wives, your daughters, and the wives of true believers to draw their veils close around them. That is more proper so they may be recognized and not molested" (33:59) (see also 24:30–31). The historical context for what is "proper" is that Arabian women before Islam were scantily attired and often topless; as a result, they were abused by men.[21]

Zepp quotes Jane Smith, formerly of the Harvard Center for the Study of World Religions, on why Muslim women dress the way they do:

> Regardless of their degree of liberation, Muslim women value modesty as well as prize and retain their femininity. They find particularly odious, as do Muslim men, the sexual permissiveness of Western society. Whether the control exercised by Muslim men over their women is viewed as protection or exploitation, the fact remains that liberal and conservative Muslims alike are appalled and disgusted by women's open display of themselves and the sexual freedoms seen as part of the general emancipation of women in the West. . . . To cite the expressive commentary of Fatima Mernissi, "While Muslim exploitation of the female is clad under veils and buried behind walls, Western exploitation has the bad taste of being unclad, bare, and overexposed."[22]

Polygamy

Islam permits a man to have more than one wife under certain conditions. It is a conditional permission and not a matter of necessity. A man may be permitted to have up to four wives. All the wives enjoy the same rights and privileges. A prerequisite of polygamy is equality of treatment and provisions for the wives. The permission to have more than one wife is given to alleviate some social and moral problems and is considered an emergency matter.

The Qur'an states, "If ye fear that ye shall not / Be able to deal justly / With the orphans, / Marry women of your choice, / Two, or three, or four; / But if ye fear that ye shall not / Be able to deal justly (with them), / Then only one, or (a captive) / That your right hands possess. / That will be more suitable, / To prevent you / From doing injustice."[23]

This Qur'anic passage refers to what happened in the Battle of Uhud, in which many slain Muslim men left behind widows and children. To protect and provide for these widows and children, other men took them as wives and adopted their children. Consequently, a revelation came to the prophet.

This verse from the Qur'an allows a man to have more than one wife but only if he deals justly with all his wives. Another verse says that a person is unable to deal justly between wives, thus giving permission to the man but also giving a discouraging note: "Ye are never able / To be fair and just / As between women, / Even if it is / Your ardent desire."[24]

It is thought that Muhammad himself had nine to twelve wives and/ or concubines. He married his first wife at age twenty five when she was fifteen years his senior. After her death he married widows and divorcees and the young daughter of Abu Bakr, his early convert and first caliph. She was six at the time of betrothal, and the marriage was consummated when she was nine.

By divine commission the Qur'an grants Muhammad the right of wives. "O Prophet! We have / Made lawful to thee / Thy wives to whom thou / Hast paid their dowers; / And those whom thy / Right hand possesses out of / The prisoners of war whom / Allah has assigned to thee; / And daughters of thy paternal / Uncles and aunts, and daughters / Of thy maternal uncles /And aunts, who migrated / (From Makkah) with thee; / And any believing woman / Who dedicates her soul / To the Prophet if the Prophet / Wishes to wed her—this / Only for thee, and not / For the believers at large."[25]

There has been much discussion about the motives and manners of Muhammad's marriages and relationship with women. It is generally understood that he married for political alliances, for diplomatic purposes, and to provide a family life for widows and orphans. Some have surmised that he had pity on helpless women, that he was approaching old age and had no sons, and that there were sexual attractions.[26]

The Hadith report many sayings and experiences which Muhammad had with his wives. Muslims accept these as truthful and authoritative. These traditions add information beyond the Qur'an on the status of women as well as on polygamy. Muhammad in the Hadith always serves as an example for Muslims.

Muhammad had female captives in addition to his twelve wives. Sexual rights were a part of possessing female captives. Prophet Muhammad would have had the right to accept sex from these women. Tradition reports,

> Narrated Anas: The Muslims said amongst themselves, "Will she (i.e., Safiya) be one of the mothers of the believers (i.e., one of the wives of the Prophet) or just (a lady captive) of what his right hand possesses?" Some of them said, "If the Prophet makes her observe the veil, then she will be one of the mothers of the believers (i.e. one of the Prophet's wives), and if he does not make her observe the veil, then she will be his lady slave." So when he departed, he made a place for her behind him (on his camel) and made her observe the veil.[27]

The sex life of Muhammad is seen in the following tradition: "Narrated Qatada: Anas bin Malik said, 'The Prophet used to visit all his wives in a round, during the day and night and they were eleven in number. I asked Anas, 'Had the Prophet the strength for it?' Anas replied, 'We used to say that the Prophet was given the strength of thirty (men).'"[28]

Traditions tell of the way the Prophet greeted his wives and in return they would bless him. At times they would argue with him. Umar, who was to become a caliph after Muhammad's death, had a daughter married to the Prophet. He blamed the arguments on the youngest wife, Aisha, whom he regarded as too young and vain and as favored by Muhammad.

A tradition states, "Narrated Aisha: That the Prophet married her when she was six years old and he consummated his marriage when she was nine years old, and then she remained with him for nine years (i.e., till his death)."[29] Muhammad married six-year-old Aisha when he was over fifty. Muslim apologists insist that she had her first period at nine years of age.

Muhammad had difficulties with his wives over his preferential treatment of Aisha. The Qur'anic revelation indicated that a man was to regard all his wives with equality. However, various traditions portray his favoritism toward his youngest wife.

"Narrated Abu Musa: Allah's Apostle said, 'Many amongst men reached (the level of) perfection but none amongst the women reached this level except Aisha, Pharaoh's wife, and Mary, the daughter of Imran. And no doubt, the superiority of Aisha to other women is like the superiority of Tharid (i.e., a meat and bread dish) to other meals.'"[30]

> Narrated Urwa: (The Prophet) then said to (Um Salama), "Do not hurt me regarding Aisha, as the Divine Inspiration do not come to me on any of the beds except that of Aisha." On that Um Salama said, "I repent to Allah for hurting you." Then the group of Um Salama called Fatima, the daughter of Allah's Apostle, and sent her to Allah's Apostle to say to him, "Your wives request you to treat them and the daughter of Abu Bakr on equal terms." Then Fatima conveyed the message to him. The Prophet said, "O my daughter! Don't you love whom I love?" She replied in the affirmative and returned and told them of the situation. They requested her to go to him again but she refused. They then sent Zainab bint Jahah who went to him and used harsh words saying, "Your wives request you to treat them

and the daughter of Ibn Abu Quhaba on equal terms." On that she raised her voice and abused Aisha to her face so much so that Allah's Apostle looked at Aisha to see whether she would retort. Aisha started to reply to Zainab till she silenced her. The Prophet then looked at Aisha and said, "She is really the daughter of Abu Bakr."[31]

The wives of Muhammad were jealous over his favoritism of Aisha. They sent his daughter and another to ask him to be more equal in his treatment of all of them. He responded in two ways. First, he said that revelation had come to him when he was in bed with Aisha and not with the others. Secondly, he asked them to love Aisha whom he loved, thus asking them to accept his preference for her. Other traditions indicate that Aisha was jealous of Muhammad's spending extra time with the other wives.

Polygamy, thus, was entirely acceptable in the Qur'anic teachings. The Prophet was not limited to four wives as other Muslim males were. The traditions indicate many characteristics of the married life and the treatment of women and wives by Muhammad. He was a lover, a provider, and an arbiter between his wives. There were times of harmony and times of disharmony in his married life.

In contemporary Islamic societies polygamy is little practiced. Some nations that observe Islamic Shari'a prohibit polygamy. It appears that few Muslims take seriously the injunction that a man may have up to four wives. Perhaps economic demands as well as the equality of time spent with each wife discourage its practice to any significant degree.

Traditional Family Lifestyles

The Arab Muslim family is usually large, strong, and closely knit. It is the basic unit of society. It is usually a patriarchal family with the father as head and the mother as the home nurturer, although more women are working outside the home. One's family is the source of reputation and honor, and most social activities revolve around the family unit. Perhaps the tie between mothers and sons is the most important relationship within the family.

Children are loved and often indulged with special attention. Discipline is strict, and children are taught to respect their parents and elders. Excessive praise for another's children is considered bad luck (the evil eye) for the family. The extended family is important, and close familial relationships are expected with both paternal and maternal relatives. Often, cousins are just as close as brothers and sisters. Parents are proud

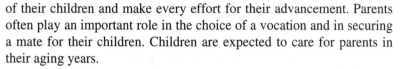

of their children and make every effort for their advancement. Parents often play an important role in the choice of a vocation and in securing a mate for their children. Children are expected to care for parents in their aging years.

Generally, there is a separation of males and females, especially in the public arena. Dating is not common, and it is often restricted to cousins when allowed. Women are protected and restricted by Islamic law and tradition. A woman's behavior, in particular, reflects upon her family's honor and reputation. Extramarital sex is strictly illegal and prohibited by Islam. A girl is protected by her brothers. The honor of the man also is based on how well he protects the women in his care.

SOCIAL LIFE

The ideal Islamic society is the community *(umma)* or brotherhood of Islam whose morals and manners and institutions find their legitimacy in the Qur'an and their patterns in the model of the life of the Prophet. The umma established by Muhammad cut across all lines of race, class, tribe, and ethnicity. Religion was integrated with society, and the new community was Muslim.

Outlines for the social patterns in Islam can be seen in the Qur'anic admonition,"O ye who believe! / Fear Allah as He should be / Feared, and die not / Except in a state / Of Islam."[32]

In a sermon during the pilgrimage in Mecca, Muhammad told his followers that their lives and properties were sacred and inviolate. He admonished them that the blood feud practices in the days of ignorance and paganism were to be abolished. Slaves were to be fed and clothed as their owners. "Know that all Muslims are brothers unto one another. You are One Brotherhood. Nothing which belongs to another is lawful unto his brother unless freely given out of good will."[33]

Muhammad declared the inviolability of a man's person, property, and honor. Muslim law establishes the principal crimes: murder, damage to body, fornication and adultery, theft and highway robbery, and consumption of alcoholic beverages. All of these are punished. The punishment for damages against a person is retaliation: life for life, eye for eye, tooth for tooth.

Positions within society and seats of power came in the development of the Islamic community. The growth of cities brought a division within society. The town dwellers established homes and a settled life, while the nomads were transitional over territories. The centers of government and political power usually were in the urban areas, and the nomadic tribes usually were placed in positions of deference and dependence to those seats of power.

A new aristocracy developed. Prior to Islam, tribal nobility and blood kinship were the measurements of status. Islam brought a new class or status. The Muhajirun were the fellow emigrants who left Mecca for Medina to help Muhammad build his new community, the umma. The Ansar were the helpers or natives of Medina who welcomed Muhammad and the emigrants and became Muslims in the new community. Thus, the early followers of Islam became associated through common bonds of religion, not necessarily kinship or tribal loyalties.

Other groups who claimed rank were the Hashimites, who were kin to Muhammad through common descent from Hashim, his great-grand-father, and the Alids, who traced descent from the prophet's son-in-law Ali through his martyred son Husein. The divisions of society at the time of the Caliph Umar about A.D. 650 are described as follows:

> I commend to you the fearing of God, with whom is no asso-ciate; and I commend to your favour the early Muhajirun, that you may recognize their past services; and I commend to your favour the Ansar—approve their good deeds and pass over their misdeeds; and I commend to your favour the inhabitants of the cities, for they are the support of Islam against the enemy and the gatherers of tribute. And exact no tribute from them except by their favour and consent. And I commend to you the inhab-itants of the open country, for they are the originals of the Arabs; and it is of the essence of Islam that you should take part of the superfluities of the wealth of their affluent ones and remit it to the poor among them; and I commend to your favour the people under "protection." Do battle to guard them and put no burden on them greater than they can bear, provided they pay what is due from them to the Muslims, willingly or "under sub-jection, being humbled."[34]

People described as under protection were non-Muslims who had no legal rights in the state and were permitted to exist on the payment of the poll tax *(jizya)* as provided by the Qur'an. Those to whom the Book had been brought were exempt from attack if they paid the tax. The People of the Book were the Jews, Christians, Sabians, and Zoroastrians; these peoples had been given the scriptures in the past.

With the coming of Islam to Persia, there arose a class of interpreters of the Qur'an and the traditions of law called the *ulama* and *qadis*. They had their rankings in society. The different grades of society in Persia about A.D. 1032 included the king, the provincial governors and tax gatherers, the vizier, landowners, peasants, ulama and qadis, and police officers.

In modern Islamic societies religion continues to play an important part in determining social status. Descent connected to the Prophet is prestigious and advantageous. A pilgrimage to Mecca gives one added status in the community. There is the political class who exercises power. There are the economic classes who control the market places and businesses and industries. There is often the new intelligentia class educated outside Muslim countries who return to their native lands as diplomats and engineers and technocrats. There is also the class of religious leaders such as the ayatollahs and sheikhs, who exercise power according to the strength and opportunities of Islam in the society.

Much of social behavior for Muslims is caught up in their families, for it is with their immediate and extended families that they spend time. Next to their families good Muslims give time and energies to their religious activities at the mosques and to the many observances of the Islamic calendar. The following paragraphs look at the vices and virtues of social behavior and social graces and courtesies.

Greetings and Postures

The traditional greeting is *salam alekum* (peace be on you). The response is *we alekum salam* (and on you be peace). The Qur'an tells Muhammed to greet others by saying "Peace be upon you."[35] This is also the greeting given to the blessed in paradise.

Muhammad is reported to have said, "There are no two Muslims who meet and shake hands but their sins will be forgiven before they separate." Greeting is a religious obligation. "'Peace!' a word (of salutation) from a Lord most merciful!"[36] Muslims also may shake hands, and men may embrace one another in greetings while kissing each cheek. It is standard in greetings to inquire about a person's health and family and to make polite conversation before engaging in serious matters.

Tradition is precise about sitting arrangements. When in public worship in the mosque, sitting is on the floor, usually on carpets. Those of superior status always sit above others when there are social gatherings. One never exposes the bottoms of one's feet or shoes towards others. Often, shoes are removed upon entry in buildings, and always they are left at the entry of the mosque before assuming the prayer positions inside.

The prophet adopted ten qualities from his culture and handed them down: cleaning teeth, cleaning the nose with water at the time of prayer, cleaning the mouth likewise, cleaning finger joints, washing with water after urinating, clipping the mustache, shaving pubic hair, cutting nails, not cutting the beard, and removing hairs under armpits.

The right hand is used for eating, and the left hand is avoided because Muslims believe that Satan uses the left hand. Also, the left hand is generally taboo, because it is the hand the Muslim uses in relieving himself. To beckon another person, all fingers wave with the palm facing downward. Sometimes, it is impolite for a man to cross his legs. Generally a person keeps both feet on the ground or floor.

Arab Muslims place great emphasis on formality and protocol in greetings, visitations, hospitality, and business transactions. Deference must be given to elders. In an initial business meeting, it may be the better time for the Arab to discuss and demonstrate the ideals of Islamic and Arab civilization than for any objective analysis or problem solving of business and commercial interests. Polite conversation and the serving of refreshments are more appropriate than heavy stuff which may come at a later time. Refreshments are always offered to guests, including the customer in the shop. It is good etiquette to refuse refreshments several times before yielding to the host's persistent offer.

Except for close friends and relatives, one will not visit another without an invitation. Arab Muslims may invite friends or business acquaintances for afternoon refreshments or for a meal. It is an offense to the host if hospitality is refused. Sometimes it is appropriate for the guests to take flowers or candy to present to the host. Usually one does not compliment the possessions of the host, for there is a tradition that it is a social obligation that the host upon receiving the compliment should give the guest the object. However, one may offer genuine compliments on the home, food, children, and accomplishments.

Distance and Touching

Arabs seem to have the need to feel the presence of other people. It is said that some Arabs like to feel one's breath on their face. Thus, they may get close in conversation, gesticulate with animation in their voices, and speak in loudness. Closeness between the sexes in public is considered obscene. But a male may hold the hand of another male friend as they proceed down the street. This is a custom and does not suggest a homosexual relationship.

Names of Individuals and Families

Muhammad taught that there were good names and bad names. The best names are associated with religious character and may express some relationship to God or an attitude toward God. They include Abd'allah (servant of God) and Abdu'r Rahman (servant of the Merciful One). A name of anathama is Maliku'l-amlak (King of Kings), for only God may be called King of Kings.

The prefix Abu means "father of," and Umm and Ummu mean "mother of." For example, Abu Musa means "father of Moses." Ibn means "son of," as Ibn Hasan, son of Hasan. Sometimes a person is named after his occupation. Hasan al-Hallaj is Hasan the dresser of cotton. Some are known for their birthplace. al-Bukhari is a native of the town of Bukhari.

The most common name for a male is Muhammad, which means "highly praised by God." Ahmad, Mahmud, Hamid, and Hamud are derivatives of the same root word. Other common names include Ali, Musa (Moses), Yusuf (Joseph), Da'ud (David), Ibrahim (Abraham), Hasan, Husein, and Ishaq (Isaac).

Common female names are Fatima (daughter of Muhammad), Khadija (first wife of Muhammad), A'isha (young wife of Muhammad), Jamila (pretty), and Najma (star). The Kurdish ruler/warrior whom the Crusaders knew as Saladin had many names and titles: al-Malik al-Nasir al-Sultan Salah al-Din Yusuf ibn Ayyub which is translated "The Victorious King, Sultan, Redressor of the Faith, Joseph, son of Job."

Often at the time of birth a Muslim cleric will come to the bedside and whisper the name in the ear of the newborn. Ancient Arabic names are used as well as those of Hebrew origin. Arabic personal names are not limited to Arabs, but they are shared by other peoples who have been influenced by Islam. Names which follow in some degree the forms above may be found wherever there are Muslims, from Africa to Indonesia.

Charms and Amulets

Charms and amulets are used across the Islamic world, although they are condemned by the purists. They are expressions of popular Islam. They may be composed of bone, shells, beads, silver and gold. Their forms may be lockets or beads or other symbols. They may be worn around the neck or arms or stitched on clothing or carried on the auto dashboard or placed in an obvious place on a stand or table in the home.

Prominent on the charms are inscriptions from the Qur'an as well as figures of individuals. The hand of Fatima is a very popular symbol, especially among the Shi'ites. It is worn around the neck. The fingers are interpreted as the five saints: Muhammad, Ali, Fatima, Hasan, and Husein.

Animals

A dog is considered unclean. It is a term of vilification against one's enemies, especially against unbelievers. A dog is only justifiable for herding, hunting, and protection. If a dog comes into contact with food or eating utensils or the surroundings of the mosque, there is impurity, and rituals of cleansing are necessary. Satan is believed to appear in the form of a black dog.

The camel is an animal for transportation and brings other amenities to its owner. It is mentioned in the Qur'an as an example of God's wisdom and kindness. It may be sacrificed at special celebrations and festivals, and it is an object of zakat. A tradition says that Muhammad looked with favor upon the cat as a pure animal, saw cattle as a gift of God, and appreciated horses.

Parents and the Elderly, Relatives and Neighbors

It is said that in the Islamic world there are no old people's homes. The Qur'an says, "Thy Lord hath decreed / That ye worship none but Him, / And that ye be kind / To parents. Whether one / Or both of them attain / Old age in thy life, / Say not to them a word / Of contempt, nor repel them, / But address them / In terms of honour. / And, out of kindness, / Lower to them the wing / Of humility, and say: / My Lord! bestow on them / Thy Mercy even as they / Cherished me in childhood.'"[37]

To care for parents in their aging years is an honor and a blessing. One is to remember that when one was a helpless child one's parents preferred one to themselves. Mothers are especially honored by the prophet who taught that paradise lies at the feet of mothers. To serve one's parents is a duty second only to prayer.

With respect to other relatives Muslims are taught from the Qur'an: "And render to the kindred / Their due rights, as (also) / To those in want, / And to the wayfarer: / But squander not (your wealth) / In the names of a spendthrift."[38] As to neighbors, the prophet teaches that one is not a believer who eats his fill when his neighbor beside him is hungry; and one is not a good Muslim whose neighbors are not safe from his injurious conduct.[39]

Slavery

A slavery system was in place in ancient society before Muhammad, and Muhammad included that system in his new religion. It appears that slavery was considered a part of the natural order of things. Muhammad recommended the humane treatment of slaves and counseled that the freeing of them was a kind act. The abolition of slavery as a system is not suggested either in the Qur'an or in the traditions of the prophet.[40]

In Islamic history some slaves acquired great status and wealth. Aybak, the favorite slave of Muhammad Ghuri, the chief and founder of Islam in India, was the first of the slave kings of Delhi. The Mamluk sultans of Egypt were of similar origin. Series of dynasties were founded in the Middle East by the Turkish tribes during the twelfth and thirteenth centuries. The Seljuks originally purchased slaves as bodyguards, and the slaves later were appointed to the highest offices in the state.

In early Islam the practice was established not to take captives from among Muslims and not to enslave Muslim Arabs. The slave was regarded by law as an inferior being both morally and physically. Normally the slave's evidence was not acceptable in a court of law. A tradition reports that both Muhammad and Ali rendered counsel that no Muslim could be killed for a protected non-Muslim (Jew or Christian) and no free man for a slave.

Slaves were permitted to marry, but the consent of the owner was required. The Hanafi and Shafi'i law schools permitted only two wives for a male slave while the Malikite school allowed four. The Qur'an allowed a Muslim to marry his own slave girl if she were a Muslim. However, some law schools held that the Muslim must free her in marriage. There were no restrictions upon concubinage with slave girls.

The emancipation of slaves was considered a commendable act in the Qur'an and the traditions. Slaves could become free in various ways. The woman slave became free upon her master's death, as did the children she had as his wife or concubine. The slave who came into the possession of an owner who was kin to him in the direct line could be freed. Freedom of a slave could be an act of piety as recommended by the Qur'an. The slave in emancipation became the freedman or client of his late owner. The slave received benefits from the owner and gave him patronage in return.

During the caliphates and Islamic empires, thousands of slaves, both black and white, were imported. Great profit was involved as well as the provision of a labor force. In the earlier days black slaves came from Libya and upper Egypt, and white slaves came from Syria and central Asia. Beautiful slave girls came to the harems of the Baghdad caliphate from Spain and Italy. Egypt, North Africa, and South Arabia became the chief markets for black slaves from Africa.

In 1925 slaves were bought and sold at Mecca. In the Treaty of Jedda in 1927 between the British government and King Ibn Saud, the slave trade was suppressed in Arabia. Other Muslim lands and societies have either prohibited slavery or suppressed it or tolerated it in more isolated areas. The veiled Tuaregs of the Sahara have slaves. Their two categories include household slaves and outdoor slaves. Local law regards the slaves as chattel.

Virtues and Vices

Muslims are to cultivate social virtues and avoid social vices. Islam does not condone frivolous pleasures, lying, slander, arrogance, boasting, scheming, obscenity, insult, spite, envy and inconstancy. It encourages kindness, generosity, feeding the poor, visiting the sick, escorting the deceased to the grave, honoring the aged, and peaceful relations. A Muslim should be the first to give greetings and should restrain anger. One's word is to be one's bond.[41]

Traditional Cultural Assumptions

In summary, the following are general characteristics of Muslim thinking and acting:

- Islam is the one true religion. It is inconceivable that anyone would want to be anything but a Muslim.

- When non-Muslims learn about Islam and realize that it is the one true way, they will convert.

- The Qur'an and associated laws and customs found in the Shari'a, the Sunnah, and the Hadith are the final arbiter in any dispute, argument, and legal question.

- Male members of the family have the right and the obligation to maintain the family honor.

- All good things, including education, jobs, marriage, housing, and recreation, come through the family. The individual is an intricate part of the family.

- The preferred marriage partner for any male is the daughter of his paternal uncle.

- A woman fulfills part of her duties as a wife by bearing male offspring.

- One should be careful in a greeting not to inquire about another's wife but about the family.

- One should not offer food or drink with the left hand. It is for cleansing oneself.

- The woman's place is in the home.

- To tell a guest no is impolite. One will do one's best to oblige a guest.

- One must offer a guest food and/or drink.

- If someone admires something one owns, then one should offer it.

- It is a son's duty to take care of his parents in their aging years.

- The future is in God's hands. It would be presumptuous for one to predict the future or even to assume there will be a future.

- Knowledge is power. One reluctantly and judiciously shares it.

ECONOMIC LIFE

Commerce, business, and trade in Islam find their principles and practices in the Qur'an and in the life of Muhammad.[42] He married a wealthy businesswoman and evidently was a successful merchant.

The Qur'an provides specific instructions for the economic life of individuals and the community.[43] One should make a living through hard work and honest ways. All business should be conducted with frankness and honesty. Honest trade is permitted and blessed by God. Thus, honest and decent work, warnings to cheaters, and the forbidding of usury or taking interest on loans are all emphasized in the Qur'an.

"And the Firmament has He / Raised high, and He has set up / The Balance (of Justice), / In order that ye may / Not transgress (due) balance. / So establish weight with justice / And fall not short / In the balance."[44] "Woe to those / That deal in fraud—/ Those who, when they / Have to receive by measure / From men, exact full measure, / But when they have / To give by measure / Or weight to men, give less than due. / Do they not think / That they will be called / To account?— / On a Mighty Day, / A Day when (all) mankind / Will stand before / The Lord of the Worlds."[45] The traditional role of commerce is seen against the backdrop of God holding a balance sheet over humankind in their actions and dealings. The Last Judgment is a reckoning of a person's accounts in a book of balances. Deeds are weighed, and each soul is held in pledge for the deeds committed. Good deeds merit good rewards.

The noted Muslim scholar Ibn Khaldun of the fourteenth century wrote,

> It should be known that commerce means the attempt to make a profit by increasing capital, through buying goods at a low price then selling them at a high price, whether these goods consist of slaves, grain, animals, weapons, or clothing material. The accrued amount is called profit. The attempt to make such a profit may be undertaken by storing goods and holding them until the market has fluctuated from low prices to high prices. Or the merchant may transport his goods to another country where they are more in demand than in his own. Therefore, an old merchant said to a person who wanted to find out the truth about commerce: "I shall give it to you in two words: buy cheap and sell dear."[46]

Islam has much to say about God, religion, and commerce. Generally, it encourages private property and the accumulation of wealth. Commerce is a superior work, and tradition reports that Muhammad said that the trustworthy merchant will sit in the shade of God's throne at the Day of Judgment.

Muhammad's Example

Muhammad was both prophet and chief administrator of the commerce of the fledgling and emerging community. He required the conquered by formal treaties to give a percentage of income and properties. A special tax was required of Christians. Muhammad received one-fifth of all captured booty and accepted private gifts. He took all booty which was won by negotiation.

Because he was the total leader of the community in all religious, political, and social affairs, Muhammad had many obligations. His expenses were heavy. He provided extensive hospitality and gave fine gifts. As was the mandate on other Muslims, he, too, was required to give generously as commanded by the Qur'an to family, orphans, beggars, and friends.

Thus, the example of Muhammad demonstrates that in Islam there is no contradiction between wealth and piety. Those who have are under the guidance of the Qur'an which urges the wealthy to do good works, reminds them that riches for their own sake are condemned, and that there is a Day of Judgment when the scales are brought out and the balance of good and evil is weighed.

A tradition reports that Muhammad passed by a pile of grain. He put his hand into the middle of it, and his fingers touched moisture. He said, "O merchant, what is this?" The merchant replied, "It has been damaged by rain, O Apostle of God." Muhammad replied, "If that is the case, why not put the damaged grain on top of the pile so that people can see it?" Then he concluded, "Whoever practices fraud is not one of us."[47]

Usury

Usury, the taking of interest on loans, is specifically forbidden in the Qur'an. "Those who devour usury / Will not stand except / As stands one whom / The Evil One by his touch / Hath driven to madness. / That is because they say: / 'Trade is like usury,' / But Allah hath permitted trade / And forbidden usury. / Those who after receiving / Direction from their Lord, / Desist, shall be pardoned / For the past; their case / Is for Allah (to judge); / But those who repeat / (The offence) are Companions / Of the Fire; they will / Abide therein (forever). / Allah will deprive / Usury of all blessing, / But will give increase / For deeds of charity; / For He loveth not / Creatures ungrateful / And wicked."[48]

Scholars speculate that the background for the prohibition of taking interest came with the situation in Medina. Muhammad appealed for aid from the Jewish tribes. The Jews refused but offered to lend money at interest. In this way they were refusing to accept Muhammad as prophet. Also, the idea underlying usury has been argued that all believers are brothers and therefore ought to assist one another financially without taking additional interest money.

In present Islamic societies there are variations on the acceptance and rejection of usury. Islamic nations do business with non-Muslim business and financial institutions as well as nations. American, European, and Japanese financial principles and practices depend on interest rates, and these principles have influenced Islamic practices.

Customs and Contracts in Business

A strong tradition among Muslims is memorization of the Qur'an by heart. Consequently, over the centuries Muslims have relied on oral tradition and the conduct of business on a verbal basis. In a traditional Shari'a court, only oral evidence is accepted at the disallowance of written evidence.

Honor and saving face are important, and one is honor bound to stand by an agreement. Intention is more important than action. For example, if a merchant bought food during a famine in order to hoard it and sell it at a higher price, the Shari'a rules it wrong even though the contract for purchasing the food was valid. Morality takes precedence over a contract.

Shari'a requires that a contract be completed in three days. In the modern world this is impractical, and Muslims make adaptations to this requirement through options and other means. To conclude an agreement is not to be confused with the bargaining process that preceded it. Bargaining is a way of life, and the art of compromise involves giving and taking without losing face.

It is illegal to sell that for which the exact quality and quantity is unknown. Likewise, it is illegal to sell that which would cause harm in delivery or which has no use.

It is said that the three worst vices are folly, meanness, and falsehood. Lies which avert harm and bring benefit may be justified, but they are still vile. A man who boasts of his possessions, although he is telling the truth, is nevertheless vile. The vilest of all men is he who boasts of what he has not.

"Business transactions enjoy a great deal of attention from Islam. Honest trade is permitted and blessed by God. This may be carried out through individuals, companies, agencies and the like. But all business deals should be concluded with frankness and honesty. Cheating, hiding defects of merchandise from the dealers, exploiting the needs of customers, monopoly of stocks to force one's own prices are all sinful acts and punishable by the Islamic Law. If one is to make a decent living, it has to be made through honest ways and hard endeavor."[49]

The Arab Muslim takes a relaxed view of the use of time. To rush into something is considered an insult and a possible disaster. "On" or "about" time is followed for appointments or meetings rather than "exactly at." There is little pressure of time. If Allah wills things to happen, they will; why worry and rush? For the Arab a relationship is more important than a transaction. A favorite saying is "En shallah," meaning "If Allah wills."

Islam views the future as in the prerogatives of Allah, and in human hands it is at most relative and at least to be handled with care and caution. Muslims are not bound to terms or contracts which are unfavorable even if found unfavorable down the road. Long-term commitments to business agreements may be weakened over time. Precision in beginning and concluding dates for a project is limited.

POLITICAL LIFE

According to Kenneth Cragg, to study the history and theology of Islam "is to encounter the most resolute and unperturbed of all faiths in placing trust, and finding pride, in political religion."[50] As in social and economic life, political life follows the teachings of the Qur'an. Islamic political and governmental life adheres to the principles and practices of a theocracy, that is, rule in the name of God. Although Islamic societies through the centuries have had various forms of governments, for the most part they have honored Islamic law to varying degrees.

Early Islam under the rule of Muhammad was nascent in formulating its governance. The Prophet's rule in Medina has been characterized as "The Constitution of Medina." The Ottoman Empire reigned under a caliph who administered Islamic law. In modern times Turkey, the seat of the former Ottoman Empire, basically has had a secular government; the constitutions of Saudi Arabia and Iran state that they rule under Islamic law.

Early Character of the Islamic State

In A.D. 622 Muhammad fled Mecca to go to Medina to assume leadership in establishing peace and stability among the tribes. He continued to have revelations from God which had begun in Mecca in A.D. 610. He implemented what has been referred to as "The Constitution of Medina." This document defined the rights and duties among those who accompanied Muhammad from Mecca, those new believers in Medina who accepted his message, and the Jewish tribes in the area. It established the umma, the community of believers, and the guidelines for living and rules for relationships with non-believers.

All matters were to be referred to Muhammad. Rules were set to pay blood money and to ransom captives. The community of believers made peace together and took revenge against their enemies together. No war was to be declared except through the Prophet. Jews were given their religious rights and guidelines to exist in relationship to the umma.

The constitution gave Muhammad the authority and power to be not only prophet, which authority he already had from the Qur'an, but also political leader, judge, and commander-in-chief. All disputes were handled by him to give out justice in the name of God. He had power to give security guarantees to tribes. As military chief he defended Medina and initiated raids on rebellious tribes. One-fifth of the spoils from battle went to him. He appointed some to perform functions for him such as collecting taxes.[51]

Islam's Heartland

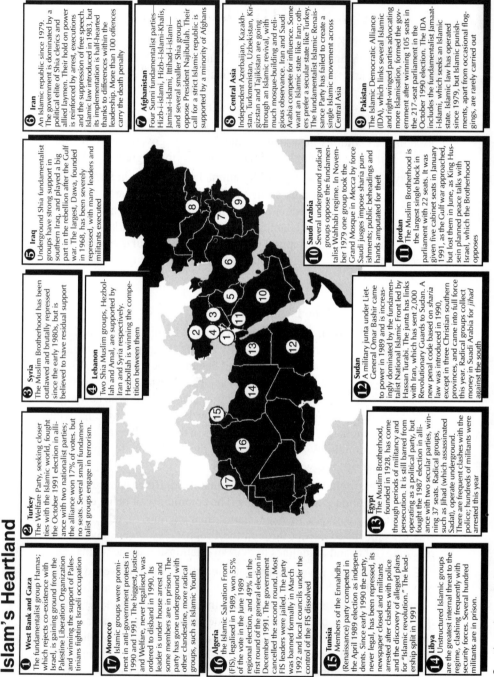

① West Bank and Gaza
The fundamentalist group Hamas, which rejects co-existence with Israel, is gaining ground from the Palestine Liberation Organization and winning the support of Palestinians fighting Israeli occupation

② Turkey
The Welfare Party, seeking closer ties with the Islamic world, fought the October 1991 election in alliance with two nationalist parties; the alliance won 17% of votes, but no seats. Several small fundamentalist groups engage in terrorism.

③ Syria
The Muslim Brotherhood has been outlawed and brutally repressed since the early 1980s, but is believed to have residual support

④ Lebanon
Two Shia Muslim groups, Hezbollah and Amal, are supported by Iran and Syria respectively. Hezbollah is winning the competition between them

⑤ Iraq
Underground Shia fundamentalist groups have strong support in southern Iraq, and played a big part in the rebellion after the Gulf war. The largest, Dawa, founded in 1968, has been severely repressed, with many leaders and militants executed

⑥ Iran
An Islamic republic since 1979. The government is dominated by a political elite of Shia clerics and allied laymen. Their hold on power is reinforced by arrest, executions and the suppression of free speech. Islamic law introduced in 1983, but its implementation is half-hearted thanks to differences within the leadership. More than 100 offences carry the death penalty

⑦ Afghanistan
Four Sunni fundamentalist parties—Hizb-i-islami, Hizb-i-Islami-Khalis, Jamiat-i-Islami, Ittihad-i-islami—and several smaller Shia groups oppose President Najibullah. Their call for a strict Islamic republic is supported by a minority of Afghans

⑧ Central Asia
Independent Azerbaijan, Kazakhstan, Turkmenistan, Uzbekistan, Kirgizstan and Tajikistan are going through an Islamic revival, with much mosque-building and religious observance. Iran and Saudi Arabia compete for influence. Some want an Islamic state like Iran; others prefer a secular state like Turkey. The fundamentalist Islamic Renaissance Party has failed to create a single Islamic movement across Central Asia

⑨ Pakistan
The Islamic Democratic Alliance (IDA), which links several Islamic and right-winged parties advocating more Islamisation, formed the government after winning 105 seats in the 217-seat parliament in the October 1990 election. The IDA includes the fundamentalist Jamaat-i-Islami, which seeks an Islamic state. Islamic law has operated since 1979, but Islamic punishments, apart from occasional floggings, are rarely carried out

⑩ Saudi Arabia
Several underground radical groups oppose the fundamentalist Wahhabi regime. In November 1979 one group took the Grand Mosque in Mecca by force. Saudi juges impose sharia punishments; public beheadings and hands amputated for theft

⑪ Jordan
The Muslim Brotherhood is the largest single block in parliament with 22 seats. It was given five cabinet seats in January 1991, as the Gulf war approached, but lost them in June, as King Hussein planned peace talks with Israel, which the Brotherhood opposes

⑫ Sudan
A military junta under Lieutenant-General Omar Bashir came to power in 1989 and is increasingly dominated by the fundamentalist National Islamic Front led by Hassan Turabi. The junta has links with Iran, which has sent 2,000 Revolutionary Guards to Sudan. A new penal code based on sharia law was introduced in 1990, except in three Christian southern provinces, and came into full force this year. Radical groups collect money in Suadi Arabia for jihad against the south

⑬ Egypt
The Muslim Brotherhood, founded in 1928, has come through periods of militancy and persecution. It is still barred from operating as a political party, but fought the 1987 election in alliance with two secular parties, winning 37 seats. Radical groups, such as Jihad (which assassinated Sadat), operate underground. There are frequent clashes with the police; hundreds of militants were arrested this year

⑭ Libya
Unstructured Islamic groups are the greatest internal threat to the regime, clashing frequently with security forces. Several hundred militants are in prison.

⑮ Tunisia
Members of the Ennahdha (Renaissance) party competed in the April 1989 election as independents. Since early 1990 the party, never legal, has been repressed, its newspaper closed and militants arrested after clashes with police and the discovery of alleged plans for "Islamic revolution." The leadership split in 1991

⑯ Algeria
the Islamic Salvation Front (FIS), legalised in 1989, won 55% of the vote in the June 1989 regional election, and 49% in the first round of the general election in December 1991. The government cancelled the second round. Most FIS leaders were jailed. The party was banned formally in March 1992 and local councils under the control of the FIS dissolved

⑰ Morocco
Islamic groups were prominent in anti-government protests in 1990 and 1991. The biggest, Justice and Welfare, never legalised, was ordered to disband in 1990. Its leader is under house arrest and some members are in prison. The party has gone underground with other clandestine, more radical groups, such as Islamic Youth

Countries and areas shaded have a Muslim majority. Apologies to Bangladesh, Indonesia and Malaysia (credit: *The Economist* April 4, 1992.)

In pre-Islamic Arabia tribes were based on blood kinship. The umma (community) under Islam was based on religious affiliation. It became the Brotherhood of Islam with Muhammad receiving messages from God and giving directives to the people. The enemies of the community are the unbelievers and idolaters. They are like hostile tribes. There is to be no intermarriage with them. The community pays Zakat (Qur'anic mandated giving) for its security and protection and well-being, while non-Muslims pay jizyah for its protection.

The Muslim community was established in Medina in close association with three events as announced by the Qur'an. They were the Hajj (pilgrimage), the jihad (struggle or warfare), and the direction (Qibla) of prayer toward Mecca. All three have a major impact on the community's life and constitution.[52]

Contemporary Political Expressions

From its beginning Islam has been not only a religion but also a state which has everything required for life. Previously, the eras of the various caliphates and dynasties have been reviewed. The last great vestige of a monolithic Islamic political and legal system ended with the fall of the Ottoman Empire in 1924, after a ruling span of four hundred years. The latter half of the twentieth century has seen within Islamic societies government by kings and presidents, some ruling according to Islamic law and others adhering to secular courts.

Islamic leaders gathered in London in 1980 and issued a statement concerning the establishment of an Islamic Order. Only God confers legitimacy on governments, rulers, and institutions. An Islamic government follows the mandatory principles stated in the Qur'an and in the Sunnah. God's resources are to be used to serve justice, to promote goodness and virtue, and to eliminate evil and vice. These resources are to be shared equitably by all. "Islam aims at creating a model society. Its strategy is to mold the individual in accordance with the tenets of Islam, to organize and mobilize within a social movement for progress and development, and to establish an Islamic Order by building society and state, their institutions, and policies at national and international levels."[53]

The document emphasizes three concepts: brotherhood, justice, and consensus. It does not mention individual liberty or political freedom. Brotherhood is fundamental in Islam. Once one becomes a believer and thus a Muslim, one must not be attacked by fellow Muslim believers and one is protected from non-believers. The Qur'an repeatedly teaches justice. "We sent aforetime / Our messengers with Clear Signs / And sent them down with them / The Book and the Balance / (Of right and wrong), that men / May stand forth in justice."[54] The consensus (ijma) of the community may be utilized as an instrument for political change.

Muhammad Hamidullah points out that there are four duties of the Muslim state: the executive, legislative, judicial, and cultural. The *executive* means that sovereignty belongs to God; it is a trust which is administered by man for everyone's well-being. The *legislative* is found in the Qur'an which is the Word of God and source of law in all of life, spiritual as well as temporal. The *judicial* holds that all men are equal before the law. By *cultural* it is meant that the Word of God alone should prevail in the world. It is the duty of every Muslim and of every Muslim government not only to follow the Divine Law but also to organize foreign missions to help others know about Islam.[55]

According to another Muslim scholar, Mumtaz Ahmad, Muslim jurists have emphasized three important features of an Islamic state: umma (community), shari'a (law), and caliphate (leadership). The three spheres of legislative activity in a Muslim national state are to enforce laws which have specifically been laid down in the Qur'an and the Sunnah; to bring all existing laws into conformity with the Qur'an and Sunnah; and to make laws as subordinate legislation which do not violate the Qur'an and Sunnah.[56]

Ahmad continues that the example of the prophet's governance in Medina cannot provide solutions for the state today. With the fragmentation of dar al-Islam (the community or house of Islam) into separate principalities, a different set of criteria resulted. The original idea of consensus, universal participation, and mutual consultation collapsed. Legal scholars began advising Muslims to obey whoever was in power.

Should Islam allow autocratic/monarchical rule as well as some form of elective government? This debate was revived during the constitutional movement in Turkey late in the nineteenth century. Most Muslim thinkers believe the rule of autocratic kings is prohibited and that a constitutional or representative form of government either with or without a king is the only government permissible. A minority view holds that the average Muslim, being almost totally ignorant of Islam and its values, cannot realistically be expected to choose the right leader to represent him. Thus, a head of state must appoint a shura (council) to advise him, but it is not legally binding.[57]

The Qur'an seems to require that authority be vested in leaders whose ability and competence are suited for rule. It treats power as trust and draws up basic rules for the exercise of power. It makes every person accountable for all his capacities. And it requires power to be used to aid justice and mercy.[58]

The state which is governed in accordance with Islamic law is dar al-Islam (community or nation of believers or peace.) If the Islamic state is politically or economically subjugated by a non-Muslim power, it becomes dar al-harb (the community or nation of war or unbelievers). The state under subjugation has two choices. There may be jihad (struggle or war) to gain independent status, or there may be Hegira (migration) to another territory.[59]

Many Muslims desire an Islamic state. But its form and substance, the nature of legislation, the source of power and leadership, whether it is democratic or monarchical or other, is up for debate. Given the history and traditions of Islam and its presence in many cultures and nations, there is little consensus.

In discussing the political life in Islam, it is appropriate also to present the relationship of religion and politics in the state. The religion of Islam was from the beginning a synthesis with politics and the community or state. Bernard Lewis, a noted historian of Islam, has written that "such pairs of words as Church and State, spiritual and temporal, ecclesiastical and lay, had no real equivalents in Arabic until modern times, when they were created to translate modern ideas; for the dichotomy which they express was unknown to the medieval Muslim mind. The community of Islam was Church and State in one, with the two indistinguishably interwoven; its titular head, the Caliph, was at once a secular and a religious chief."[60] That Islamic state was a theocracy in theory and practice. God was considered the source of the state's power and law, and the caliph was God's representative. Orthodoxy meant the acceptance of the caliph's rule, and criticism or rejection was apostasy or heresy.[61]

The founder of the Muslim brotherhood in Egypt, Hassan al-Banna, wrote,

> My brothers, you are not a philanthropic society, nor are you a political party, nor an organization with a specific and limited goal. You are a new spirit flowing through the heart of this nation. You will revive it through the Quran. A new light will scatter the darkness of materialism through the knowledge of Allah. If people ask you: what is your message? answer: we proclaim the Islam which was given through Muhammad, and government is part of it and freedom is one of its commandments. And if people tell you: but this is politics, say: this is Islam. If they say to you: you are spreading a revolution, answer them: we are

the proclaimers of truth and peace which we believe and of which we are proud. If you revolt against us and stand in the way of our cause, God has already given us the right to defend ourselves and you would have become the oppressing revolutionaries.[62]

al-Banna was rooted in Sunni Islam, the orthodoxy of that branch. In Iran, Shi'ite Islam had its representative in Ayatollah Khomeini, who said,

You must show Islam as it truly is. You must make Islam known according to its basic truth so that the young generation may not imagine that the theologians at Najaf (in Iraq) and at Qom (in Iran) believe in the separation of religion from politics, or that they are exclusively preoccupied with matters of ritual purity and personal hygiene! Certainly they are concerned about politics. It was the imperialists who, through their control of educational programs, spread the idea of the separation of religion from the state. It was the imperialists who fooled the people into imagining that the theologians were incapable of being involved in the affairs of state and of society. Was religion isolated from politics in the days of the Prophet?[63]

Thus, during the latter half of the twentieth century, change within and among Muslim states has been evident. Arab nationalism was given credence and practice as it still is. However, problems existed. Former president Sadat of Egypt undermined the value of socialism and raised questions in Muslim minds about its usefulness. The Shah of Iran undermined the value of capitalism and raised questions about its usefulness among Muslims. People began looking around for other workable solutions. If neither secular socialism nor secular nationalism succeeded, then a possibility might be a revived form of Islam. Thus, the resurgence of the Muslim brotherhood in various parts of the Islamic world is evident. The revolution of the Ayatollah in Iran occurred and has continued in the Islamic Republic of Iran.

Islam has much to say with regard to human rights not only of Muslims but also of non-Muslims in the state. Full human rights are guaranteed non-Muslims by the Shari'a. It gives protection to their lives and property and to their houses of worship. They can also apply their own cannon laws to their affairs. Shari'a may not be imposed upon them, but they may apply on occasion to the Islamic court to settle their cases. The state also has to extend its welfare service to them.

Origin, race, and color are not bases for distinction or differentiation. All people are equal before the Shari'a. Cooperation with all members of the society is an obligation. Non-Muslim citizens within the great Islamic empires enjoyed equal status with Muslims and often a privileged and flourishing status. They were physicians, secretaries, and treasurers. They were translators. They were exempted from military service and from the payment of Zakat. They were required to pay a poll tax from which women, children, the elderly, and the poor were exempted.

A tradition about the prophet states, The Prophet, peace and blessings be upon him, said to his Companions once: Do you know what is the right due a neighbor? It is as follows: You should extend to him your assistance if he should seek your help, and your support whenever he needs it. Lend him whatever he may ask to borrow from you. If he should be in need, hasten to provide for his need. Visit him if he falls sick. If he should die, participate in his funeral. Extend your congratulatory greetings to him on happy occasions and your condolences on the occasion of misfortune. Do not raise your building so as to prevent the wind blowing in his house unless he grants permission to you to do so. And do not hurt him or his feelings in any manner. If you bring fruits home, send him some; otherwise let him not see it and let not your children stir the jealousy in the heart of his children by seeing it in their hands. Let not the odor of your cooking reach his nostrils unless you let him share it.[64]

8

ISLAMIC ANSWERS
TO CONTEMPORARY ISSUES

INTRODUCTION

D uring the fourteen hundred years of its existence, Islam has moved from the Arabian peninsula to all continents. The heartland of Islam continues to be in the Middle East and South Asia, the places of its birth, formative years, grand empires, huge mosques and shrines, and stimulating educational centers. Yet its population centers and its accommodation to other cultures and traditions is widespread. Indonesia is the largest Muslim nation, but African nations are well represented in its family. Millions of Muslims live in China, India, and the former Russian republics of central Asia.

Islam has faced transition and change, unity and diversity, and struggle (jihad) within itself as it has met forces of modernization and westernization and the challenge of other cultures. Commerce and trade, international politics and banking, the technological revolution, and the thirst of peoples for improvement in their health and education and housing and jobs have brought Islamic nations and peoples to interface with the nations and peoples of the world.

The oil wealth which certain Islamic nations have enjoyed since the early 1970s has increased huge expansions in their economies, an influx of outside peoples and institutions to assist them in development, and a challenge to their traditional life and culture. Millions of Muslims study in the universities of Europe, the United States, China, Japan, and other non-Muslim environments and have been educated and trained in western and far-eastern technology as well as ways of thought and life.

Islamic philosophers, theologians, scientists, medical personnel, educators, and political leaders have been challenged in their basic Muslim beliefs, practices, and values. In a highly industrialized society, what effect do time schedules and daily work requirements have upon praying in the mosque five times daily or in fasting during the month of Ramadan? How is the role of women in Muslim society affected by the feminist movement? When Muslims are a minority in a society, how do they view their responsibilities to government and its leaders? What are their ideas about freedom of religion and religious liberty and separation of church and state when they are a minority and when they are a majority?

This chapter explores the unity and diversity and the challenges and tensions within Islam as it responds to life in its surroundings of tradition and change. Issues of sexual relationships, contraceptives, and abortion will be surveyed. What is the Islamic perspective on AIDS and on homosexuality? What are Islam's teachings on suicide and euthanasia? What does jihad mean in terms of war and peace? What is the role and status of women as the twenty-first century approaches? What are basic human rights?

Some answers to these challenges may be simple, others complex. Some answers will come directly from the Qur'an, some from Muslim tradition, and others from the insights of Islamic scholars and non-Muslim observers. However, Islam will have some answer or direction for each challenge that it faces.

BIRTH CONTROL AND CONTRACEPTION

The primary objective of marriage is the preservation of the human species. Islam encourages couples to have many children, and it allows the husband and wife to plan for their family with proper conditions.

The common method of contraception at the time of Muhammad was *coitus interruptus*, the withdrawal of the penis from the vagina just before ejaculation, preventing the entry of semen. One tradition reports that a follower came to Muhammad to seek his advice. He told him that he had a slave girl with whom he wanted to have relations but did not want her to become pregnant. Was coitus interruptus permitted? He told Muhammad that the Jews of the community said coitus interruptus was a form of burying your child. Muhammad replied that the Jews were wrong, and if God wishes to create a child, one cannot prevent it. This was interpreted to mean that despite using coitus interruptus, a drop of semen still might reach the vagina without one's knowledge, and thus result in conception.[1]

The Qur'an has no categorical statement about contraception. It does condemn infanticide.[2] Scholars basically rely on the general Qur'anic teachings and those of the Prophet while employing analogical reasoning. Thus coitus interruptus is permissible but conditional in that it deprives a woman the right to experience sexual fulfillment and to have children. Most jurists agree that the permission of the wife is necessary to secure her right to have children and not negate it if both agree on this form of contraception. She may consent to the temporary loss of her right.[3]

The jurist-scholar al-Ghazali (d. 1111) ruled that coitus interruptus was justifiable. He cited three reasons: to protect the wife's life from risk of childbirth; to prevent excessive hardship on the family; and to consider an undue financial burden.[4]

Generally, there is a scale of criteria for the acceptance or prohibition of a matter arrived at by jurists and scholars and which helps establish the validity of the tradition. The criteria are as follows:

- Halal—good and encouraged without restriction

- Mandub—desirable or recommended in general

- Mubah—permissible, neither encouraged nor discouraged

- Makkruh—generally blameworthy, hated, improper, undesirable

- Haram—bad by nature, absolutely unlawful[5]

In summary then, the Qur'an has no explicit reference to contraception and birth control. The Prophet through his sayings indicates no prohibition of coitus interruptus. Five schools of jurists rule that it is undesirable and improper (makkruh), though not unlawful or prohibited.

Other methods of contraception are also considered. The douche, condom, diaphragm, and pill are all makkruh, that is undesirable but not unlawful (haram). Each woman should avoid that which might threaten to harm her health.

Islam prohibits irreversible methods of contraception such as vasectomy, tubal ligation, and hysterectomy. Jurists have used the prohibition against castration as an analogy to consensus against methods of sterilization. They prevent procreation and are an affront to the nature of the creation of God.[6]

Infertility is defined as the failure to have a pregnancy within a year of regular sexual intercourse without the use of contraceptives. A tradition of Muhammad reports, "marry women who will love you and give birth to many children for I shall take pride in the great number of my ummah (nation)." [7] The Qur'an says that God bestows children and leaves barren whom He wills. Infertile women appeal to God to cure them. Some resort to polygamy, amulets, and foster children. The Qur'an permits a man to have up to four wives within certain conditions. Thus, Islam has ways to cope with infertility.

Biotechnological innovations related to birth control, infertility, and abortion are presenting challenges to Islam. Any actions must not contradict the Qur'an or the traditions of the Prophet. Masturbation is prohibited. Artificial insemination in order to gain seed for the wife may meet the higher goals of birthing a child. Sperm banks are condemned as an illegitimate act. In vitro fertilization must be restricted to a single ovum but is still questionable. Surrogate parentage is illegitimate.

Various Islamic nations have considered and implemented family planning. Some are more successful than others. Pakistan initiated a family plan for the years 1965–70. The ulama (Islamic clergy) opposed it because it:

- resembled infanticide

- was unnatural to human nature

- demonstrated disbelief in the providence of God

- ignored the Prophet's admonition to increase in numbers

- would lead to disastrous social consequences

- was part of a conspiracy of western imperialists against developing nations.[8]

ABORTION

Abortion is the termination of a pregnancy. It may be spontaneous or by intervention. Islamic concern is only with abortions occurring as a result of human intervention. Abortion then is the expelling of a fetus inside a woman's womb before the end of the natural period of gestation.

No Qur'anic statements deal directly with abortion. Islam generally upholds the sanctity of life.[9] There are justifications for ending life.

Punishment for highway robbery may include execution.[10] Adultery is dealt with by one hundred stripes.[11] Muhammad added stoning. Apostasy for one who renunciates Islam may have fatal consequences.[12] The Prophet is reported to have said to kill one who changes his religion. Apostasy is treason, for it is against one's God, family, and community. Murder demands a just retribution.[13] Jihad or holy war also results in killings.[14]

Thus, the status of the fetus in the womb must be examined. Considerations include:

- the humanity of the unborn

- the right of the unborn

- the future physical, mental, and social health of the unborn

- the wishes of the father and mother[15]

The Qur'an states, "We created you / Out of dust, then out of / Sperm, then out of a leech-like / Clot, then out of a morsel / Of flesh, partly formed / And partly unformed, in order / That We may manifest / (Our Power) to you; / And We cause whom We will / To rest in the wombs / For an appointed term, / Then do We bring you out / As babes."[16] Tradition holds that after 120 days the fetus has a soul.

Muslim jurists agree that after the fetus is completely formed and has a soul, abortion is forbidden, and is also considered a crime if performed. If pregnancy occurs from illegitimate sex, abortion is viewed only as a temporary solution, for Islam advocates early marriage. Therefore, sex outside of marriage which results in pregnancy does not justify abortion.[17]

Rape does not necessarily justify abortion; however, violent rape resulting in pregnancy may. Islam is commissioned to create an environment or society in which rape is not encouraged. A pregnancy in which the fetus is determined to be possibly mentally deformed does not warrant abortion. Muslims are counseled to stay away from drugs and to exercise patience.

If the continuation of the pregnancy would result in the death of the mother, then following the general guideline in the Shari'a of choosing the lesser of two evils would prevail, and abortion would be appropriate.

al-Ghazzali distinguishes between contraception and abortion:

> Contraception is not like abortion. Abortion is a crime against an existing being. Now, existence has stages. The first

stages of existence are the settling of the semen in the womb and its mixing with the secretions of the woman. It is then ready to receive life. Disturbing it is a crime. When it develops further and becomes a lump, aborting it is a greater crime. When it acquires a soul and its creation is completed, the crime becomes more grievous. The crime reaches a maximum seriousness when it is committed after it (the fetus) is separated (from the mother) alive.[18]

Islam teaches that every human being has a right to live (be born), and to live as long as God permits. No one may be deprived of life except for legitimate crime. Abortion, with few exceptions, is unallowable. A basic Muslim understanding places any discussion of abortion in the context of marriage and sex.

Thus Islam does not look at sex as an end in itself, but as a means to an end. The end of sex according to Islam is to have children. So, it is not allowed in Islam that a woman can have an abortion simply because it is her wish to do so, under the pretext of keeping her beauty and to avoid responsibility. This is considered as selfishness. Should a pregnant woman make abortion without any justified reason such as the expectation of risk on the mother's life, then this act amounts to murder according to Islam.[19]

HOMOSEXUALITY

Homosexuality is abhorrent to Islam and is condemned. The Qur'an contains the story of Lot and his people and the experience of sexual deviation. Muslims point out the following:

- Allah condemned sexually deviant behavior in the time of Lot and does so now.

- The Qur'an makes a lie of the argument that homosexuality is by birth for it points out that the people of Lot were the first to originate this shamefulness.

- "Do you commit lewdness / Such as no people / In creation (ever) committed / Before you? For ye practise your lusts / On men in preference / To women: ye are indeed / A people transgressing / Beyond bounds."[20] Homosexuality is not a natural inclination.

- The view of homosexuality to state its lifestyle publicly and openly is corrupting. It is offensive to society and in violation of Qur'anic teachings. "Do ye indeed approach men, / And cut off the highway?— / And practice wickedness / (Even) in your councils?"[21]

- When sexual deviancy requests and/or forces itself on society, the answer must be no. "And his people gave / No answer but this: / They said, 'drive them out / Of your city: these are / Indeed men who want / To be clean and pure.'"[22] The righteous are not required to share the same space as the homosexuals.

- The vice of homosexuality is linked with violence and aggression against others. The people of Lot who practiced this vice in their councils were also highwaymen (robbers).

- The story of Lot also shows the confederation and cooperation between the male and female deviants. Some of the women were impressed by this deviation among the men and they liked it. One was Lot's wife. God destroyed her along with her people and saved Lot and the other members of his family.[23]

Muslim theologians consider homosexuality a major sin. Islam has a high view of marriage and the family. Marriage is the norm for the female, and teenaged girls often marry. This early age undercuts the potential for lesbianism. Males frequently marry in their twenties. Premarital heterosexual experiences are discouraged. A sexual option for men before marriage is homosexuality, just as prostitution is an option for females. Whatever the extent of homosexual behavior may be in Islamic cultures, it is viewed as aberrant behavior.[24]

Dr. El Ashi observes that the Qur'an considers homosexuality to be against human nature. "It is harmful to man and it betrays one basic goal of sex, namely: procreation within the limits of marriage only. That is why it is prohibited to practise homosexuality."[25]

AIDS

In an article titled "AIDS—A Concern for Muslims" in a Muslim journal, Sheik N. Hassan, M.D. writes, "AIDS is a worldwide problem and involves more than an illness. It is a problem for all of humanity and not even the most devout Muslim should ignore it. Anyone, including Muslims, would be naive to think that AIDS is not his or her concern.

Every person must learn about it, know how to prevent it, and teach these preventive measures to others."[26]

AIDS is the acronym for Acquired Immunodeficiency Syndrome. It spares no one because of national origin, race, religious affiliation, or even personal practices. It is a disease that affects the immune system of the body, and the body becomes disabled to ward off diseases. The disease was identified about 1981. AIDS is a virus which is known as the Human Immunodeficiency Virus (HIV). There is no specific therapy for HIV, but it can be treated or controlled for some time.

The clinical manifestation of AIDS includes infections, tumors, dementia, body wasting, loss of appetite, weight loss, debility, and death. The effects of AIDS are physical, mental, and social. The median survival from the time of the development of AIDS to death is about one year with about ten percent of patients being alive after one year. With physical deterioration, long hospital stays, social stigma with its accompanying isolation and loneliness, there is despair, despondency, and depression. There are physical, emotional, and financial stresses upon family and friends. Caring for patients is very costly.[27]

Certain factors are known risks for contracting AIDS, including: illicit intravenous drug use; homosexuality; bisexuality; multiple sex partners or sexual relations (even once) with an infected person; babies born to mothers who are HIV positive; accidental punctures with needles contaminated with the virus; and transfusion with HIV contaminated blood and blood products.

The only known effective therapy for AIDS is prevention. Islam holds strict views on God's purposes in creation for human beings, for the health of individuals, for marriage and the family, and for the cleanliness and purification of the body as well as the soul.

While distributing needles to drug addicts and passing out condoms to young people may help curtail the spread of AIDS, they are in reality not practical.

> These efforts to control AIDS actually encourage behavior that is haram—behavior which Muslims must not engage in, condone, or be silent about. The solution of the problem of AIDS is very simple: strong moral behavior. This means:
>
> (1) the absolute abstinence from illicit drug use; and
>
> (2) the absolute abstinence from sex outside of marriage.

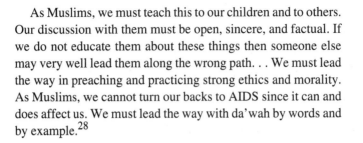

As Muslims, we must teach this to our children and to others. Our discussion with them must be open, sincere, and factual. If we do not educate them about these things then someone else may very well lead them along the wrong path. . . We must lead the way in preaching and practicing strong ethics and morality. As Muslims, we cannot turn our backs to AIDS since it can and does affect us. We must lead the way with da'wah by words and by example.[28]

EUTHANASIA AND SUICIDE

According to the Islamic view, death ends a person's opportunity to perform good deeds. It also transforms a person from one kind of existence to another. The afterlife of either reward or punishment reflects what an individual has done during temporal lifetime.

With regard to suicide, Abdul Muhammad Khouj writes,

Some people, especially those unhappy with their lives, may think that life ends with death. Thus, they try to commit suicide or to get killed in one way or another. In Islam, this belief is invalid because the individual's life does not end with this worldly life, but extends to other periods of existence. For this reason, the person who has committed suicide is considered an unbeliever who was a victim of misconception and false imagination. Temporal life is a trial period for the hereafter. Allah says, "Did ye then think that We had created you in jest, and that ye would not be brought back to Us (for account)?" In this sense, a Muslim should not wish to die or to be killed. Anyone who has taken his own life has violated Allah's order—that humans do not have the right to commit suicide. "Nor kill (or destroy) yourselves: for verily Allah hath been to you Most Merciful. (4:29)"[29]

Two representative Hadith deal with suicide.

"Narrated Abu Huraira: The Prophet said, 'Whoever purposely throws himself from a mountain and kills himself will be in the (Hell) Fire falling down into it and abiding therein perpetually forever; and whoever drinks poison and kills himself with it, he will be carrying his poison in his hand and drinking it in the (Hell) Fire wherein he will abide eternally forever; and whoever kills himself with an iron weapon, will be carrying that weapon in his hand and stabbing his abdomen with it in the (Hell) Fire wherein he will abide eternally forever."[30]

"Narrated Jundub: Allah's Apostle said, 'Amongst the nations before you there was a man who got a wound, and growing impatient (with its pain), he took a knife and cut his hand with it and the blood did not stop till he died. Allah said, '"My slave hurried to bring death upon himself so I have forbidden him (to enter) Paradise"'."[31] Ahmed Ibn Hanbal reports similar traditions about suicide.[32]

Thus, there is a severe penalty for a Muslim to take one's life. Hell is the reward, and one suffers the torments eternally. Allah alone gives life, and He alone takes life. To take one's life is to disobey and turn from the path of Islam.

Khouj writes that anyone believing in Allah should expect difficulty in this life. Therefore one should accept problems with patience and endurance. True believers know that hardships come from Allah and not from anyone else. Allah is merciful to those who repent and seek righteousness.

How is death determined in Islamic jurisprudence? Dr. al-Butee has written that death is the complete departure of the soul or life from the body. The evidence in Islamic law is the absence of the pulse and the uninterrupted cessation of the heartbeat. Dr. al-Butee cautions that brain death cannot be considered a clear-cut evidence that death has occurred. It is mere speculation on the part of physicians. He concludes that as long as the heart is beating, the occurrence of death cannot be confirmed. Disconnecting life-support systems is not considered killing or a cause of death for the patient. True life does not come from machines.[33]

WAR AND PEACE

If there is one word which non-Muslim peoples have seen in the press or heard over the media since the 1970s, it has been *jihad*. Together with the word *ayatollah*, the two have become synonymous with Muslims. Muslim writers claim the media has distorted the teachings and practice of Islam by misinformation and inflammatory usage.

It is appropriate to raise some questions: Was Islam spread at the point of the sword in its beginnings and expansion? Is the Muslim emblem the Qur'an or the sword? Were the Muslims imperialists and colonialists seeking loot and power in empire building? What are Islamic understandings of war and peace and how do their perspectives bear on their relationships to non-Muslims in nation building and government?

Marcel A. Boisard, writing from his Islamic perspective, asserts that the "traditional Western prejudice which portrays Islam as a belligerent religion gave rise to a derogatory and permanent definition of the Muslim 'holy war.' The term leads us to believe that Muslims are supposedly encouraged to take up arms in order to impose the faith by force, annihilating those who reject it. The generic term of jihad means 'effort', perhaps a violent one, but in no way specifically a military one."[34] Boisard states that the passionate ardor for the cause of Allah leads one to exert the effort to live according to his law and the struggle (jihad) to have his justice done.

According to Boisard, Muslim jurists hold to four types of "holy war;" the war waged by the heart, the tongue, the hand, and the sword. The war of the heart is the internal spiritual and moral struggle. It is the most important and meritorious war. It leads to victory over the ego. The war of the tongue is for speaking the truth of Islam and the war of the hand is for setting forth good moral example for the community and for non-Muslims. "Finally, the 'jihad of the sword' corresponds exactly to armed conflict with the enemies of the Islamic community and foreign leaders who either persecute the believers or restrict the freedom of conscience of their subjects. It results from the rejection of oppression and from the dynamic conception of justice and mercy."[35]

John Kelsay, a western non-Muslim scholar, raises the following questions: How does one measure the justice of war in general and in particular cases? What are the rules of war? Who has the authority to declare war and when?[36]

Islam offers two choices to humanity. The way of heedlessness or ignorance *(al-jahiliyya)* leads to religious and moral error and chaos. The way of submission *(al-islam)* is to follow the admonitions of Allah in the Qur'an. "The way of heedlessness and the way of submission are seen as institutionalized in the existence of Islamic and non-Islamic political entities. The former may be described as the territory of Islam (dar al-islam); the latter is the territory of war (dar al-harb)."[37]

In classical Sunni Islamic scholarship, the territory of Islam is viewed as the territory of justice and peace. In contrast, the territory of ignorance is full of disorder and strife and is a continual threat to Islam. Boisard points out that the enemies of God are those who threaten the existence of the Islamic community, those who persecute Muslims and, finally, polytheists. "Islam and polytheism, which stands as the enemy of Muslims, cannot coexist. Pagans have to choose between faith or the sword."[38]

Kelsay observes that for the Muslim the peace of the world cannot be fully secure until people come under the protection of Islam. He points out that in classical Sunni Islam there is a program of action, namely jihad, to help bring about the territory of Islam. For force to be used in extending the territory of Islam and thus to achieve peace, Sunni theorists set down certain rules:

- There must be a just cause (the refusal of a non-Islamic political entity to acknowledge the sovereignty of Islam).

- There must be a declaration of Muslim intentions (The Muslim ruler must invite the adversary to accept Islam or to pay tribute and acknowledge the Muslim authority.).

- There must be right authority (the proper Muslim head of state or ruler).

- The war must be conducted based on Islamic values (right intent for the cause and in the path of God).[39]

Kelsay takes issue with the observations of the noted Islamicist Bernard Lewis with respect to conceptions of war in Islam. Lewis points out that Muhammad was not only a prophet of a religion but also a ruler and a commander of a community. Muhammad's leadership involved a state and its armed forces. Lewis contends that if the Muslim soldiers are fighting for God, it follows that their opponents are fighting against God. "And since God is in principle the sovereign, the supreme head of the Islamic state—and the Prophet and, after the Prophet, the caliphs are his viceregents—then God as sovereign commands the army. The army is God's army and the enemy is God's enemy."[40]

Kelsay argues against the view of Lewis in that the Islamic tradition suggests that the idea of religion as a *casus belli* provides a way to limit the occasion and the damage of war. Holy war is not equivalent to total war. The jihad tradition, so Kelsay points out, is the special military aspect of a "working politico-military doctrine" by which Muslims attempt to foster relations between peace, order, and justice in human affairs.

The general mission of all Islamic tradition is to demonstrate to the world the values associated with pure monotheism, to command good, to forbid evil, and to bring about justice. Islam wants to create a political entity that reflects Islamic values. It is interested not only in avoiding conflict but also in creating a just society. This is where the Islamic view of peace leads.

Marcel Boisard in his work *Jihad: A Commitment to Universal Peace* states, "The 'holy war' (jihad) is in effect that instrument which if needs be must impose the reign of Islam, in other words, peace and justice under the protection of the revealed law—upon a recalcitrant and aggressive 'world of war.'"[41] An armed holy war is against the enemies of God, apostates, secessionists, disturbers of the public safety, monotheists who refuse to pay the capitation tax, and in defense of the frontiers. Monotheists are the People of the Book (Jews and Christians) who showed hostility toward Islam and refused the payment of the tax. They would have a choice of faith and acceptance of the Qur'an or pay the tax or war.[42]

In a discussion of religion and world order in the context of the reference to world order by the United Nations and other world leaders, Kelsay writes, "In encounters between the West and Islam, the struggle is over who will provide the primary definition to world order. Will it be the West, with its notions of territorial boundaries, market economies, private religiosity, and the priority of individual rights? Or will it be Islam, with its emphasis on the universal mission of a transtribal community called to build a social order founded on pure monotheism natural to humanity. Who will determine the shape of order in the international context?"[43]

Many Muslim scholars think that the non-Muslim media has distorted Islam's views and practices of war. Thus they write to set the record straight. Hammudah Abdalati writes, "The Qur'an makes it clear that, whether we want it or not, war is a necessity of existence, a fact of life, so long as there exist in the world injustice, oppression, capricious ambitions, and arbitrary claims."[44] Thus, Islam recognizes war as a lawful and justifiable action for self-defense and the restoration of justice, freedom, and peace.

The Qur'an states, "Fighting is prescribed / Upon you, and ye dislike it. But it is possible / That ye dislike a thing / Which is good for you, / And that ye love a thing / Which is bad for you. / But Allah knoweth, / And ye know not."[45]

Abdalati continues, "Muslims are commanded by God not to begin hostilities, or embark on any act of aggression, or violate any rights of others."[46] For the Qur'an says, "Fight in the cause of Allah / Those who fight you, / But do not transgress limits; / For Allah loveth not transgressors. / And slay them / Wherever ye catch them, / And turn them out / From where they have / Turned you out; / For tumult and oppression / Are worse than slaughter; / But fight them not / At the Sacred Mosque, / Unless they (first) fight you there; / But if they fight you, / Slay them.

/ Such is the reward / Of those who suppress faith. / But if they cease, / Allah is Oft-Forgiving, / Most Merciful. / And fight them on / Until there is no more / Tumult or oppression, and there prevail / Justice and faith in Allah; But if they cease, / Let there be no hostility / Except to those / Who practise oppression."[47]

War, then, is the last resort for Muslims. Abdalati writes, "Islam is the religion of peace; its meaning is peace; one of God's names is peace; the daily greetings of Muslims and angels are peace; paradise is the house of peace, the adjective Muslim means Peaceful. . . . If non-Muslims are peaceful with Muslims or even indifferent to Islam, there can be no ground or justification to declare war on them. There is no such thing as religious war to force Islam on non-Muslims, because if Islam does not emerge from deep convictions, from within, it is not acceptable to God. . . . If there is any religion or constitution to guarantee peaceful freedom of religion and forbid compulsion in religion, it is Islam, and Islam alone."[48]

Another Muslim scholar, Muhammad Hamidullah, asserts that:

> a just struggle cannot be anything except a holy act. All war is forbidden in Islam, if it is not waged for a just cause, ordained by the Divine law. The life of the Prophet provides reference to only three kinds of wars: defensive, punitive, and preventive. In his celebrated correspondence with the Emperor Heraclius of Byzantium, in connection with the assassination of a Muslim ambassador in the Byzantine territory, the Prophet proposed three alternatives; "Embrace Islam—if not, pay the jizah." To establish liberty of conscience in the world was the aim and object of the struggle of the Prophet Muhammad and who may have a greater authority in Islam than he? This is the 'holy war' of the Muslims, the one which is undertaken not for the purpose of exploitation, but in a spirit of sacrifice, its sole object being to make the Word of God prevail. All else is illegal. There is absolutely no question of waging war for compelling people to embrace Islam; that would be an unholy war.[49]

Then what were the reasons for waging war by Muhammad's militias and by succeeding Muslim armies? Abdalati suggests there are four reasons. Muhammad, being the Prophet of God, tried to approach the rulers of the neighboring territories to invite them to accept Islam. They not only rejected his gracious invitation but also persecuted him and declared wars against the Muslims. Later, all Christendom, including

Spain and France, was at war with Islam. "The adventure of the Muslims in Europe has also to be seen in the light of these circumstances. The fact that all Christendom was operating as one power is proven by the unquestionable authority of the Roman papacy over Christians. It is also proven by the general mobilization of Christian powers against Islam during the Crusades of the Middle Ages and even of the first quarter of this twentieth century. So when Rome sanctioned war against Islam, the Muslims could not be denied the full right to fight back on any battleground—whether in Palestine or in the Fertile Crescent, Italy or Hungary. This is what took them to Spain and Southern France. They could not afford to be encircled from all around by the mighty power of Rome and Persia."[50]

Abdalati continues that the second reason for waging war was that because there were no telecommunication systems in those earlier days, the Muslims had to make direct and personal contacts by crossing borders. Because of the dangers involved, they had to cross with large groups which may have appeared like armies although they were not. "They had, by the order of God, to make Islam known to the outside world."[51] In crossing the borders, some who had been under the oppression of the foreign powers of Rome and Persia welcomed the Muslims. Others accepted Islam. Those who did not accept Islam were asked to pay the tribute or tax equivalent to the Islamic tax, the zakat.

Those who rejected Islam and refused to pay the tax "made it hard for themselves. . . . In a national sense, that attitude was treacherous; in a human sense, mean; in a social sense, careless; and in a military sense, provocative. But in a practical sense it needed suppression."[52]

Thirdly, when one surveys what the Qur'an says about injustice and oppression, and what one finds in the people ready for and joyful to receive liberation at the hands of the Muslims, one can see the justification of crossing borders and bringing the religion of peace, according to Abdalati.

Fourthly, Abdalati discounts the motivation for war as economic gain through looting and booty. He concludes, "The fact remains that Islam is the religion of peace in the fullest sense of the term; that unjust war was never among its teachings; that aggression was never its tenets or tolerated by it; that force was never employed to impose it on anyone; that the expansion of Islam was never due to compulsion or oppression; that misappropriation was never forgivable by God or acceptable to Islam; and that whoever distorts or misrepresents the Islamic teachings will do more harm to his own self and his associates than to Islam. Because it is the religion of God and the straight path to Him, it survived under the most difficult conditions, and it will survive to be the safe bridge to happy eternity."[53]

THE ROLE OF WOMEN

The Arabian environment out of which Islam emerged has influenced its teachings and practices on the role and status of women in marriage, family, religion, and other social, economic, and political areas of life. However, Muhammad was able to introduce deep changes in these areas. Female infanticide was prohibited unconditionally by the Qur'an.

It stated, "Even so, in the eyes of most / Of the Pagans, their 'partners' made alluring / The slaughter of their children, / In order to lead them / To their own destruction, / And cause confusion / In their religion. / If Allah had willed, / They would not have done so: / But leave alone / Them and their inventions."[54] Muhammad denounced and forbade female infanticide, and it disappeared from Arabia in early Islamic times.

In the early Muslim era women in general were subject to the authority of the nearest male kin, either to father or brother or husband whose right over the wife was similar to his rights over other properties. The husband was to keep the honor of his wife inviolate.

In marriage the bridegroom paid a sum of money, known as *mahr*, to his prospective bride. This was to be her money. However, the wife was still to be under the husband's authority, and he was entitled exclusively to her services.

The husband received one-half of the *mahr* if there were no children. He received one fourth if there were children. However, there was no mutual ownership of property between husband and wife. He retained full control over his possessions and she over hers; he was to provide completely for her sustenance in food and clothing and housing. A woman could receive a portion of her parent's inheritance, although a man could receive the portion of two females.

The Qur'an reflects the view of women in various ways as do the traditions of Muhammad. In the Qur'an when idolators are denounced for worshiping the goddesses al-Lat, al-Uzza, and al-Manat, the question is asked ironically, "What! For you / The male sex / And for Him, the female? Behold, such would be / Indeed a division / Most unfair!"[55]

In another statement about women, it is said, "Those who believe not / in the Hereafter, name / The angels with female names."[56] To unaccommodating women, particularly wives, it is written, "Men are the protectors / And maintainers of women, / Because Allah has given / The one more (strength) / Than the other. . . . As to those women / On whose part ye fear / Disloyalty and ill-conduct, / Admonish them (first), / (Next), refuse to share their beds, / (And last) beat them (lightly); / But if they return to obdeience, / seek not against them / means (of annoyance.)"[57]

Baydawi, a thirteenth-century commentator highly respected by Sunnis, comments on the Qur'anic passage 4:38 which deals with Allah's preference of the male over the female "in the matter of mental ability and good counsel, and in their power for the performance of duties and for the carrying out of divine commands. Hence to men have been confined prophecy, religious leadership, saintship, pilgrimage rites, the giving of evidence in law-courts, the duties of the holy war, worship in the mosque on the day of assembly (Friday), etc. They also have the privilege of electing chiefs, have a larger share of inheritance and discretion in the matter of divorce."[58]

The rights and duties of women are specified in Islam. Although there are differences between men and women, women have the rewards of paradise equal to men. On earth wives are never required to earn income, for husbands are to assume this duty. If wives had a certain lifestyle from their families before marriage, like having servants in the home, then the husband is to provide such if affordable.

Before Islam a man could take an unlimited number of wives, depending upon his capacity. The Qur'an allowed a man to have two, three, or four wives simultaneously, as long as he could treat all with equity.

Muhammad himself received a special revelation giving him the right to unlimited number of wives: "O Prophet! We have / Made lawful to thee / Thy wives to whom thou / Hast paid their dowers; / And those whom thy / Right hand possesses out of / The prisoners of war whom / Allah has assigned to thee; / And daughters of thy paternal / Uncles and aunts, and daughters / Of thy maternal uncles / And aunts, who migrated / (From Makkah) with thee; / And any believing woman / Who dedicates her soul / To the Prophet if the Prophet / Wishes to wed her—this / Only for thee, and not / For the Believers (at large)." [59]

Traditions report that the Prophet encouraged his male followers to marry numerous wives who preferably should be free women and virgins. Also, no woman should be married without her consent. If a man married more than four wives, there is no stated prohibition except the general threat of hell fire for wrongdoers.

Today in Muslim societies it is rare for a man to have more than one wife. Economically it is difficult. Also, laws demanding separate establishments for families make it almost impossible to have several families scattered throughout an area. Many Muslim nations, because of public conscience and the impact of modern education and mores, have placed restrictions on polygamous marriages, careful not to conflict with Qur'anic injunctions; these have discouraged men from having more than one wife. Polygamy was abolished in 1926 in Turkey, and restrictive legislation has curtailed it in Egypt, Syria, Iran, and other Muslim nations.

Muslim men may marry any woman except an idolatress, that is, chaste women to whom the Book has been given.[60] The Hanafi law school interprets this to mean a man may marry up to four Jewish and Christian women. The Shafi'i school makes it impossible to marry non-Muslim women. Muslim women may marry only a believer.

Although the Qur'an permits the marriage of a Muslim with a female slave, certain law schools place restrictions. There are no restrictions on the possession of unmarried female slaves in concubinage by their owner, but the Hanafi law school prohibits a Muslim man from marrying his own or his son's female slave, and also a Muslim woman from marrying her male slave.

A divorced woman or a widow must under certain conditions wait before another marriage. The waiting period will reveal if there is a pregnancy which would then mean that the former husband had obligations.

Islam fixed no age limits for marriage, though it was generally understood that the girl was not to be given to the man until she was ready for sexual intercourse. In Muslim societies governments have set certain age limits. They vary from an unusual age of twelve to an older eighteen.

The central feature of the marriage is the contract, and it includes a payment (mahr) to the wife. The amount of the payment may depend on the affluence of both parties and on the status, goods, and pedigree of the woman. The payment belongs to the wife and not to her family or her husband. The marriage contract often stipulates whether the prospective bride is a virgin, and this may mean not only more honor in the marriage but also a higher payment.

Another form of marriage developed in Islam called *mut'a*. A *mut'a* arrangement between a man and a woman was not for the establishment of a home nor for having children. It was simply to provide a man a wife for a specific time while he was away from home, in military service or for other reasons. It was a personal arrangement with no kin involvement.

In cases of charges of adultery the Qur'an required, "If any of your women / Are guilty of lewdness, / Take the evidence of four / (Reliable) witnesses from amongst you."[61] This charge was practically impossible to obtain. It was said that those who accuse a chaste woman of fornication and then cannot bring four witnesses should themselves be scourged with eighty stripes.

A husband who accuses his wife of adultery and who is unable to bring the necessary evidence may testify four times that he speaks the truth and that he does not lie.[62] If a woman is able to swear a five-fold oath that her husband lies, she may escape any punishment, but the marriage is annulled, and the divorce occurs. In actuality, no justification is demanded of the man in divorcing his wife. But the wife does not have the same privilege.

Certain laws make provisions for divorce based on religion. A woman may claim a divorce from her husband when, both being non-Muslims, she becomes a Muslim and he refuses. If the husband becomes a Muslim and the wife refuses to become a Muslim, then the law must decide between them. Annulment of a marriage may occur on the grounds of sexual incapacitation.

The veiling and seclusion of women has been a part of Muslim life. Muhammad commanded his wives and daughters and the wives of believers to wear long veils when they went out in public.[63] It is believed that he received this revelation before his rise to power and when his followers were open to insult. It is reported that one member of his family refused to abide by the veil. His wife's niece, A'isha, did not wear the veil despite the protests of her husband.

Muhammad gave certain rules for modest conduct and chastity. "Say to the believing men / That they should lower / Their gaze and guard / Their modesty; that will make / For greater purity for them: / And Allah is well acquainted / With all that they do. / And say to the believing women / That they should lower / Their gaze and guard / Their modesty; that they / Should not display their / Beauty and ornaments except / What (must ordinarily) appear / Thereof; that they should / Draw their veils over/ Their bosoms and not display / Their beauty except / To their husbands, their fathers."[64]

Baydawi, the thirteenth-century commentator, writes that wives of believers when they go out of doors should not be like female slaves in their garb, leaving their hair and face uncovered; they should let down part of their robes that no miscreant may expose them to harmful comments when he discovers them to be free-born women. The interpreters differ however on the meaning of "letting down the veil." Some say it means they must cover their faces and heads, showing nothing but one eye. Others say the forehead only need be covered.[65]

It is not known specifically when the harem system and the seclusion of women began to be general. By the time of Harun al-Rashid, about

150 years after the death of Muhammad, the harem system was fully established. Women among the richer classes were shut off from the household and were under the charge of eunuchs. Among nomadic tribes and in the countrysides, women often were not veiled and were not strictly secluded or separated from men.[66]

After the fall of the Ottoman Empire in 1924, Kemal Ataturk led Turkey in reforms and the secularization of much of society. He forbade women to wear the veil in public. Shah Reza in Persia also forbade the veil in public. However, in 1926 the ulama of Saudi Arabia would not allow women to be unveiled in public. Women thus use the veil or appropriate clothing according to the interpretations made of the Qur'an and of tradition by the ruling political order and/or by the ulama.

The seclusion or prohibition of women from praying publicly in the mosque has varied over time. To pray in public is one of the most obvious demonstrations of a Muslim believer's faith. An early tradition reports that Muhammad allowed women to pray in his presence and to go to the mosque with their husbands' permission. Generally, the formal prayer times at the mosque are attended by Muslim men. In some cultures women may go to the mosque to pray covered properly; however, they are segregated from the men in a special place.

In contemporary Islam, cultural traditions do affect the roles of women in society. Traditionally in Riyadh, Saudi Arabia, a woman may not drive a car, hold a job, or travel anywhere without a male member of her family. In public a woman wears a floor-length black robe and a black veil pulled over her head to be modest in public according to the Qur'an and to avoid the lustful glances of men.[67] Each day the streets are patrolled by bearded men of the Committee for the Propagation of Virtue and the Suppression of Vice to warn and/or apprehend violators of the Islamic codes.

Across the Red Sea from Saudi Arabia, Muslim women in Egypt walk freely and unveiled. The interpretation of the Qur'an and the traditions is more liberal for these women. A woman may maintain a modest appearance by covering shoulders, arms, and legs. Eastward across the Persian Gulf in Karachi, Pakistan, women have different roles. A woman instructs pilots for the national airlines. At a governmental vocational school, some four hundred neatly uniformed girls repair electric motors and televisions.

Women go unveiled in Indonesia, which is more than ninety percent Muslim. One area of Sumatra is matriarchal. Women pray their daily prayers at home in Pakistan. In Egypt and Indonesia women attend mosques, and they pray separately from men.

In some countries polygamy is banned by civil law unless the first wife gives her permission. A man may divorce his wife by simply saying four times "I divorce you!" But in Pakistan a local council has the authority to attempt to bring reconciliation. Tunisia has banned divorce by proclamation by the man. Women also have the right to seek divorce.

For adultery such obvious proof is required in the charge that the death penalty and flogging are rare in many countries. However, in Saudi Arabia in 1977 Saudi Princess Misah was shot for adultery in Jedda and her lover was beheaded.[68]

The Muslim scholar, Muhammad Hamidullah, writes that Islam demands that a woman should remain a reasonable being. He says that the Prophet Muhammad taught that the golden mean is the best of things. He writes, "If one wants to compare or contrast her position in Islam with that in other civilizations or legal systems, one should take into consideration all the facts, and not merely isolated practices. In fact, in regard to certain aspects of morality, Islam is more rigid and more puritan than certain other systems of life in our times."[69] He makes the following observations about the role and status of Muslim women:

- The position of mother is very exalted in Islamic tradition. The Prophet Muhammad said that even paradise lies underneath the feet of mothers.

- With regard to the role of wife, the Prophet said that the best among men is the one who is best towards his wife.

- The birth of daughters is hailed as good over against the pagan practice of female infanticide.

- Nature has not granted a perfect equality between man and woman but different avocations and functions.

- Woman is considered equal to man in certain respects and not so equal in others; this is better seen in a woman's obligations and rights.

- In religious matters her first duty is to believe in the oneness of God, which is the only means of salvation in the hereafter.

- Women are exempted for feminine reasons from certain religious duties such as prayer, fasting, and pilgrimage, with opportunities for possibly making them up later. Islam is lenient and considerate of women.

- Women are to refrain from the vices of alcohol and gambling.

- Women are to be warned of the vices of fornication and adultery.

- Women are counseled to be modest in dress to diminish the occasions of attractiveness and to be protected from wicked men. And women may engage in every profession that suits them—nurses, teachers, singers, cooks, judges—to earn their livelihood and to develop their skills.

- Women should not marry for beauty or wealth but for religious devotion. A woman should be a pious wife.

- Divorce should be a last resort after reconciling means have been employed.

- Women have a most absolute right over their property.

- Shares of inheritance of women vary according to conditions. The shares of men are greater than those of women. A woman is given a dowry, a financial gift at marriage, which is solely hers. Women do not have the financial obligations that men do. Therefore, men may receive a greater share of inheritance.

- Women may be in a relationship of polygamous marriages. Polygamous marriages are more in harmony with the requirements of society than other systems of law which in no way permit polygamy. However, the wife must give permission for the husband to take another wife.

- In divorce there is a unilateral right of the man to divorce his wife. Women may also acquire a similar right while contracting the marriage.[70]

In a pamphlet produced and distributed by The Institute of Islamic Information and Education of Chicago entitled, "Women's Liberation Through Islam," the writers assert that the women's liberation movement was not begun by women but was revealed by God to Muhammad. "The Qur'an and the Traditions of the Prophet (Hadith or Sunnah) are the sources from which every Muslim woman derives her rights and duties."[71]

The pamphlet presents the following points:

- *Human Rights:* "Islam, fourteen centuries ago, made women equally accountable to God in glorifying and worshiping Him, setting no limits on her moral progress. . . . Since men and women both came from the same essence, they are equal in their humanity.

Women cannot be by nature evil (as some religions believe) or then men would be evil, also. Similarly, neither gender can be superior because it would be a contradiction of equality." (Qur'an 4:1).[72]

- *Civil Rights:* A woman has the basic freedoms of choice and expression. She is free to choose her religion (Qur'an 2:256). Islam encourages women to give their opinions and ideas. "A Muslim woman chooses her husband and chooses to keep her name after marriage." Her testimony is valid in legal disputes.[73]

- *Social Rights:* Women should seek knowledge through education including the Qur'an and the Hadith. They have an obligation to promote good behavior and condemn bad behavior. "While maintenance of a home, providing support to her husband and bearing, raising and teaching of children are among the first and very highly regarded roles for a woman, if she has the skills to work outside the home for the good of the community, she may do so as long as her family obligations are met."[74]

- *Political Rights:* "A right given to Muslim women by God 1400 years ago is the right to vote." Women may voice their opinions and participate in politics. Women also may hold important positions in government.[75]

- *Economic Rights:* The Qur'an says, "By (the mystery of) The creation of the male and female—Verily, (the ends) ye Strive for are diverse" (92:3–4). Men and women are different with unique roles, functions, and skills. Women are given the nurturing role, and men have the guardian role. Women are given the right of financial support by the husbands (Qur'an 4:34). "Muslim women have the privilege to earn money, the right to own property, to enter into legal contracts, and to manage all of her assets in any way she pleases. She can run her own business and no one has any claim on her earnings including her husband" (Qur'an 4:32; 4:7).[76]

- *Rights of a Wife:* Marriage is a relationship of mutual rights and obligations based on divine guidance. Each spouse protects the other and hides the faults and compliments the characteristics of the other (Qur'an 30:21; 2:187). The first right of a wife is to receive mahr, a gift from the husband. The second right is maintenance. The husband must provide her food, shelter, and clothing

(Qur'an 65:7). "God tells us men are guardians over women and are afforded the leadership in the family. His responsibility for obeying God extends to guiding his family to obey God at all times."[77] Spouses have a need for companionship and sex, and marriage is designed to meet those needs. For one spouse to deny this satisfaction is to invite temptation to seek it elsewhere.

- *Duties of a Wife:* A wife is to guard her husband's secrets, property, and marital privacy (Qur'an 4:34). She should allow no one to enter the house whom her husband dislikes nor to incur expenses which he disapproves.

- The pamphlet concludes: "The Muslim woman was given a role, duties and rights 1400 years ago that most women do not enjoy today, even in the West. These are from God and are designed to keep balance in society; what may seem unjust or missing in one place is compensated for or explained in another place. Islam is a complete way of life."[78]

HUMAN RIGHTS

Human rights in Islam have been granted by God. No legislative assembly or government has the right or authority to make any changes in the rights conferred by God. The charter and resolutions of the United Nations cannot be compared with those rights sanctioned by God. Those of the United Nations are not applicable to anybody while those of God are applicable to every believer. Every Muslim administrator will have to accept and enforce the rights given by God.[79] The Qur'an states, "If any do fail to judge / By (the light of) what Allah / Hath revealed, they are / (No better than) Unbelievers."[80]

Human rights in an Islamic State include the following:

- *The security of life and property.* The Prophet said, "Your lives and properties are forbidden to one another till you meet your Lord on the Day of Resurrection." The Prophet also said concerning the *dhimmis* (the non-Muslim citizens of the Muslim state), "One who kills a man under covenant (i.e., dhimmi) will not even smell the fragrance of Paradise."[81]

- *The protection of honor.* The Qur'an states, "O ye who believe! / [Do not] defame nor be / Sarcastic to each other / By (offensive) nicknames: / Avoid suspicion as much / (As possible). . . And spy not on each other, / Nor speak ill of each other / Behind their backs."[82]

- *Sanctity and security of private life.* The Qur'an states, "And spy not on each other"(24:27).

- *The security of personal freedom.* Islam teaches the principle that no citizen can be imprisoned unless his guilt has been proven in open court.

- *The right to protest against tyranny.* Under God power delegated to man becomes a trust. Caliph Abu Bakh said, "Cooperate with me when I am right but correct me when I commit error; obey me so long as I follow the commandments of Allah and his prophet; but turn away from me when I deviate."[83] The Qur'an says, "Allah loveth not that evil / Should be noised abroad / In public speech, except / Where injustice hath been / Done."(4:148).

- *Freedom of expression.* "Islam gives the right of freedom of thought and expression to all citizens of the Islamic state on the condition that it should be used for the propagation of virtue and truth and not for spreading evil and wickedness. . . It was the practice of the Muslims to inquire from the Holy Prophet whether on a certain matter a divine injunction had been revealed to him. If he said that he had received no divine injunction, the Muslims freely expressed their opinion on the matter."[84]

- *Freedom of association.* People have freedom to form parties and organizations subject to certain general rules.

- *Freedom of conscience and conviction.* Islam states, "Let there be no compulsion / In religion."(Qur'an 2:256) .

- *Protection of religious sentiments.* Individuals have the right of protection of religious sentiments and nothing may be said or done to encroach upon that right.

- *Protection from arbitrary imprisonment.* The individual has a right not to be arrested or imprisoned for the offenses of others. The Qur'an states, "Nor can a bearer of burdens / Bear another's burden." (35:18).

- *The right to basic necessities of life.* Islam recognizes the right of needy people for assistance. The Qur'an stipulates, "And in their wealth / And possessions (was remembered) / The right of the (needy)." (51:19).

- *Equality before the law.* Individuals have absolute equality before the law.

- *Rulers not above the law.* A tradition tells of a wealthy woman arrested for theft and brought before the Prophet with the recommendation she be spared punishment. The Prophet replied, "The nations that lived before you were destroyed by God because they punished the common-man for their offenses and let their dignitaries go unpunished for their crimes; I swear by Him Who holds my life in His hand that even if Fatima, the daughter of Muhammad, had committed this crime, I would have amputated her hand."[85]

- *The right to participate in the affairs of state.* The legislative assembly or shura composed of the executive head of government and members of the assembly should be elected by free and independent choice of the people. The Qur'an states, "Their affairs by mutual Consultation" (42:38).

ISLAMIC FUNDAMENTALISM: STRUGGLE BETWEEN TRADITION AND CHANGE

Islamic fundamentalism is a term used mostly in the Western press to portray the resurgent Islam of the last quarter of the twentieth century. *Fundamentalism* as a word has no counterpart in Arabic. However, its present usage refers to attempts by various Muslim thinkers and groups to return to the roots of Islamic ideology and practice.

The characteristics of Islamic fundamentalism are several and make for a general profile. Truth in a literal sense has been given by Allah. The guide to every condition of life is found in three sources. They are in descending priority, the Qur'an, the Sunnah (the sayings and doings of Prophet Muhammad), and the Shari'a (the codification of the rules and principles in the Qur'an and the Sunnah).[86]

Islamic fundamentalism returns to a classical Islamic worldview in which the world is partitioned into two parts. There is the world or territory ruled and administered by Islam, and there is the world or territory which is un-Islamic and disobedient and not under the rule of the Qur'an, the Sunnah, and the Shari'a. Islam must bring the disobedient world under its domain.[87]

The son of the late Ayatollah Khomeini of Iran, Ahmad Khomeini, has said, "Iran's Islamic revolution has awakened all the Islamic countries. . . . Islam recognizes no borders. We cannot put off establishing Islamic governments and administering the divine laws. The objective of the Islamic Republic and its officials is none other than to establish a global Islamic rule. . . . Political means and methods may differ, but no revolutionary Muslim ever forgets the objective."[88]

The sentiments of Ayatollah Morteza Mutahhari of Iran prior to the establishment of the Islamic state are as follows:

> Imagine some group that says to the Muslims who are delivering the call of Islam to a nation: "You have no right to say what you are saying. We do not allow it." In these circumstances it is not permissible for us to fight with that nation, with those people who are blameless and unaware. But is it permissible for us to fight against that corrupt regime which props itself up with a putrid ideology that it uses like a chain around the necks of people to imprison them in blind alley isolated from the call of truth; a regime which acts as a barrier against that call? Is it permissible for us to fight that regime so as to remove that obstacle? Or, in real terms, is it permissible for us to fight against that prison of repression or is it not? In view of Islam this is permissible, for this itself would be a form of uprising against *zulm*, against injustice and oppression. It may be that the *mazlum*, the wronged, the oppressed, are not aware of the nature of the injustice and have not requested our help, but in fact there is no need for them to request it.[89]

Mohammad Mohaddessin has written, "Islamic fundamentalism is based upon a medieval and totalitarian ideology. It interferes in the most trivial personal matters of the citizenry, imposing a repressive system that eliminates all avenues for free political, social, and economic activities. Furthermore, owing to its nature, this ideology recognizes no geographic boundaries and, therefore, elevates the export of revolution, crisis, and disruption of all norms of international relations to the top of its agenda."[90]

Lewis points out that the struggle between good and evil in early Islam acquired both political and military dimensions. The warriors of Islam were engaged "in the path of God." The logic followed that Muslims were fighting a war on behalf of God. Since God was the sovereign and head of the Islamic state or *umma*, the Prophet Muhammad, and the rulers succeeding him, acted on behalf of God. God thus commanded the state, and the army and others acted and fought on God's behalf. Thus, non-Muslim opponents who fought against the Islamic state fought against God.

The decades after World War II have seen a rise in resurgent Islam and often-militant Islam. Lewis observes that there was little Muslim interest in the West until the Second World War, the rise of the prominence of oil, and the post-World War II development of Muslim businessmen and students traveling to the West.

The Second World War brought further intrusions of the West into the heartland of Islam and encouraged the birth of the nation of Israel in 1948. Oil gave prominent Muslim nations both political and economic power in the modern world. Travel and education of Muslims in the West gave them tools of science and technology which they could utilize in their homelands, but these also brought a certain alienation among them against western values and cultures.

Muslims remembered the glory days of the Middle Ages when Islam was dominant. They regretted the loss of that world to the advancement of the USSR and the West. They lamented the invasion of their own lands by western rulers or their substitutes and of western values and ways of life. They detested the challenges within their own homes of emancipated women and rebellious children, infected by western intrusions. Islam under these kinds of foreign threats needed revival and restoration.

Islamic fundamentalism, thus, castigated the West, especially the United States of America. The United States became the "enemy of God" and "the Great Satan." Western values were equated with corruption, materialism, and immorality.[91] The imposing western cultural, economic, and diplomatic presence in Muslim countries signaled Muslims to arise, to throw out these hostile intrusions, and to restore true Islam.

Bernard Lewis has observed that Muslims have accused the West, particularly the United States, of sexism, racism, and imperialism institutionalized in patriarchy and slavery, in tyranny and exploitation. However, Lewis theorizes that what is truly evil and unacceptable to Muslims is the dominance of infidels over the true believers, i.e., the Muslims under the domination of infidels. This domination is blasphemous and unnatural. Thus, the true faith of Islam must be protected from insult and abuse.[92]

Lewis further observes that the struggle of Islamic fundamentalism is against secularism, an evil neopagan force, and modernism, the process of holistic change. The United States is held as the prototype of secularism and modernism, as well as the expression of the Judeo-Christian heritage.

Lewis cites two examples of radical Muslim reactions against the United States. In November 1979, a mob burned the United States embassy in Islamabad, Pakistan. The stated cause was protesting the seizure of the Great Mosque in Mecca by Muslim dissidents. What American involvement was there to cause the burning of its embassy?

In February 1989, the United States Information Service Center was attacked in Islamabad by angry crowds in protest of the publication of Salman Rushdie's *Satanic Verses*. The book had been published first in London and later in the United States. Why was not the British embassy attacked? Lewis concludes that Islamic fundamentalism is a clash of civilizations, that of Islam with the Judeo-Christian heritage and secularism and the worldwide expansion of both by the West and especially the United States.[93]

Samuel Huntington, a professor at Harvard University, has written about Islam and the West. He contends that the two are in for continuing confrontations. *The Economist* reports,

> There is good reason why the culture of the Muslim world is regarded by many people as the West's only real ideological competitor at the end of the 20th century. . . . Islam claims to be an idea based upon a transcendental certainty. The certainty is the word of God, revealed syllable by syllable to Muhammad in a dusty corner of Arabia 1,400 years ago and copied down by him into the Koran. As a means of binding a civilization together, there is no substitute for such a certainty. Moreover—and this is not happening anywhere else—new recruits are flocking to join this claim to certainty. Whether it is because of the repeated defeats inflicted upon Muslims by the outside world, or because of the corrupt incompetence of most of their governments, the past 25 years have seen a huge growth in what outsiders call Islamic fundamentalism. Muslims themselves hate the phrase, but it is not inaccurate. A large number of people who feel ashamed of the past few centuries want to show they can do better. To do that, they need to rediscover a sense of identity. And to do that, they turn back to the Koran. You can call it a revival, or a resurgence; but it is also a return to the foundations."[94]

Islamic fundamentalism is far from being a monolithic and unified movement under the aegis of one person or a single organization. It houses an ideology of returning to the foundations of Islam, and it expresses itself in a myriad of thinkers and movements. It shelters a network of extremist factions.

Although there is an outcry against western ideas, values, and lifestyles, Muslims in the fundamentalist movement do not hesitate to employ western products and practices of modernity. Governments in Muslim countries use western models of parliamentary and constitutional forms. Tanks, televisions, and T-shirts are bought and become symbols of prestige. Cokes and McDonald's hamburgers, with colorful billboards, beckon Muslims in their lands to eat and drink. Within Islamic fundamentalism there is struggle between tradition and change.

Judith Miller interviewed two leaders of Islamic resurgence and reported the interview in *Foreign Affairs*.[95] Hassan Abdallah al-Turabi of the Sudan is leader of the Muslim Brotherhood. "He is the power behind the Islamic regime, which has ruled Sudan since 1989, when a military coup destroyed Sudan's inept democracy. In the past 30 years Turabi has transformed the Muslim Brotherhood from a marginal group into a powerful political force, one that Sudan's traditional parties were forced to include in their ruling coalition."[96]

Sheikh Muhammed Hussein Fadlallah of Lebanon, a descendant of the Prophet Muhammad, is the leader of the Hezbollah, the party of God, and is a prolific poet, scholar and influential Shi'ite cleric. Miller has written, "Hezbollah's kidnappings, hijackings and car-bomb attacks in the early 1980s helped drive America from Lebanon, and the Party of God remains the major opponent of Israel's self-declared 'security zone' in southern Lebanon. Under Fadlallah's guidance Hezbollah has not only captured the largest bloc of seats in Lebanon's parliament, it has developed a large and passionate following among young Shiite Muslims, now the largest religious group in what was once a predominantly Christian country."[97]

Turabi and Fadlallah have never met but have begun a correspondence. "Both expressed absolute certainty that only Islam can fill the vacuum left by the failures of Western-inspired Arab nationalism and other imported ideologies.... Both dismissed Saddam Hussein as a fraud, an Islamic pretender... both were even more hostile to the American led forces that drove Iraq's troops from Kuwait.... Both leaders detest Saudi Arabia, a less obvious competitor and an early patron of their charitable and political works."[98] Turabi said, "The Saudis, with their monarchy and secular laws and secular elites, had propagated a very conservative Islam throughout the Middle East for years. But the gulf war has shattered the dynasty's legitimacy. Now, even the Saudis face a full-fledged Islamic movement that will no longer be bought off."[99]

Fadlallah also had little affection for the Saudi regime "despite the fact that it bans alcohol, strictly segregates the sexes, and has made sharia, or Islamic law, the law of the land—all ostensible goals of most radical Islamic movements, including Hezbollah." He dismissed "as cosmetic Riyadh's recent well-publicized rapprochement with its sub-stantial Shiite population. The agreement, he complained, solved only one one-thousandth of the problem. The Shiite minority of Saudi Arabia are citizens of the tenth degree."[100]

Both men distanced themselves from Iran. Turabi denied that Iran operates training camps in the Sudan and denied that the Sudan harbors members of the Hezbollah, Hamas, and other Islamic liberation groups. Judith Miller reported that, despite this denial, she had interviewed such people during her stay in the Sudan. "Turabi's and Fadlallah's belief in Islam's ultimate triumph is accompanied by their certainty of America's decline."[101]

Turabi said that democracy does not require multiple parties, the right of any individual to stand for office or spend money campaigning for it, or the right to advocate a view that contradicts the Qur'an. "For both Turabi and Fadlallah the western notion of democracy is alien. For both men, no parliamentary majority, however large, can nullify God's law as codified in Islamic law."[102]

Thus, Islamic fundamentalism is expressed in various writers, leaders of nations and factions, and in the actions of both devoted Muslim believers and in Muslims who are politically and militarily active. The intellectual writers, Muhammad Abdul and Hasan Banna, view Islam over against colonialism and imperialism and secular modernism; Islam is a fusion between the civil and religious domains. The Islamic state becomes the beacon of the governance and life of the people.[103]

The revolution of 1978–79 established the Islamic Republic of Iran, advised and governed by the vision and practice of Ayatollah Khomeini. That vision included a return to the teachings of the Qur'an, the tradi-tions of Prophet Muhammad, and the institution of the Shari'a law. The political leadership of the Sudan, influenced by Islam, has attempted to turn the nation into an Islamic one governed by Shari'a criminal law.

In Egypt, the Muslim Brotherhood and various Muslim factions have criticized the government's economic programs as well as its drift toward western materialism and values. President Anwar Sadat was assassinated. Xenophobia has reigned among these militant factions against the West and against westerners in Egypt.

Eric Davis has noted "a consistent pattern of recruitment into the Muslim Brotherhood and affiliated radical Islamic groups from the 1930s through to the 1960s. This pattern is marked by the prominence of an urban professional middle class: schoolteachers, clerks, low-level bureaucrats and more recently—with the development of technical education—engineers." Davis further wrote "an important qualification: most of the Islamic militants are recent migrants into urban areas who have had a traditional upbringing in the rural areas."[104]

In Algeria the rise of Islamic fundamentalism resulted in its victorious representation in the Algerian parliament only to be taken away by the established government. Internal war has continued within the country between the Muslim militants and the Algerian armed forces and police. Thousands have been killed, including a significant number of westerners.

In parts of Asia, Africa, the Middle East, Europe, and the United States, various groups who espouse Islamic fundamentalism engage in the political process to win legitimacy in local government. Some groups are militant in using physical force to obtain their objectives through terrorist activities including the bombing of planes, cars, and buildings. Some groups attack segments of the population.

In conclusion, various Islamic fundamentalist groups express the following concerns in varying degrees and expressions:

1. A concern about the degeneration of the Islamic faith

2. A call for a jihad, a struggle and warfare, to rescue the Islamic community from decline and to establish its true and correct standing as the umma

3. A return to the essentials of Islam founded on the Qur'an, the Sunnah, and the Shari'a

4. A critique of and an attack upon any forms of colonialism and imperialism advanced both by outside and western influences and tolerated by leaders within Islam

5. A judgment against the moral decadence of western values seen in the light of secularism and modernism and compared to the Islamic "straight path to God"

6. An affirmation of the rights of Palestinians for a homeland and a condemnation upon Zionism.

9

GLOBAL ISLAM

MUSLIM REGIONS, PEOPLES, LEADERS

F rom its beginning Islam has been a missionary and mobile religion. From Mecca to Malaysia and in between in fourteen hundred years, it has spread its beliefs, practices, worldview, cultural values, material wealth, and spiritual aspirations. Its sixth pillar of faith, jihad, has been expressed as holy efforts, struggles, and sometimes wars on behalf of Allah.

Where Islam has moved, Muslims have carried the preachments of their Prophet Muhammad, built their mosques for prayer and worship, and considered it their mission to encourage others to come to submission to their God. The very word *Islam* means submission.

As the twenty-first century approaches, there are over 1 billion Muslims around the globe. They are present on all continents and in most countries. There are 527 million Muslims in Asia, 306 million in the Middle East, 129 million in Africa, 50 million in Eurasia, 17 million in Europe, over 5 million in North America, and hundreds of thousands in South America.

The largest Muslim population centers are not in the Middle East, but in Asia. The four largest Muslim populations are found in Indonesia with 170 million, Pakistan with 118 million, India with 106 million, and Bangladesh with 103 million. Forty-three percent of the world's Muslims live in these four countries.

165

Islam: A Survey of The Muslim Faith

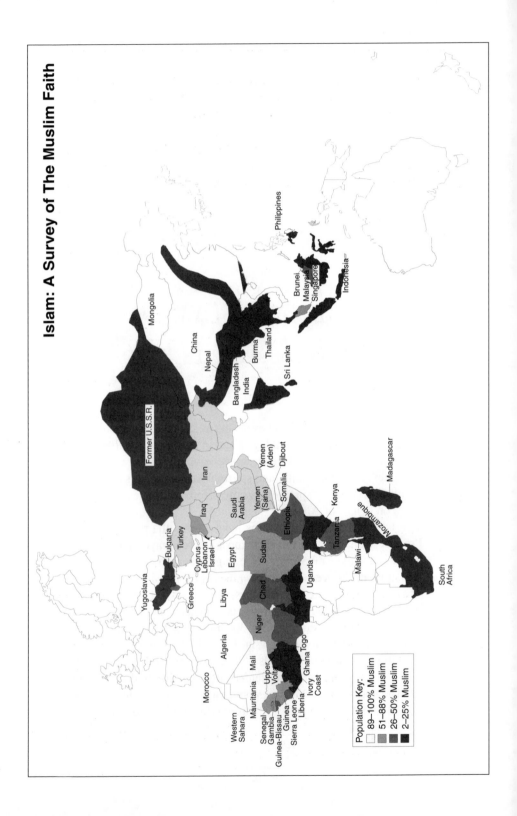

Population Key:
- 89–100% Muslim
- 51–88% Muslim
- 26–50% Muslim
- 2–25% Muslim

In the Middle East there are 24 countries each with more than 1 million Muslims. Iran has 56 million followed by Turkey with 55.5 million. Yemen is 99.91 percent Muslim, and Saudi Arabia is close behind.

Africa, including North Africa, has 26 countries with more than 1 million Muslims. Egypt with more than 46 million Muslims has the largest Muslim population, Nigeria has some 45 million, and the Sudan some 20 million. Somalia has the highest percent of Muslims with 99.96 percent.

Seventeen million Muslims live in Central and Western Europe. France has 5 million, followed by Germany with 2 million, Bosnia with 1.7 million, England with 1.5 million, Bulgaria with 1.25 million, and Italy with 1 million. Many Muslims have come from North Africa, Turkey, Iran, the Arab nations, and India and Pakistan.

The United States, with over 5 million Muslims, is the only country in the Americas with over 1 million. Argentina has over 400,000 Muslims, followed by Canada with over 200,000, Brazil with over 150,000, and Panama with over 100,000 Muslims.

Why and how has Islam grown and spread so rapidly and extended itself so far? There are several reasons.

- Islam teaches and encourages large families. High birth rates, especially when one is born a Muslim in family and culture, add to Islamic population.

- Islam began as a religion closely associated with urban life and trade and travel. Muslim merchants and educators and diplomats and students and religious leaders have not hesitated to build mosques in the countries and cities where they have migrated and studied and settled.

- Islam is a missionary religion engaged in jihad, holy efforts for God, and both individual Muslims and the Muslim community are involved in missions.

- Islam, though a complex religion, presents itself with clarity and simplicity in its six basic beliefs and its five pillars or practices, which makes it appealing to those searching and asking for religious answers and directions.

- Islam is amenable to certain religious and cultural traditions of others and is able to incorporate them into itself. Polygamy and saint veneration are two examples.

Both unity and diversity characterize Muslim peoples. This diversity raises a question: Who speaks for Islam worldwide? More particularly, who in Asia or Africa or the Middle East or the United States has the authoritative voice to represent Islam?

The Mufti of Lebanon speaks from one side, the Ayatollah of Iran from another. How do Muslims in Lebanon differ from those in Iran? How does the training of Islamic scholars and preachers in the great theological schools of Qum, Iran, differ if at all from the Egyptian theological centers at al-Azhar University in Cairo, or in the theological center at Kufa, Iraq?

Islam is variously associated with leaders in many countries. They are seen praying in mosques. They are heard uttering the word "jihad" against their Muslim neighbors or against the "Satanic West." So has Ayatollah Khomeini of Iran uttered "jihad" against both Iraq and the United States, and so has President Saddam, of Iraq declared jihad against much of the world.

What is the role of the king of Saudi Arabia as the guardian of the two holiest cities of Mecca and Medina in his kingdom? What kinds of Muslims are King Hussein of Jordan, President Assad of Syria, President Mubarek of Egypt, King Hasan of Morocco, and the numerous other presidents and clerics of Muslim-dominated lands and governments?

What kinds of governments exist in Islamic lands? What is allowed to co-exist with Islamic rule by the Qur'an and the Tradition, and by laws that may be more Western-oriented in their principles and interpretations?

This chapter reviews various global regions, giving special attention to predominantly Muslim countries. Highlights of each region and country will include the form of Islam, the peoples who are called Muslims, and the characteristics of Muslim cultures and leaders.

MIDDLE EAST

The Middle East is the heartland for three monotheistic, prophetic, and ethical religions—Judaism, Christianity, and Islam. Abraham, Moses, David, Jesus, and Muhammad are major religious figures about whom stories are remembered and told among Jews, Christians, and Muslims. Synagogues, churches, and mosques are centers of worship and celebration throughout the religious calendar year. The cities of Jerusalem, Mecca, and Medina hold holy memories for the individual religions.

Land, dwellings, and holy cites have been prayed over and fought over for centuries. Jerusalem, which inspires dreams of unity and peace, has long been a battleground for territorial rights. Christians and Muslims have fought for the "holy land." Jews and Muslims have waged war for Palestine. Iran has battled Iraq for land and water and resources and control of holy Shi'ite shrines. Iraq has warred against neighboring Kuwait as well as against other Muslim nations and non-Muslim nations. Turkey has fought the Kurdish tribal peoples, as have Iran and Iraq. Many groups with Islamic names have battled one another and Israel for land and for control of Palestine and for the governments of their respective lands.

Countries and peoples of the Middle East have been pawns in world wars and objects of colonialistic adventures. In recent history Middle Eastern oil has been a source of economic prowess and political clout for Muslim nations such as Saudi Arabia, Iran, Iraq, and the smaller gulf nations.

Since the 1960s tumult and terrorism have pervaded much of the Middle East. Outside powers have aided the establishment of the State of Israel, but this has caused decades of resistance by Muslim countries against the "Zionist intrusion." The Palestinian people have waged combat to regain land and rights in Palestine. Terrorist activities have caused untold loss of human life and property.

Saudi Arabia

Islam originated in Arabia in the seventh century, and it has played a major role in the life of the region ever since. Today the Kingdom of Saudi Arabia is the heartland of Islam. Muhammad was born there, Islam was born there, and it is the site of Islam's two holy cities, Mecca and Medina. Muslims face toward Mecca for daily prayer and millions make the annual pilgrimage to this land.

In the eighteenth century a religious scholar of the central Najd, Muhammad Bin Abd al-Wahhab, allied with the ruler of the oasis town of Diriyah, Muhammad Bin Saud, to call Arabia back to orthodox Islam. Wahhab's orthodoxy is known as Wahhabism, though his followers prefer to be known as Unitarians or followers of the Hanbali school of law. His movement was a return to early Islam and condemned superstition, saint worship, lax sexual practices, and other accretions.

Wahhab's movement faltered during the nineteenth century, but emerged as a power in the early twentieth century. By 1925 it held Mecca and Medina and Jeddah.[1] The al-Saud family also came to power again and captured Riyadh in 1902. By 1932 the Kingdom of Saudi Arabia was founded by King Abdul Aziz al-Saud.[2]

Saudi Arabia now has a population of some 17 million. The population is 93.4 percent Muslim; 79 percent are Sunni, mainly of the Wahhabi sect; 13.4 percent are Shi'ite, mainly Arabs on the Gulf coast and Iranians; and 1 percent are Ismaili. Christians make up 4 percent of the population and include expatriate Filipino, Korean, Indian, Arab, and Western.

Three major cities are: Riyadh, the capital, with 1.3 million population; Jiddah with 1.6 million; and Mecca with 550,000. Mecca's population swells with some 2 million pilgrims each year, and the 1 billion Muslims of the world are required to face Mecca in prayer five times daily.

Saudi Arabia has the Qur'an for its constitution and the Shari'a as the base for its legal system. It is an absolute monarchy and has been ruled by the Sa'ud family for decades. Its administration, commerce, and diplomacy are closely controlled by the large royal family.

The Kingdom is a leader in working for worldwide Islamic unity. The Muslim World League and the Organization of Islamic Conference have their headquarters there. The League controls vast sums of money to propagate Islam around the world. Much aid is given to countries sympathetic to the Kingdom, and the Palestine Liberation Organization through the years has received a generous amount. The world's largest printing presses are located in the country and each year produce some 28 million Qur'ans used to extend Islam globally.

The Saudi Arabs of Saudi Arabia are among the most influential and wealthiest people in the Islamic world. They are holders of 25 percent of the world's known oil reserves. Their gross national product of over $100 billion, based mostly on natural petroleum reserves, is used to develop their nation and to benefit other undeveloped countries, including many Muslim countries. The Saudis are large contributors to the Islamic Development Fund, to the Islamic Development Bank, and to the Islamic Organization for Science, Technology and Development.[3] They also provide funds and personnel to establish and maintain mosques and programs in many countries, including the recently liberated republics of the former USSR, including Kazakhstan and Uzbekistan.

Saudi Arabia exercises a trust in acting as guardian of the sacred shrines of Islam at Mecca, the birthplace and pilgrimage center of Islam, and at Medina, the prophet's burial place. King Fahd adopted the official title of Custodian of the Two Holy Mosques. Each year the Saudi government provides funds to maintain the mosques and to prepare for the more than one million pilgrims who come annually on the Hajj.

With renovations and improvements the mosque at Mecca will accommodate over one million worshipers. The expansion of the Prophet's mosque in Medina will increase the capacity of worshipers from 28,000 to 455,000. Improvements also will be made to transportation, accommodations, and health care facilities.[4]

A strong custom among both Saudi men and women is special clothing. Men wear a thobe, a simple garment of wool in the winter and cotton in the summer. A *ghutra* is worn around the head for protection against wind storms. Women wear long veils that cover the length of the body. Women adhere to strict dress codes for their purity and honor. Islamic vice-squads called *muttawa* patrol stores, restaurants, and streets to enforce dress codes and closings at prayer times. The most publicized case was in 1979: the Princess was shot and her lover beheaded.

Saudi Arabia denies religious freedom among the natives. Workers from other countries may under certain conditions maintain their own religious activities, but expatriate Christians live under tight surveillance. They can build no churches. Other religions are strictly forbidden. No Christian may enter the city of Mecca. Saudi Arabia funds the building of mosques, the sending of Muslim missionaries, the establishment of Islamic study centers on university campuses, and the distribution of Islamic literature in other countries.

The Persian Gulf War in the early 1990s highlighted the tension between Saudi traditions and the modern world. Saudi women saw American military women driving vehicles, even flying planes. Some Saudi women took to the streets in protest to demand their right to drive automobiles.

Jordan

Formerly known as Transjordan, the modern state of Jordan was formed in 1920–1922 by British authorities in Palestine. It originally consisted of the lands to the east of the Jordan and to the west of Syria, Saudi Arabia, and Iraq. In 1950 the land west of the river which was not part of the state of Israel was annexed to Jordan. During the Arab-Israeli war of 1967, Israel took the West Bank, including the eastern part of Jerusalem. In this action, Israel seized control of the three holy sites: the Temple Mount, the Holy Sepulchre, and the Dome of the Rock. The Islamic world has continued to demand the return of its holy sites as well as the restoration of the land to the Palestinians.

The population of Jordan is about 3.8 million. Since the Gulf War of 1991, 300,000 Palestinians and 80,000 Iraqis have fled to Jordan. Amman is its capital with 1.2 million population. Jordan is 96 percent Arab with 2 million Palestinians and 1.4 million East Bank Jordanians. Sunni Islam is the official religion. The constitution prohibits discrimination and promotes freedom of other religions, but Muslims are prohibited from changing their religion.

King Hussein succeeded his grandfather King Abdullah, who was assassinated while he prayed in the mosque of the Dome of the Rock in Jerusalem. The eighteen-year-old Hussein was with his grandfather at the time. He opened the Jordanian royal parliament on May 2, 1954.

As a member of the Hashemite family of Mecca, he traces his kinship from the Prophet Muhammad. The King has faced four perennial challenges: (1) settlement of the Israeli problem; (2) relations with other Arab states; (3) the Palestinian refugees; and (4) the establishment of a financially free Jordan and the raising of the living standards for the people.

During his reign of over forty years, King Hussein has fought Israel alongside other Arab nations. He has battled the Palestine Liberation Organization within his own borders, and his army routed them out of the country. From time to time, he has had strained relations with his Arab neighbors, including Syria and Egypt. He supported Iraq in its war against Kuwait and other Arab nations and the West. For a time, his support alienated him from his Arab neighbors and the West.

King Hussein has survived the political, religious, and social changes in the Middle East. It is said that he has promoted the welfare of his people foremost, and this devotion to his people has made for a lengthy reign. He has attempted to relate to the various constituencies in his country. He has a special relationship with the sheikhs of the bedouin tribes. A sheikh said of the King, "He knows us all by name, and the names of our fathers—and their fathers. He does not have to ask our help, we will be there."[5] In recent times the King also has sought good relations with the less extreme wing of the Muslim Brotherhood. Members of the Brotherhood have been permitted to run for seats in parliament, while in most other Arab countries they have been outlawed or restricted.[6]

King Hussein has worked with clear goals: to promote the interests of his own peoples; to promote aid without political strings; to oppose communism in all its guises; to defend the Holy Land and the frontiers of Jordan; and to support Arab causes against Israel.

In recent times the King refused to condemn Iraq's takeover of Kuwait and became alienated from some of his Arab neighbors as well as from the West. Hussein did not send forces into the Gulf War, but his resiliency has improved relationships with Arab states. He has signed a peace accord with Israel. He has continued to support the rights of the Palestinian people. His economy has continued to be fragile and dependent on outside aid, especially from the United States.

The King has been described as a Muslim of strong faith. His grandfather taught him passages from the Qur'an, took him to the mosque for prayers, and often reminded him of his descent from Prophet Muhammad. It is said that he developed an unswerving trust in Allah.

Under the King's leadership, Christianity has been granted freedom. Christians represent about five percent of the population. Most of the Christians are from the ancient Greek Orthodox Church. King Hussein has faced West often in his education in England, in his marriages to British and American wives, and to the Western nations for aid and military assistance programs. Currently, he is married to an American.

Iran

The history of Iran is long. Arfa described the last monarch of Iran as heir to 500 kings, belonging to 40 dynasties, who governed or reigned over Iran for 2,500 years.[7] The Persian Empire was led by kings such as Cyrus, Darius, and Artaxerxes.

Iran has faced many invasions. The Greeks, the Arabs, and the Mongols came. Notably, the Arabs brought Islam to Persia in the seventh century A.D. In the early part of the twentieth century Russia and England divided the country into areas of influence.

In the 1960s and 1970s under the monarchy of Shah Muhammad Reza Pahlavi, oil-rich Iran achieved a strategic position politically, economically, and militarily not only in the Middle East but in the world arena.[8] In 1979 Ayatollah Khomeini brought revolution under the banners of Islamic revivalism, deposed the Shah, and established the Islamic Republic of Iran.

Persians constitute the largest ethnic group in the country, about sixty-five percent, but there are many ethnic minorities: Kurds, Azerbaijanis, Lurs, Baktiaris, Qashqais, Baluchis, and Arabs.

Shi'ite Islam was established as the official religion by the Saffavid dynasty in 1502. In 1907 it became recognized in Iran's first constitution as the official state religion, known as the Ithna Ashari (Twelver) branch of Shi'ah. Some ninety percent of Iranians are adherents of this branch. There are also Sunni Muslims. Other religious minorities include Jews, Zoroastrians, Christians, and Baha'i. Under the monarchy the minorities were officially recognized except for the Baha'is, who often faced discrimination and persecution. Under the Islamic Republic of Iran, religious minorities have been maltreated, some individuals harassed, and others persecuted. There has been a systematic attempt to repress the Baha'i community with many known executions.

Two forces worked at cross-purposes before the Iranian revolution of 1979: the traditional Iranian clergy struggled with the modernizing and secularizing influences of Reza Shah Pahlavi before World War II and of his son from the 1950s to his exile in 1979.[9]

The Constitutional Revolution of 1905–1907 stated that no laws adverse to Islam would be considered by the Iranian assembly. The clergy were thus given influence in the establishment of the moral and social order according to Islamic law, the Shari'a. However, the secularization of Iranian society initiated by Reza Shah and continued by his son Muhammad conflicted with the vision and plan of the clergy.

The Pahlavi kings emulated the liberal reforms of Kemal Ataturk in neighboring Turkey. They basically replaced Islamic law with secular legal codes following the French Civil Code. Educational reforms, which were modeled after Western patterns, undermined the Islamic schools and seminaries led by the clergy, who taught the traditional pedagogy. The modernization of Iranian society brought changes to the role of women, who were legally required to abandon the veil.

This commitment to Westernization and secularization increased with the accession of Muhammad Reza Shah Pahlavi in 1953 and his White Revolution.[10] Opposition developed especially among the merchants, urban poor, and landless peasants. Opposition forces, especially the disenchanted masses, identified with the Muslim clergy, first through underground activities and then openly. Movements such as the Fedayeen-i-Islam (Devotees of Islam) and the Mujahadin-i-Islam (Defenders of Islam) began in the 1950s. There were assassinations of prominent Iranians and members of the dissident groups were purged and killed.[11]

Ayatollah Khomeini, a leading cleric, was exiled by the Shah in 1964. From his exile in Iraq and later (1978) in France, he masterminded the plans that resulted in the revolution of 1979.[12] The Shah's secret police, SAVAK, had become very repressive against any dissent. By the 1970s protests by students on the campuses had become a concern to the government. Other leading ayatollahs within Iran had begun to criticize the regime at great risk. A new organization of urban guerrillas emerged, the Mujahadin-i-Khalq, founded along the lines of the earlier Fedayeen-i-Islam.

By early 1978 Ayatollah Khomeini's influence had grown to network effectively with many of the dissenting organizations and movements in Iran. Other influential leaders within Iran had included Ali Shariati, a revolutionary thinker; Massoud Rejavi, leader of the Mujahadin; and Mehdi Bazargan, leader of a more moderate group.

The government collapsed in January 1979, and the Shah and his government went into exile. Ayatollah Khomeini returned to a tumultuous welcome in February, and a referendum in March voted in an Islamic Republic.

The takeover of the United States Embassy by radical students and the holding of American hostages from November 1979 until January 1981 helped consolidate radical Islamic groups against the secular liberal wing represented by President Banisadr and Foreign Minister Ghotbzadeh. Banisadr later fled the country, and Ghotbzadeh was executed for treason.

A long and bloody war between Iran and Iraq from 1980 to 1988 inflicted hundreds of thousands of casualties upon Iran. Aliakbar Rafsanjani climbed through the ranks to become President. Ayatollah Khomeini issued a death sentence against British author Salman Rushdie for his publication of *Satanic Verses.*

Ayatollah Khomeini died in June 1989, with Ayatollah Ali Khamanie succeeding him as the titular religious head of Iran and Rafsanjani as political leader and commander-in-chief. It remains to be seen what if any part Ahmed Khomeini, the son of the previous ayatollah, may play in the politics of Iran.

Since its inception in 1979, the Islamic Republic has been based upon Islamic law. Committees of radicals used as informal police have patrolled the streets to remind women and others of proper dress and manners. Influential Christian leaders in Iran have been imprisoned on various charges, and several have been murdered in the streets. Some observers have stated that the Baha'i community has been nearly bereft of its leadership.

Iran continues to sell its oil and to arm itself. It has had running battles with the Kurdish peoples along its borders, but it did not involve itself in the Persian Gulf war.

Iraq

The population of Iraq is 22.5 million and is divided along both racial and religious lines: 75 percent Arab; 18 percent Kurd; the remaining 7 percent Assyrian, Turcoman, Armenian, and Persian. Some 90 percent are Muslim with the remaining 10 percent comprised of a variety of

Christian groups and the Yazidi and Sabaean communities. Arab Muslims belong to both Sunni and Shi'ite branches of Islam. Half of all Iraqis are Twelver Shi'ites; less than a quarter of all Iraqis are Sunni Muslims; most Kurds are Sunni.[13]

Baghdad is the capital with some 4.7 million people. Other major cities include Basra with 1.5 million; Mosul with 1.2 million, and Suleimaniya with 1 million. Four of the major shrines of Twelver Shi'ites are located in Iraq, namely Kadhimain, Samarra, Karbala, and Najaf; the latter two are especially important. Thus, the Shi'ite population in Iraq has had much in common with their counterparts in Iran.

The British set up the modern state of Iraq in 1920 with Faisal, son of Sharif Husain of Mecca, as the first ruler. He could trace his descent to the Prophet Muhammad. Iraq gained its independence in 1932. The strongest political groups in Iraq were the communists and the Arab nationalists. The Sunni, from remnants of leadership in the former Ottoman Empire, had more power than the Shi'ite, who tended to be the uneducated and urban poor. The Revolution of 1958 came on the heels of secularist themes such as development, progress, and equality.

The Islamic clergy of Najaf formed an association known as al-Da'wa al-Islamiyya, the Islamic Call, in 1968. A leading Iraqi cleric, Ayatollah Muhammad Baqir al-Sadr, called for a social and political order based upon Islamic principles. This was at the time that the exiled Ayatollah Khomeini lived in Najaf from 1964–1978.

The secularizing Ba'ath party came to power in 1968, emphasizing Arab nationalism. It launched efforts to suppress and contain the Kurds in 1975 which have continued, and it moved against the clerics and the al-Da'wa, which had affirmed the Iranian revolution. By 1978 the government had arrested and executed the leading cleric, Ayatollah al-Sadr, and his sister.

Saddam Hussein rose to power within the Ba'ath party and became President of Iraq. Iraq initiated the war with Iran that lasted from 1980 to 1988, ostensibly to overthrow the Islamic Republic and to prevent the export of the Iranian revolution to Iraq. Saddam Hussein assumed an Arabic-Islamic image with a program of mosque-building and large donations to the shrines at Karbala and Najaf. He has had his family lineage traced to Prophet Muhammad.

The most recent history of Iraq has included its building of a nuclear reactor which the Israelis destroyed with air strikes, its prolonged war with Iran, and its launching of the Persian Gulf War by invading Kuwait. The latter brought the coalition of the forces of both Muslim nations and non-Muslim nations, uniting to defeat the Iraqis and to begin the process of dismantling its nuclear capacity under the auspices of the United Nations.

Pan-Arab socialism rather than Islam has been the ideology under the Baathist regime. President Saddam Hussein from time to time has called for a jihad in the name of Islam against the West. Under his leadership Iraq launched a massive modernization process funded by the wealth of oil deposits.

Also, President Hussein has battled the Kurds and the Shi'ites. Religious minorities have been favored if they demonstrated political loyalty. Christians, with 3.3 percent of the population, have increasingly been given freedom of worship and expression since 1968. A recent foreign minister of Hussein's government was a Christian.

Israel

The nation of Israel came into existence in 1948 after many decades of turmoil between the Jewish and Arab Palestinian settlers on the land.[14] The Zionist movement arose after publication of Theodore Herzl's book on Zionism in 1897. The British government's Balfour Declaration of 1917 supported the right of Jews to have land in Palestine. Soon, waves of immigrant Jews converged on Palestine. When the League of Nations' mandates failed, war ensued with Israel fighting her Arab neighbors. After major wars of 1947–1948, 1952, 1967 and 1973, Israel controlled Palestine proper, including Jerusalem, and occupied the Gaza Strip adjacent to Egypt, the West Bank adjacent to Jordan, and the Golan Heights adjacent to Syria. Its border with Lebanon was insecure, and consequently it extended its border into Lebanon.

Jerusalem is the capital with 544,000 people, although the international commumity recognizes Tel Aviv as the capital, with a population of 1.5 million. The major holy sites of Judaism, Christianity, and Islam are located in the old city of Jerusalem. The Temple Mount has been the center of dispute and sometimes warfare between Jews and Muslims.

Jews comprise over 81 percent of the country's people. There are Jewish immigrants from 102 nations. Arabs make up 15.8 percent, including 700,000 Israeli Arabs and 50,000 Bedouins. Other peoples are Druze, Egyptians, Adygey, Greek, and Samaritans. There is freedom for all religious groups within their own faith communities except for Jewish Christians, who are denied any legal standing as a religious body. Religious preferences include 81.4 percent Jews of various groups, including traditional, orthodox, and reform; 14.5 percent Muslims, mostly Sunni Palestinian; 2.3% percent Christians of Catholic, Orthodox and Protestant backgrounds; and 1.6 percent Druze.

The only major peace movement which has come to fruition occurred when President Anwar Sadat of Egypt recognized the legitimacy of the state of Israel in the late 1970s. Sadat signed a peace accord, visited Jerusalem, and received the return of the Sinai from Israel, which it had battled over and won in the 1967 war.

In the occupied West Bank in 1993, there were 120,000 Jewish settlers and 1.1 million Palestinians. In the occupied Gaza Strip in 1993, there were 4,000 Jewish settlers and 700,000 Palestinians.[15] The latter are occupied people without a vote. In Israel proper Arab voters number nearly one-third of a million; Druze 8 percent; Christians 15 percent; and Sunni Muslim 77 percent. These groups represent 18 percent of the electorate of Israel. Indications are that the Arab vote is being cast for Arab political parties.

In December 1987, the *intifada* (stone throwing) began when young men hurled stones at Israeli soldiers. This protest movement resulted in many lost lives and injuries. The Palestine Liberation Organization (PLO) issued a proclamation in 1988 from Algiers, calling for a Palestinian State in the name of Allah with its capital in Holy Jerusalem.

In September of 1988, a new Islamic group, Hamas, arose in Gaza opposing the leaders of the intifada and the PLO. Hamas, meaning "Movement for Islamic Resistance," became a major force in Gaza, the West Bank, and Israel proper. The Hamas Covenant calls on Palestinian Muslims to wage jihad (holy war) on Israel as the only answer to the Palestinian problem. It calls for an Islamic state.

A peace treaty was signed between the Palestine Liberation Organization and Israel on September 13, 1993, on the White House grounds in Washington, D.C. Between that date and March 4, 1994, some thirty-three Israelis and more than a hundred Palestinians died in violent clashes both in Israel and in the occupied territories. King Hussein of Jordan signed a peace treaty with Israel in the fall of 1994.

Since its formation in 1948, Israel has faced hostilities and warfare, inside and outside its borders. The 1991 Gulf War with scud missiles hitting Israel from Iraq brought internal turmoil to the population. Israeli government and society have been polarized by military setbacks in Lebanon, the restlessness of the occupied populations, terrorist attacks against the military and civilian population, and the rapid development of the Jewish settlements in the occupied territories. Pressure has increased for a settlement of the Arab-Israeli conflict. The future of the occupied territories, whether it be annexation, limited autonomy, or a Palestinian state, has been the subject of heated national and international discussions.

Religion and politics are intertwined within Israel and outside of it. Palestinians want land and nationhood. Muslims want guardianship over their holy places. Jews insist on their own integrity over the Temple Mount.

Lebanon

Lebanon has been a crossroads of the Middle East for many years. Many invaders, entrepreneurs, and political/religious sects have impressed its peoples. In 1920, France took control of the Syrian provinces of the Ottoman Empire which are known today as Syria and Lebanon. In 1943 the French agreed to independence for Lebanon and Syria.

A National Pact was formed which relied on the census of 1932 for elections and appointments to the government. That census gave Christians an edge in population. Lebanese life was complicated by religious, sectarian, political, and territorial questions. The following arrangement was worked out:

- the president was to be a Maronite Christian;
- the prime minister was to be a Sunni Muslim;
- the speaker of parliament was to be a Shi'ite Muslim;
- the minister of defense was to be a Druze; and
- the foreign minister was to be a Greek Orthodox.

During the last several decades, the 1932 census has been disputed, and it has been argued that there are more Muslims in Lebanon than Christians.[16]

The total population of Lebanon is estimated at 3.3 million. The Arab population of 86 percent includes Lebanese 68 percent and others 14 percent (Syrian, Palestinian, and Egyptian). Other peoples are 14 percent (Armenians, Kurds, and Assyrians).

Lebanon is the only Arab state that is not overwhelmingly Muslim. There is freedom of religion. There are seventeen recognized religious communities: five Muslim, one Jewish, and eleven Christian. A factor in the unrest in Lebanon has been the rapid rise of the Muslim population, especially of the underrepresented Shi'ite community.

Muslims represent 53 percent of the population. Shi'ite Muslims are 33 percent, mainly located in the south, in the Bekaa Valley in the east, and in Beirut. Sunni Muslims are 20 percent, resident in Beirut, Tripoli, Sidon, and the northeast; they include Syrians and Palestinians. Christians comprise 38.7 percent of the total population with predominance among the various Catholic and Orthodox communities. They are located particularly in east Beirut and in central and north Lebanon. The Druze are 7 percent with great presence in the Chouf mountains east of Beirut.

In the 1960s and 1970s Lebanon was caught up in the politics of her neighbors against Israel and in the Palestinian plight. By 1975 full-scale civil war broke out. Some 400,000 Palestinian refugees had fled into Lebanon by that time. The Palestine Liberation Organization took up residence under the direction of Yasser Arafat . Israel invaded and occupied Beirut in 1982. Israel carved out a free zone in southern Lebanon. The Syrian army occupied parts of Lebanon. The Iranian revolution of 1979 inspired Shi'ites to make Lebanon a training ground for various militias.

Strikes, demonstrations, road blocks, bombings, and fighting became a daily affair. Lebanon divided increasingly along political/religious lines. Sometimes Muslims fought Muslims; sometimes Christians fought Christians; and sometimes Christians and Muslims fought each other. The Syrian army imposed a measure of stability in 1992 and opened the way for the Taif agreement of 1992 and a new Lebanese government. Under Syrian oversight the government has begun to exercise control over much of the country.

The Syrian army still occupies parts of Lebanon. Israel continues to have its free zone in southern Lebanon; and the various sectarian groups have their territories, militias, and agendas. The civil war which lasted from 1975 to 1992 wreaked havoc and devastation on the economic and political life of the country. Lebanon is now attempting to reconstruct its national life.

The following have been the principal factions in Lebanon:

- *Amal:* An armed Shi'ite organization organized in the early 1970s, Amal has been led by Nabih Berri and has been linked to Syria. A rival to the PLO and Hezbollah, one group split off in the early 1980s as Islamic Amal, which may have been linked with hijackings and attacks on U.S. and French troops in Lebanon.

- *al-Fatah:* This is the largest of the groups making up the PLO headed by Arafat.

- *Hezbollah:* Known as "the party of God," this is a militant Shi'ite group linked to Iran.

- *Progressive Socialist Party:* This represents Lebanon Druze and is led by Walid Jumblat. It is considered opportunistic in its alliances.

- *South Lebanese Army:* This is a mercenary army financed and directed by Israel. It is comprised mostly of Christians and coordinates patrols in the free zone carved out by the Israelis in the south.

- *The Lebanese Forces:* Formed in 1980 with the merging of several Maronite militias by President Bashir Gemayel, this group favors closer relations with the West.[17]

There are many other smaller factions, including Islamic Jihad, which is thought to be comprised of small cells of terrorists. Lebanon has attempted to rebuild its infrastucture since the end of the civil war. What alliances can be consolidated to bring unity for political stability remains to be seen.

Syria

The Mimbar (Pulpit) inside the great Umayyad Mosque in Damascus, Syria (Author took photo)

Syria became independent from France in 1946. Its estimated population is 15 million. The Arab population is 85 percent, including nearly one million Bedouins and a half million Palestinians. The other 15 percent are comprised of Kurds, Turks, Armenians, Assyrians, and Gypsies.

Prior to 1973, Islam was the state religion. Since then Syria has been a secular state with Islam recognized as the religion of the majority. The minorities are given definite rights and privileges. Muslims comprise 90.5 percent, including 75.1 percent Sunni, 11.7 percent Alawite, and 2.7 percent Druze. Christians are 8 percent, with various communities of Orthodox, Catholic, and Protestant. There are four thousand Jews.

The capital of Syria is Damascus with 1.9 million people. The city of Aleppo has 1.6 million. Damascus and Aleppo are said to be the oldest continually inhabited cities in the world.

The Ba'ath party gained control in Syria in 1963. It was the political movement of renaissance which sought to unite Marxist socialism with Arab nationalism. By 1970, Hafiz al-Assad had become president.

Assad was raised in poverty and within the Alawite sect.[18] The Alawites were considered a heretical sect of Shi'ite Islam. He was the first Alawite ever admitted to the Homs Military Academy. Upon joining the Ba'ath party, he rose to the positions of Air Force general and Minister of Defense. After he became president, he brought Alawites into the government, the military, and the Ba'ath party.

The Syrian Muslim fundamentalists have considered the Alawites atheists.[19] The Muslim Brotherhood looked upon Assad with disdain. The Imam Musa Sadr, leader of the Lebanese Twelver Shi'ite community, issued a fatwa (official Islamic opinion) in 1973 proclaiming the Alawites an authentic Shi'ite sect. However, even since this action of approval, President Assad has never received the favor of fundamentalist Islam.

Syria looked to the USSR for aid until its dismemberment in the early 1990s. Syria has waged war with Israel since the Israeli state was formed. It lost the Golan Heights to Israel in the 1967 war. The Heights continue to remain the negotiating point in the recent peace talks. Syria sent its occupying army into Lebanon in the late 1970s; some have suggested that Syria still dreams of Lebanon being a part of the greater Syria. It sided against Iraq in the Gulf War and contributed forces.

President Assad has faced internal dissension. There were clashes of citizens and Islamic groups against government forces in the 1970s and 1980s. The most serious clash was in February 1982 with a fundamentalist-led full-scale insurrection led by the Muslim Brotherhood in the city of Hama. According to estimates, 20,000 were killed before order was restored.[20]

The Syrian government tightly regulates Islam, and some consider it a terrorist state. It has struggled in the 1990s with the challenges to become a full-fledged cooperating nation in the international milieu.

Turkey

Turkey became a secular state under the leadership of Kemal Ataturk upon the demise of the Caliphate and the Ottoman Empire in 1924. Islam was repressed with the government's takeover of the legal, educational, and religious institutions.

The population of Turkey is over 61 million. There has been pressure on ethnic minorities to conform to Turkish culture. Turks (up to 81 percent), Kurds (up to 19 percent), and Arabs (about 1 percent) make up the major ethnic groups. Muslims comprise 99.8 percent of the country, with Sunnis in predominance.

Islamic political parties emerged in the 1960s and 1970s. Some have promoted the idea of an Islamic state. The government has become more sensitive to Islam although it still wields an oppressive hand against extremists. Turkey borders Syria, Iraq, Iran, and the former Soviet republics of eastern Europe. Various influences pervade Turkey from alliance with NATO to the Kurdish uprisings in its east and along the borders, particularly with Iraq.[21] Also, its proximity to the conflicts in the Balkans has increased its strategic importance.

Ankara serves as its capital city with a population of over 2.5 million. Other major cities are Istanbul (Constantinople) with over 7 million, Izmir (Smyrna) with about 1.8 million, and Adana with over 900,000.

Palestine Liberation Organization (PLO)

The Palestine Liberation Organization (PLO) began in 1964 at the first Arab summit meeting, and the Palestine Liberation Army was assembled in the same year. The circumstances of their founding can be traced back further than the founding of the state of Israel in 1948. In 1895, Theodore Herzl, founder of the Zionist ideology to establish a homeland for the Jewish people in Palestine, wrote that when the Jews occupy the land they must take gently the private property of the estates assigned to them and try to spirit the penniless population across the border. In 1917 the British government promulgated the Balfour Declaration which projected a national home for the Jewish people in Palestine that would not prejudice the civil and religious rights of existing non-Jewish communities.

In 1918 there were 56,000 Jews in Palestine and 644,000 Arabs; that is, 8 percent of Jews lived on 2 percent of the land. Between 1918 and 1948, waves of Jewish emigrants entered Palestine. These emigrants soon clashed with Arab Palestinians. The League of Nations recommended the creation of a Jewish state, an Arab state, and Jerusalem as an international city. Palestinians opposed the plan and war resulted.

Yasser Arafat said that at the time of the war the Zionists occupied 81 percent of the land, uprooted a million Arabs, and destroyed 385 out of 524 Arab villages. Palestinian Arabs left for surrounding territories, especially Jordan. Later, hundreds of thousands became entrapped in the occupied territories of the West Bank and Gaza.

Yasser Arafat helped organize the Palestine Liberation Organization (PLO) and became its titular leader in 1969. Born in Jerusalem in 1929, he moved to Jordan and Lebanon with his family in the late 1940s. He studied at Cairo University and joined the Egyptian army. In 1959 he went to Beirut and entered Palestinian politics.

In the late 1960s Arafat endorsed the PLO covenant, including the following points: Only Jews who lived in Palestine before 1917 should be citizens in a Palestinian state; Only Palestinian Arabs deserve the right of self-determination; warfare against Israel is legal and should be pursued militarily.

Seven groups united under the PLO umbrella, including Fatah, which served as the guerrilla army with training bases particularly in Lebanon and Syria; the Popular Front for Liberation of Palestine; and the Palestine National Front. From the late 1960s until recently, the PLO through its various organizations and constituents had the ultimate purpose of defeating Israel and establishing a Palestinian state for the Palestinian Arabs in the occupied territories and for the hundreds of thousands of refugees scattered throughout the Middle East and in other parts of the world.

The life of the PLO and its leader has had a cycle of highs and lows.[22] The PLO has been in favor and out of favor with Arab nations, including Jordan, Syria, Lebanon, Egypt, and Saudi Arabia. The Jordanian army drove the PLO out of Jordan in the early 1970s. PLO forces were cornered and driven out of Lebanon by Israeli forces. Arafat sided with Iraq in the Gulf War and again fell into disfavor with its chief banker, Saudi Arabia.

The PLO has been associated with plane hijackings, terrorist bombings, and the killing of targeted individuals and populations. In November 1974, Arafat was invited to address the United Nations General Assembly, and the PLO was granted permanent observer status by the UN.

In September 1993, following a series of secret meetings, the PLO and Israel agreed formally to recognize each other and signed a Declaration of Principles on Palestinian Self-Rule in the Occupied Territories. Since the signing hundreds have lost their lives in both Israel and the West Bank and Gaza in fighting between Israeli forces and Palestinian individuals and groups as well as in suicide bombings especially in Jerusalem and Tel Aviv.

NORTH AFRICA AND SUB-SAHARA AFRICA

In its first century, Islam moved from Arabia through the heartland of the Middle East and across North Africa into Spain. North Africa, including Egypt, Tunisia, Libya, Algeria, and Morocco, became Islamized within the various cultures of tribalism and/or Christianity. In its early history Christianity had taken hold in centers like Alexandria and Carthage, and giants of the early church like Augustine, Tertullian, and Cyprian had made names for themselves.[23]

Greek and Roman influences also held sway along the North African coast. Yet basically North Africa was Arabicized and Islamized by the early medieval times. The later history of the area saw the armies of Napoleon enter in the 1790s, and the encounter with European culture began. Later, the British were to influence Egypt, the French to impact Algeria and Tunisia, and the Italians to colonize Libya.

Islam has remained the dominant religion of North Africa along with traditional tribal institutions and values. Christianity has a scattered presence in North Africa; the Coptic Christians of Egypt are the largest Christian community. Political leadership has varied across the area from King Hasan in Morocco to President Gadhafi of Libya. All the countries from time to time have taken stands with other Arab nations against Israel and have had up-and-down relationships with European nations and the United States. Each country has at times been more traditionally Islamic, at other times more secularized in institutional life and behavior. For several years the PLO has had its headquarters in Tunisia.

Sub-Sahara Africa has been rich in tribalism and in religious traditions. Christianity and Islam stand beside traditional religion across the countries. Christianity spread from Palestine to North Africa and Ethiopia in its first several centuries. Its spread to sub-Sahara Africa was diminished by the Arab-Muslim conquest of North Africa in the seventh century A.D.

Not until the fifteenth century was Christianity brought to the area by Portuguese traders. In the nineteenth and twentieth centuries in particular, missionaries from the Roman Catholic Church and Protestant churches in Europe and America came. They brought western medical technology and education. Churches were built across the African landscape.

Islam was introduced into Africa within one hundred years after the death of Muhammad. In later centuries Muslim traders brought their religion from North Africa and from across the Red Sea to affect African tribes and empires. Tribal chiefs led whole tribes to adopt Islamic beliefs and practices. However, there was syncretism of tribal ways with those of Islam.

Traditional religion has remained strong. The African concept of the High God, ancestor veneration, and practices of divination and rites of passage have been influential in daily life.

African nations have claimed their independence from European colonial powers since World War II. Independence was followed by the natural pains of conflict and challenge between tradition and change, the old ways and modernization, and between tribal leadership and nomadic ways and those of urbanization and the national state.

Egypt

With 60,470,000 people, Egypt[24] is one of the most populous nations of the region. Its capital, Cairo, unofficially has some 14 million. Cairo claims to be the intellectual capital of Islam with the prestigious al-Azhur University. Islam is the state religion with 85.4 percent Muslim. The Christian population is 14.2 percent with Coptic Christians the majority. Christianity came to Egypt soon after the death of Jesus and established churches and theological centers. Its ethnic populations include Egyptian 86.4 percent (Arabic-speaking with descendants of the ancient Coptic-speaking peoples of biblical times); Arab 6.2 percent (Bedouin, Sudanese and others); Nubian 3 percent; Berber 2 percent, and Gypsy 2 percent.

Islam entered Egypt within two decades of Muhammad's death (A.D. 632). The Fatimid Dynasty ruled Egypt and its environs during the Middle Ages. The Ottoman Empire influenced Egypt from the early 1500s until its collapse in 1924. Napoleon's army entered Egypt in the 1790s to initiate the process of modernization and colonialism of much of the area.

> The relationship between Islam and politics in Egypt, which had been intertwined and inseparable, began to change with the rise of a "modern" Egypt under the rule of Muhammad 'Ali (1805–1849). The forces of modernization which the Ottoman leader unleashed by creating a modern army (building factories to arm, clothe and feed this army), sending the educational missions to Europe and introducing cash crops such as cotton, together with the influx of Levantines and Europeans as merchants and entrepreneurs, began a process of modernization which continued unabated until the mid-twentieth century. Gradually during this period the ideology of Egyptian nationalism, which consciously separated Islam from politics, became the dominant ideology.[25]

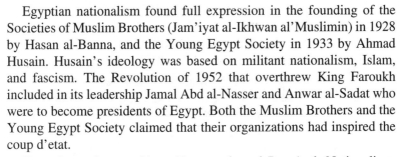

Egyptian nationalism found full expression in the founding of the Societies of Muslim Brothers (Jam'iyat al-Ikhwan al'Muslimin) in 1928 by Hasan al-Banna, and the Young Egypt Society in 1933 by Ahmad Husain. Husain's ideology was based on militant nationalism, Islam, and fascism. The Revolution of 1952 that overthrew King Faroukh included in its leadership Jamal Abd al-Nasser and Anwar al-Sadat who were to become presidents of Egypt. Both the Muslim Brothers and the Young Egypt Society claimed that their organizations had inspired the coup d'etat.

Upon becoming president, Nasser adopted Pan-Arab Nationalism. His struggle with the Muslim Brothers was over power, not ideology. Their conflict continued over the years with their leaders' imprisonment and occasional release. Nasser built mosques and Arabicized the educational system. However, in the 1960s he introduced his plan of "scientific socialism," and once again was opposed by the Muslim Brothers. They regarded the plan as incompatible with Islam, and many were imprisoned. Their leader at the time, Sayid Qutb, had more influence than the founder ever had and inspired offshoot movements such as the violent al-Jihad. Qutb was executed by the government in 1966.

Nasser promoted his pan-Arabism around the Middle East. He nationalized the Suez Canal and went to war over it with Israel in 1956. After dissidents assassinated Nasser in 1970, Anwar Sadat became president. He attempted to accommodate the Muslim Brothers and other dissidents by releasing some from prison and including them in consultations with the government. However, Sadat never succeeded in containing or co-opting them. He was assassinated by the al-Jihad organization in October 1981, while reviewing a military parade in Cairo.

Under mounting pressure from within Egypt and from Arab neighbor states, Sadat launched a surprise attack upon Israel on the Jewish high holy season of Yom Kippur in 1973. After advancing into the Sinai, having caught Israel by surprise, the Egyptian army was later routed. Thereafter, the Egyptian economy became weak. The population grew restless. Sadat saw peace as a means for stability and for growth.

At the time of his death, President Sadat was the only Arab leader and the only Muslim to have signed a peace treaty with Israel. President Carter of the United States had held the Camp David Peace Accords in Washington and served as mediator between President Sadat and Prime Minister Begin of Israel. The result was a visit by Sadat to Israel, the signing of the peace accord, his worship at the sacred mosque on the Temple Mount, visits of Israeli government officials to Cairo, and the return of the Sinai to Egypt.

Under the leadership of President Mubarak, there has been a quiet stability in the Egyptian economy. Egypt sided with Saudi Arabia and other Arab neighbors along with the United States and others in sending forces to drive Iraq out of Kuwait. The peace with Israel has held.

However, there have been continuous clashes between the government and militant Islamic organizations, including the Muslim Brothers and al-Jihad. The government has attempted to incorporate the Muslim Brothers into the political system with elections to parliament. Even so, there have been murders of government officials, clashes with the police, and disruption of transportation and the lucrative tourist business. The al-Jihad organization and its splinter groups are of a different ideological school of thought from the Muslim brothers.

According to Muhammad Abd al-Salam Faraj, who wrote *The Absent Obligation*, "The rulers of Muslims today are in a state of apostasy from Islam. . . they are Muslim in name only even though they may pray and fast and claim to be Muslims."[26] Thus, the author writes that the primary obligation of all Muslims is to declare jihad and fight against the present regimes, the enemy within, that is the rulers of Muslims, in order to achieve the Rule of God.

Libya

Islam and politics have been intertwined in the development of modern Libya. In the nineteenth century, the Sanussiya, an Islamic reformist movement, migrated to Libya from Arabia. Its purpose was to proselytize and to reform the Islamic way. It centered around lodges headed by religious sheikhs. These lodges became centers of learning and military outposts. Rulers of the Ottoman Empire relied on the lodges to collect taxes. The movement spread to neighboring Chad.

The Sanussiya resisted the Italian colonial powers. King Idris I, the first head of state upon Libyan independence in 1951, was a leader of the Sanussi Order. The present leader of Libya, Mu'ammar Gadhafi, has a view of religion and politics which bears the legacy of the Sanussi Order. Gadhafi considers Islam a reformist movement, a source of change and progress in harmony with the laws of science.

Since the 1970s, the Libyan government has controlled Islam, constraining the ulama and placing its own religious leaders in the mosques. The major Friday sermons in the mosques have been restricted to spiritual rather than political matters. The government supervises religious endowments (Awqaf), which have provided the main source of the income of the ulama.

A major critic of Gadhafi was the Grand Mufti of Libya, Sheikh al-Zawi. He spoke out against taxing individuals because of Libya's tremendous oil revenue and against breaking the law of usury. He resigned in January 1984 in protest of these matters and of his own harrassment.

The Muslim Brotherhood criticized the government for its liberal view on women and for its view that individuals could interpret the Qur'an for themselves. The Hizboal-Tahri al-Islam (Islamic Liberation Party), a major organization in Libya, has been repressed. Hangings by the government have occurred; students have been arrested; and mosques have been raided. Gadhafi criticized the wearing of the veil by women as a work of the devil.[27]

The population of Libya is about 5.5 million. The Arabs make up 77 percent. Berbers are nearly 10 percent. Expatriates are 11 percent and include many laborers, mainly Egyptian, Sudanese, North African, Chadean, Pakistani, and Bangladeshi. Sunni Islam is the state religion, and Muslims comprise 96 percent of the population. The Christian minority of about 3 percent is strictly monitored. Tripoli is the capital with nearly a million people.

Morocco

Morocco has a population of over 29 million. Of these 64.7 percent speak Arabic. They are culturally Arab but predominantly Berber with Arab mixture. Berbers make up 34.8 percent with three main language groups. The Berbers were nominally Christian until Islam came with the Arab armies in the seventh century.

Islam is the state religion, and Muslims represent 99.8 percent of the people. Other religious groups, few as they are, are tolerated. The present ruler, King Hasan II, is believed to have descent from the Prophet Muhammad. He is associated with *baraka* (spiritual power attributed to saints). There have been good relations between the king and the religious leaders. On the popular level Sufi orders have played a great part in Islamic life in Morocco. The institutions of brotherhoods, shrines, and saints have been related to these groups.

In 1972, a militant Islamic movement in the Association of Islamic Youth was organized and divided into five groups. They viewed the monarchy as corrupt and as subservient to the West. The government has arrested and jailed some followers of this movement. King Hasan has enjoyed a relatively peaceful reign. The dominant political issue since 1974 has been the occupation of the Western Sahara and the subsequent warfare it has brought. Hasan has built the largest mosque in the world in Rabat.[28] Rabat, the capital, has just over 1 million in population. Other major cities include Casablanca with 4.5 million people, the ancient Islamic center of Fez with 800,000, and Marrakech with some 800,000.

Tunisia

Islam is the state religion of Tunisia. Muslims comprise 99.5 percent of the population. The government of Tunisia, tending at times to be secularist, has been sensitive to the issues of religion in its society and in its relationship with worldwide Islam. The headquarters of the PLO are located in its capital of Tunis. Tunis has a population of 1,225,000.

In 1987 the Islamic Jihad bombed four tourist hotels. Seven of the ninety arrested were sentenced to death. Tensions brought the ouster of President Bourguiba, and President Ben Ali assumed power. He granted amnesty to 2,487 prisoners.[29]

Algeria

Islam in Algeria has long been associated with politics. A nation of over 29 million, Arabs from Arabia brought Islam to North Africa on their way to Spain in the seventh century. In modern Algeria, during 130 years of French colonial rule, Islam served as a source of national identity. Muslims comprise 99.4 percent of the population. The Catholic and the Protestant churches of Algeria are the only Christian bodies officially recognized. Algiers serves as the capital with just over 3 million people.

In 1931, Sheikh Ben Badis set forth the role which Islam would play when he stated, "Islam is my religion, Arabic my language, Algeria my fatherland."[30] In 1956 followers of Ben Badis joined with the Front du Liberation Nationale (FLN) in the war of independence against France. Thus, Islam mobilized support which led to the new state in 1962. Ahmed Ben Bellah, a leader in the FLN, headed the government. Islam became the religion of state in the new constitution, but the government did not make Shari'a a part of the legal system, nor were Muslim jurists given voice in the affairs of government.

The government appointed a minister of religious affairs with the authority to name and dismiss clergy, review Friday sermons, administer religious endowments (Awqaf), control religious publications, and set up Islamic institutes of higher learning. Orthodox Muslims were displeased.

In 1964 the first autonomous Islamic organization emerged, known as al-Qiyam ("the values"). It was the precursor to the fundamentalist movements of the 1980s and 1990s. The Boumedienne regime suppressed it and killed its leader in 1967. However, Islamic revivalism reemerged in the mid-1970s. It opposed the government's nationalization of property and its shift to the left. By the end of the 1970s the organization Ahl al Da'wa ("People of the Call") was formed. Boumedienne had died, and the Iranian revolution was influencing the disenchanted Muslims of Algeria

Ahl al Da'wa became very organized and active. It desired that the Shari'a be the basis for governing. It wanted a strict dress code for women and the prohibition of alcohol in public places. It took over mosques with its ideology, clashed with police, and attacked public places.

In the 1980s the government arrested its leaders and began a systematic campaign to abolish them. The campaign was ineffective, and the government attempted a gesture of peace by releasing prisoners and providing money to construct mosques. The Islamic groups were not to be appeased.

In 1988, riots occurred to protest shortages, reduced subsidies, and high unemployment. The army was brought in and hundreds were killed. Attempts were made at appeasement. In 1989 a new political party was formed, the Islamic Salvation Front, and it was approved by the government of President Chadli. An informal Islamic Shura (a consultative council) made up of Islamic leaders was formed.

By the 1990s the Islamic Salvation Front had become powerful enough to win elections. Algeria's military junta rejected the Front's election victories in 1992, declared one million votes fraudulent, and clamped down on the Front and several other groups. President Chadli resigned. Violence and civil war ensued. Some estimate that some 30,000 may have died in the violence.[31]

The temporary president, Mohammad Boudiaf, was assassinated. In 1994 a weary military chose Brig. Gen. Zeroual as president. Some eighty foreigners and two dozen journalists have died. Thus, fundamentalist Muslims are at war with their government to bring it into line with orthodox Islam. There are many factions and parties against the government which include Armed Islamic Movement, Expiation and Sin, Exile and Redemption, Faithful of the Sermon, and Bridges of God.

Nigeria

Nigeria is the most populous African nation with about 120 million people. These include some 47 percent Muslim (Muslims claim up to 60 percent), 34 percent Christian, and 19 percent tribal beliefs. There are six hundred ethnic groups which include the Hausa, Yoruba, and Ibo. Nigeria gained its independence in 1960 and since has had several military coups which installed military governments. Its capital, Abuja, has 379,000 people; other major cities include Lagos with 5,686,000 and Ibadan with 2 million.

A basic political and social cleavage with religious overtones exists between the north and the south. The north has major tribal-ethnic groups like the Hausa, Kanuri, and the Fulani with traditional Muslim roots. The south includes the Ibo and the Yoruba with Christian backgrounds.

Northern Muslims have been heavily influenced by Arab Islam. They have sought a special place for the Shari'a (Islamic law) in the affairs of government. Their desire to rule Islamic jurisprudence has concerned the Christian Nigerians. In the civil wars of 1966, Ibos were killed. Thus, Muslims became known for their killing of Christians.[32]

In the 1970s and 1980s fundamentalist Muslim sects agitated and caused uprisings in Keno and Gombe against the ruling authorities. The Nigerian army put them down and killed thousands. In 1986 President Babangida, a Muslim, changed Nigeria's observer status at the Islamic Organization to that of a full member. Christian Nigerians inferred from this action that the government of Nigeria considered the country a Muslim state. The government has moved to establish Shari'a courts in the federal judicial system in the provinces. It also imposed a political nominee as Sultan of the largest Hausa emirate. Riots resulted in Sokoto.

The military coup in November 1993 installed General Abacha as head of government. A promise was made, which appears to be a perennial promise, to have a constitutional convention to bring about national reconciliation. Thus, the military rules a fragmented Nigeria. There are many political parties. The Fulani and Hausa of the north are organized under local monarchs called Emirs; the family is the social unit among the Ibos.[33]

Thus, religion and politics amidst tribal, ethnic, and religious cleavages and confrontations have exemplified conflict and change within Nigerian society. Islam has continued to be a main player in this context.

Sudan

Sudan, with a population of about 29 million, occupies the largest territory of any African nation. It gained its independence from Britain in 1956. Its ancient history revolved around the Pharaohs of Egypt and the Nubian peoples. Christianity came to the Sudan in the sixth century, but the country remained basically traditional; it adopted Islam in the thirteenth century, although Islam was stronger in the north than in the south.

There are over 140 ethnic groups with non-Arabs accounting for 64 percent and Sudanese Arabs 36 percent. Khartoum, its capital, numbers over 1.5 million. It is estimated that since 1985, 1.5 million deaths have occurred through war, genocide and famine. Over 5 million southern Sudanese have been internally displaced.

The Sudan was declared an Islamic Republic in 1983. Muslims are 70 percent with Sunni Islam in dominance. Almost the entire indigenous northern population is Muslim. There are several powerful Sufi orders, and the largest is the Ansar, the followers of Mahdi. Christians comprise 19 percent, most of whom live in the south, in the Nuba mountains, and in Khartoum's southern section. Traditional religions comprise 9.9 percent.

Much of Sudan's history has revolved around coalition governments and military rule. Many political parties have existed. Colonel Jaafar Mohammad al Nimeri was elected president in 1971. A constitution was adopted in 1973. Nimeri attempted to impose Islamic law on the provinces south of Khartoum. By 1983 the government enforced Islamic law throughout the country. A person found guilty of armed robbery had his right hand and left foot chopped off as an example to all. Alcoholic beverages were strictly forbidden.[34]

Under Nimeri, Sudan descended into economic chaos, and an influx of refugees from Ethiopia made things even worse. While Nimeri was traveling abroad, the Sudanese military carried out a coup. In 1986 elections were held and a coalition headed by Dr. Sadiq al-Mahdi won. He was named prime minister. Dr. al-Mahdi was the great-grandson of the founder of the Ansar sect of Islam. In the 1880s Mohammad Ahmad declared himself the Mahdi, an Islamic term for the one after the Prophet who is to return and rule the earth. He established an Islamic state that continued until victory of British colonialism in 1898.

In the midst of chaos al-Mahdi attempted to rule by coalition and to tone down the implementation of Islamic law by the government. His government collapsed in August 1987. The Muslim Brotherhood joined with the National Islamic Front led by Hassan Tourabi to form a government. Tourabi drafted even stricter versions of Islamic law. An armed robber was sentenced to crucifixion, and the penalty for conversion from Islam to Christianity was death.

Meanwhile, the ethnic group in the south, the Dinkas, led by Col. John Garang, formed the Sudanese People's Liberation Army to combat the northern government. Garang's revolutionaries have prevented any voting in the south of the Sudan. Moderate Muslims in the National People's Assembly have acted to tone down the proclamations of Tourabi.

The Sudan has lived in chaos. There is religious antagonism and civil war. Some of the worst droughts in the world hit the Sudan. The worst floods in the twentieth century hit Khartoum and its environs in 1988 and left more than two million homeless and starving. About 2.5 million refugees from the south camped in and around Khartoum.

In mid-1989 a military coup ousted from office and imprisoned al-Mahdi, infuriating the Muslim fundamentalists. General Omar Hassan al-Bashir emerged as leader of the Revolutionary Council. He was named president to rule by decree until elections could be held.

The Sudan was split in 1994 into twenty-six states where there were formerly nine. Little had changed, with the refugee problem intensified, corruption rampant, revolutionary forces still in the south, and food shortages magnified. The United States, after some years of aid, cut off aid and classified Sudan as a terrorist state exporting violent Islamic fundamentalism.[35]

A primary issue has continued to be the Islamization of the Sudan and whether it would be moderately Islamic or fundamentally Islamic. Besides natural disasters and political turmoil, there has been much warfare and persecution of both Christians and moderate Muslims. Since 1985 in particular there have been attempts to eliminate a viable Christian presence in parts of the country through bombings and destruction of churches and Christian villages, massacres with mass crucifixions in some areas, the killing of Christian leaders, and a food-for-conversion policy for refugees banished to desert areas around Khartoum.[36]

FAR EAST AND SOUTH ASIA

Islam eventually spread to South Asia and the Far East. It reached India soon after Muhammad's death in the seventh century. India, included in South Asia, was the home of Hinduism and Buddhism, and Islam became a significant religion alongside of them. After centuries of conflicts and battles focused on the religions and politics of these world religions, especially between the Hindus and the Muslims, Muslims founded their homeland with the partition of India and Pakistan. However, many Muslims remained in India. Also, Afghanistan has been an Islamic country since soon after the death of the Prophet.

The Far East was opened to Islam much later by Muslim merchants and traders. After the fourteenth century, Indonesia, Malaysia, and the Philippines were fertile grounds for Muslim advance. Each country had its special cultural and ethnic roots. All had their indigenous traditional beliefs of tribalism and/or animism.

Indonesia had Hindu and Buddhist influences centuries before Islam arrived to dominate its religious culture. Malaysia has had its Chinese roots, but in recent history has embraced Islam as a state religion. The Philippines has been predominantly Roman Catholic with a variety of other religious expressions, including a strong Muslim minority.

Thus, the Far East is the home of the world's most populous Muslim country, namely, Indonesia. Malaysia, though far from the heartland of Islam, has made Islam its state religion. And South Asia, especially the countries of India, Pakistan, and Afghanistan, has significant populations of Muslims engaged in a variety of religious and political expressions.

Indonesia

Indonesia has the largest Muslim population in the world, with some 170 million Muslims out of a population of about 196 million. Most Indonesians are of Malayo-Polynesian ethnicity, a mixture of Polynesian, Mongolian, Indian, and Caucasian of ancient origin; this group represents 95 percent of all Indonesians. Other ethnics are Chinese (about 3 percent) and European (about 2 percent). There are also small groups of Christians, Hindus, and Buddhists with a basic tradition of tribal/animistic characteristics.[37]

Indian cultural and religious influences came into Indonesia about the beginning of the Christian era. Hinduism and Buddhism mixed with popular animistic/tribal beliefs and practices to form a complex and unique culture. Islam came to Indonesia from India about the eleventh century. It spread slowly until by the sixteenth century a majority of the people had become Muslim.

Colonial rule of the Dutch East India Company dominated Indonesia until the rise of nationalism in the twentieth century. The Japanese invaded Indonesia and remained until their defeat in 1945. Indonesia became a republic in 1949 under the leadership of Sukarno, who moderated between the communists and the army. Sukarno ruled until the army clashed with the communists. The army won after much violence. One of its generals, Suharto, seized leadership and deposed Sukarto in 1966.

Suharto has held the presidency since 1967, and at 71 years of age was elected in 1993 to another term as president. He is a strong leader who has ruled under a system known as *Pancasila democracy*. This ideology for governing is based on five principles: nationalism, democracy, internationalism, social justice, and belief in one God. All political parties must accept Pancasila. The armed services play an important role in the political process through Golkar, the official government party.[38]

Islam has made its presence felt. During the colonial period Islam became a unifying symbol against Dutch rule. The first mass nationalist party was Sarekat Islam. After the Dutch left in 1949, Muslims in West Java and other regions were under the influence of a radical Muslim movement, Darul Islam, to establish an Islamic state. Communists attempted to take over Indonesia in 1965 and 1966, but Muslim organizations helped government forces destroy them.[39]

Tensions have existed between Muslim organizations and the Suharto government since the late 1960s. Muslim organizations have been critical of the secularity of government, of the government's positions on marriage laws, the perceived weakness of religious teaching in the schools, and the weakness of the statement on God in the Five Principles. The government has used terms in prison to oppose religious activism and Muslim extremism.[40]

Malaysia

Malaysia is a neighbor to Indonesia. Its population is nearing 19 million. Half are Malayo-Polynesians, a mixture of Polynesian, Mongol, Indian, and Caucasian. About forty percent are Chinese, and ten percent are Indian.[41] The capital, Kuala Lumpur, has 1,475,000 people.

There are two distinct divisions in Malaysia. Peninsula Malaysia (PM) is on the west and a part of mainland Asia; East Malaysia (EM) consists of the territories of Sarawak and Sabah on the northern third of the island of Borneo. Sunni Islam is the official religion in PM, and there is pressure to make Islam dominant in EM where it is the minority.

Estimates of the major religious groupings are Muslim, 55 percent; Christian, 8.6 percent; Buddhist 7 percent; Hindu, 6 percent; and Chinese religions, 18 percent.

Before Malaysia's independence in 1957, it lived under the colonialism of the Dutch and the British, as well as the invasion of Japan during World War II. Tension has existed between the ethnic Chinese and the Malays, most of whom are Muslim.

Two political problems appeared in 1985–1986: first, political struggles between political parties, especially the National Front, the dominant United Malay National Organization (UMNO), and the Malayan Chinese Association (MCA); second, the increase in militant Islam. Islam is the state religion, and Muslims enjoy certain special privileges. Islam came to Malaysia in the Muslim expansion of the sixteenth century. Officially, there is freedom of religion for other faiths. The prime minister, Dato Seri Dr. Mahathir Mohammad, heads the UMNO and faces the challenges of coalition building, honoring the state religion Islam, and building the economy.

Malaysia is a federation of states, and each state has a Sultan who heads the Islamic religious affairs. In recent years a conservative Muslim organization, the Parti Islam Sa Malaysia, has opposed the government and has called for an Islamic revival. Women have been asked to wear appropriate clothing. Gambling has been condemned. The proselytizing of Muslims has been prohibited. A rise in Muslim youth organizations has occurred (about 45 percent of Malaysians are under age fifteen). More involvement in Islamic international organizations and affairs has been implemented. The prime minister has voiced anti-Zionist sentiments in public statements.[42]

Johnstone has observed,

> The Muslim half of the population has been politically and socially divided through an extremist minority pressing for radical Islamic reforms and the formation of an Islamic state. This has brought stress to the whole country, an acceleration of Muslim missionary activities among non-Muslims and also discriminatory legislation and actions against non-Muslims. . . . All non-Muslims, and Christians in particular, are suffering a creeping erosion of religious freedom. Intimidation, discrimination and bureaucratic obstructionism are widespread in PM but also occur in EM.[43]

Philippines

The Philippines has an estimated population of nearly 70 million. Malayo-Polynesians comprise 93 percent of the people, but there are also Chinese, Negritos, Europeans, and persons of mixed ethnicity. Ninety percent are Christians, mostly Roman Catholics; Islam claims about 8 percent, and the rest practice animist/tribal religious traditions. Metro Manila, its capital, has a population of 10 million. The constitution guarantees freedom of religion. The Philippines is the only country in Asia with a Roman Catholic majority.

The Muslim minority in the southern Philippines has long sought to attain independence. Its history goes back to the colonial era. Fifty thousand died from clashes with government forces in the 1970s. Muslims comprise 4 million of the 14 million inhabitants in the contested area.

Recently, the government proposed to let the will of the people in the contested ten provinces decide their local autonomy.[44] The Muslims, however, are the majority in only five of the ten provinces, and they have wanted to dominate all of them. There have been cycles of violence and cease-fires.

Brunei (Brunei Darussalam)

Brunei is a nation of only about 277,000 people enclosed by the East Malaysian states of Sarawak and Sabah. Malays make up most of the population with a significant Chinese minority. Brunei is officially a Muslim nation (Darussalam means abode of peace) led by His Majesty, the Sultan of Brunei, Bolkiah Mu'izzaddin Waddaulah. The Sultan has two wives. He studied in England and was crowned by his father in 1968 as the twenty-ninth ruler.

There have been no political parties and little opposition to the regime. Multicultural diversity is acceptable with the Malays established in their Islamic traditions. The Sultan promotes Islam through schools, the media, and through observances. The Sultan has curbed Islamic extremism, although he has criticized Israel and voiced support for the Palestinian cause. In recent times, Freemasonry and the Jehovah's Witnesses have been banned.[45]

India

Islam entered India soon after Muhammad's death. Hinduism and Buddhism originated there centuries before the advance of Islam. There may be over a hundred million Muslims in India, but Islam remains a minority religion representing about 11 percent of the population among the predominant Hindus. The population of India is 904,800,000.

India is a secular state that guarantees freedom of religion. Its religious make-up includes Hindu, 78.8 percent; Muslim, 11 percent; Christian, 2.6 percent; Sikhs, 2 percent; and Buddhists, traditional religions, Jains, Parsi, and Baha'i. Islam is a widespread minority, but it has a majority in the states of Kashmir and Lakshadweep; it is growing among certain castes. The Muslim secessionist movement in Kashmir is in armed conflict with the government.

The history of India has involved tensions, conflicts, and accommodations among the religions. Islam has been no exception. In modern times during the independence struggles led by Gandhi against British colonialism, the Muslim League led by Muhammad Ali Jinnah broke with Gandhi and demanded that the British create a Muslim state. Pakistan was carved out of India in 1947. Eight million Muslims left to form the state of Pakistan. One million lost their lives in rioting and fighting. Gandhi was assassinated in 1948 by a dissident.

The majority Hindus have clashed with Muslims over a variety of issues, including representation and power in government and government protection of mosques built over Hindu sacred sites. Most residents of the Indian state of Kashmir are Muslims, and they have perennially clashed with the government. In 1988 there were attempts at secession. In 1989 Muslim separatists called themselves mujahedin (holy warriors) and stated that their conflict with the government was a holy war (jihad).[46]

Pakistan

After much rioting and bloodshed, Pakistan was created from partition by India in 1947 in order for Muslims to have an autonomous state. It has a population of over one hundred million with a plurality of Muslims. Sunni Islam is the predominant branch following the Hanafi school of law. There are also Shi'ite and Ahmadi Muslims.

From the first, Pakistan has struggled over the proper form of Islam. The Ahmadis were founded as a sect in the Punjab in the mid-nineteenth century by Mirza Ghulam Ahmad. He claimed to be the Madhi, a Muslim savior type, destined to rule the nations. His movement was rejected by orthodox Islam in his day, but today there may be five million Ahmadis in Pakistan. General Zia ul-Haq, while president of Pakistan, declared them non-Muslims in 1984.

Pakistan has at times considered becoming a fully functioning Islamic state. Jamaat-i-Islami was founded as a religious party by Maulana Maududi, expressing militant and fundamentalist Islamic views. It has clashed with leaders who lean toward secularism.

In the 1960s a series of Family Law Ordinances became controversial. The Ordinances curbed polygamy, barred child marriages, made divorce for women more humane, and made equality for a non-Muslim the same as for a Muslim.

The Orthodox pressured changes in the government. Bhutto became prime minister in 1972. With a parliament sensitive to orthodoxy, Islam became the state religion under the constitution. However, the government resisted the pressures of requiring the veiling of women and corporal punishment for theft and adultery. In 1977 Bhutto was deposed by a military coup led by General Zia ul-Haq, who initiated a period of Islamization. He implemented the Islamic legal code. Punishment for theft was the amputation of hands. The evidence of two women in court was necessary to contradict that of one man. Zakat (alms tax) was introduced. The government was criticized by non-Muslim minorities, women's groups, and human rights groups. There were Shi'ite-Sunni clashes in 1983, 1984, and 1987 with many deaths. In August of 1988 Zia was killed in a suspicious plane crash.

The election of Benazir Bhutto, a woman and graduate of Harvard University and daughter of the former prime minister, has been a test case for an Islamic nation. She has moved slowly to dismantle the foundations of Zia's Islamic reforms. There has been much tension within the government and among the religious and political parties. There have been bombings of mosques with loss of lives and the murder of two United States diplomats stationed with the U.S. consulate. Also, Muslim groups strongly protested Rushdie's *Satanic Verses*.

Afghanistan

Afghanistan is a nation of about 20 million. There are twenty languages with Pushto dominant and Dari the language of business and government. Islam became the religion of dominance with the Islamic advance eastward from Arabia in the seventh century A.D. The major branch of Islam is Sunni following the Hanafi school of law. There is a sizable Shi'ite minority.

In 1973 King Zahir Shah was deposed. Mohammad Daoud initiated a bloodless coup in reacting to Russian influence and the rise of Islamic fundamentalism. Daoud was overthrown in 1978 by Marxist-oriented Mohammad Tarik. The Soviet invasion of Afghanistan in 1979, coupled with next door neighbor Iran's Islamic fundamentalist-inspired revolution, caused widespread conflict in the country. The Soviets installed Babrak Karmal to head the government, and the Iranian government of Ayatollah Khomeini aided the Afghan fundamentalists to fight the Soviet army and Karmal.

Between 1985 and 1987 the mujahedin *(Muslim holy fighters)* operating out of Pakistan fought the Soviet-supported Afghan government. The United States gave aid to some of the fighting groups. In 1987 Dr. Najibulah was elected president and drafted a new constitution declaring Afghanistan an Islamic nation. The various political factions and fighting groups gave little positive response to this proclamation.[47]

In 1988 the Geneva Accords resulted in the Soviets' departing the country after severe military losses and internal unrest in their own country over their policies. Moderate and fundamentalist Muslim groups continue to oppose each other, and they have done little to resolve the country's problems. Millions of refugees have fled the country, most to Pakistan. Unrest has continued.

People's Republic of China

Islam was introduced into China during the Tang Dynasty (A.D. 618–906) by Arab and Persian merchants and by Muslim soldiers brought in to stop a rebellion in the interior. With a population of more than one billion, there are more than thirty million Muslims who make up ten minority groups. Nine of these groups live between the provinces of Xinjiang and Kansu and attempt to live in balance between the communist rulers and the growing influence of global Islam.[48]

The largest Muslim minority is the Hui, some nine million of whom are Sunni Muslims scattered across China. They are the only Chinese-speaking Muslim group. The second largest Muslim minority is the Uygurs, who number almost nine million. They live primarily in the Xinjiang province which is adjacent to the new republics of the former Soviet Union. There are significant numbers of Uygurs in the republics. There may be as many as 14,000 mosques among the Uygurs.

The Uygurs are one of nine Muslim ethnic groups in their province. Others include Kazakh, Hui, Kirghiz, Uzbek, and Tajik. Nationalistic feelings have emerged among these Muslim peoples, and China is very sensitive to this possibly explosive challenge.

The Kazakhs, the primary ethnic group of the new republic of Kazakhstan, have some one million in China.

RUSSIA AND THE COMMONWEALTH OF INDEPENDENT STATES

By the early 1990s the Union of Soviet Socialist Republics (USSR) under the rule of Communism had come to an end. Under the USSR, religions had been suppressed and their adherents often persecuted. Russia now had become the Russian Federation, and many other republics had become independent.

The Commonwealth of Independent States were formed in 1991 by the Minsk Agreement and the Alma-Ata Declaration. Azerbaijan, Kazakhstan, Kyrgyzstan, Tajikistan, Turkmenistan, and Uzbekistan are all nations with roots in Islam. Tartarstan, Bashkortostan, and Chuvashia, seeking independence from Russia, are also of Turkic background.[49]

These emerging nations have experienced the initial phases of transition from dependency and often suppression by the USSR and from the atheistic ideology and practice of Communism. Political organizations, economic plans, and religious and cultural institutions have been explored and set in motion. Islam, being a major religious and cultural orientation suppressed by Communism, has begun to be considered.

Iran, Saudi Arabia, and other Muslim nations have looked to the emerging republics as fertile grounds for Islamic missions and revivalism. Muslim clerics have been sent. Islamic institutes have been established to train the peoples in the teachings and practices of Islam. Old mosques have been renovated, and new mosques are being built. Qur'ans have been sent, and translations are being made in the vernacular languages.

The freedom and independence of these republics is so recent that patterns of what forms and functions Islam may have in them are not yet clear. However, both outside the republics and within them, Islam is being seriously considered once again as a viable and visible religion.

Azerbaijan

Azerbaijan is a country with a population of over 7 million, according to a 1991 census. It borders Iran to the south, to the west Armenia, to the northwest Georgia, and to the north the autonomous Republic of Daghestan. Its capital is Baku with 1.8 million people. The Azerbaijanis are 80 percent Muslim with Shi'ites 56 percent and Sunnis 24 percent. The Sunni follow the Hanafi school of law. The Muslim Board of Transcaucasia is based in Baku. It has religious jurisdiction over the Muslims of Armenia, Georgia, and Azerbaijan. The chairman of the Directory is a Shi'ite, and the deputy chairman is a Sunni.[50]

The non-religious comprise 17.3 percent. Many Azerbaijanis were atheists before 1990. Christians are 2.67 percent, and almost all are non-indigenous.

Kazakhstan

Kazakhstan has a population of approximately 17 million. It borders to the south the republics of Turkmenistan, Uzbekistan, and Kyrgyzstan; to the east the People's Republic of China; to the north the Russian Federation and a coastline with the Caspian Sea. Alma-Ata is its capital with over a million people. Kazakhstan has been the depository of much of the former USSR's nuclear arsenal.

The major religion of the Kazakhs is Sunni Islam, representing about 40 percent of the population. Most Kazakhs are influenced by Folk Islam. By 1991 there were an estimated 230 Muslim religious communities with a newly opened Islamic institute in Alma-Ata. In 1990 the Muslim authorities in the country established an independent Muslim leader called a mufti.[51] Saudi Arabia, Turkey, and Iran have sent Muslim missionaries and have given aid for mosques, Qur'ans, and Islamic theological education.

Christians represent about 27 percent, and non-religious and other about 33 percent of the peoples.

Kyrgyzstan

Kyrgyzstan is a small, land-locked republic bordering Kazakhstan to the north, Uzbekistan to the west, Tajikistan to the south, and to the east the People's Republic of China. The population is about 4.7 million. Its capital is Bishkek with 631,000 people. Most Kyrgyz are Sunni Muslims (60 percent) of the Hanafi school. Many follow Folk Islam influenced by pre-Islamic shamanism. In 1991 there were sixty operating mosques of which eighteen were opened in 1991. Muslims in Kyrgyzstan are officially under the spiritual jurisdiction of the Directorate of Central Asia based in Uzbekistan. The Directorate chief leader in the country is called a *kazi*.[52]

Kyrgyzstan is basically a secular state with the guarantee of religious freedom. Non-religious comprise 30 percent, Christians nearly 12 percent; there are also a few Jews and Buddhists.

Tajikistan

Tajikistan is bordered to the north and west by Uzbekistan, to the northeast by Kyrgyzstan, to the east by the People's Republic of China, and to the south by Afghanistan. The population is estimated to be 6.3 million. Its capital is Dushanbe with 602,000. Muslims comprise 82.3 percent of the population with the majority Sunni Muslims of the Hanafi school; there is a minority sect of Shi'ites. The Muslim Board of Central Asia has jurisdiction in the country, and its chief representative is called a kazi.[53] Battles have ensued over government policy between communists and the alliance of conservative Muslims and democrats. Muslims have increased the number of mosques from 120 in 1991 to 2,100 in 1993.

The non-religious are 13.2 percent, and the Christians are 4.2 percent. There are a few Jews.

Turkmenistan

Turkmenistan borders Uzbekistan on the north and Kazakhstan on the northwest, and is bordered on the west by the Caspian Sea. To the south is Iran, and to the southeast is Afghanistan. Its population is estimated to be four million. Its capital is Ashkhabad with 407,000 people. The Turkmen are basically Sunni Muslims with some representation of Sufism. Ashkhabad was the only Central Asian capital without a functioning mosque until 1989. It is under the spiritual jurisdiction of the Muslim Board of Central Asia based in Uzbekistan with its leader called a kazi.[54]

The religious make-up is 76 percent Muslim, 18.2 percent non-religious, 5.7 percent Christian, and a few Jews. Government policy is a secular state with freedom of belief.

Uzbekistan

Uzbekistan borders Kazakhstan to the north, Kyrgyzstan to the east, Turkmenistan to the south, and Tajikistan to the southeast. It also shares a short border to the south with Afghanistan. The population is estimated to be 23.4 million. Tashkent is its capital with 2.5 million people.

The government declared a secular state with freedom of religions. The religious composition of the population is 68.2 percent Muslim, 26 percent non-religious, 4.7 percent Christian, and a few Buddhists, Jews, and Baha'i. Most Uzbeks are Sunni Muslims, but there are small communities of Wahhabis, the more conservative branch of Muslims. The Muslim Board of Central Asia is located in Tashkent with a mufti as its head.[55]

Russia

Russia is the world's largest country, extending across eleven time zones between the Baltic and the Pacific. Its population of some 153,646,000 is comprised of Indo-Europeans, 89.3 percent (Slavs, Caucasus peoples, others); Turkic/Altaic, 8 percent (Turkic, Altaic, Finno-Ugric); Semitic and other Siberian peoples. Moscow, its capital, has a population of 9 million.

Its Czarist empire collapsed in 1917, followed by the Communist revolution. Multiparty democracy was begun in 1990, and the Communist party was banned. President Yeltsin, a reformist democrat, has battled politically the ex-Communist leadership over political and economic reforms. A number of its constituent republics have considered independence from Russia.

The Communist government promoted atheism and repressed and restricted all religions. The present government guarantees freedom of religion. Major religious communities include Christians, 56.3 percent; Muslims 8.7 percent; and a few Jews, Buddhists, and animists. The non-religious population is about 32.7 percent. Muslims are represented mainly by Turkic and Caucasus peoples.

EUROPE

Islam came to Europe with the Islamic advance from the Arabian peninsula through Palestine and North Africa into Spain before it was halted by Christian forces in France in A.D. 732. Later, Islam was to enter eastern Europe and become embedded in Albania and Yugoslavia in particular. After 1950, Muslims in greater numbers came into Europe. The growth in Europe has been rather rapid, largely because of immigration and the influx of refugees.

Islam is the second-largest religion in France and possibly England. There are large concentrations of Muslims in Germany, Albania, Belgium, Bulgaria, and in the formerly united Yugoslavia.

Developing Islamic nations have sent their citizens to Europe for education and training. Muslims have gravitated to Europe for work opportunities to send their earnings back home to their families. They have followed their former colonial rulers to their native cultures to study, work, and settle down in the familiar culture of the language learned and the habits ingrained.

There may be as many as 20 million Muslims in Europe. They have become citizens of their adopted countries. They have built mosques and started their own Qur'anic schools. They have become politically active. Whereas they could never have the freedoms of expression and the quality of life they desire in their Muslim homelands, they have relished their new lives in European culture.

Albania

Until the Communist takeover in 1944, 70 percent of the people professed Islam. In 1967 religion was abolished, and Muslim leadership was purged. In 1976 the constitution prohibited religious organizations. Recently, the government has been more open to religious expressions.[56]

Yugoslavia

Muslim populations in Yugoslavia include Albanians, Macedonians, Montenegrins, Serbs, and Turks. Until the early 1970s there was little Muslim interest in or display of a national consciousness. Muslims were spread widely over the country and the totalitarian government held all in check. Most Muslims lived in Bosnia-Herzegovina.

The Communist government in 1988 gave Muslims the status of a nation. Thus, Muslims began asserting themselves with their national interests, and polarization among them occurred, first in Bosnia-Herzegovina and then in Croatia. The rise of Islamic fundamentalism aided their newfound aspirations. During the 1990s there has been war between the Muslims in Bosnia and the Serbs.[57]

France

Islam is France's second-largest religion after Christianity. Waves of immigrants have come to France from their former colonies in North Africa. Ayatollah Khomeini lived in exile there in the final year before he returned to Iran to establish the Islamic Republic. Many French Muslims cannot vote because of their immigrant status. Many younger Muslims tend toward secularism.[58]

Germany

Many Muslim immigrants from Turkey and Yugoslavia find work in Germany to send monies back to their families. Slowly, Muslims are becoming a political force in Germany.[59]

England

The largest ethnic minority in Great Britain is comprised of Muslims. They have come from the Gulf states, from Saudi Arabia, from Iran, from Pakistan and India, from North Africa, from sub-Sahara Africa, and from other Muslim societies. Many receive vast sums of money from oil-rich Muslim nations of the Middle East for financing mosques and programs. The largest sect is Barelwi, which receives financing from Libya and Iraq. The minority sect is Peobandi, which receives funds from Saudi Arabia.

Muslims have established several organizations to coordinate their activities, including the United Kingdom Council of Imams and Mosques. They have even sought to form the basis for a political party. They have tried to establish Muslim schools similar to those of the Church of England and the Roman Catholic Church.

Muslims have objected to publication of Rushdie's *Satanic Verses*. It was in England that the manuscript of *Satanic Verses* was photocopied and sent around the world to alert Muslim peoples of its blasphemy. On December 2, 1989, eight thousand Muslims demonstrated against the book. It was the largest ethnic demonstration in England. Muslims burned a copy of the book in a large public gathering.[60]

10

MUSLIMS IN AMERICA: A GROWING RELIGION

INTRODUCTION

I slam has been a religion on the move since its inception in the Arabian peninsula in the seventh century. The Middle East is its heartland today with the special holy cities of Mecca, Medina, and Jerusalem, but it has significant numbers of followers in Asia, Africa, and Europe. Indonesia, far from the Middle East, has 170 million Muslims, making it the world's largest Muslim country. Europe may have as many as 20 million Muslims. There are about one billion Muslims around the globe, second only to the number of Christians. Thus, Islam has been a highly mobile and missionary religion.

North America is also experiencing the advance of Islam. The Muslim vision and mission of Islam are centered in a worldview that divides the world into two territories: the household of Islam and the household of the ignorant, the disobedient, and the non-Muslims.

Therefore, Muslims look at the world as a fertile ground either to restore or to plant the beliefs and the practices of Islam. Muslims, thus, are ones who submit to Allah (God). They build their mosques as places of worship and prostration before God, places where they gather to pray, to hear the Qur'an, and to experience community. They commit themselves to jihad, both a personal struggle to achieve peace with God and a community struggle to establish their Islam in societies where Muslims live.

Americans have come to know about Muslims and their religion primarily from the mass media's presentations over the last several decades. Words and phrases such as Islamic jihad (warfare), ayatollah (Muslim leader), and Hezbollah (Muslim terrorist group) account for much of the information Americans receive and upon which they form various images and stereotypes. The following questions will elicit data about Islam which it is hoped will be of assistance in understanding Islam's expressions in America:

- When did Muslims come to America?

- Why did they come?

- How many Muslims live in the United States?

- What are they doing?

- What is the difference between an ayatollah and a Saddam Hussein?

- Are there Shi'ites in America?

- Why do Muslim women wear a headcovering?

- Is there a difference in the Islam of a Malcolm X and a Louis Farrakhan?

- What kind of Muslim would blow up the Trade Center in New York City?

- What do Muslims have against Jews?

- Why do Muslims deny that Jesus Christ was crucified?

- Why are Muslims building hundreds of mosques across the United States?

Estimates of the number of Muslims in America vary from three to ten million. There are Muslim visitors who may stay shorter or longer periods; there are immigrants; there are American converts; and there are African-Americans who are raising their generations in Islam. The American Muslim Council (AMC) reported in the fall of 1992 that Muslims exceed 5.5 million. Some scholars predict that, with continuing growth, they will outnumber the Jews by 2015 to become the second-largest religion of America.

Signs of Islamic growth in America are more than just numbers. There are some six hundred mosques and Islamic centers, and others are under construction. New York has eighty-two, and California has fifty-nine.[1] Many include Qur'anic schools that teach Muslims to read the Qur'an in Arabic and to pray the formal prayers. Some Muslim communities have begun their own public schools.

In December 1993 the first Muslim chaplain in the United States armed forces was sworn in at the Pentagon. "Imam Abdul-Rasheed Muhammad, born a Baptist 40 years ago in Buffalo, stood at attention Friday as his wife pinned on his uniform the double bars signifying the rank of Army captain and a crescent-shaped chaplain's crest designed for Friday's ceremony."[2] His appointment as chaplain was a response to the expanding number of Muslims enlisting in the military or converting to Islam in the ranks. Imam Muhammad was assigned to Fort Bragg, North Carolina. He was the first non-Judeo-Christian to be appointed chaplain.

On February 6, 1992, Wallace Deen Muhammad was invited to offer the prayer to open the session of the United States Senate. He is an African-American whose father, Elijah Muhammad, a former Baptist, led the founding of the Nation of Islam in America in the 1930s. Louis Farrakhan succeeded Elijah Muhammad, and Wallace Deen Muhammad founded the American Muslim Mission. Before 1992, only clergy representing Protestantism, Roman Catholicism, and Judaism had offered prayers.

In early 1994 Louis Farrakhan was courted by congressional politicians and the NAACP, even though his close associate had created a furor over his addresses which denigrated both Jews and Christians. Farrakhan also associated with Jesse Jackson when Jackson ran for the presidency in 1988.

Thus, Islam has grown rapidly in the United States since World War II and is now highly visible, but its roots go back several centuries. This chapter explains American Muslims by examining immigrant Muslims, nativistic Muslims, small groups of Muslims, the Nation of Israel, the American Muslim Mission, and orthodox Islam in America. Immigrant Muslims may or may not be citizens of the United States, but they express their faith and practice in various institutional settings. Some have been in America long enough to have generations of Islam in their families. Nativistic Muslims are primarily those African-Americans who have converted to Islam and who may be followers of various sects within greater Islam.

IMMIGRANT MUSLIMS:
TRANSITIONAL MUSLIMS AND CITIZENS

Muslims may have entered the Americas as early as 1717. Scholars have noted records of Arabic-speaking slaves who refrained from eating pork. Perhaps a fifth of all slaves brought to the Americas from Africa in the eighteenth and nineteenth centuries were Muslims, but most of these converted to Christianity.

ISLAM AMONG AFRICAN-AMERICANS

1921	**AHMADIYYA MOVEMENT** in Islam
1925	**MOORISH TEMPLE OF SCIENCE** with Noble True Ali
1933	W. D. Fard's **Temple of Islam** in Detroit. Chief follower Elijah Muhammad; Fard disappears
1935-1975	**NATION OF ISLAM** with Elijah Muhammad headquartered in Chicago
1958	Khalifa Hamas Abdul breaks with Nation of Islam and establishes **Hanafi Center**
1964	Clarence 13 X expelled from Nation of Islam, establishes **Five Percent Nation Islam**
1964	Malcolm X and Wallace D. Muhammad expelled from Nation of Islam; Louis Farrakhan replaces Malcolm X as national spokesman
1964	Macolm X establishes **Muslim Mosque, Inc.**
1965	Malcolm X assassinated; Muslim Mosque, Inc. disintegrates
1969	Wallace Muhammad reinstated by Elijah his father
1970	**NUBIAN ISLAMIC HEBREWS** established by Muhammad Ahmed Abdullah

---

Newell S. Booth Jr. reports that some Muslims from the Middle East, the Balkans, or India came to the Americas throughout the colonial period and into the late nineteenth century. "They came as individuals, and there was no real Islamic presence. There is a reference to 'Moors' living in South Carolina in the 1790s. In the 1850s several Muslims came to the United States to help introduce camels in the Southwest. That project failed but a man called Hajj Ali stayed and became a pros-

1975	Elijah Muhammad dies
1975	Wallace D. Muhammad assumes leadership of Nation of Islam. Wallace changes name to Warith
1975	**BILALIAN COMMUNITY** replaces Nation of Islam under Warith D. Muhammad
1976	Silas Muhammad breaks with Warith D. Muhammad; Silas begins **Lost, Found Nation of Islam**
1977	**WORLD COMMUNITY OF ISLAM** in the West replaces Bilalian Community under Warith D. Muhammad
1977	Louis Farrakhan breaks with Warith D. Muhammad; re-establishes original **Nation of Islam** (Elijah Muhammad)
1978	John Muhammad breaks with Warith D. Muhammad; forms **Nation of Islam** under John Muhammad
1978	Caliph Emanuel Muhammad breaks with Warith D. Muhammad; forms **Nation of Islam** under his name
1980	**AMERICAN MUSLIM MISSION** replaces World Community of Islam in the West; Warith D. Muhammad leads in direction of Sunni Islam
1985	American Muslim Mission decentralized; Warith D. Muhammad presides over South Side Temple in Chicago

pector in California. The first known American convert to Islam was (Mohammed) Alexander Russel Webb, who, in 1887, encountered Islam in the Philippines, where he was consul."[3]

By 1875 Muslims had begun to migrate to the United States, especially from the area known today as Syria and Lebanon. The Ottoman Empire was beginning to crumble, and Muslims looked west for opportunities. Men came to find work, then brought over their families. Most were unskilled and uneducated people who found work in shops and factories, but some opened their own businesses.

Four Waves of Immigration

Haddad writes of four waves of Muslim immigrants.[4] The first wave came before World War I and was composed especially of Muslims departing the demise of the Ottoman Empire.

The second wave also came primarily from the Middle East and settled in the American Midwest. Booth reports that many were attracted to Detroit after Henry Ford offered workers five dollars a day. In 1919 they built a mosque in Highland Park. When Ford opened a plant in Dearborn, Muslims moved to South End. The Sunni Muslims built a mosque in 1936. The Shi'ite Muslims acquired a building as their center. "The South End of Dearborn developed into the only area in North America with the outward appearance of a Muslim town, complete with coffee houses, grocery stores, and restaurants catering to the Arab-Muslim population."[5] Other mosques were built in Cedar Rapids, Iowa, in 1934 and in Edmonton, Alberta in 1938. The second wave was halted by World War II.

The third wave came after the war and lasted until the mid-1960s. Islamic societies were in transition, especially in the Middle East and in Eastern Europe. Some fled to America from political oppression—Palestinians who became refugees with the establishment of the state of Israel, and Muslims fleeing revolutions in Egypt, Syria, Iraq, Yugoslavia, Albania, and the Soviet Union. Many were affluent and highly educated, and they settled in various cities.

The fourth wave began coming after 1967 and continues. President Johnson had introduced liberal immigration laws, and many Muslims who came were educated, Westernized, and fluent in English. They came from many countries. Developing Muslim countries sent their youth to American colleges and universities for education and training. American foreign aid and sales to these countries encouraged them to seek technical training in the United States. The developing oil wealth of these countries enabled them to send tens of thousands of youth to America to gain the skills needed for development. It is estimated that in the early 1960s there were a little over 100,000 Muslims in the United States among the immigrant population.

Some have estimated that the number of Muslim students in the United States may be as high as 750,000. It is known that in 1980, about the time of the Iranian revolution, there were over 50,000 Iranian students and thousands of Arab and Malaysian Muslim students. Wherever immigrants and students have gone, they have usually formed Muslim associations and built mosques or rented centers for their religious activities. Many immigrants have settled down and have become citizens.

Muslim Organizations

Immigrant American Muslims have formed various organizations to meet their community needs including some major voluntary national organizations.[6]

The *Federation of Islamic Associations* (FIA) was formed in 1954 primarily by Lebanese Americans "to promote and teach the spirit, ethics, philosophy, and culture of Islam." It publishes the *Muslim Star* and is vigilant against anti-Arab and anti-Muslim media.

The *Muslim World League* was founded in Mecca in 1962; it is an international organization with an office in New York City. The League has various programs, including the distribution of Islamic materials, financial assistance to Muslims and mosques, and assistance to Muslims in prison.

The *Muslim Student Association* (MSA) began in 1963 with the aid of Saudi Arabia to counter the Arab Student Organization supported by the Nasser regime of Egypt. It is considered the largest and most active Muslim group. In its monthly journal, *Islamic Horizons*, the stated purpose of MSA is "the advancement of unity among Muslims. . . conveying the message of Islam to non-Muslims and removing misconceptions about it and . . . working with Muslims and non-Muslims to address common concerns to improve the quality of life for all. . . " Many alumni of MSA who have settled in the United States have formed three professional organizations: the Islamic Medical Association, the Association of Muslim Social Scientists, and the Association of Muslim Scientists and Engineers.

The *Islamic Society of North America* (ISNA) was formed in 1982 to meet the needs of Muslim students and Muslim American citizens. One of its main objectives is "to advance the cause of Islam and Muslims in North America." The MSA now functions as an agency of ISNA.

The *Council of the Masajid* operates out of the Muslim World League office in New York City and promotes cooperation among mosques in the United States as well as internationally. It gives counsel on constructing and maintaining mosques.

The *American Muslim Council* (AMC) was formed in June 1990 with the purpose of "filling a void and providing an indispensable service to the American-Muslim community." It further states, "The American-Muslim community is not an alien community. It is part and parcel of mainstream America. The notion that the moral principles in the United States are based on the Judeo-Christian teachings is inaccurate. More precisely, it is based on the Judeo-Christian-Muslim teachings." The AMC calls on Muslims to join the council to "ensure that the American-Muslim community is recognized as a constructive force in the political life of this country." The AMC set up a Legal Department in 1992 to handle cases concerning issues such as child custody, religious rights, and hate crimes against Muslims. Its goal is to set up a Muslim American Bar Association.

NATIVISTIC ISLAM I: SMALL GROUPS

Noble Drew Ali and the Moorish Science Temple of America

In the early twentieth century some four million American blacks left the rural south, where they had been sharecroppers. They headed for cities of the northeast and midwest to find new work opportunities and to escape Jim Crow segregation. But many only exchanged southern rural poverty for northern urban poverty. They were to become the feeding ground for black militant and separatist movements. Mamiya and Lincoln write, "At stake in all black militant and separatist movements are two fundamental concepts or values: freedom and identity."[7]

Noble Drew Ali, born Timothy Drew in rural North Carolina in 1866, founded the Moorish Science Temple of America in 1913 in Newark, New Jersey. Little is known of his earlier life. Evidently he traveled extensively, including in the Middle East, where he was given the title "Ali" during a visit to Mecca. He was one of the migrants from the south to the north and became a street corner preacher in Newark.

Drew had his own ideas about the history and identity of blacks in America. He taught that blacks were not of Ethiopian origin but Moors with Islam as their religion, descendants of the Moabites of Canaan with their homeland in Morocco. Before the American Revolution blacks were free and flew their red Moorish flag. Continental Congress robbed them of their nationality and put them in slavery. Thus, during slavery they forgot their true religion of Islam and adopted Christianity. Drew asked President Woodrow Wilson to return the flag which he said had been kept in Independence Hall since 1776.

Drew's movement grew from its inception in 1913 in Newark, opening temples in Detroit, Chicago, Harlem, Pittsburgh, and southern cities. It is estimated that by the time of his death there were up to 30,000 followers. In 1928 the name of the organization was changed from the Moorish Temple of Science to the Moorish Science Temple of America. He published *The Holy Koran* in 1927, a sixty-page document of Moorish Science beliefs.[8]

Noble Drew Ali taught that Christianity opposed the interests of blacks. Jesus was a black man who was executed by Romans while attempting to redeem the black Moabites. Drew saw Islam as a way to unite blacks. Thus, his change of name and his counsel to his followers to be known as Moorish Americans were ways whereby he hoped to change their sense of identity and ethnic background.

Drew issued "nationality and identification cards" to his followers.

> Each card was stamped with the Islamic symbol of the star and crescent, accompanied by an image of clasped hand and a circumscribed 7. It announced that the bearer honored "all the Divine Prophets, Jesus, Mohammed, Buddha, and Confucius" and pronounced upon him the "blessings of the God of our Father Allah." The card identified its presenter as a "Muslim under the Divine Laws of the Holy Koran of Mecca, Love, Truth, Peace, Freedom, and Justice," and concluded with the assertion "I am a citizen of the United States." Each card was validated by the subscription "Noble Drew Ali, The Prophet."[9]

Difficulties developed as the movement grew. Each Thursday was the traditional day off from work for domestics. Males would wear red fezzes and on Thursdays the more aggressive ones would bump whites on the sidewalks and flash their identity cards as a sign of their new identity, status, and power. Racial confrontations occurred. There were clashes with police. Noble Drew Ali finally ordered the practice stopped.

Some leaders grew rich by selling relics, magical charms, Old Moorish Healing Oil, and Moorish Purifier Bath Compound. When Ali intervened to prevent this exploitation, his leadership was challenged and eventually he was killed. His death remains unresolved. Some of the circumstances leading to his death are as follows. While Ali was out of town, his business manager was killed during an internal struggle within the movement. Upon Ali's return, he was arrested and charged with murder and released on bond. Weeks later, he died mysteriously. Speculation was that he was beaten by police or by dissident followers.

At his death the movement split into several factions. Some temples still remain active, especially in Chicago. Friday is the sabbath for Moors. They pray three times daily toward Mecca. Jesus is prominent in their worship. Many Moors were early converts to the black Muslim movement.

The Ahmadiyya Community of North America

The Ahmadiyya Community of North America is named after its founder, Mirza Ghulam Ahmad, who was born in the Punjab of India. In India his early followers were known as the Qudianis. In 1889 he proclaimed himself as the Mahdi whom the Prophet Muhammad foretold would come toward the end times. The Ahmadis believe that Mirza Ghulam Ahmad received revelations from Allah; that he was given a prophet roll as the Mahdi; and that his mission was to purify Islam and to convert the world to Islam.

Dr. Mufti Muhammad Sadiq brought the Ahmadiyya movement to America in 1921. His original intention was to convert Islamic immigrants to the movement, but there was much success among African-Americans. Chicago became the official headquarters of the movement and the site of its first mosque. By 1940 membership in the United States had approached nearly ten thousand.

The Ahmadis' most important centers were in Chicago, Cleveland, Kansas City, Washington, and Pittsburgh. One of their major characteristics is the practice of *purda,* which requires the separation of women from men in public places and specifies modest dress for women, usually with a head covering and a face veil.

Orthodox Islam has long criticized the movement as heretical. The Muslim World League has warned against "the prodigal Qadiani sect which is considered a germ in the body of the Islamic *umma.*"[10] They caution that the movement is apostate because it teaches that their founder is a prophet, affirms belief in the second coming of Jesus, makes the birthplace of their founder a pilgrimage site, and declares that jihad is unIslamic. The admadis are to be treated as unbelievers.

The Ahmadiyya Movement continues to be very missionary in propagating what they consider to be true Islam. They publish and distribute their own version of *The Holy Qur'an.* They support missionaries and aggressively seek converts. Their numbers in the mid-1990s are over five thousand. Scholars note that the movement in its earlier days among the African-American community had a significant impact on the development of African-American Islam as a reaction to American racism.

Ansaru Allah

Isa Muhammad, an African-American, began the Ansaru Allah in 1970 with headquarters in Brooklyn. He was influenced by the black movements of his time, including the Moorish Science Temple and the Nation of Islam. However, he criticized their assumptions and roles as prophets and launched his own movement to correct and supersede those before him. He moved away from racist doctrines of the teaching of the Qur'an, projecting himself as the divinely inspired interpreter.

In 1988 Isa Muhammad retired as leader of the Ansaru Allah. He came out of retirement to write a book under the pseudonym Rev. Dwight York entitled *360 Questions to Ask the Orthodox Sunni Muslims*. He attacked the Sunni, especially those of Saudi Arabia, and called them liars. Sunni Muslims have attacked his authority as an interpreter of the Qur'an and rejected many of his doctrines, especially his teaching that women do not have spirits. It is estimated that there are several hundred Ansaru Allah followers in the United States.[11]

The Nubian Islamic Hebrews

The Nubian Islamic Hebrews movement was founded in New York City in 1970 by Muhammad Ahmed ibn Abd'ullah, a man of Sudanese background. His followers consider him the expected successor to the Prophet Muhammad. They believe that the Nubian (black) race goes back to Adam and Eve. Due to Noah's curse upon Canaan, Canaan's skin was turned pale. He became the father of all pale-skinned races. Some Nubians intermarried with the outcast children of Canaan. From these unions came the Chinese, East Indians, Eskimos, Indonesians, Japanese, Koreans, Malayans, Pakistanis, and Sicilians. All of these races are regarded as black, although they are mixed.

The Nubian Islamic Hebrews also believe that two other nations came from Abraham: the Ishmaelites and the Israelites. Just as the Israelites were held in Egyptian bondage, so were the Ishmaelites held in American bondage for over 400 years. From this bondage came the Nubians (blacks) of North America and the Caribbean. The American Nubians consider themselves Hebrews. Their theology is a mixture of Jewish, Christian, and Muslim beliefs. Their leader is Siddid al Imaan Isa al Haahi al Madhi, the great-grandson of the founder.

The Hanafi

Hamaas Abdul Khaalis (Ernest T. McGee) joined the Nation of Islam in 1950 in an attempt to bring it in line with orthodox Islam. In 1958 he broke with Elijah Muhammad and founded the Hanafi movement based in Washington, D.C. In 1973 five members of the Nation of Islam brutally murdered seven Hanafis, including five members of Khaalis' immediate family.

In 1977 Hanafis in Washington attempted to stop the screening of the movie "Mohammad Messenger of God" by seizing the District Building, the Islamic Center, and the B'nai B'rith Building. They killed one person and took one hundred hostages. Khaalis demanded that the killers of Malcolm X be turned over to him and that Wallace Deen Muhammad and the boxer Muhammad Ali be brought to him. Although none of these demands was met and the crisis was over in two days, it demonstrated an intense hostility by Khaalis toward the Nation of Islam with which he had been involved. He was sentenced to a prison term of 21 to 120 years. His movement continues to adhere to the basic tenets of Sunni Islam.

The Islamic Party of North America

The Islamic Party of North America was organized in 1972 in Washington, D.C. at the Masjid-al-Ummah. Their purpose is to propagate Islam through study of and commitment to it. They study both classical and contemporary writings on Islam. Their publication is *al-Islam,* which is distributed internationally. They provide many services, including counseling, programs for alleviating hunger, and the offering of properly slaughtered meat *(halal)* to Muslims at fair prices.

United Submitters International

Rashad Khalifa (1935–1990) founded the United Submitters International with headquarters in the mosque in Tucson, Arizona. Born in Egypt, he came to the United States in 1959, obtained a doctorate in biochemistry from the University of California at Riverside, married a native of Tucson, became a U.S. citizen, and presided over the Tucson mosque for eleven years.[12] On January 31, 1990, he was stabbed to death in the Tucson mosque. Haddad and Smith write,

> It is not difficult to imagine why Khalifa knew that he had enemies or why the preaching of his understanding of the message of Islam would be so difficult for many in the Islamic community to understand. Khalifa's explanation of the miracle of the Qur'an as proven by his computer analysis of its structure, and his con-

clusion that the key to the book is in the number nineteen, first excited and challenged the Muslim world. Many who were initially persuaded, however, became disenchanted (and some became outraged) when he used this analysis to announce the year of the End of the World, denounced two verses of the Qur'an as "satanic" in origin, severely attacked Muslims in general and Arab Muslims in particular for the idolatry of following the Hadith and the Sunna, and revealed his own designation as God's messenger in the line of Abraham and Muhammad.[13]

Khalifa's murderer was never apprehended. Since his death his followers in Tucson have continued their community and the dissemination of his teachings. They continue to promote the removal from Islam of teachings they consider impure.

The American Druze Society

The Druze had their beginnings in the eleventh century A.D. in Egypt with roots in Islam. Their founder was al-Hakim. They have kept their beliefs and practices in secret from the uninitiated and non-members. Druze first came to the United States from the Middle East in the 1870s. Today the American Druze Society has its headquarters in Troy, Michigan. It is estimated that there are five thousand Druze in North America.[14]

NATIVISTIC ISLAM II
ELIJAH MUHAMMAD, MALCOLM X, WALLACE MUHAMMAD, LOUIS FARRAKHAN, AMERICAN ORTHODOXY

In the 1930s a movement began in America that would eventually have wide appeal among African-Americans. Under the banner of Islam it developed a religious ideology based on racial purity and segregation, and it developed a personality cult in its leaders.

In 1865 slavery officially ended in the United States. The indigenous African-American church experienced great growth. As blacks sought to establish their identity and place in society, the black church addressed their needs. The African-American church associated with Pan-Africanism, becoming involved in cultural and economic development in the United States and in missions in Africa.

The theological direction of the church was changed by events both at home and abroad. As Reconstruction ended in the South, white supremacy fostered racist terrorism and intimidation among the slaves.

As the industrial revolution in the northern United States flourished and as a wave of European immigration came, African-Americans were eliminated from the skilled labor force. Colonialism in Africa stifled the African-American church's mission. The church thus abandoned its Pan-African approach in its ministry. This created a vacuum in dealing with dignity, African identity, and world significance.

Into this vacuum in the African-American experience stepped individuals and movements in competition with the church. They included W. E. B. Dubois with his emphasis upon education; Marcus Garvey and the United Negro Improvement Association; a few black Jewish sects; and several Islamic-oriented black nationalist sects.

The Nation of Islam, whose followers the media labeled as black Muslims, began in the 1930s with its leaders W. D. Fard and Elijah Muhammad. By the 1960s Malcolm X had achieved fame equal to that of Elijah Muhammad and was murdered in 1965. By the time of the death of Elijah Muhammad in 1975, the Nation of Islam had several million followers with many mosques and other religious institutions across America.

Elijah's son, Wallace Deen Muhammad, assumed the leadership of the Nation and transformed it into an orthodox Islamic institution named The American Muslim Mission. Whereas worldwide orthodox Islamic leaders considered the Nation of Islam under Elijah Muhammad a heresy, they welcomed the leadership of Wallace Muhammad into orthodoxy.

Not all followed Wallace into orthodoxy. Louis Farrakhan, who had been a close associate of Elijah Muhammad, assumed leadership of the Nation of Islam and continued the ways of his mentor. Farrakhan's Nation has been ostracized by worldwide Islam and by Wallace's movement. By the mid 1980s Wallace had closed The American Muslim Mission and had become a spokesman for mainline Islam in America.

Spokespersons for orthodox Islam in America include immigrants, naturalized immigrants, and American converts such as Wallace Deen Muhammad, who has had great appeal to the African-American community. The other major expression of Islam in America has been represented by the Nation of Islam under Louis Farrakhan.

NATION OF ISLAM WITH ELIJAH MUHAMMAD AND MALCOLM X

Origins

A man appeared in July 1930 on the streets of Detroit selling silk. He was to inspire the founding of the Nation of Islam. His name was Fard

Muhammad, although he had several other names: W. D. Fard, Wali Farrad, F. Muhammad Ali, and Mr. Farrad Muhammad. Little is known of his life. Some say he was of Arabic background. Fard Muhammad, the name used by leaders in the movement, told others that he was "the supreme leader of the universe" and that he had come to deliver "the lost-found nation of Islam." His early followers accepted his teachings that God is black, that the white man is the devil, and that the black race is supreme.

As the movement grew, organizations were formed. The University of Islam included elementary and secondary schools. The Training and General Civilization Class taught Muslim women sewing and cooking. The Fruit of Islam taught Muslim men the arts of defense and security. The name of the movement was changed from the Lost-Found Nation of Islam in the Wilderness of North America to the Nation of Islam.

Little is known of what happened to Fard Muhammad. Some say he was involved in a power struggle and disappeared. Some reports indicate he was jailed in Detroit in 1932, ordered out of Detroit in 1933, then jailed again in Chicago. Elijah Muhammad, who succeeded him, said that he disappeared on March 19, 1934, just as mysteriously as he had appeared in 1930.

Elijah Muhammad

In Detroit in August 1930, Elijah Muhammad met Fard Muhammad and began following his teachings. Elijah had been born Elijah Poole to a Baptist preacher in Georgia in 1897. He moved with his wife Clara to Detroit in 1923 to find work in factories. Upon meeting Fard he quickly rose to be Fard's chief Minister of Islam. He helped Fard build the first temple in Detroit as well as to launch other organizations. Upon Fard's disappearance, Elijah gained ascendancy and moved to Chicago to the temple he had established in 1932. There he set up his headquarters.

Eric Lincoln writes that "Elijah Muhammad was almost single-handedly responsible for the deification of Fard and for the perpetuation of his teachings in the early years after Fard disappeared."[15] Fard Muhammad thus became Allah in person, and Elijah became the Messenger or Prophet of Allah. This deification of Fard was celebrated annually in February on Fard's birthday and was called the Savior's Day Convention.

Elijah Muhammad continued to build his Nation of Islam on Fard's teachings. A basis for those teachings was a story known as "Yacub's History." This story taught that original humanity was the black race. Their religion was Islam, and they founded Mecca. A special tribe of blacks called Shabazz was created. This tribe was the ancestor of the Negroes in America.

Yacub was the God of 6,600 years ago. Being black, he decided to create a new race of white people. The white race was a race of devils with no black substance and no affinity with Islam. Yet, the white race was made the world's ruler. In good time God was to appear, destroy the white race, and restore the black race to its rightful leadership. Thus, God appeared as Fard Muhammad.

As the civil rights movement emerged in the 1950s, the Nation of Islam under Elijah Muhammad grew and established various institutions. The headquarters continued in Chicago. Reports vary as to the number of mosques and members. By 1959 estimates ranged from 70,000 to 250,000 as reported by the Nation of Islam. In 1962 the media speculated there were 10,000 core members while Elijah Muhammad claimed 500,000. Mosques had been built in the major cities, including Chicago, Detroit, New York, Atlanta, Miami, and Washington. Certainly, the Nation of Islam had good growth in the fifteen-year period between 1950 and 1965.

Malcolm X

Born Malcolm Little in Omaha, Nebraska, on May 19, 1925, Malcolm X was the son of a black Baptist minister who was inspired by the teachings of Marcus Garvey. His family was harassed by the Ku Klux Klan and his home was burned when he was four. An orphan at thirteen, he went to live with his sister in Boston. By 1942 he had moved to Harlem, where he engaged in drugs and prostitution.

After moving back to Boston, he was caught burglarizing homes. He served six years in prison. While in the Norfolk Prison Colony, he became a Muslim in 1948. Upon his release in 1952 he went to Detroit, where he found work and assumed the name Malcolm X. He was named assistant minister at Temple No. 1 in Detroit the summer of 1953.

Elijah appointed him minister at the prestigious Harlem Temple No. 7 in June 1954. He assisted in establishing temples in Boston, Philadelphia, Atlanta, and Los Angeles. In 1957 he founded and printed the weekly newspaper, *Muhammad Speaks*, which became nationally known. He married Betty X in 1958, and they had four daughters.

Elijah Muhammad had placed great confidence in Malcolm X as his chief spokesman, and Malcolm X had devoted himself in complete obedience and devotion to Elijah. During the 1950s, the press called him, "the angriest Negro in America." Later this would change.

The Nation of Islam

Malcolm X was the most vocal and visible advocate of Elijah's status as prophet and of his most unorthodox teachings of Islam. "What the Muslims Believe" according to Elijah Muhammad was a regular statement that appeared weekly in *Muhammad Speaks*. The main points were these:

1. One God—Allah

2. The Qur'an and the scriptures of all the prophets of God

3. The truth of the Bible, though it is now corrupted and must be reinterpreted

4. Allah's prophets and their scriptures

5. Mental resurrection

6. Judgment, which will take place first in America

7. Immediate separation of Negroes and white Americans

8. Justice, whether under God or not (respect U.S. laws)

9. Integration is hypocritical and deceptive

10. Muslims should not fight, especially for the United States

11. Muslim women should be respected and protected as others

12. Allah appeared in the Person of Master W. Fard Muhammad in July 1930

13. Fard was the Christian Messiah and the Muslim Mahdi

Alongside the column "What the Muslims Believe" appeared a description of "What the Muslims Want":

1. Freedom

2. Justice

3. Equality of opportunity

4. Separate state/territory

5. Release of all Muslims from prisons

6. An end to brutality and mob attacks against Negroes in the U.S.

7. Equal employment opportunities

8. Tax exemption for Negroes

9. Equal education (separate schools for boys to age sixteen and for girls to age eighteen, with girls guaranteed a college education)

10. No race mixing

Basic to the "beliefs" and "wants" is an ideology of racial superiority and separatism meshed with a veneer of Islamic terminology and practice. "Yacub's History" is still prominent: God is black; the black race is original and pure and superior; the white race is a grafted race, impure and of the devil; the white race is associated with Christianity and both have enslaved the black race and are therefore evil; Islam is the original and natural religion of the black race; Allah has condemned the white race and will restore the black race to its legitimate place.

A lifestyle was demanded and taught to the members of the Nation of Islam. Hygiene was essential: neat clothes, daily baths, teeth brushed, and hair combed. Prohibitions included alcohol, narcotics, tobacco, gambling, dancing, extramarital sex, lying, frivolous activities like movies, and the eating of pork. Members who disobeyed these injunctions were suspended until they redressed their ways.

Members of the Nation of Islam were encouraged to open businesses and to buy from one another. Small stores were begun, including grocery stores, dress shops, barber shops, meat markets, cleaners, and restaurants. The Nation purchased some farm land and apartment buildings.

The Nation offered some schooling in and around the mosques. Women and girls were taught and trained in domestic matters, and men were prepared to defend their families and themselves in times of struggle. Though the idea of a separate nation for blacks was voiced, there was little done to implement it.

Elijah and Malcolm X at Odds

In 1963 Elijah named Malcolm the first National Minister of the Nation. Yet there were tensions. Malcolm had become the foremost spokesman for the movement, speaking around the nation on university campuses and before television media. Southwick described him as a handsome, tall, red-haired, light-skinned man who relished speaking to the masses and who had the talent of a fine though devious lawyer.[16]

A power struggle began between other leaders and members of Elijah's family and Malcolm. The weekly *Muhammad Speaks* began giving him less press. Mass rallies were less promoted where he had spoken.

Malcolm visited Elijah's son Wallace, whom he trusted to discuss his own status and rumors about Elijah.

Malcolm had heard for years of Elijah's affairs with women and even his adultery, but he had refused to believe any of it. Tension developed when two former secretaries implicated Elijah Muhammad in paternity suits. His fears were given substance; Malcolm conversed with women who had brought paternity suits against Elijah. He also learned that his Messenger and Prophet considered Malcolm a dangerous threat.

Malcolm visited Elijah in Arizona in April 1963. In response to questions about the women's charges, Elijah is purported to have said, "When you read in the Bible how David took another man's wife, I'm David. . . You read about Lot, who went and laid up with his own daughter. I have fulfilled all those things."[17]

Soon after Malcolm's visit to Elijah, President Kennedy was assassinated. Elijah had ordered his ministers to refrain from commenting on the assassination. However, when Malcolm was asked his opinion of it, he commented that it was a case of "the chickens coming home to roost." This was the beginning of the end for Malcolm in the Nation of Islam. He was suspended from all his duties by Elijah. His world which revolved around Elijah Muhammad crumbled. He said, "And that was how, after twelve years of never thinking for as much as five minutes about myself, I became able finally to muster the nerve, and the strength, to start facing the facts, to think for myself."[18]

Malcolm left the Nation in early 1964 to form his own black nationalist group, the Muslim Mosque, Inc. For the first time he traveled to the Middle East, visiting Muslim peoples and making the pilgrimage (Hajj) to Mecca. He changed his name to El-Hajj Malik El Shabazz. He returned speaking about the brotherhood of the races he experienced on his pilgrimage and saying that the white man is not inherently evil but is a product of a racist society. He continued, however, to speak militantly about solving black problems in America. He criticized the moderate approach of Martin Luther King in the civil rights movement.

Late in 1964 Malcolm X formed the Organization of Afro-American Unity (OAAU), which would include blacks of all faiths, with the hope that it would fulfill what the Nation of Islam had only preached.[19] Malcolm's vision was that black/white brotherhood could not occur until black people first were united. After achieving this state of unity, black and white coalitions would be possible.

The breech between Malcolm X and Elijah Muhammad appeared irreversible. Elijah had prohibited Malcolm from participating in the civil rights movement as his chief associate, and Malcolm had described the Nation as too sectarian. Some speculate that Malcolm wanted to carry the militant rhetoric of the Nation into action. Lincoln has written, "Malcolm X was a true revolutionary. It is not inconceivable that, given the time, the means and the opportunity, Malcolm X would have committed an act of violence."[20]

The Nation of Islam vilified Malcolm while still praising Elijah. In many issues of *Muhammad Speaks,* Malcolm was called "the worst hypocrite Islam has produced," a traitor, "a cowardly hypocritical dog." Although Elijah never directly called Malcolm's name, he suggested that he was the chief hypocrite of all.

In issues of *Muhammad Speaks,* Elijah was called the word of God made flesh and blood, the Elijah of Malachi, and the Jesus of St. John. Elijah was said to be the end and Seal of the Prophets. These were the words and sentiments of the followers of Elijah which surely were not prohibited by Elijah himself. Malcolm X later admitted, "I believed in him not only as a leader in the ordinary human sense, but also I believed in him as a divine leader. I believed he had no human weaknesses or faults, and that, therefore, he could make no mistakes and that he could do no wrong."[21]

Death Takes Malcolm and Elijah

Malcolm became the target of many threats. An official in Temple No. 7 in Harlem was ordered to kill him, but he refused and defected to Malcolm. Malcolm's home was firebombed on February 14, 1965; he stated that the Nation of Islam or the Ku Klux Klan might be responsible. He said, "There is no group in the United States more capable to carry out this threat than the Black Muslims. I know because I taught them myself."[22]

On February 21, 1965, as he addressed about four hundred members of his Organization of Afro-American Unity in Harlem's Audubon Auditorium, Malcolm X was murdered. His three assassins were identified as former members of the Nation of Islam.

The true motives for his murder were never established at the trial and conviction of his assassins. Lincoln has written, "Always a popular folk hero for the angry black masses who shared with him the brutalities of American racism and the hope for a retributive Armageddon, in death Malcolm X loomed even larger than in life. A whole generation of African-American youth who were born too late to have savored his style or heard his rhetoric made him the guru of their aspirations. Popular culture celebrates his memory with Malcolm X clubs, Malcolm X caps, Malcolm X T-shirts. . . His autobiography was turned into a film. . . ."[23]

Rise of Wallace and Farrakhan

After Malcolm X's murder, Elijah named Louis Farrakhan as the National Representative of the Nation of Islam and as the minister of Temple No. 7 in Harlem. Farrakhan had been trained by Malcolm. Farrakhan had been a successful calypso singer in night clubs and was an accomplished violinist. Lincoln contrasts his style as a low-keyed, scholarly approach compared to the polemical way of Malcolm.[24] Farrakhan emerged as a popular representative for Elijah until Elijah's death in 1975.

Another close associate of Elijah Muhammad was Raymond Sharrieff, his son-in-law and the Supreme Captain of the Fruit of Islam. Sharrieff monitored any unorthodoxy among the members and provided security for Elijah and for the various temples around the nation. He also supervised the business affairs of the Nation, keeping a careful eye on them for Elijah Muhammad.

The Nation's holdings increased during the 1960s to include a 625-acre farm in Michigan, a 3,600-acre farm in Alabama, and a 4,350-acre farm in Georgia. But late in 1973 reports of difficulty surfaced. Poor management and cash-flow problems troubled this seventy-million-dollar empire. It obtained a loan of $3 million from Libya.

Factionalism and conflict had developed within the Nation and with other smaller groups outside of it. Tensions arose between the nation and the founder of the Hanafi Sunni Islamic movement. Hamaas Abdul Khaalis had been a member of the Nation but left it to form a Hanafi center in Harlem in 1968. He wrote letters to the ministers of the Nation criticizing Elijah Muhammad and inviting them to leave the Nation, rejecting Elijah and his teachings.

Internally, dissidents arose criticizing members of Elijah's family and other leaders for using monies of the Nation for personal gain, for wasting funds, and for failing to work on common concerns with other black groups. Raymond Sharrieff was wounded by gunfire in one incident. A shootout between some Muslims and police in Baton Rouge, Louisiana, left three blacks and two policemen dead. These events happened when some dissidents of the Nation went across the country in an attempt to recruit followers.

By late 1973, Elijah Muhammad became ill and with his wife's death he further withdrew. Frequently, his articles in *Muhammad Speaks* were reprints. The newspaper reported his death on February 25, 1975. There was some confusion over his death, because *Muhammad Speaks* ran a headline stating: "He Lives On!" Some of the members believed that he had not died and would appear at the Savior's Day Convention the next day.

Elijah had died. Some said that his latter years witnessed a certain mellowing in his teachings. *Time* reported that he had kept busy investing money rather than "inflaming Muslim passions." His 1974 Savior's Day address lacked the usual mention of whites as devils, though he did say that blacks were divine.

Elijah had ruled over the Nation of Islam since 1934, some forty-one years. The teachings and practices of Islam were a mere cover for his racial ideology. Worldwide Islam did not give him any recognition as a leader, and in fact condemned him and considered his movement a heresy. He had contributed to the massing of tens of thousands of African-Americans together for a fresh identity and a continuing hope for self-esteem and self-improvement.

However, he was to leave a legacy of deception, corruption, and financial chaos. His son, Wallace, was to succeed him and transform the Nation of Islam into a new entity. His chief associate, Louis Farrakhan, was to assemble his hardcore followers and to continue the legacy of Elijah Muhammad as the Nation of Islam.

THE AMERICAN MUSLIM MISSION AND WALLACE DEEN MUHAMMAD

Wallace Deen Muhammad

Upon his father's death, Wallace D. Muhammad became the leader of the Nation of Islam. He spoke at the Savior's Day Convention in Chicago on February 26, 1975. Elijah's approval of his successorship is assumed, although the process in the succession immediately after Elijah's death is unclear.

Wallace tells that, when his mother was pregnant with him, Fard Muhammad wrote his name Wallace with chalk on the door. He also wrote, "My personal answer would be it was God's intention. It was God's plan. But I have also heard my Father Himself say that when I was born or I was conceived in my mother, He had been born as the Servant, the Messenger of God, who manifested Himself with W. F. Muhammad; and by me being born at the time when He was in contact with His Saviour, the God in Person, helped to form me, not only as child of his loins, but a child for the Mission."[25]

Wallace was born in Hamtramyck, Michigan, on October 30, 1933. He went to high school in Chicago, which was the headquarters of the Nation of Islam. He held various jobs while serving in the Fruit of Islam. From 1958 until 1960 he was the minister of the Philadelphia temple, which Malcolm X had helped found. Married three times, twice to the same wife, he had five children when he assumed leadership of the Nation. He was imprisoned from October 1961 to January 1963 for refusing to report to the draft.

Wallace was not always in favor with his father. He was suspended from the Nation twice and readmitted. In 1964 he accused his father of immorality and deception and said that the movement was politically ineffective. Nevertheless, at his ascension as leader, he was praised by many of the ministers of the temples and also by Raymond Sharrieff his brother-in-law and Captain of the Fruit of Islam, by boxer Muhamad Ali and by Louis Farrakhan, the National Representative of the Nation and minister of Temple No. 7 in Harlem.

Changes in the Nation of Islam

Wallace Deen Muhammad had a vision to reinterpret his father's teachings and to bring the Nation in line with worldwide orthodox Islam. In an early address Wallace indicated that his leadership would not solely emphasize color and racism. He desired to present the "Divine mind and the Divine will." He referred to his father's work as the First Resurrection, dealing with mental, moral, and physical renewal. His own work was to be the Second Resurrection, with particular emphasis on the spiritual. As he asserted his leadership, some wanted to divinize him while others wanted more democracy in decision making and operations of the Nation.

Gradually, Wallace established his own teachings and organizational changes. He was careful to honor the memory of the Nation's beginning with Fard Muhammad and his father Elijah, but he was committed to alter the Nation radically. He thought of God as the Divine Mind and humanity as a part of that Mind. He no longer considered Fard Muhammad to be God, nor God to be black.

Wallace gave increasing attention to the concepts of Islam. He wrote that blacks must use their intelligence to come into the full light of al-Islam.[26] The Divine Mind becomes known to man in the Qur'an. Correct knowledge aids man to advance to the spiritual level of existence.

The notion of the white race as the devil was changed to a mental perspective, a falsehood. Thus, evil was in the mind. Wallace believed Christianity and the Church gave birth to the white devil mentality and became the agents which spread it around the world. He said that the Church presented Christ on the cross as a white god. The Church led black people to worship a white god and thus kept them in oppression. Wallace kept only the parts of Christianity and the Church which he, himself, could properly interpret from the Bible. He affirmed the prophethood of Jesus as taught by Islam. Wallace considered himself a *mujeddid,* that is, a reviver/restorer of religion.

By October 1975, members began calling themselves Bilalian Muslims. Bilal was an Ethiopian slave who became the muezzin of Prophet Muhammad and rose to considerable status after the Prophet's death.

Muhammad Speaks was changed to *Bilalian News.* These name changes pointed the Nation to its roots in Africa, the Middle East, and Islam. By late 1976 the Nation of Islam's name had been changed to the World Community of Islam in the West (WCIW). The WCIW's mission now was the restoration of pure Islam, while returning to the Qur'an for truth. The WCIW also would work with others for the well-being of all people.

The financial situation of the Nation was already in jeopardy when Wallace assumed leadership—deficits in business enterprises; farms in arrears, long-term loans of $9.5 million. Old businesses were sold. Legal fees of Muslim criminals were no longer paid. Ministers of the temples were placed on fixed salaries. By 1978 Wallace was praised as saving the Nation from bankruptcy.

Staff personnel and ministers whom Wallace distrusted were replaced or transferred. Louis Farrakhan was moved from the Harlem temple to a temple in Chicago, some say so that Wallace could keep a closer eye on him. By 1978 Farrakhan had left the WCIW to rebuild the former Nation of Islam upon the teachings of Elijah Muhammad.

Wallace initiated changes in titles, roles, and administrative functions. Rather than Chief Minister, Wallace became the Chief Imam. The minister of each temple became an imam. This change represented a move from non-Islamic to Islamic terms. Wallace desired to relinquish his administrative duties and concentrate on spiritual responsibilities.

A Council of Imams was formed in 1978, composed of six imams of temples who would manage the affairs of WCIW. They represented temples in Chicago, Washington, New York City, Atlanta, Houston, and Los Angeles. The Council was appointed by Wallace and not elected, demonstrating that Wallace was consolidating power within his leadership.

Islamic institutions and practices received attention. Wallace stopped using the phrase "Peace be upon Him" after the utterance of his father's name. The phrase in traditional Islam was only used for the bona fide prophets of orthodox Islam. Whereas his father had required members to fast during the month of December, Wallace changed fasting to the month of Ramadan. Unlike his father, he encouraged his members to take the pilgrimage (Hajj) and began planning trips with the assistance of the Muslim World League.

Temples were renamed mosques (*maesjid* singular; *masajid* plural); chairs were removed and members sat on the floors. Wallace taught the members the correct form of prayer, and the Arabic language was taught for use in prayer. By the end of 1978 the WCIW was moving toward a more acceptable expression of Islam in theology and practice.

In the early years of Wallace's leadership there was consistent growth in numbers, mosques, and programs. By late 1978 there were 142 mosques in the United States. Estimates of members ranged from 25,000 by police accounts to 500,000 by the WCIW and between 250,000 to 300,000 by other sources.[27]

Two of the primary institutions under Elijah were changed. The Fruit of Islam was disbanded. The University of Islam continued with the name changed to Sister Clara Muhammad Elementary and Secondary Schools. Clara was Elijah's wife. Each mosque became the center of religious and social life for members.

Wallace formed the Committee to Remove All Images of the Divine (CRAID), an attempt to discourage display of pictures and crosses. New World Patriotism Day was begun to encourage citizenry in the political process of both local and national politics. Wallace even waved an American flag at the first occasion in 1977.

Wallace's movement became increasingly Americanized in the early 1980s. The American flag appeared alongside the WCIW in the *Bilalian News*. Children in the Sister Clara schools recited the pledge to the American flag each day. Wallace praised the efforts and progress made in civil rights and encouraged the members to become involved.

American Muslim Mission

In April 1980 the World Community of Islam in the West changed its name to the American Muslim Mission. In November 1981 the *Bilalian News* became the *World Muslim News*. Circulation was between 40,000 and 50,000. The American and WCIW flags were moved from the front page to the top of Wallace's column. By May 1982 *World Muslim News* had been changed to *A.M. Journal*. The flags reappeared on the front page of the *A.M. Journal*. Thus, in the early 1980s there were attempts to portray Wallace and his movement in both universalistic and in local terms with words in the titles of journals and organization of 'World' and 'American.'

The Committee to Remove All Images of the Divine was activated under the American Muslim Mission. From meetings in local mosques to conventions with up to 10,000 present, efforts were made to promote the removal of all divine images from all houses of worship, specifically pictures and statues of Jesus from churches. Wallace said that the pictures of a white Jesus were deceiving black Americans into believing they were inferior to white Americans as they had to look at a white divine image.

In May 1981 the American Muslim Mission (AMM) announced that the Illinois state board of education had approved a teacher training college to be launched by AMM; Imam Matthew Hamidullah was named president. Hamidullah was a native of North Carolina and at the time was Resident Imam of the Elijah Muhammad Maesjid in Chicago. The basic purpose of the school was to train teachers for the Sister Clara Muhammad Schools. It was announced that the college would open a campus in Sedelia, North Carolina, just outside Greensboro, after the national boarding high school was begun there. Its name would be the American Muslim Mission Teachers College.

Classes did begin on the Sedalia campus, but a shortage of funds soon forced its closing. There had been conflict in the leadership of AMM in operating and raising funds for the school and the property. Hamidullah resigned. Wallace D. Muhammad criticized both Hamidullah and the Council of Imams over the handling of the school and its closure. It had become evident that there were leadership problems within AMM including Wallace.[28]

Wallace changed his name in 1980 to Warith, which means "inheritor." Thereafter, he was known as W. Deen Muhammad; he insisted that Warith was a name difficult for non-Muslims to pronounce. He was also called Imam and President. His writings included *As the Light Shineth from the East* and *Prayer and al-Islam*. Wallace appeared to have high self-esteem. Often it appeared that he equated himself with Jesus. "Not even the tomb could keep him down. Not even 2,000 years of being absent from the world could hold him back. Here he is. Take a look at him." This he said as an audience roared its approval.[29]

He spoke of himself as being in the line of prophets and also among the great civil rights leaders. He thought that he combined the best of his father Elijah Muhammad and Martin Luther King. His followers also looked upon him as a special leader. He was hailed as the greatest leader since the Prophet Muhammad. An oath of allegiance was first given to him and then to the program. Members were encouraged to read what he had written, to listen to his tapes, and to be taught his teachings concerning the Qur'an.

Troubles in the American Muslim Mission

By the middle of 1982 Wallace appeared to make a significant change in his role as leader of AMM. He announced that he would no longer have ties with the Council of Imams and that he would have no responsibility for any mosque or for the newspaper. The Council of Imams had been appointed by Wallace and oversaw the general administrative functions of AMM. The imams were to be the moral examples of the community. They were to abstain from alcoholic beverages and should not be in public alone with a woman except their wives. They were to respect each other's territory and be able to recite the Qur'an in times of prayer and in sermons.

In the summer of 1982 the first regional imam was voted out of office by the Council. Imam Adulalim Shabazz of Detroit was dismissed from his mosque and from his seat on the Council of Imams. The cited reasons were that he had disobeyed authorities and had not provided acceptable leadership. He had been critical of Warith's decisions. Shabazz wrote to Warith D. Muhammad, inferring basically that what had been heralded as a democracy within AMM was in reality a dictatorship led by Warith.

Later, Imam Khalil Abdel Alim, resident imam of the Washington, D.C. mosque and regional imam of the Southeastern United States who served on the Council of Imams, was asked to resign by the Council. He had evidently questioned a decision by Warith. Thus, when one questioned the authority of Warith, it became clear there was no room for disagreement or for another opinion. Shabazz and Alim signaled a wider conflict with the AMM.

In 1983 Warith spoke out more often about the imams. He said that most of them were unqualified. In September 1983 the editor of *A.M. Journal* openly sided with Warith against certain dissensions within the ranks of the imams. Communication broke down between the imams and Warith, and they refused to attend a session which Warith requested.

Warith was quoted as saying that some of the imams were Christians, some atheists, and some agents. He brought three Muslims before the people in the Elijah Muhammad Masjid in Chicago in November 1983 to answer charges he had made against them. One was the former imam of the masjid in which they met. Speculation about the charges was that the three had some involvement with Louis Farrakhan. They were relieved of their responsibilities in AMM.

Farrakhan was seen as fomenting trouble within the AMM. Warith was quoted as saying, "You know what (Minister Louis) Farrakhan will not admit is because he wants to get a following that will give him dollars like he used to get and won't demand any moral justice, any moral purity, and won't demand that he take an intelligent stand on truth whether it be against black consciousness or whether it be against black nationalism. He doesn't have that in him. He didn't come to Allah for pure Quran. He didn't come to Allah for a Book that has no crookedness in it. He came to Allah for the promise of plenty of money, good homes, and friendships in all walks of life."[30]

Besides the internal dissension among the imams toward Warith and besides the conflict with Louis Farrakhan, what broke the back of the AMM and caused Warith's withdrawal and its collapse may have been the Estate Trial. At issue was whether the money collected by Elijah Muhammad belonged to his estate or to the organization. Elijah had no will at death. The Illinois inheritance laws were changed soon after his death so that children born outside of legal marriage might be considered heirs of the estate. Some of Elijah's illegitimate children brought suit, and the AMM was brought into court.

Millions of dollars were awarded to family members. Legal fees for the AMM were exorbitant. It appeared that the AMM would have to sell off its properties. Bankruptcy seemed a possibility.

In June 1983 Warith gave a speech in Harlem in which he said, "Pretty soon, in order to stay in this community, with the benefit of attending our community meetings and identifying with us as a member, you're going to have to be a producer! If you aren't giving in Zakat, you're going to have to give at least five hours work. You're going to have to give money or you're going to have to give your time—you're going to have to give labor. Money, labor, and open support for what I represent. That's our American right, and we're going to take every bit of it."[31]

Demise of the American Muslim Mission

The AMM National Convention soon followed in Georgia with 12,000 in attendance. Conflict between Warith and other leaders continued. In November a statement appeared in the *A.M. Journal*: "Imam W. Deen Muhammad is no more the leader for the masajid and centers throughout the United States. Imam Muhammad is only responsible for the masjid in Chicago where he is Resident Imam."[32] Warith also announced the formation of the Muslim American Community Assistance Fund. He said that monies given to this fund would be used to spread Islam in the United States. Thus, Warith had set the stage for the disintegration of the AMM. He moved from its Chicago headquarters to California. In 1985 the movement was officially integrated into the general Muslim community in the United States. Its members are now known simply as Muslims.[33] Warith has continued to represent an Islamic perspective akin to orthodox Islam and in contrast to that of Louis Farrakhan in the Nation of Islam.

Eric Lincoln has written, "By 1985 the transition from a cosmocentric, race-based community of believers in search of Armageddon to the anonymity of unchallenged inclusion in one of the world's great spiritual communions had been substantially completed. . . . Having set the parameters and served as exemplar for the spiritual metamorphosis of his once Lost-Found Nation, Warith Deen Muhammad was ready for recognition and reassignment."[34] Muslim leaders, especially of the Middle East, turned to him as the titular head of Muslim interests in the United States. He lectured at universities and churches and synagogues. On February 5, 1992 he addressed military leaders at the Pentagon. The next day he gave the invocation on the floor of the United States Senate, praying to Allah "the Most Merciful Benefactor, the Merciful Redeemer" on behalf of the President of the United States and every member of Congress. Imam Muhammad was welcomed by international Islam and by the political leaders of the United States. He had forged a new place within religious pluralism and had gained respect and acceptance which he never had in the old Nation of Islam.

THE NATION OF ISLAM AND LOUIS FARRAKHAN

Louis Farrakhan: Life with Elijah

Louis Farrakhan became prominent within the Nation of Islam under the leadership of Elijah Muhammad during the 1960s and 1970s. After Elijah's death in 1975, he left the movement led by Elijah's son, Wallace Muhammad, whom he considered a liberal reformer, to continue the Nation and the basic teachings of Elijah his mentor.

Born in the Bronx on May 11, 1933, Louis Eugene Farrakhan grew up in Boston. He was active in the Episcopal Church and an honor student and track standout at Boston English High School. He attended Winston-Salem Teachers College in North Carolina for two years. He became a singer/musician and married Betsy Wolcott. In 1955, playing for a nightclub engagement, he was invited to hear Elijah Muhammad, leader of the Nation of Islam.[35]

After joining the Nation, Farrakhan changed his name to Louis X. He became the chief of the Fruit of Islam, the Nation's security force, in Boston and later head of the temple there. When Malcolm X was murdered in Harlem in 1965, Elijah Muhammad named Farrakhan to succeed Malcolm as National Representative of the Nation of Islam and to be the minister of Malcolm X's former mosque, Temple No. 7 in Harlem. Lincoln has written that the choice of Farrakhan was an attempt to diminish the influence which Malcolm X had.[36] Farrakhan represented Elijah throughout the Nation of Islam until Elijah's death in 1975.

Separation from Wallace

Immediately after the death of Elijah Muhammad, in February 1975, Farrakhan receded into the background. There has been speculation that he was the one who was supposed to succeed his leader and mentor. Instead Elijah's son Wallace assumed the mantel, but Farrakhan soon emerged as a popular spokesman for the Nation. As Wallace took control of the Nation, he reassigned Farrakhan from Harlem to the temple in Chicago. Some have viewed this move as a way Wallace could keep the reigns on Farrakhan, who would be nearby.

In mid-1975 Farrakhan denied rumors of a power struggle within the Nation. He continued to represent Wallace across the country. But by 1977 Farrakhan's articles had disappeared from the *Bilalian News*.

Farrakhan reappeared in the press in March 1978 announcing plans "to rebuild the Nation of Islam in line with the doctrine of the late Elijah Muhammad."[37] He rejected Wallace's new approach, including his encouraging blacks to work with whites.

Wallace Muhammad stated that Farrakhan left because he "has not understood and accepted the psychology and gradualism for the total religious transformation of the Lost-Found Nation of Islam in America."[38] Evidently there had been friction between Wallace and Farrakhan, or at least Farrakhan felt that Wallace no longer appreciated and supported him. Wallace contended that he offered the temple in Harlem back to Farrakhan, but Farrakhan never responded.

From 1979 to 1983 Farrakhan was the object of much criticism by Wallace and his leaders. Perhaps Farrakhan with his own new movement was causing friction among his former colleagues. He was called many names including "a voice of Satan." One of the key imams of Wallace wrote, "Farrakhan, so-called orthodoxism, blackness, following the Honorable Elijah Muhammad, materialism, jealousy, envy, personality cult worship, education elitism, suspicion, and distrust of leadership, all are voices of Satan."[39]

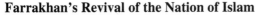
Farrakhan's Revival of the Nation of Islam

The *A.M. Journal* in early 1983 carried an article presenting Farrakhan's objections against Wallace and the American Muslim Mission:

1. Confusion. "That once alive quickened mind, that inspired a whole people with its discipline, hard work, cleanliness, courtesy, righteousness and fearlessness, is now confused."

2. That "all work in the way of self-independence has ceased."

3. That the feet of the former NOI under the leadership of Imam Warith Deen Muhammad are "nailed to the acceptance of the status quo. The feet that walked after the Law of God are nailed to the acceptance of the sport and play of this world's life."

4. That the movement led by Imam Warith Deen Muhammad represents death, and that the old Nation of Islam had to die so that it could be resurrected under Farrakhan's leadership.

5. That there is no "honor for the father (Elijah Muhammad) in his own house."

6. That the Honorable Elijah Muhammad was "made to appear a weak, immoral man, a trickster, guilty of misrepresenting himself, God and the Truth, and even a devil."

7. That Imam Muhammad hates his father.[40]

Smith writes, "While some distortion may have resulted from the *A. M. Journal's* presentation of Farrakhan's position, his perspective on the changes brought about by Warith was clear. They had undermined the stability of the Nation of Islam, weakened its effectiveness, and disgraced its foremost leader."[41]

Farrakhan set out to rebuild the Nation of Islam on the foundations laid by Elijah Muhammad. Teachings on the nature of God, Yacub, and the white man remained intact. The statements under Elijah, "What the Muslims believe" and "What the Muslims want," have been preserved. The newspaper *The Final Call* was resurrected with the same title as under Elijah in 1933.[42]

Many members of the movement under Elijah and Wallace who had fallen away returned to Farrakhan. Some brought new recruits. It is estimated that there are between 70,000 and 100,000 followers of Farrakhan's Nation of Islam. He has remained popular among African-American students.

Controversy has followed him.

The stabilization of the new Nation of Islam coincided with the emergence of Jesse Louis Jackson and Operation PUSH (People United to Save Humanity) into the national spotlight. Farrakhan, becoming a strong supporter of Jackson, was soon thrust into the spotlight as he moved around the country and made several controversial remarks. During the 1984 presidential campaign he became embroiled in Jackson's difficulties with the Jewish community. During a radio speech in March he called Hitler a 'great man' and was vilified in the press as an anti-Semite. The Anti-Defamation League published a monograph attacking him. Jackson tried to distance himself from Farrakhan's remarks but refused to separate himself from the Muslim leader.[43]

Farrakhan has continued to build his Nation. There are over eighty mosques. He purchased the showpiece mosque of Elijah's regime in Chicago, refurbished it as his headquarters, and named it Maryam Mosque after the mother of Jesus. In an unprecedented move, he did what no other Muslim group dared: he appointed Sister Ava Muhammad, a New York attorney, to be a minister in the Nation of Islam. He has gained much attention for his clean-up campaigns in black neighborhoods, and he has used his Fruit of Islam security to patrol drug-infested areas of inner cities.

Lincoln writes, "Farrakhan has done more than keep the faith: he has enlarged and enhanced it with a new vision and new perspectives."[44] His recent book *A Torchlight for America* and weekly addresses that appear in his newspaper *The Final Call* depict his teachings. *The Final Call* claims to have the largest circulation of any black periodical in the United States.

Farrakhan appeared on the cover of *Time* (February 28, 1994), and the issue included two cover stories. In citing problems Farrakhan has caused many groups in America, it continued,

> Above all, he is a problem for an America that is increasingly multiracial and multicultural and is consequently in growing need of tolerance and mutual respect. His success underscores two ugly truths of American life. A great many black Americans view their white fellow citizens with anger. And a great many white Americans view their black fellow citizens with fear. Farrakhan's call for separatism and economic "reparations" and his assertion of black racial superiority win respect

from millions of blacks, even among those who wish he would stop calling Jews "bloodsuckers." While most whites are apt to think his abusive rhetoric should be ignored if not silenced, many blacks think he is saying some things America ought to hear.[45]

"A *Time*/CNN poll of 504 African-Americans by Yankelovich Partners last week found 73 percent of those surveyed were familiar with him. . . and two-thirds of those familiar with Farrakhan viewed him favorably. Some 62 percent of those familiar with him said he was good for the black community; 63 percent said he speaks the truth; and 67 percent said he is an effective leader."[46]

The Million Man March

Louis Farrakhan called for a million black men to march in Washington, D.C. on October 16, 1995. The purpose of the march was to inspire a moral and spiritual rebirth among African-American men. Farrakhan's fellow organizer was Benjamin Chavis, former N.A.A.C.P. executive director who was stripped of that title in 1994 for alleged misuse of funds and sexual harassment.

Farrakhan stressed that he was not "asking anyone to march under the Islamic banner. "Whoever will, let him come."" However, his chief of staff said the march was a handy gauge of Farrakhan's popularity. All the marchers "are coming because they support Louis Farrakhan. He's become a major, major factor in this country."[47]

The march occurred on October 16. Estimates of the numbers of participants varied from 400,000 to 860,000. Speakers on the platform located on the Mall between the Washington Monument and the Capitol included Jesse Jackson, Benjamin Chavis, and Louis Farrakhan. Farrakhan spoke for over two hours. He asked the marchers to pledge themselves to self-reliance and to respect for women. He promised to launch a nationwide voter registration drive to make African-Americans into a "third political power."[48]

Responses to Farrakhan's leadership in the march were varied. Laura Washington, African-American editor and publisher of the Chicago-based *Reporter,* a newsletter on race relations and poverty issues, wrote, "I abhor his racist and bigoted statements. They are counterproductive and unfair. But it is important for whites not to put too much stock in what he says." He is "the leader of a black fascist sect. His people are disciplined, orderly, militant, reminiscent of the Brownshirts. But they are not Hitler Youth taking over society. He may be a hysterical preacher of hate, but he is not about to take control of anything. He is not about to march into your neighborhood."[49]

New York civil rights activist Michael Mayers, an African-American, said about Farrakhan's history and the march, "It is racist, it is sexist, it's regressive, it's divisive. . . . All the reasons for opposing the march can be summed up in two words, Louis Farrakhan. Louis Farrakhan is the apostle of black racism and antisemitism."[50]

Marchers spoke affirmatively of the goals of the march. They saw Farrakhan as an inspirational African-American leader rather than as the head of the Nation of Islam. *Time* observed that "by speaking to the deepest needs of African-Americans at a time when other black leaders have been conspicuously silent, Farrakhan has injected himself into the very heart of the ongoing racial debate. . . . He has forced every thinking black man in America to make a painstaking decision about his march. He was, finally, where he wanted to be—on everyone's mind, whether they like it or not."[51]

The Million Man March was the vision of Louis Farrakhan. He was the chief organizer. He was the main platform speaker. He gained the major exposure in the mass media with articles featuring his picture in the leading newspapers and magazines and with appearances on television talk shows. His security guards, the Fruit of Islam, had been seen in the mass media providing protection for the attorneys of O. J. Simpson in the trial in Los Angeles. They were also conspicuous in the crowds and on the platform at the march on the mall.

In an interview given to *Newsweek,* Farrakhan spoke on a number of issues. He said there was little moral outrage voiced at the plight of the black community in America, particularly against the circumstances of the black male. He said that whites demonize blacks. On the day of the march he pointed out there were no arrests, no drunkenness; there was "only the utmost courtesy between brother and brother." On politics in 1996 he said there would be no party loyalty among blacks. "We intend to create a third force or a third power out of Republicans, Democrats and independents."[52]

Farrakhan had been quoted earlier as referring to Jews as "bloodsuckers." He replied that all he had done was explain the function of a leech. A leech takes but it never gives anything to what it takes. "I mentioned that back in the '40s and '50s some of the merchants who were Jewish owned the tenement buildings, the businesses, the pawnshops, and they drew from the black community. And later they were replaced by Palestinians and other Arab merchants, then by Vietnamese and Koreans.

These are persons that generally take from the community but don't give back. I said there are even some blacks who do the same thing."[53]

Farrakhan said of himself that he was "a nightmare" to some but "a dream come true" to others.[54] National television journalist Ted Koppel said that Farrakhan may have to be called one of the most influential leaders in black America. After the march some U.S. congressmen called for a presidential commission on race relations.

Farrakhan and his Nation of Islam have great appeal despite his theology and beyond it. He has identified important issues and found support in many communities. He has attacked the welfare system, stating that it subsidizes single women to have babies. He has criticized the government for spending more money on prisons than on education.

The Nation of Islam runs counseling programs for drug addicts, alcoholics, and street gang members. His young men in the Fruit of Islam have patrolled the streets of ghettos to ward off drug sellers and users. Louis Farrakhan and the Nation of Islam have offered African-Americans an alternative for religious and community life. Three events in 1995 thrust him into the national spotlight: (1) the arrest of Qubilah Shabazz, daughter of Malcolm X, for plotting to kill Farrakhan in retaliation for what she believed was his role in her father's death; (2) the deployment of the Fruit of Islam to provide security for the attorneys of O. J. Simpson in Los Angeles; (3) the Million Man March.

The Million Man March in Washington has presented another platform for Louis Farrakhan and the Nation of Israel to demonstrate their presence in American society and to align themselves with the concerns of African-Americans. The future will reveal the significance of his ideas and teachings on race, black separatism, and anti-Semitism. An interesting observation will be how, if at all, his ideas will continue to follow those of Elijah Muhammad, founder of the Nation of Islam and Farrakhan's hero.

ORTHODOX ISLAM IN AMERICA

Peoples, Mosques, and Associations

Muslims in America are both ethnically and theologically diverse. They are immigrants, visitors, students, African-Americans, citizens, Sunnis, Shi'ites, Sufis, and a variety of other sectarian types. American Muslims are estimated to be 42 percent African-American; 24.4 percent Asian Indian; 12.4 percent Arab; 5.2 percent African; 3.6 percent Persian; 2.4 percent Turk; 2 percent South Asian; 1.6 percent American white; and 5.6 percent other. They live from coast to coast although they have larger concentrations in twenty-two major U.S. cities. There are hundreds of mosques and Islamic centers as well as Muslim organizations.

Mosques vary in shapes and sizes. The Islamic Center of Washington, D.C., is located among the embassies on Massachusetts Avenue and has traditional Middle Eastern architecture and decor. The mosque near Toledo, Ohio is built near the intersection of two major interstate highways on former farmland. Made of white block with rising minarets, it stands out on the landscape. With an ultramodern kitchen and dining hall to feed one thousand and a paved parking lot for a thousand vehicles, it serves Muslim needs for a several-state area.

Mosque outside Toledo, Ohio which serves for worship and study for area Muslims.

The mosque on the campus of Shaw University, a Baptist school in Raleigh, North Carolina, is located on the upper level of the international studies building. Built with monies donated by the Saudi Arabian government, it is named The Mosque of the Late King Khalid Ben Abdul Aziz Al Saud.

The Islamic Center of Raleigh is a two-story brick building across the street from the soccer field of North Carolina State University. At the weekly Friday noon prayers and sermon, hundreds gather to hear the sermon from the cleric of the mosque who came from Damascus, Syria and has gained American citizenship.

The *Boston Globe* reported, "With its $5 million grant from Saudi Arabia, Harvard University will move into the vanguard of a national boom in Islamic studies spurred by the growing power of religious movements in the Arab world and generous gifts from the Saudis and other Arabs. Harvard will use the grant ... to establish a center for

242

Islamic legal studies. Meanwhile, University of Arkansas officials said they are closing a deal with the Saudis for $23.5 million to fund a Middle Eastern studies program at the Fayetteville campus, which will include the study of Islam."[55]

The Islamic center in Denver, Colorado, sponsors a grade school and will soon open a K-12 school for its Muslim children. One of the goals of the school is to provide Muslims a place for learning their language, culture, and history. A Muslim community has been formed in New Mexico; Dar al-Islam publicizes its boarding school as a place to protect children from immorality, violence, and drugs which are in the public schools.

The Islamic community in Cedar Rapids, Iowa may be a typical story of the growth of a Muslim people. In the early 1920s Syrian and Lebanese immigrants rented a building for a mosque with only twenty members. After World War II, Muslims from Afghanistan, Albania, Indonesia, Iran, Pakistan, Russia, Senegal, and Turkey joined the community. There were 150 members by 1970, and by 1980 there were 250. They started a "Sunday school." The government of Egypt gave money to build a library and Islamic study center. It started a monthly magazine, *The Voice of Islam.*

On university campuses with significant numbers of Muslim students, there are Muslim Student Associations with a network with others across the nation. Ten thousand Muslims serve in the U.S. armed services with their own Muslim chaplain. Many organizations, such as the American Muslim Council, have goals to strengthen the Muslim communities and to educate the American public about Islam.

In 1980 the U.S. Congress adopted a resolution recognizing fourteen centuries of Islam and pledged to improve the understanding of Islam in America. The resolution was sent to the leaders of every Muslim country. The National Council of Churches sent a congratulatory letter to all Islamic organizations in America on this 1400th-year celebration.

Wallace Deen Muhammad, the founder of the American Muslim Mission and the leading figure of the African-American Muslims, received the Walter Reuther Humanities Award and the Four Freedoms Award. The governments of Saudi Arabia, Abu Dubai, and Qatar named him the only trustee for the distribution of funds to all Muslim organizations in America. Thus, Wallace Deen Muhammad has assumed or has been recognized as the de facto leader of Muslims in America. He was the one called upon to offer the opening prayer for the U.S. Senate in 1992.

Muslim Beliefs and Practices in America

The basic and essential beliefs and practices of Islam are uniform among Muslims around the world. Muslims in America and Muslims in Africa, Asia, the Middle East, and Europe are required to believe and practice the basic tenets of the Qur'an.

Many converts to Islam as well as its interpreters and critics claim that the beauty of the religion is in its simplicity and clarity. Without denying the depth of its theology and philosophy, they say that a Muslim can easily state the major beliefs of the religion and perform its practices without confusion or complexity.

There is a universal distinctiveness of its beliefs and practices which may appeal across cultures. Basic beliefs include God, angels, prophets, sacred scripture, and eternal judgment. Basic practices include the confession, prayer, giving, fasting, pilgrimage, and missions.[56]

Muhammad made certain that his followers knew that there was a definite law to be followed regardless of geographical location or social position in life. The Muslim holy book, the Qur'an, contains the very words which Allah revealed to Muhammad through the angel Gabriel. The Qur'an is the road map for a Muslim community or nation to follow, as it mandates the complete life in community. Therefore, the individual religious lifestyle blends into a unified community lifestyle with Allah as the only God, Muhammad his prophet, and the Qur'an as the infallible record of law and order.

Islam informs all people that it appreciates its roots in the Hebrew-Christian tradition. However, it quickly states that the Qur'an clarifies, refines, and gives the final and correct revelation through its prophet to Jews and Christians. Islam teaches that the Bible has been corrupted through its interpretations and translations.

Muslim lifestyle is based on certain key beliefs. Allah is the one and only God and does not share his divineness with any other creature, including Jesus. There have been prophets through history, including Abraham and Jesus. However, Muhammad is the final prophet with the final revelation.

Allah's revelation has been recorded in the Hebrew and Christian scriptures, but the Qur'an is the final and unabridged revelation. Human life is lived out in a history that has a beginning and an end. Life is lived under the judgment of Allah, and at its conclusion there are punishments in hell and rewards in heaven. The beliefs of Islam, then, are monotheism, prophets, holy scriptures, a strong ethical life, and a judgment day.

These beliefs provide the backdrop for the daily practice of Islam. Some Muslims, especially among the intelligentsia, say emphatically that one may become a Muslim by accepting the confession, "There is no deity but Allah, and Muhammad is the messenger of Allah." In this view the confession is sufficient, and other practices may be performed at the discretion of the individual.

However, most Muslims would agree that there are six major practices in Islam which characterize the religious lifestyle and which are mandatory:

1. *Confession.* The confession that there is only Allah and Muhammad is his prophet is prayed and chanted by of Muslims daily.

2. *Prayer.* The practice of prayer is perhaps the most rigorous and time-consuming expression. Prayer is a stated ritual five times a day. There are ceremonies of washing and purification before prayer. There are specific words and regular genuflections as one dramatizes the relationship to Allah.

3. *Fasting.* A Muslim fasts once a year for one month. No food or drink is consumed from sunrise to sunset. The monetary value of the food or the food itself which would have been consumed is given to the poor. Fasting is considered healthy for the body as well as a way to provide for the needs of the less fortunate.

4. *Alms.* Muslims are required to be fastidious in giving certain percentages of their monies and properties to the causes of Islam. Their giving supports the maintenance and operation of the mosques and provides the livelihood of the clergy.

5. *Pilgrimage.* Each Muslim is required to make the pilgrimage to Mecca once in a lifetime if funds are available and if there is good health. Millions visit the shrines at Mecca and Medina each year.

6. *Jihad.* A Muslim is obligated to be a missionary for the faith, that is, to be on holy conquest (jihad) for Allah. Islam has expanded around the globe because of its missionary impulse.

The Muslim lifestyle takes shape most visibly and dramatically in the religious life and activities associated with the mosque. The mosque symbolizes unity and universality in Islam. The leader of the mosque (imam) serves as the model for the Muslim lifestyle. The people imitate the imam in his words and actions in the prayer rituals. The imam interprets the law of Islam through sermons and classes. The people give their offerings to him to provide for mosque activities. He often leads the pilgrimage journey.

The Muslim calendar influences the lifestyle of Muslims in every nation. The calendar is followed assiduously. That means Muslims pray together in the mosque at stated hours, fast at the same time, take the pilgrimage at the same month, hear the sermon at the stated hour, and celebrate countless religious days together. Although Muslims may do religious duty individually, the main thrust of Islam is to reflect a religious lifestyle in community and in the brotherhood of Islam. Therefore, the Muslim lifestyle affects the family, the vocation, the economic and political life, and the relationship between Muslims and non-Muslims.

Islam teaches that the world is divided into two spheres. There is the territory of obedience (dar al-Islam) and there is the territory of war (dar al-harb). John Kelsay writes about the two choices which the teachings of Islam offer to humanity. "The way of war or heedlessness or ignorance, all characteristic of the non-Islamic world, lead to religious moral error and chaos. The way of obedience or submission is to follow the admonitions of Allah in the Qur'an. Islam has the mandate to control and subdue and if possible to convert the unbelieving world. Unbelievers, therefore, must submit to certain political and religious realities under the dominance and tutelage of Islam."[57]

Islam in America is growing in numbers of adherents, mosques and organizations, and in influence in communities and upon the government. As it grows it will continue to be involved in the challenges of living in a democratic society. As with all religions, it will have to live within the framework of the Constitution and the Bill of Rights. The essential matters of freedom of religion, religious liberty, and relations between religions and the political order will have to be a part of its existence, as well as relationships with government, other religions, and various communities.

11

THE ENCOUNTER BETWEEN ISLAM AND CHRISTIANITY

CHRISTIANITY AND THE BEGINNINGS OF ISLAM

Muhammad (A.D. 570–632) lived in the Arabian peninsula at a time when Christianity was facing both consolidation and schism. For over two hundred years, Christians had been divided by controversies over the nature of God and of Jesus Christ. Church councils agreed that Jesus Christ was fully God and fully human, but heretical groups differed among themselves, some asserting that he was more divine than human, others stating that he was more human than divine. Most Christians in Arabia, Palestine, Syria, Iraq, and Egypt belonged to schismatic groups. These Monophysite and Nestorian churches had been declared heretical and were expelled by the church councils.

It is not known exactly what were the influences of Christianity upon the people of the Arabian peninsula or upon the religious thought and experience of Muhammad. There was no Arabic translation of the Bible, although there may have been some translations of passages of it in monasteries or similar places.

Ibn-Ishaq, a noted Arab historian, reported that Waraqa ibn-Nawfal, the cousin of Muhammad's wife Khadija, was a Christian and had some knowledge of the books. Perhaps he was familiar with some passages in the Syriac language. Muhammad, along with other Meccan merchants, had traveled to Gaza and Damascus and Christian Abyssinia, but little is known of their contact with Christians. W. Montgomery Watt concludes that "people in Mecca knew of the existence of the Jewish and Christian religions, but had little accurate information about them."[1]

THE QUR'AN AND CHRISTIANITY

In the seventh century the Arabs had no historical documents. There may have been some inscriptions, but reading was limited, and they basically depended upon oral tradition. There is a tradition that Muhammad was illiterate. Muhammad began receiving visions about A.D. 610 and these continued until near his death in 632. The content of the visions was kept on various parchments and other artifacts, and by 651 the Qur'an had been codified. Muhammad received these visions while he was in Mecca and Medina.

The Qur'an is considered by Muslims to be a perfect word from God. Thus, what the Qur'an says about any matter, be it marriage or Christianity, is correct and acceptable. Thus, for Islam the Qur'an is the sourcebook for whatever is true about Christianity as a religion, as a people, and as a way of life. It sets the record straight about who Christians are, what they may or may not believe correctly, and about their relationship with God. Whatever is in the Bible and however Christian history has developed over six hundred years up to the time of Islam are true only as they do not contradict that data in the Qur'an.

As stated above for Arabs in the peninsula and for Muhammad in particular the knowledge of and relationships with Christians were limited. Early passages in the Qur'an refer very favorably to Christians. "Those who believe (in the Qur'an), / And those who follow the Jewish (scriptures), / And the Christians and the Sabians / Any who believe in Allah / And the Last Day, / And work righteousness, / Shall have their reward / With their Lord; on them / Shall be no fear, nor shall they grieve."[2]

Muhammad fled from Mecca to Medina in 622. He had difficulties with some of the Jewish tribes, and received a revelation which portrayed the Christians quite favorably in comparison with the Jews.

> Strongest among men in enmity / To the Believers wilt thou / Find the Jews and Pagans; / And nearest among them in love / To the Believers wilt thou / Find those who say, / "We are Christians": / Because amongst these are / Men devoted to learning.[3]

Later in the chapter there will be data concerning the theological and doctrinal differences between Islam and Christianity. However, the next passage of the Qur'an will refer to Jesus and the Gospel (Injil). For Muslims the Gospel is the revelation given to Jesus for his era and the people. However, the Bible has been corrupted over time, and the correct Gospel is only what is in harmony with the Qur'an. The same is true with the Jews and the Torah. Muslims look upon Jesus as a great prophet, but Jesus is not seen as divine or as the incarnate Son of God.

Another passage speaks well of Christians but less favorably of the monastic tradition.

> And bestowed on him / The Gospel; and We ordained / In the hearts of those / Who followed him Compassion and Mercy, / But the Monasticism / Which they invented / For themselves, / We did not Prescribe for them: / (We commanded) only / The seeking for the Good / Pleasure of Allah; but that / They did not foster / As they should have done.[4]

As Muhammad established his Islamic community, the *umma*, he appealed to both the Jews and the Christians to accept Islam or to be a part of the community by paying a designated tax. The next passage indicates that they would not accept him as prophet and relied on their own beliefs.

> "The Jews say: 'The Christians / Have naught (to stand) upon"; / And the Christians say: / 'the Jews have naught / (To stand) upon.' Yet they / (Profess to) study the (same) Book. . . But Allah will judge / Between them in their quarrel / On the Day of Judgement.[5]

Another passage may suggest disputes among Christians:

> From those, too, who call / Themselves Christians, / We did take a Covenant, / But they forgot a good part / Of the Message that was / Sent them: so We estranged / Them, with enmity and hatred / Between the one and the other, / To the Day of Judgement.[6]

The Qur'anic account of the annunciation to Mary and the birth of Jesus (Isa.) are long passages.[7] The annunciation is similar to that found in Luke 1:26–38, but the description of the birth story is very different from that of the Bible. No mention is made of Mary's relationship to Joseph, of the journey to Bethlehem, or of the manger scene. Muslims accept the virgin birth of Jesus by Mary but deny the divinity of Jesus.

Jesus' mission as a prophet and messenger also includes references to the miracles of his speaking while a baby in the cradle and of his turning clay into birds. The virgin birth is also implied.

> He shall speak to the people / In childhood. . . She said: "O my Lord! / How shall I have a son / When no man hath touched me? / He said: "Even so: Allah createth / What He willeth: When He hath decreed / A Plan, He but saith / To it, 'Be,' and it is! and Allah will teach him / The Book and Wisdom, / The Law and the Gospel, /And (appoint him) /A messenger to the Children / Of Israel . . . In that I make for you / Out of clay, as it were, / The figure of a bird, / And breath into it, And it becomes a bird / By Allah's leave."[8]

Central to Christianity are the beliefs in the divinity of Jesus Christ and His crucifixion on a cross. The Qur'an denies both. Concerning the death of Jesus the Qur'an states:

> "That they rejected Faith; /That they uttered against Mary / A grave false charge; / That they said (in boast), / "We killed Christ Jesus / The son of Mary, / The Messenger of Allah"— / But they killed him not, / Nor crucified him, / But so it was made / To appear to them, / And those who differ / Therein are full of doubts, / With no (certain) knowledge, / But only conjecture to follow, / For of a surety / They killed him not—Nay, Allah raised him up / Unto Himself.[9]

Another passage about the death of Jesus reads:

> Behold! Allah said: / 'O Jesus! I will take thee / And raise thee to Myself / And clear thee (of the falsehoods) /Of those who blaspheme; / I will make those / Who follow thee superior / To those who reject faith, / To the Day of Resurrection; / Then shall ye all / Return unto me, / And I will judge / Between you of the matters / Wherein ye dispute.[10]

The words "it was made to seem to them" are interpreted by Muslims to mean that someone else was substituted for Jesus on the cross, possibly Judas. Another view is that Jesus fainted on the cross, was removed, recovered, and went on his mission of preaching.

The divinity of Jesus is denied in the Qur'an. Included in this denial is the Christian doctrine of the Trinity. The Qur'an asserts that Mary was considered one person of the Trinity, and also assumes that Christians understand Jesus to be "son" in a physical sense. When the Qur'an uses the term "People of the Book," it refers to Christians and Jews who in their own Gospel and Torah received revelations through their prophets Jesus and Moses. However, the books were later corrupted. The following passages illustrate the Islamic understanding of the divinity of Jesus.

O People of the Book! / Commit no excesses / In your religion: nor say / Of Allah aught but the truth.

Christ Jesus the son of Mary / Was (no more than) a Messenger of Allah, / And His Word, / Which He bestowed on Mary, / And a Spirit proceeding / From Him: so believe / In Allah and His Messengers. / Say not "Trinity": desist: / It will be better / For you: For Allah is One God: / Glory be to Him: / (Far Exalted is He) above having a son.[11]

They do blaspheme who say: / "Allah is Christ the son / Of Mary." / But said Christ: / "O Children of Israel! / Worship Allah, my Lord / And your Lord." Whoever / Joins other gods with Allah— / Allah will forbid him / The Garden, and the Fire / Will be his abode. There will / For the wrongdoers / Be no one to help. / They do blaspheme who say: / Allah is one of three / In a Trinity: for there is / No god except One God.[12]

And behold! Allah will say: / "O Jesus the son of Mary! / Didst thou say unto men, / Worship me and my mother / As gods in derogation of Allah? / He will say: "Glory to Thee! / Never could I say / What I had no right / (To say). Had I said / Such a thing. Thou wouldst / Indeed have know it. . . . Never said I to them / Aught except what Thou / Didst command me / To say, to wit, 'Worship / Allah, my Lord and your Lord'; / And I was a witness / Over them whilst I dwelt / Amongst them; when Thou / Didst take me up / Thou wast the Watcher / Over them, and Thou / Art a witness to all things.[13]

The Qur'an teaches that Christians were people of the Book who had received truth through their prophet Jesus. However, the Gospel became corrupted. Their beliefs deviated from truth. Muhammad brought the perfect truth in the Qur'an. Yet they refused him as prophet, and thus refused the correction of their beliefs.

CHRISTIANS AS PEOPLE OF THE BOOK AND AS DHIMMIS

Between A.D. 622 and A.D. 632, Muhammad established the Islamic community, the umma. It was an Islamic state. He fulfilled the leadership roles as prophet, ruler, military chief, and judge. Paganism, polytheism, and atheism were intolerable to the Islamic community. Peoples of these beliefs were considered the Dar al-Harb, the land of the ignorant or of disbelief. They were realms and peoples to be brought under the authority of Islam through jihad. Thus, from the beginnings of Islam, the community and the caliphates could not exist side by side with idolatry.

Muhammad initiated the system of protected minorities known as the *dhimmis*.[14] Both Jews and Christians fit this category since they were the People of the Book mentioned in the Qur'an. They were given protection by the state; they were given certain rights in their own religious practices. They could maintain their faith and worship within their own families. They were restricted from propagating their faith or seeking converts outside their own families.

In return Christians were to pay the tax to the state and meet certain conditions as a protected minority. Islam expected them to acknowledge the ultimate truth of Islam although they were not compelled to become Muslims. Thus whereas pagans and idolaters were given the choice of accepting Islam as their religion, or the sword, Christians could become the community of the protected. The protected status of Christians and Jews has been a part of the Shari'a wherever Islam has been the dominant political power.

In the Islamic umma, a change of faith for a Muslim was considered political treason. However, the dhimmis or permitted minorities could remain in the religious communities or become Muslims. Through the centuries they accepted minority status, for it was better than persecution. They lived by permission of an empire and by the authority of Islam. Kenneth Cragg describes the Islamic community and the dhimmis: "Although Jews and Christians often came to occupy important positions in the management of financial, educational, or in Ottoman days, military aspects of the caliphate, this fact should always be seen in

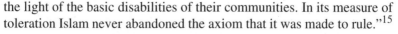

the light of the basic disabilities of their communities. In its measure of toleration Islam never abandoned the axiom that it was made to rule."[15]

By the time of the Ottoman Empire, the minorities were grouped in "the millet system." The word *millet* comes from the Qur'anic term, *millah,* meaning community. It came to mean any religious group of dhimmi status which could administer its own personal laws of marriage, divorce, and inheritance and its own community education. Thus, religious communities such as Copts, Greeks, Armenians, Maronites, Syriac Christians, and others maintained their own communal identity. The millet system, however, existed within the dominance and permission of Islam. Religious minorities have existed in various forms of the millet system to the present day.

CHRISTIANITY UNDER EARLY MUSLIM RULE

Under the second caliph Umar (634–644), Islam began an expansion which was to last for a hundred years. By the year 750, Islam had spread across the Middle East, across North Africa into Spain, and across Iraq and Iran to Central Asia, including Bukhara, Samarkand, and the Punjab. Asia Minor remained within the Christian Byzantine Empire.

Muslim expansion was facilitated by the classic Arab raid, the *razzia.* It was a quick and sudden attack on a pasturing group. Often the men would run away, leaving the Muslims with the booty. Often there was little loss of life. As Islam expanded with its people and armies, the raid became more expanded. Battles ensued between the Muslim and Byzantine and Sassanian armies.

Groups realized that they could avoid attack by submitting to the Islamic state by becoming Muslims or by becoming protected minorities as Christians could do. Some of the Monophysite writers of the seventh century viewed the rise of Islam as a sign of the judgment of God against the sins of the Orthodox Christian Church. Later, under the Ottoman Empire, "millets" were developed where entire Christian communities lived in specific areas of a city or region. Their patriarchs served as the religious representatives to the Islamic state. Christians abided by their own internal laws of religion, paid taxes to the state, and abided by the rules not to proselytize among the Muslims.

Watt has written, "On the whole Muslim colonialist regimes behaved very fairly towards their minorities and did not oppress them. The worst that could happen was that in a time of crisis a mob could get out of hand and attack minorities, but this was rare. Apart from this, however, the members of the minorities always felt that they were second-class citizens, excluded from the Muslim elite and from many government positions, Moreover, while a Muslim man could marry a woman from the minorities, a man from the minorities could not marry a Muslim woman."[16] In the status of protected minority, Christians lived under Islamic colonialism, "but it was a relatively benign form of colonialism."[17]

EARLY MUSLIM POLEMICS AND APOLOGETICS

The Qur'an had criticized Christians for their exclusiveness, and had attacked the Christian teachings on the divinity and crucifixion of Jesus and on the Trinity. During the early centuries of Islamic development and expansion, Muslims wrote polemics against Christianity and engaged in discussions with Christians.

It must be remembered, however, that Islamic law (Shari'a) demanded the punishment of death for apostasy from Islam. This law placed great danger upon Christians to share the gospel with Muslims. It also meant that Christians should exercise great caution in discussing Christianity with Muslims. However, there were examples of various relationships between Muslims and Christians.

With the beginning of the Umayyad dynasty in 661, Damascus became the first center of Islamic power beyond Mecca. The Syrian Christians (Jacobites) made up much of Caliph Mu'awiya's army. Mansur Ibn Sarjun, the former controller of the Byzantine government, continued to serve the Muslim caliphate. His grandson, John, grew up as a playmate with Yazid, the Caliph's son. John later became the Bishop of Damascus. John of Damascus wrote *Dialogue Between a Saracen and a Christian,* an apologetic for eighth-century Christianity. His aim was to equip Christians to understand Muslims whom he considered heretics and to prepare them to face Muslims in argumentation.

Caliph al-Mahdi in A.D. 781 had conversations with Timothy, the head of the Nestorians in Iraq. He asked why Christians faced the east in worship, why they worshiped the cross, and why they were not circumcised. He accused Christians of believing that God married a woman and had a son. He asked how having a son could be possible without genital organs. He asked how Jesus could die if Jesus is God.

R. W. Southern has described some of the issues that Islam presented to Christianity:

> To acknowledge one God, an omnipotent creator of the universe, but to deny the Trinity, the Incarnation, and the divinity

of Christ was an intelligible philosophical position made familiar by many ancient thinkers. Likewise, to profess the immortal-
ity of the soul, the existence of a future state of rewards and
punishments, and the need for such good works as almsgiving
as a requirement for entry into Paradise was recognizable in this
same context. But what was to be made of a doctrine that denied
the divinity of Christ and the fact of his crucifixion, but ac-
knowledged his virgin birth and his special privileges as a
prophet of God; that treated the Old and New Testaments as the
Word of God, but gave sole authority to a volume which inter-
mingled confusingly the teachings of both testaments; that accepted the philosophically respectable doctrine of future
rewards and punishments, but affronted philosophy by suggest-
ing that sexual enjoyment would form the chief delight in Paradise?[18]

Among works of Muslim polemicists from the ninth century is a *Ref-
utation of the Christians* by al-Jahiz, who died in 868. In Islamic Spain,
Ibn-Hazm (d. 1064) wrote the *Kitab al-Fisal* to refute the views of non-
Muslim philosophers and Muslim heretical sects. Ibn-Hazm knew of the
theological controversies between Melchites, Jacobites, and Nestorians
over the nature of Jesus Christ and argued that apparently only half of
Christ died. He argued that Jesus received a Qur'an-like scripture from
God and proceeded to demonstrate how little of it was preserved in the
actual Gospels.[19] It appears that Ibn-Hazm had a copy of the New Testament or the Bible which informed his polemical statements.

al-Ghazali, a noted theologian of the eleventh century, had a different
spirit of refutation of Christianity from Ibn-Hazm.[20] In one work he
speculates that a Muslim becomes distressed if asked to repeat the
Islamic confession, the Shahada, substituting the name of Jesus for that
of Muhammad: There is no god but God, Jesus is the messenger of God.
He went on to say that the use of Jesus' name was acceptable, taking into
account that Christians are erroneous in two matters concerning the
background for this statement when they believe that "God is the third
of three," and when they deny the prophethood of Muhammad.

In his most famous work, *The Revival of the Religious Sciences*, al-
Ghazali quotes a number of Jesus' sayings which are relevant to the life
of a Muslim Sufi. He presents a sympathetic discussion on the names of
God toward the concept of incarnation with the Sufi idea of "becoming
characterized with the characters of God."

ENCOUNTERS IN MEDIEVAL EUROPE
AND THE CRUSADES

Seven thousand Muslims invaded Spain in A.D. 711. They extended their raiding expeditions from their stronghold in North Africa. By 716 they had occupied all of Spain and Narbonne in southern France. In a battle with the Christian armies of Charles Martel in 732, they were defeated in their further push into Europe.

Many Christians in Spain converted to Islam, though the exact figures are unknown. Christians had the option of being a protected minority, a dhimmi. Although the Umayyad Caliphate fell in Damascus in 750, Umayyad leaders still ruled over Spain until about 1000. After A.D. 1000, various Christian kings made intrusions into the Muslim hegemony. The Muslim Kingdom of Granada survived until 1492.

Prior to the crusades there was a revival of religious feelings across Europe, particularly with reference to the establishment of more monasteries and more pilgrimages to shrines. The ultimate pilgrimage was to the Holy Sepulchre in Jerusalem. Thirty years before the first crusade of 1099, it is said that seven thousand people traveled from the Rhine to Jerusalem, led by an archbishop and three bishops. In 1076 a Turkish emir who took control of Jerusalem under the aegis of the Ottoman Empire placed difficulties upon the Christian pilgrims.

Pope Urban II called for a crusade in 1095 to liberate Jerusalem and the Holy Land. Earlier, the Byzantine Christians had suffered a serious defeat by the Muslims in 1071 and had to withdraw from much of Asia Minor. Thus, the crusades occurred for various reasons—commercial rivalries between Genoa and Venice, rivalries between the emerging nations of Europe, and the Pope's desire to reunite Christendom under his leadership, and mounting resentment toward the Muslims over their control of the Holy Land.

Steven Runciman wrote, "The crusades form a central fact in medieval history. Before their inception the centre of our civilization was placed in Byzantium and in the lands of the Arab Caliphate. Before they faded out the hegemony in civilization had passed to western Europe. Out of this transference modern history was born."[21]

Armies assembled in Constantinople in 1097, marched south through Asia Minor, and captured Jerusalem from the Muslims in 1099. Four Crusader States were established: kingdom of Jerusalem, principality of Antioch, and the countries of Edessa and Tripoli. Then, Muslims recaptured Edessa in 1144. In 1187 the renowned Muslim General Saladin recaptured Jerusalem from the Christians. Some estimate there were eight crusades. Christian armies captured Acre and a part of the Palestinian coast in 1191 and held them for a hundred years.[22]

Muslims have continued to remember the crusades as having been instigated by violent and corrupt Christians. The Pope and other leaders have been viewed as foolhardy. At the time of the crusades the Middle East was divided into smaller independent Muslim states which were fighting with one another. By late eleventh century the consolidation of the states under strong Muslim leadership brought an end to Christian control in the Holy Land.

For Muslims at some distance from Jerusalem, the crusades were a distant distraction. The caliph at Baghdad knew of them but had little power to intervene. The Seljuq dynasty, whose centers were hundreds of miles east of Baghdad and who were the real power in the Islamic world of the day, showed little interest in the distant frontier.

Saladin became the major Muslim leader in the region with power to dislodge the crusaders. Saladin had become master of Egypt and by 1174 was recognized as the sultan of the entire region from Mosul to Cairo.[23] He set out to defeat the crusaders and captured Jerusalem in 1187. Saladin had engaged in jihad against the Christians in the area before the recapture of Jerusalem. An event which sparked his mission of jihad had been the sinking of a Muslim pilgrim ship on the way to Mecca in 1182 by a Christian vessel.

Some later Muslim writers saw the crusades as a Christian jihad against Muslim lands and peoples. Some have viewed them as the beginning of European colonialism. Colonel Gadhafi of Libya has said that the Napoleonic invasion of Egypt in 1798 was the ninth crusade, and the establishment of the state of Israel was the tenth crusade with the aid of Christian America.[24] Muslims through the centuries have used the crusades as illustrations of the worst that is within Christianity. In their schools, from the sermons in their mosques, and from their various writings, Muslims remember the crusades as a Christian blight upon Islam.

The encounter with Islam deeply impressed Christians during this period. Watt describes the perception of Byzantine Christians toward Islam as a vicious caricature: "After all, the Muslims were the great enemy who had wrested from the Empire many flourishing provinces, such as Egypt and Syria including Palestine, the original home of the Christian faith, and who remained a constant military threat on their southern and south-eastern frontiers."[25]

Byzantine theologians from the eighth to the thirteenth centuries described Islam not only as a Christian heresy but as a false religion displaying idolatry. Muhammad was considered a false prophet and even the anti-Christ. Some said the followers of Muhammad worshiped him as a god:

> One explanation for the origin of Islam was that Muhammad was a cardinal who failed to get elected pope and, in revenge, seceded from the church. It was commonly believed that Muhammad had trained a dove to sit on his shoulder as a prop to deceive followers into thinking that he spoke as one inspired by God. Another exceedingly degrading and widespread story reported that Muhammad had been killed by swine while in the process of urinating. The list goes on and on.[26]

Dante described a mutilated Muhammad languishing in the depths of hell. Christians viewed the Qur'an as a false scripture with distortions of the Bible, with additions by Muhammad, and with materials included from the heretical Manichaeans. However, in Spain, where Muslims lived alongside Christians especially during Christian rule, often Muslims were seen as reasonable people.

The golden age of Islamic civilization occurred under the Abbasid dynasty centered in Baghdad. The interchange of ideas along with polemics continued from the Damascus days. Arabic translations were made of the philosophical works of Aristotle, Plato, neo-Platonists, and many of Galen's medical writings. Christians were called on for much of the translation work from the Greek language.

The Nestorian patriarch was allowed to maintain his headquarters in the Islamic capital of Baghdad while the Jacobite Christians were denied direct access to the caliph. Nestorian missionaries were allowed to travel in Muslim territories during the eighth and ninth centuries, establishing bishoprics in India, China, and central Asia.

Several schools of Islamic theology developed in and around Baghdad during this era. Two of the schools, the Mu'tazilites and the Sunni Ash'arites, had differences over the doctrine of God. al-Ashari, founder of the Ash'arites, initiated dialogical theology *(kalam)* as an Islamic theological method. Thus, while Christian Europe was in the Dark Ages, Islamic scholarship, science, medicine, and mathematics were transmitted to Europe via North Africa and Spain by noted Muslim scholars like Avicenna (Ibn Sina; 980–1037) and Averroes (Ibn Rushd: 1126–1198).

The encounter with Islam led some Christians to seek more information about the religion. Peter the Venerable, abbot of the monastery at Cluny from 1122 to 1156, commented in his writings on the crusades, "There had grown a strong conviction that the avowed purposes and

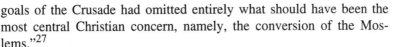
goals of the Crusade had omitted entirely what should have been the most central Christian concern, namely, the conversion of the Moslems."[27]

Peter administered a monastic movement with 10,000 monks in 600 monasteries throughout western Christendom. On a year's journey into Spain, Peter set out to give European Christians an accurate account of Islam and to criticize the errors of Islam. Among his writings he penned, "I attack you not as some do, by arms, but by words; not with force, but with reason, not with hatred, but in love. . . . I love; loving, I write you; writing, I invite you to salvation."[28]

Peter the Venerable collected Latin works translated into Arabic, and under his influence the Qur'an was translated into Latin. Bernard of Clairvaux criticized him for his work. Peter countered on the basis that Islam was a Christian heresy and Christians needed to know Islam in order to respond to it. Peter's efforts to understand Islam had particular weight when Martin Luther and Philip Melanchthon in 1543 wrote introductions to the publication of translations of the Qur'an and other Islamic writings.

Thomas Aquinas, although not a student of Islam, wrote about Islam in his *Summa contra Gentiles*. Like Peter the Venerable, he desired the conversion of Muslims. The writings of Peter the Venerable and Thomas Aquinas provide the basic perceptions of Christianity toward Islam until about the nineteenth century. Watt summarizes the perceptions under four headings:

1. Islam is a false and a deliberate perversion of truth.

2. Islam is a religion which spreads by violence and the sword.

3. Islam is a religion of self-indulgence.

4. Muhammad is the Antichrist.[29]

Watt observes that just as the Islamic perception of Christianity omitted much, so did Christianity's perception of Islam.

About the time of Aquinas, Francis of Assisi said that love instead of the crusading spirit should be demonstrated toward Muslims. He studied Islam and during the crusades went to Egypt in 1219 to preach to the sultan. After hearing the Muslim call to prayer, he asked the monks to ring church bells to announce worship services. His spirit of brotherhood influenced others to relate to the Islamic world.

Raymond Lull (1232–1316), a Franciscan missionary, was born to a wealthy Roman Catholic family on an island off the coast of Spain that had been regained from the Muslims at the time of his birth. He committed himself to a mission among the Saracens, considered the most hated and feared enemies of Christians. He wrote, "I see many knights going to the Holy Land beyond the seas and thinking that they can acquire it by force of arms, but in the end all are destroyed before they attain that which they think to have. Whence it seems to me that the conquest of the Holy Land ought . . . to be attempted . . . by love and prayers, and the pouring out of tears and blood."[30]

Lull's relationship to Muslims was pursued through apologetics, education, and evangelism. He spent nine years in learning the Arabic language. He wrote some sixty books, many of them devoted to Christianity and Islam. He established monasteries as training grounds with emphasis upon the Arabic language. At the Council of Vienna he persuaded leaders to have Arabic offered in the European universities, which he believed would encourage dialogue between Christians and Muslims.

Lull traveled to Algeria and Tunisia, preaching and holding dialogues with Muslims. Several times he was banished. In 1315 when he was over eighty years of age, Lull met his martyrdom in Algeria after preaching and arguing with Muslims. They stoned him to death. Lull combined both a spirit of love toward Muslims and a strong polemic toward their beliefs and practices. Perhaps his fanaticism and theirs met to end his life.

A different spirit toward Islam was exemplified by Nicholas of Cusa (1401–1464). In the Renaissance culture, he traveled widely and wrote from his experiences in churchly and intellectual circles. In his *De Pace Fidei* (*Concerning the Harmony of the Faiths*), he wrote of an imaginary dialogue between seventeen members of various religious traditions. The result of the conversations was a fundamental unity in religion in spite of the diversity of rituals and beliefs. His later work, *Cribratio Alchorani* (*Shifting of the Qur'an*), was written to refute Islam in its errors in the Qur'an. Nicholas attempted to deal with Islam fairly and accurately.

TOWARD THE MODERN ENCOUNTER BETWEEN ISLAM AND CHRISTIANITY

Turkish tribes poured into Anatolia and Asia Minor after the eleventh century. Led by a series of khans, most notably by Gengis Khan, they defeated the Muslim rulers. Eventually the Mongul Turks were converted to Islam. Later, the Ottoman Turks gained ascendancy and fought the Byzantines. They were known as warriors for Islam against Christianity.

Before 1400, the Ottomans had conquered several provinces of the Byzantine Empire including Greece and Bulgaria. In 1453 Mehmet II captured the city of Constantinople, later named Istanbul. A longstanding Islamic dream had been achieved. Byzantine Christianity had lost its long struggle with the Turks and the Muslims to keep its autonomy. Sunni Islam under the Ottomans launched an empire that was to last until the twentieth century. Eastern Orthodox Christianity became subservient to Islam.

The Greek Orthodox Patriarch became responsible to the Ottoman sultan and became the head of the Christian millet (community). As the Ottomans extended their territories, they established other Christian and Jewish millets. The Armenian Patriarch in Istanbul had authority over the Monophysite Copts of Egypt, the Jacobite Syrian Orthodox, the Nestorians in Mesopotamia, the Maronite Catholics, and others. The Ecumenical Patriarch of Constantinople had jurisdiction over the Melkite Greek Orthodox of Antioch, Jerusalem, and Alexandria.

Syria and Egypt, under Mameluke Turkish rulers, succumbed to the Ottomans in 1517. Hungary was ruled by them by 1526. They established a navy in the Mediterranean Sea, besieged Vienna, and had a war with Spain. Their empire included Algeria, Tunisia, Iraq, and parts of the Arabian peninsula, and they had a fleet in the Indian Ocean.

The Protestant Reformers of the sixteenth century were preoccupied with matters other than Islam. Even so, Martin Luther's writings portray an abiding hostility toward Islam. He wrote in the context of the danger of the intrusions of Ottoman Turks into the Christian lands. He wrote castigating the Qur'an as a "foul and shameful book" and describing the Turks as devils following their devil god. In his *On War Against the Turks*, Luther wrote about the Qur'an,

> He (Mohammed) greatly praises Christ and Mary as being the only ones without sin, and yet he believes nothing more of Christ than that He is a holy prophet, like Jeremiah or Jonah, and denies that He is God's Son and true God. . . . On the other hand, Mohammed highly exalts and praises himself and boasts that he has talked with God and the angels. . . . From this anyone can easily see that Mohammed is a destroyer of our Lord Christ and His kingdom. . . . Father, Son, Holy Ghost, baptism, the sacrament, gospel, faith, and all Christian doctrine are gone,

and instead of Christ only Mohammed and his doctrine of works and especially of the sword is left.[31]

By 1700 the Ottoman Empire was declining. The Empire faced the Holy Alliance of Austria, Poland, Venice, and the Pope. Greece gained its independence in 1829, and Algeria was occupied by France in 1830. The Empire had become "the sick man of Europe." After its defeat in the Balkan War of 1912-1913 and the havoc of World War I, it ended. In 1922 Mustafa Kemal Ataturk abolished the Empire and established the Republic of Turkey.

European colonialism began in earnest in Muslim territories with the occupation of Algeria by France in 1830 and the control of Tunisia. Italy gained Libya in 1912. After World War I, the Ottoman Empire was divided with mandates given to France over Syria and Lebanon, while the British looked after Jordan and Palestine. Islam felt a major intrusion into its heartland with the Balfour Declaration of 1917 in which the British guaranteed the Jews a national homeland in Palestine. Waves of immigrant Jews came with the establishment of the nation of Israel in 1948.

A Muslim Prayer	A Christian Prayer
In the name of God, Most Gracious, Most Merciful. Praise be to God, The Cherisher and Sustainer of the Worlds; Most Gracious, Most Merciful; Master of the Day of Judgment. Thee do we worship, And Thine aid we seek. Show us the straight way, The way of those on whom Thou hast bestowed Thy Grace, Those whose (portion) Is not wrath, And who go not astray.	Our Father which art in heaven, Hallowed be thy name. Thy kingdom come, Thy will be done in earth, As it is in heaven. Give us this day our daily bread; And forgive us our debts, As we forgive our debtors; And lead us not into temptation, But deliver us from evil. For thine is the kingdom and the power and the glory, for ever. Amen. (Matt. 6:9–13, KJV)

MISSIONARIES AND ORIENTALISTS AND ISLAM

Islam has always declared that it is apostasy for Muslims to convert to Christianity. Thus, Muslims have not looked kindly on Christian missionaries coming to their lands. They have also associated the mission-ary movement with the colonialism of Europe and America.

However, the modern missionary movement of the nineteenth cen-tury initiated a new awareness and appreciation of the religions of other peoples. Missionaries took languages and religious cultures seriously. Together with Western scholars, they gathered significant data on reli-gious traditions.

Missionaries were associated with the Portuguese, with the Dutch in Indonesia, and with German and Belgian missions in Africa. For the most part British administrators in India and Malaysia and Nigeria refrained from full support of missionaries in their territories. However, medical and educational work by missionaries were often supported by the colonial powers. And many Muslims took the opportunity to attend Christian educational institutions as well as to receive medical care from Christian medical centers and practices.

One of the most famous chaplains for the East India Company was Henry Martyn. He arrived in India in 1806, and during his short time became one of the greatest Bible translators in Central Asia. William Carey had seen his great talents as a linguist and encouraged him. His major contributions were the translation of the New Testament into Hin-dustani, Persian, and Arabic. In 1812 while living in Iran, he perfected his Persian translation with the help of the finest scholars there. He died that fall at the age of thirty-one.

Thomas Carlyle gave the West a positive perspective on Islam. In his series on *Heroes and Hero Worship*, he gave a lecture on Muhammad as "The Hero as Prophet." Carlyle pointed out the good qualities of Muhammad and evaluated him as a sincere and pious individual.

Islam surely knew what were the major perceptions of Christians toward them as the twentieth century approached. A pamphlet published by the Religious Tract Society of London in 1887 by Sir William Muir was entitled "The Rise and Decline of Islam." It portrayed the same ste-reotypes of the medieval perspective toward Islam as already enunci-ated: the falsehoods of its teachings; its spread by violence and the sword; sexual indulgence; and the unseemly character of Muhammad.

In India and Iran there occurred debates between Muslims and Chris-tians. Carl Gottlieb Pfander, a German, went to India to work with the Church Missionary Society. He debated publicly with Muslims in Iran and in British India. In his book *Balance of Truth*, which was translated into Urdu, he presented the superiority of Christianity and critiqued Islam. By 1852 a Muslim scholar, Maulana Rahmat Allah Kairanawi, wrote *Revelation of Truth* to refute Pfander. Rahmat Allah also publicly debated Christian teachings. He employed the new European biblical critical methods to condemn the missionaries' message. He emphasized how the Qur'an abrogated the Bible and the false teaching of the Trinity.

W. H. Temple Gairdner (1873–1928) served as a missionary to Egypt. His hero had been General Charles Gordon, who had been killed by the Sudanese Mahdists in 1885. He saw Islam as a challenge to Christianity and spent twenty-eight years in Cairo.

At the same time, more information was becoming available in the West as orientalists studied the language, cultures, and religion of Islam. In 1932 Sir Hamilton Gibb edited the book *Whither Islam?* which described Islam in North Africa, Egypt, India, and Indonesia. In 1946 he delivered lectures in Chicago on "Modern Trends in Islam." In 1949 Gibb wrote the book *Mohammedanism: An Historical Survey.* (Gibb was criticized for the use of the word *Mohammedanism* rather than Islam in his title. His publisher chose the title but Gibb's text uses only the words *Muslims* and *Islam,* and a later edition was entitled *Islam.)*

Orientalists, through language facility and translations, became more familiar with the original sources of Islam. European scholars brought modern critical methods to their studies. Scholars criticized the historicity and the authenticity of the Hadith in Islam, that is, the traditions of the Prophet's teachings and their commentaries. Notable works were Ignaz Goldziher's *Mohammedanische Studien* and Joseph Schacht's *The Origins of Muhammadan Jurisprudence.* These writers asserted that few of the Hadith were genuine history. Muslims viewed their writings as an attack on their religion and on the Islamic system of law.

The Muslim scholar Ameer Ali wrote the book *The Spirit of Islam* to counter the European perspective toward Islam. However, there was little appreciation among Muslims of the intellectual tradition of the West, especially of historical-critical scholarship. Watt writes of one line of Muslim defense:

> One line of thought was to claim that the Qur'an had anticipated various scientific discoveries not made until centuries later, such as: the sphericity and revolution of the earth (39:5); the fertilization of plants by the wind (15:22) ; the revolution of the sun, moon and planets in fixed orbits (36:38f.); the aquatic origin of all living creatures (21:30); the mode of life of bees (16:69); the duality of sex in plants and other creatures (36:35). It was argued that, since these matters were not known to human beings in Muhammad's time, they proved that the Qur'an was of divine origin. This line of thought was taken up by a retired

French medical doctor, Maurice Boucaille, who produced a book purporting to show that, while there were many scientific mistakes in the Bible, the Qur'an was ahead of the science of its time and anticipated later findings.[32]

Another Muslim tool for proving the superiority of Islam is the *Gospel of Barnabas,* a work of over two hundred chapters and four hundred pages. The original manuscript is in Italian and came to light in Amsterdam in 1709. It was published by Christian scholars in English in 1907. A purported early Arabic version has never been found. Much of the actual materials in the Gospels of the New Testament are included, but there are many additions. Jesus speaks of Muhammad as the Messiah. Christian scholarship suggests that it was written between the fourteenth to sixteenth centuries perhaps by a Christian convert to Islam. The writer makes mistakes about Islam as well as about other matters, even placing Nazareth on the Sea of Galilee.

Muslims published an Arabic translation in 1908 in Cairo, and other translations followed in Persian, Urdu, and Indonesian. Muslims have used the *Gospel of Barnabas* to illustrate the falsehood and inaccuracy of Christianity and to buttress their own prophet Muhammad and their religion.

Eventually, scholars began to call for a more objective study of and relationship toward Islam. One of them, Louis Massignon (1883–1962), had become a Christian partly through the study of the Muslim mystic and martyr, Hallaj. He called for a more open dialogue between Christianity and Islam.

Samuel Zwemer, called the Apostle to Islam, more than anyone else focused the attention of the world on Islam in about 1900. Some consider him the strongest influence in calling attention to the Muslim world since the mission of Raymond Lull in the thirteenth century.[33] He and others formed their own mission, the American Arabian Mission, and Zwemer sailed for Arabia in 1890.

After his mission work in Arabia and Bahrain, he moved to Cairo in 1912. There he found a more open Muslim society. Many were impressed with his intellectual presentation of Christianity. He gained access to influential leaders on the renowned Muslim campus of al-Azhar. Sometimes he spoke in audiences with two thousand Muslims present. For seventeen years Zwemer made Cairo his headquarters, and from there he traveled the world, speaking, raising funds, and establishing work among Muslims in India, China, Indonesia, and South Africa.

Ruth Tucker has written that Zwemer "dwelt with Muslims on a plane of equality—sharing his own faith (a very conservative theology) as he sought to learn more about theirs, always showing them the utmost respect. Although his converts were few—probably fewer than a dozen during his nearly forty years of service—he made great strides in awakening Christians to the need for evangelism among the Islamic peoples."[34]

In 1929 he joined the faculty of Princeton Theological Seminary. His life had been fully devoted to the Islamic world. He served as editor of the prestigious journal *The Muslim World*. He wrote some fifty books and numerous articles. A part of his legacy continues in the Samuel Zwemer Institute of Muslim Studies in California.

William W. Stennett has written of the change in approach beginning in the twentieth century.

> For years. . . .the manner of proclaiming the Gospel to the Moslem was primarily through argument. The missionary felt that he must by logical proof compel the intellectual acceptance of Christianity. This approach came to be known as 'The Great Moslem Controversy.' Some of its greatest adherents were men like Raymond Lull, Henry Martyn, Karl Pfander, and many others. They preached and wrote and, though different in many respects, had confidence in an approach that had practically passed out of existence. Its passing began around the turn of the century. At the Cairo Conference in 1906 the controversial method was discussed and it was agreed that polemic should be avoided whenever possible, but that when it could not be avoided, it should always be conducted in the spirit of patience, fairness, and love.[35]

Islam was given a boost at the World Parliament of Religions held outside Chicago in 1893. Leading figures from world religions were introduced to the American public and gave lectures. Alexander Russell (Muhammad) Webb, who had served as a diplomat with the United States government and was a convert to Islam, was a major speaker on behalf of Islam. Also, George Washburn, a Presbyterian missionary who served as president of Roberts College in Turkey, gave a scholarly presentation on the comparisons of Christianity and Islam.

The years from 1900 until 1950 saw several world missionary conferences which began dealing with the issues of religious pluralism. The Third World Missionary Conference held in 1938 in India was influenced by the seminal work of Hendrik Kraemer, *The Christian Message in a Non-Christian World*. Kraemer set forth the position of discontinuity between the Christian revelation and various religions. Much debate ensued over this position, including the ideas of William Hocking, the philosopher at Harvard University, and E. Stanley Jones, the American evangelist.

In 1948 the World Council of Churches was founded. It initiated many consultations on the study of and dialogue with other religions. The Southern Baptist Convention, today the largest Protestant denomination in the United States, began a serious study of other religions through its Department of Interfaith Witness. The 1950s and 1960s saw serious efforts by churches and by Christian scholars to understand peoples of other religions and to prepare the churches both in dialogue with and in witness to these peoples. These efforts included the world of Islam.

The writings of William Cantwell Smith exemplify a scholarly approach from Christianity to Islam in the latter half of the twentieth century. Smith, a member of the United Church of Christ who headed the Islamic study center at Harvard University, has examined Christian and Muslim theology and philosophy and encouraged interreligious dialogue within the commonalities of both traditions. He particularly made a distinction between the personal faith and religious tradition of believers.

In a seminal paper Smith outlined various ways in which the Islamic-Christian interrelation has occurred.

> (i) To say: "Islam is a Christian heresy" is to formulate the situation in classical-Christian terms (e.g., John of Damascus); (ii) To say: "Jesus is an important member of a long line of prophets, beginning with Adam and culminating with Muhammad" is to formulate it in classical-Islamic terms. (iii) To say: "Christianity is one religion, and Islam another" is to formulate it in classical nineteenth-century terms. (iv) The most fruitful and responsible way to formulate the issue in the light of present-day knowledge and current sophisticated sensibilities, and particularly in terms of world history, the religious history of our race, is a question not yet answered.

Smith indicates that he will pursue the fourth way including more of both the first and second ways in revised form.[36]

Anglican Bishop Kenneth Cragg has been a missionary scholar, statesman, and writer on Islam. He has served the church in the Middle East and has been a welcomed lecturer in Muslim circles there. Through his many writings, including *The Call of the Minaret* and *Sandals at the Mosque,* Cragg has stated with sensitivity the deep theological gulf that separates Christianity and Islam. He has pointed out common themes in the Bible and the Qur'an as well as in religious practice.

The Roman Catholic Church paved new ground between itself and Islam with its declarations in the Vatican Council in 1964.

> Upon the Muslim, too, the Church looks with esteem. They adore one God, living and enduring, merciful and powerful, creator of the heavens and the earth and speaker to men. They strive to submit wholeheartedly even to his inscrutable decrees, just as did Abraham, with whom the Islamic faith is pleased to associate itself. Though they do not acknowledge Jesus as God, they revere him as prophet. They also honor Mary, his virgin mother; at times they call on her, too, with devotion. In addition, they await the day of judgment when God will give each man his due, after raising him up. Consequently, they prize the moral life and give worship to God especially through prayer, alms-giving, and fasting.

> Although in the course of the centuries many quarrels and hostilities have arisen between Christians and Muslims, this Council urges all to forget the past and to strive sincerely for mutual understanding. On behalf of all mankind, let them make common cause of safeguarding and fostering social justice, moral values, peace and freedom. [37]

ISLAMIC REVIVAL AND RESURGENCE

Islam since World War II has undergone revival and resurgence. A number of Muslim-dominated nations gained independence from their colonial administrators, including Jordan, Syria, Lebanon, Egypt, Algeria, and Indonesia. Peoples of these newfound republics wrestled with their forms of government and socio-religious life.

What place would Islam have in defining the identity of these nations? Lebanon, for example, attempted a consensus among the various communities of Christians and Muslims. Indonesia established religion as a major focus of its constitution with the predominant religion being Islam. Pakistan, created out of India, has debated the place of Islam in its national political life. Thus, Muslim nations have struggled to define the role of Islam in their governmental and political structures.

Revitalization and revival of Islam since 1950 have taken various forms in different countries. John Esposito, a scholar of contemporary Islam, has perceptively written:

> Islamic revivalism in its broadest sense refers to a renewal of Islam in Muslim personal and public life. Its manifestations include an increase in religious observances (mosque attendance, Ramadan fast, wearing traditional Islamic dress); a revitalization of sufi (mystical) orders; proliferation of religious publications and media programming; calls for the implementation of Islamic law; creation of Islamic banks; and the growth of Islamic organizations and activist movements.

> Growing out of this context, Islamic revivalism has led to the reassertion of Islam in politics. Incumbent governments appeal to Islam for political legitimacy and popular support for policies and programs. Opposition movements use the language and symbols of Islam to criticize established governments, and to advocate actions ranging from socio-political reform to violent revolutionary action.

> The forms that Islamic revivalism takes vary almost infinitely from one country to another, but there are certain themes: a sense that existing political, economic, and social systems have failed; a disenchantment with and even rejection of the West; a quest for identity and greater authenticity; and the conviction that Islam provides a self-sufficient ideology for state and society, a valid alternative to secular nationalism, socialism, and capitalism.[38]

The establishment of the state of Israel in 1948 caused much unrest in and among Muslim nations. Several Muslim nations of the Middle East and North Africa joined in wars against Israel, in funding opposition groups against Israel, and in seeking through the United Nations ways to present both Islamic and Palestinian concerns about the territory of Palestine and Jerusalem.

By the 1960s the industrialized nations of Europe, the United States, and Japan in particular were heavily dependent on the oil resources of

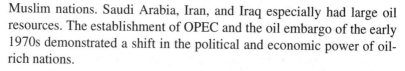

Muslim nations. Saudi Arabia, Iran, and Iraq especially had large oil resources. The establishment of OPEC and the oil embargo of the early 1970s demonstrated a shift in the political and economic power of oil-rich nations.

The Muslim oil-rich nations also used this newfound power and influence in the world to reassert their Islamic identity. Some nations allocated great sums of money to spread Islam around the world by sending Muslim missionaries, building mosques and Islamic centers, and funding programs on university campuses to promote Islam.

As some Islamic nations prospered in newfound wealth and influence, governmental programs were launched to bring their peoples socially and economically into the modern era. They sent their youth to study and train in the so-called modern nations. These leaders returned to become the educators and technocrats in the emerging industrialization and technologization of their countries. Also, many internationals were employed to assist in nation building in Muslim lands, which further introduced peoples of modern views and values into more traditional societies.

In the rapidly changing environment of these developing nations, feelings and reaction against westernization and modernization among segments of the population surfaced. Islamic traditionalists or fundamentalists viewed many of the changes as forms of colonialism and imperialism and a threat to Islamic values, institutions, and life.

Thus, in many Muslim countries there was a revival of dissident and militant Muslim groups. They attacked their own governments and their programs. They attacked the policies of foreign governments which they considered intrusions. They called for reforms and a return to Islamic infrastructures of government, law, education, and religious life. Many organizations emerged, including the Muslim Brotherhood, the Islamic Jihad, and the Mujahedin.

The major event representing Islamic revival and resurgence occurred with the formation of the Islamic Republic of Iran under the aegis of Ayatollah Khomeini in 1979. The ruler of Iran from 1951 until 1979 was Muhammad Reza Shah Pahlavi. During his reign of thirty-eight years he initiated his "White Revolution" to bring Iran into the modern era through social and economic reforms. He was a modernizer in the lineage of Kemal Ataturk of Turkey and his father Reza Shah. Heavily dependent on European and American personnel and products to implement his revolution, he spent billions of dollars of his oil revenues to modernize Iran. He brought in tens of thousands of foreign advisors and workers for education, military training, plant construction, and expansion of transportation and communication facilities.

In the Shah's rush to transform Iran into a leading modern nation with formidable armed services and weapons and a supporting industrial complex, he provoked much alienation and dissent within the population. The ulama first cautioned against too much change too fast. Then, under the leadership of Ayatollah Khomeini, they called for uprisings and demanded the ouster of the Shah. In January 1979, the Shah fled the country. A few days later, Ayatollah Khomeini arrived from his exile in Paris and initiated the changeover from the monarchy of the Shah to the Islamic Republic of Iran. Soon thereafter, the Ayatollah depicted the United States as "the Great Satan." The United States Embassy in Teheran was taken over and its personnel were held hostage for more than a year. All Christian missionaries left the country.

Major concerns of Ayatollah Khomeini had been the "corrupt" rule of the Shah in his disregard for true Islamic values and expressions and the Shah's support of the "degenerative" policies of Western governments as well as his allowance of alcoholic beverages, profane movies, and the Western model of the liberation of women. The Shah's government also had taken over the administration of the Awqaf (religious endowments) from the traditional administrators, the ulama. The Ayatollah began the movement to return Iran to traditional Islam.

Iran became the flagbearer of Islamic revivalism and resurgence. Muslim groups in other countries looked to Iran for aid and comfort. These groups have agitated for reform, for return to Islamic law, and for a cleansing from outside influences. Iran began a protracted war against its Muslim neighbor, Iraq; hundreds of thousands of Iranians lost their lives upon Ayatollah Khomeini's call to become martyrs to the cause of Allah and gain the reward of heaven.

The Ayatollah in 1989 pronounced the death sentence upon Salman Rushdie for writing *Satanic Verses,* a book Khomeini characterized as blasphemous. Rushdie was living in Britain, and Khomeini's death sentence was, in effect, a call for terrorism. This resulted in intense feelings by Muslims throughout the world. Other nations wrestled with the issues of freedom of religion, freedom of the press, and the relationship between governments when a sentence is declared on an individual in another land. Riots occurred in Pakistan, and the U.S. embassy was attacked. Protest marches were held in various countries with the largest ever by an ethnic group in London.

With the demise of the USSR in the early 1990s, most of the former Soviet republics have become independent nations. Some of these have sizable Muslims populations which had been suppressed since the Communist revolution of 1917. Islamic nations like Saudi Arabia and Iran have sent to these republics Muslim clerics and teachers, have opened Islamic training schools, have begun restoring old mosques and building new ones, and have sent financial aid to those in government sympathetic to the revival and resurgence of the Muslim faith and its way of life.

Europe and the United States have witnessed rapid growth in the numbers of Muslims and the influence of Islam. France and England, in particular, have vocal and visible Muslim leaders. Muslims are fragmented among national, ethnic, and language lines, and this has presented a challenge for any unification of Islam. In the United States, Islam has seen significant growth with some six million Muslims and over six hundred mosques and Islamic centers.

MUSLIM-CHRISTIAN ENCOUNTERS

During the last two decades, both formal and informal conferences between Muslims and Christians have been held in various parts of the world. Examples include a visit by a party of Vatican officials to the University of al-Azhar in Cairo in 1978 and a seminar sponsored by Colonel Gadhafi in Tripoli, Libya in 1976. The Seminar of Islamo-Christian Dialogue at Tripoli had teams of fifteen Muslims and fifteen Christians discuss pertinent matters between the two religions with some five hundred observers in attendance.

In the spring of 1981 the author led a group of twelve Southern Baptist leaders and twelve Muslim leaders on a weekend retreat near Los Angeles. The topics presented and discussed were: Who Are Baptists?; Who Are Muslims?; The Baptist View of Christ; The Muslim View of Christ; The Muslim View of Muhammad; The Baptist View of Muhammad; Rites of Passage in the Baptist Family; The Rites of Passage in the Muslim Family; The Role of Women Among Baptists; The Role of Women in Islam; Islam and Political Systems; and Baptists and Political Systems.

The presentations and discussions were cordial and friendly. The substance of the discussions revealed fresh information for the participants, acknowledgment of common beliefs and practices in form and function if not always in meaning, and specific and strong differences in certain theological concepts and religious experiences.

A participant closed the Baptist-Muslim dialogue with the following statements:

Kenneth Cragg wrote a book entitled, *The Call of the Mina-ret*, which has greatly influenced my thinking and feelings about Islam and Muslims. Cragg talks about the Christian and the Muslim understanding each other. Certainly, we now better understand each other's faith and practice and religious life-style. Cragg writes of service to each other. In a real sense we have served each other by sharing ourselves in knowledge, in fellowship and community around tables, and in planting por-traits of human aspirations and needs in our Christian and Mus-lim communities. Cragg calls to our attention the challenge of interpretation. We have labored to interpret to each other the very substance of the truth that grips us in both personal and community ways. And Cragg writes about patience. There has been amiability and mutual affirmation for both the member-ship of the dialogue and the life substance of our meetings.

To be sure, in our deliberations here we have recognized our differences in theological understandings and religious practic-es. Baptists are a people nurtured on the scriptures of the Old and New Testaments, committed to the premise that God was in Christ reconciling the world unto himself, structured in the church that gives fellowship and instruction and that reaches out to the alienated and displaced peoples. But Baptists shall not allow any differences to separate us from you. And we pray that any differences you have will not keep you from dialogue and fellowship with us. We shall continue to cherish our friendship. We count it a privilege to share with you who we are, our loy-alties, commitments, and responsibilities as Christians. And we desire that you communicate to us and with us the depth of your beliefs and faith.

Since 1980 the author has taken groups of students to hold seminars in mosques located in Washington, D.C., Atlanta, Georgia, and Raleigh, North Carolina. The Muslim leaders of the mosques have lectured on Islam, and several hours of discussions have ensued between the stu-dents and Muslim leaders concerning commonalities and differences between Islam and Christianity and on Islamic perspectives on political, economic, social, and religious issues and challenges worldwide. Like-wise, the author has had Muslim leaders into his classes on-campus for lectures and discussions.

Islamic resurgence also includes Muslim scholars and writers who have a fresh view toward Christianity and its teachings. M. Kamel Hussein (1901–1977), an Egyptian, wrote a novel, *City of Wrong*, which dwelt with events in Jerusalem before and after the crucifixion of Jesus. He did not deal with the controversial question of whether Jesus actually died on the cross, but in the words of Kenneth Cragg who translated it into English: "It set out to ruminate on the collective sin of Jesus' rejection on Good Friday, which it takes as an epitome of 'the sin of the world,' a sin conceived in communal pride and perpetrated in the name of religious security and Divine loyalty, and reinforced by quotation from infallible scripture and by the philosophy that at any cost in evil the triumph of the good must be assured."[39]

Another writer, Mahmoud M. Ayoub (b. 1935), a blind Lebanese Shi'ite Muslim, has a positive attitude toward Christianity but retains his Muslim identity. His book *Redemptive Suffering in Islam* has a relevance to Christian understandings of Christ and suffering. Ayoub has written various articles published in *The Muslim World*. He maintains that Christ needs to be understood within the divine plan of human history, particularly Christ the man who is one of the servants of God and Christ the word of God. Ayoub states that these ideas are in the Qur'an and provide the framework for the image of the Christ of Muslim piety.[40]

In a summary view of Christ, Ayoub writes, "Thus we see that like the Christ of Christian faith and hope, the Jesus of the Qur'an and later Muslim piety is much more than a mere human being, or even simply the messenger of a Book. While the Jesus of Islam is not the Christ of Christianity, the Christ of the Gospel often speaks through the austere, human Jesus of Muslim piety. Indeed, the free spirits of Islamic mysticism found in the man Jesus not only the example of piety, love and asceticism which they sought to emulate, but also the Christ who exemplifies fulfilled humanity, a humanity illumined by the light of God."[41]

Ayoub voices his hope for future relations between Muslims and Christians. He advocates a true ecumenism that accommodates Islam as an authentic expression of divine and immutable truth, not as a heresy of Christianity. Truth is greater than any one religious tradition or the understanding of any individual. "In order to realize this ideal, Muslims must also rethink their own understanding of the true meaning of Islam as the living up to the primordial covenant between God and all human beings and the divine reaffirmation of this covenant in a variety of expressions to this religiously pluralistic world."[42]

In Muslim-Christian relationships in the United States, where Islam has a significant presence and is growing, there are sensitivities which are called for and guidelines which may be followed in maintaining good neighborly relations. Islam in the United States is a minority religion compared to Christianity. However, with its anticipated growth rate, it will surpass Judaism in the near future as it moves toward seven to eight million adherents.

The coming of age of Islam in American society is seen in several events. The armed services have commissioned a Muslim chaplain. A Muslim cleric has offered the prayer to open the session of the United States Senate. Mass media have reported significant rituals and ceremonies of Muslim communities in their building of mosques, their observances of the fasting season and the pilgrimage to Mecca, and their viewpoints of world happenings as Islam is affected and as Islam influences those events.

As Christians and Muslims individually and as families meet one another, live beside each other, work together, and generally mix socially, there are sensitivities to be learned and observed. Especially, Christians may be informed by the following:

- When Muslims attempt to build their worship centers and practice their religious lifestyle, they sometimes encounter misunderstanding and hostility. When any religious group operates within the framework of the Constitution and Bill of Rights and the laws of the land and local communities, they have their rights and privileges for the freedom of religion and their expression of it.

- As Muslims observe their faith through special ceremonies and special events in their religious calendar, they appreciate sensitivity and reasonableness by the schools, business community, and government.

- The Muslim lifestyle in certain respects may be different from other lifestyles, and respect is encouraged.

- Pork meat and carnivorous animals are forbidden.

- Meat should be from animals slaughtered according to Islamic law.

- Alcoholic beverages are forbidden.

- Dress should be modest. Women may be veiled in public.

- Sexual intercourse is reserved for marriage.

- Ablutions for prayer require certain washings by water.

- Prayer five times daily requires specific times and a proper place.

- Muslims in principle oppose sex education in public schools.

- During Ramadan month, Muslims fast from sunrise to sunset.

- Muslims are generally the best source to learn about Islam. Clarify any terms or ideas of Islam with Muslims.

CHALLENGES OF ISLAM FOR CHRISTIANITY INTO THE TWENTY-FIRST CENTURY

Into the twenty-first century, Christianity will face a missionary and mobile Islam. Iranian Shi'ite Muslims are sending their missionaries into the new republics of Central Asia and are constructing thousands of mosques. So is the government of Saudi Arabia. Algerian conservative Sunni Muslims are battling their government for representation in politics. And the government of Egypt faces challenges from conservative Islam.

In the Far East, Malaysia with its Islamic constitution has Muslim laws for its constituents. Muslims in England want political voice in parliament. Islam is forecast to be the second-largest religion of the United States, supplanting Judaism, by early in the twenty-first century. There are more Muslims than Episcopalians in the United States.

Islam and Christianity are two of the world's foremost missionary religions. Christian history has seen attempts at missions and relationships to Muslims since the inception of Islam, but those attempts have been sporadic and few. Islam has been a missionary religion for fourteen hundred years. Especially, it has attempted to penetrate Christian places and peoples, particularly in the Middle East, North Africa, Europe, and North America. The twentieth century has been a time of advance for Islam in Europe and the United States. At the same time Christianity has not seen much advance into predominantly Islamic lands.

Thus, Christianity in particular faces the challenge of Islam's penetration and presence. Why is this so? Both are intensely missionary religions. However, Islam in its advance has had success in societies and among peoples where freedom of religion and religious liberty are present.

In many Islamic-dominated societies, Christianity has prohibitions upon its entrance and/or restrictions upon its activities. An example is that mosques may be built across the United States whereas no church is allowed to be built in Saudi Arabia. Saudi Arabia funds the building of mosques and the establishing of Islamic presence across the world. However, as an Islamic nation it will allow no freedom of religion within its society.

The challenges and opportunities for Christianity in its encounter with Islam will involve at least five considerations:

1. Christians need to see the great challenge presented by Islam as an intentional missionary religion and prioritize its resources to meet that challenge.

2. Christians need to understand Qur'anic Islam and the way it views the Bible, Jesus, and the status and needs of the human population.

3. Christians need to understand Folk Islam and the ways it differs from orthodox Islam.

4. Christians need to engage Islam in its ideals and realities of the relationships of religion and government, of freedom of religion, of religious liberty within nations and communities.

5. Christians need to study the meaning of religious change and conversion and be prepared to consider the contextualization of the Church and the Christian message in the lives of Muslim believers as well as the consequences of Christians becoming Muslims.

Christianity's Priority with Islam

Through the centuries Christianity has shown little interest in Islam and has interacted little with it. It has had its Francis of Assisi, Raymond Lull, Samuel Zwemer and others who were concerned about Muslims. It has also had its crusades. It has had other significant priorities.

Meanwhile Islam has grown larger in numbers of followers than those of Hinduism, those of Buddhism, or of any other major religion except Christianity. Islam is the one major religion that looks upon the religion of Christianity and its teachings concerning the Trinity and the divinity of Jesus as blasphemy and sin.

Christianity in relationship to Islam needs to be sensitive to the environment which influenced the views and values of Islam. That environment included confusion and chaos within the Church over doctrine. Christianity needs to prepare Christians to greet, meet, and live alongside Muslims in the schools, the workplace, and the neighborhoods. Just as every Muslim is to be a missionary on behalf of his or her faith, so Christians need to be prepared to understand Islam and to meet Muslims.

Qur'anic Islam and Christianity

In Islam's encounter with Christianity for some fourteen hundred years, its basic stand on the Qur'an has not changed. It is the word of

Allah, absolute and correct in content, detail, and language. In fact it becomes less than perfect when it is written in languages other than Arabic. The Qur'an has the final truth about all realities, all entities, all matters of life from birth to death, and all rules and regulations about religion. Although there have been schools of Islamic law since early Islam, there is little indication that Islamic scholarship tampered with the Arabic Qur'an in translations.

The greatest challenge to Christianity in Qur'anic Islam is its view of the Bible and its teachings on Jesus Christ. The Qur'an views Christians as People of the Book. By the use of "Book" it means the uncorrupted revelation given to Jesus in his time as well as to Moses in his time. However, it considers that the "Book" has been corrupted in its translations and interpretations. Although it believes that Allah revealed his law through Moses and the Torah and through Jesus and the Gospel, it dismisses the authority and credibility of the Bible because it has been corrupted and has misrepresented the original revelation of Allah.

The major difference between Islam and Christianity, between the Qur'an and the Bible, is the data concerning and the belief about Jesus. Christians need to be aware of the Qur'anic view of Jesus, its differences from the Bible, and how Muslims view Christians as they believe the Biblical data concerning Jesus.

Jesus: Similarities and Differences in the Qur'an and the Bible

There are similarities of events and stories between the Bible and the Qur'an as they view Jesus. These would include especially the miraculous virgin birth, the miracles of Jesus, and his holiness and purity. However, the overall interpretations given to them by Christians and Muslims differ. Jesus is mentioned by name in the Qur'an in ninety-three different verses in some fifteen chapters.

1. *Virgin Birth.* The birth of Jesus is related in the Bible in the Gospel of Matthew (1:18–25) and the Gospel of Luke (1:26–38; 2:1–20). Matthew 1:18 states, "Mary was espoused to Joseph, before they came together, she was found with child by the Holy Ghost." The Gospel of Luke particularly gives attention to the visit of the archangel Gabriel and the miraculous conception of Jesus. The virgin birth of Jesus has been a cardinal belief of Christianity. It has been considered a miraculous and supernatural birth.

The Qur'an gives an account of the virgin birth of Jesus in Surah 3. Mary is described as being a virgin, chosen by God, and considered with great honor. Surah 3:42 reads, "Behold! the angels said: / 'O Mary! Allah hath chosen thee / And purified thee—chosen thee / Above the women of all nations." Surah 3:45 continues, "Behold! the angels said:

/ 'O Mary! Allah giveth thee / Glad tidings of a Word / From Him: his name / Will be Christ Jesus / The son of Mary." Surah 3:47 relates, "She said: 'O my Lord! / How shall I have a son when no man hath touched me? / He said: 'Even so: Allah createth / What He willeth: / When He hath decreed / A Plan, He but saith / To it, 'Be,' and it is!'"

Thus, the Qur'an affirms the virgin birth, and Muslims believe that Jesus was born of the virgin Mary. The birth is seen as a sign (*aya*) of Allah's power and as a miraculous event. And Muslims have a high regard also for Mary. However, the Qur'an presents Jesus as the son of Mary and not as the Son of God. That would be blasphemy (*shirk*), that is, associating the divine nature of Allah with human nature. Jesus is a created being. In Surah 3 Jesus is compared to Adam in the sense that both were created by Allah and were without a father.

2. *The Miracles of Jesus.* Jesus is described in both the Bible and the Qur'an as performing miracles. All of the Gospels present miracles which Jesus performed. Jesus heals the blind who call out to him as he passes (Matt. 20:29–34); heals a man blind from birth (John 9:1–41); heals a leper (Mark 1:40–45); and raises Lazarus from the dead (John 11: 1–44). Matthew 1:21 reports that Jesus accomplished miracles to point people to his basic reason: to save them from their sins.

The Qur'an specifically mentions two miracles which the Bible does not contain. In Surah 19:27–34, Jesus speaks from the cradle to state his mission. Jesus said,"I am indeed / A servant of Allah: / He hath given me / Revelation and made me / A prophet." Surah 5:110 reports that Jesus formed a bird out of clay, and blew into it, and it came to life and flew away. The Qur'an stresses that the miracles of Jesus were performed by the permission and power of God. There is no reference to any relationship of miracles to Jesus' mission of saving people from their sins. His miracles are seen basically in the line of his being a prophet and in God's permitting him to do so.

3. *Jesus' Holiness and Purity.* The Bible teaches that Jesus was born full of grace and truth. Matthew's purpose in writing his Gospel was to show to the Jews that Jesus is the Messiah. John's Gospel begins by stating that Jesus was the Word of God. Thus, the biblical witness to Jesus and Christianity's beliefs about him have included his messiahship and his incarnation.

The word *messiah* is the Hebrew term meaning anointed. *Christ* is the Greek word used for Messiah. Messiah thus denotes the prophetic and sacrificial roles of Jesus. Jesus never used the word *Christ* to refer to himself, but he commended Simon Peter for using it of him (Matt. 16:16–17). He also admitted to being the Christ at his trial (Matt. 26:63–64).

A Comprehensive Listing of References to Jesus (ISA) in the Qur'an

Surah	Reference
2/87	We gave Jesus, son of Mary, the Evidences and aided him by the Holy Spirit.
2/136	What has been given to Moses and Jesus and the prophets.
2/253	We gave Jesus, the son of Mary, the Evidences and supported him by the Holy Spirit.
3/45	God giveth thee tidings of a word from himself whose name is the Messiah, Jesus, son of Mary.
3/52	Jesus perceived unbelief on their part.
3/55	God said, "O Jesus, I am going to bring thy term to an end and raise to myself."
3/59	Jesus in God's eyes is in the same position as Adam.
3/84	What was given to Moses and Jesus and the prophets.
4/157	For their saying, "We killed the Messiah, Jesus, son of Mary, the messenger of God."
4/163	We made suggestions to . . . the Patriarchs, to Jesus.
4/171	The Messiah, Jesus, son of Mary, is only the messenger of God, and his work which he cast upon Mary, and a spirit from him.
4/172	The Messiah will not disdain to be a servant of God.
5/17	They have disbelieved who say that God is the Messiah, the son of Mary.
5/46	In their footsteps we caused Jesus, son of Mary, to follow.
5/72	They have disbelieved who say: "God is the Messiah, the son of Mary. "
5/75	The Messiah, son of Mary, is nothing but a messenger.

A Comprehensive Listing of References to Jesus (ISA) in the Qur'an

Surah	Reference
5/78	Those . . . who have disbelieved were cursed by the tongue of David and Jesus, son of Mary.
5/110	O Jesus, son of Mary, remember my goodness to thee.
5/112	The apostles said, "O Jesus, son of Mary, is thy Lord able to send down to us a table from heaven.
5/114	Jesus, the son of Mary, said, "O God, our Lord."
5/116	God said, "O Jesus, son of Mary, was it thou who didst say. . . ."
6/85	Zachariah and John and Jesus and Elijah.
9/30	Christians say that the Messiah is the son of God.
9/31	Monks as Lords apart from God, as well as the Messiah, the son of Mary.
19/34	That is Jesus, son of Mary, a statement of the truth.
21/91	We made . . . her and her son a sign to the worlds.
23/50	We appointed the son of Mary and his mother to be a sign.
33/7	Noah, and Abraham, and Moses, and Jesus, son of Mary.
42/13	What we laid as a charge upon Abraham and Moses and Jesus.
43/57	When the son of Mary is used as a parable.
43/63	When Jesus came with the Evidences.
57/27	In their footsteps we caused our messengers to follow, and we caused Jesus, son of Mary, to follow and we gave him the Gospel.
61/6	Jesus, son of Mary, said, "O Children of Israel, I am God's messenger to you."
61/14	Jesus, son of Mary, said to the apostles, "Who are my helpers toward God?"

Geoffrey Parrinder, *Jesus in the Qur'an* (New York: Oxford Univ. Press, 1977), 18–20.

The word *incarnation* is not used in the Bible. However, many references in the Bible, including 1 Timothy 3:16 and 1 John 1:1–30, refer to the divine nature of God in Jesus Christ. Also, Jesus forgave sin (Matt. 9:2–6), assumed judgeship (Matt. 25:31), and arose from the dead (Luke 24:1–8). Christianity has maintained the full divinity and full humanity of Jesus. The primary mission of Jesus through his birth, life and teachings, death on the cross, and resurrection from the tomb, was salvation for humanity.

The Qur'an attributes the title messiah to Jesus eleven times. It never specifically defines messiah, but it is applied to Jesus during all periods of his life. The most likely meaning is similar to the Hebrew use of the anointed one. This may be tied to Jesus' miraculous virgin birth and to his being a prophet of Allah's word. Surah 5:17 states, "In blasphemy indeed / Are those that say / That Allah is Christ / The son of Mary. / Say: 'Who then / Hath the least power / Against Allah, if His will / Were to destroy Christ / The son of Mary, his mother, / And all—everyone / That is on the earth?" In the Qur'an the title messiah is used as an equipping and commissioning for the task of prophethood and teaching. The fuller role associated with salvation is found in Christian usage and not in Muslim belief. [43]

The Qur'an denies that Jesus was the incarnation of God or the Son of God. From its perspective no divinity could be associated with Jesus. Surah 19:35 reports, "It is not befitting / To (the majesty of) Allah / That He should beget / A son. Glory be to Him! / When He determines / A matter, He only says / To it, 'Be,' and it is."

Concerning Jesus and the Trinity, the Qur'an gives a word of admonition to Christians who are called People of the Book: "O people of the Book! Commit no excesses / In your religion: nor say / Of Allah aught but the truth. / Christ Jesus the son of Mary; / Was (no more than) / A Messenger of Allah; / And His Word; / Which He bestowed on Mary; / And a Spirit proceeding / From Him: so believe / In Allah and His Messengers. / Say not "Trinity": desist: / It will be better for you: / For Allah is One God: / Glory be to Him: / (Far Exalted is He) above / Having a son. / To Him / Belong all things in the heavens / And on earth. / And enough / Is Allah as a Disposer of affairs."[44]

4. *Crucifixion and Death of Jesus.* The Bible reports the death of Jesus by crucifixion. Theologians, philosophers, and historians through the centuries may have had various understandings of the meaning of the crucifixion, but the historical fact of the crucifixion has been affirmed. Christians have believed that the death of Jesus on the cross has been effective for the salvation of a sinful humanity. The Qur'an and the Bible

differ on the crucifixion. Surah 4:156–158 states, "That they said (in boast), / 'We killed Christ Jesus / The son of Mary, The Messenger of Allah' / But they killed him not, / Nor crucified him, / But so it was made / To appear to them, / And those who differ / Therein are full of doubts / With no (certain) knowledge, / But only conjecture to follow, / For of a surety / They killed him not— / Nay, Allah raised him up / Unto Himself." Surah 3:54–55 reports, "And (the unbelievers) / Plotted and planned, / And Allah too planned, / And the best of planners / Is Allah. Behold! Allah said: / 'O Jesus! I will take thee / And raise thee to Myself / And clear thee (of the falsehoods).'"

The Qur'anic references indicate that Jesus was not crucified and that God planned and made it look like they crucified him. Muslim scholars give differing explanations of these passages. Some say that Jesus hid in a niche in the wall, and one of his companions died in his place. Others say that God sent angels to protect Jesus, and Judas Iscariot was made to look like Jesus and died in his place. Some believe that Simon of Cyrene was substituted while he was carrying Jesus' cross. A traditional view held by Muslims is that the Jews tried to kill Jesus, but were unable to do so. They believe that Jesus was taken up into heaven to be with God.

One Muslim raises questions about the death of Jesus: "(1) Can the crucifixion be reconciled with the justice, mercy, power, and wisdom of God? (2) Is Jesus' death at the hands of his enemies consistent with the providence of God? (3) Is it feasible to believe that the God who forgave Adam and Eve their sin would need a sacrifice of Jesus to forgive the human race?"[45]

There appears to be confusion about the Qur'an's presentation of Jesus and the crucifixion. Other passages speak of the death of Jesus. Surah 19:33 states, "So Peace is on me / The day I was born, / The day that I die / And the Day that I / Shall be raised up / To life (again)." Thus, the Qur'an states that Jesus was not crucified, but God made it appear that he was. Muslim scholarship struggles for interpretations of Jesus and his death.[46]

5. *Resurrection of Jesus.* The Bible holds that Jesus overcame death on the cross by being raised from the tomb on the third day. Thus, resurrection follows crucifixion. Acts 2:23–24 asserts that Jesus "being delivered by the determinate counsel and foreknowledge of God, ye have taken, and by wicked hands have crucified and slain: Whom God hath raised up, having loosed the pains of death: because it was not possible that he should be holden by it." And 1 Corinthians 15:14f. states, "And if Christ be not risen, then is our preaching vain, and your faith is also vain. . . . And if Christ be not raised, your faith is vain; ye are yet in

your sins. . . . But now is Christ risen from the dead, and become the firstfruits of them that slept."

All four Gospels report that after the crucifixion the body of Jesus was placed in the tomb. On the third day the tomb was empty, and the resurrection of Jesus had occurred. Accounts of Jesus' being seen after the resurrection are recorded in Luke 24:34, 36; John 20:19; Matthew 28:16; John 20:26; and Acts 9. He was recognized by his followers.

The Qur'an reports nothing about the resurrection of Jesus. If Jesus never died, there could be no resurrection. Although the Qur'an has little to report about Jesus after his "appearance" at the crucifixion, Muslim tradition has various stories of his latter days. According to these traditions Jesus will return from heaven, battle the Antichrist, and defeat him. Jesus will confess Islam, kill all swine, break all crosses, and establish a millennium of righteousness. There is a tradition that Jesus will marry and have children.

The Bible reports the ascension of Jesus. Acts 1 states that Jesus remained on earth forty days after the resurrection, and then was taken up to heaven. Jesus attested this even according to John 16:7 and Luke 24; Peter attested it according to Acts 2:32–33, and the writer of Hebrews also attested it (Heb. 4:14). Christians expect Jesus to return. All humankind will appear before the judgment of Jesus as recorded in Matthew 25:31–46.

6. *Jesus: A Prophet among Prophets.* Jesus is assigned many titles in the Qur'an. Perhaps two of the most enigmatic are Kalima (Word) of God and Ruh (Spirit) of God. No other prophet, including Muhammad, is referred to as Word and Spirit of God. Other terms used of Jesus in the Qur'an include "servant," "spirit," "prophet," "messenger," "sign," "witness, "righteous," and "blessed." Muslims hold Jesus in high respect and honor. When they say his name, they repeat "Peace be upon him."

The title *prophet* is the most appropriate for Jesus both in the Qur'an and in orthodox Islam. There are twenty-eight prophets recognized in the Qur'an. They include Adam, Noah, Abraham, Moses, Elisha, Zechariah, John the Baptist, and Jesus. These prophets are found also in the Bible.

The five major prophets in Islam who are predecessors to Muhammad the final prophet are Adam, Noah, Abraham, Moses, and Jesus. Thus, Jesus is a predecessor to Muhammad in the line of great prophets which culminates not in Jesus but with Muhammad.

The Qur'an states in Surah 2:136, "Say ye: 'We believe / In Allah, and the revelation / Given to us, and to Abraham, / Isma'il, Isaac, Jacob, / And the Tribes, and that given / To Moses and Jesus, and that given /

To (all) Prophets from their Lord: / We make no difference / Between one / And another of them: / And we bow to Allah (in Islam)."

The purpose of the prophets is to carry the message of strict monotheism to the people of their day. "And in their footsteps / We sent Jesus the son / Of Mary, confirming / The Law that had come / Before him: We sent him / The Gospel: therein / Was guidance and light." (Surah 5:46) "And (appoint him) / A messenger to the Children / Of Israel." (Surah 3:49)

The worldview of Qur'anic Islam includes a salvation based on faith and works, a judgment, and a heaven and hell. Essential to this view are the basic beliefs annunciated above of God, angels, sacred scripture, prophets, and predestination. Also the practices of confession, prayer, almsgiving, fasting, pilgrimage, and missionary efforts are required.

Muslims hold a high view of their sacred scripture. There are no errors in it. The Qur'an has answers for all challenges in life. Christianity needs to develop an expertise in knowing the Qur'an and its teachings and implications for the religious, political, economic, and social life of a people and a community

W. C. Smith writes of the Muslim understanding of the Qur'an,

> Muslims do not read the Qur'an and conclude that it is divine; rather, they believe it to be divine, then they read it. This makes a great deal of difference, and I urge upon Christian or secular students of the Qur'an that if they wish to understand it as a religious document, they must approach it in this spirit. If an outsider picks up the book and goes through it even asking himself, What is there here that has led Muslims to suppose this from God? he will miss the reverberating impact. If, on the other hand, he picks up the book and asks himself, What would these sentences convey to me if I believed them to be God's word? then he can much more effectively understand what has been happening these many centuries in the Muslim world.[47]

Folk Islam and Christianity

Qur'anic Islam follows the formal teachings and the letter of the law embedded in the Qur'an. Folk Islam tends to combine Qur'anic Islam with other beliefs and practices of a particular culture. For example, in Folk Islam, Muhammad and Jesus may be objects of prayer or may be considered mediators to God. There are saint's shrines or mosques in many Islamic lands. These shrines are named for important leaders like

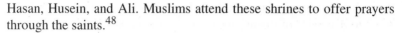

Hasan, Husein, and Ali. Muslims attend these shrines to offer prayers through the saints.[48]

Folk Islam may include power encounters with a spirit world, especially in health and healing and life decision concerns. It may incorporate fetishes and amulets. Tribal and ethnic characteristics may be expressed in Folk Islam. Sufism is considered the mystical arm of Islam. It stresses the love of God, the closeness of God, and feelings about God. The Nation of Islam in the United States may be viewed as Folk Islam as it integrates Qur'anic Islam with nativistic traditions and with the ideologies of its founders, Mr. Fard and Mr. Muhammad.

Folk Islam appears to address the heartfelt and spiritual needs of a people. It desires a God who is near and not far away. Christianity is challenged to understand the differences between Qur'anic Islam and Folk Islam and to determine if Folk Islam for Muslims addresses some of the issues and needs of humanity which may be expressed in Christianity but which may be denied or challenged in Qur'anic Islam.

Christianity and Islam: Government and Religious Freedom

In predominantly Muslim countries, Islam is expressed in various ways in religion and government and freedom of religion. Saudi Arabia places many restrictions upon the expression of Christianity; Christian missionaries are excluded and churches cannot be constructed. The Islamic Republic of Iran has placed severe constraints upon the native churches, and Christians have been persecuted and martyred. In Indonesia generally there has been religious liberty and freedom. In Lebanon, Christians and Muslims have had both peaceful and stormy times.

Christianity must be vigilant on matters of religion and government and religious liberty and freedom. Already discussed is Islam's view of the world divided into two spheres: the territory of Islam or submission to Allah and the territory of ignorance or non-submission or war. John Kelsay writes that in classical Islamic scholarship the territory of Islam is viewed as the territory of justice and peace. In contrast the territory of ignorance is full of disorder and strife and is a continual threat to Islam. Therefore, the peace of the world cannot be fully secure until people come under the protection of Islam. Kelsay points out that there is a program of action, namely jihad, to help bring about the territory of Islam.[49]

Christianity needs to engage Islam about such topics as theocracy, the relationship of religion and government, the nature of religious pluralism in a society, and the provision of religious liberty and freedom of choice in religion. The way Islam answers these topics influences the missionary nature of Christianity, the sending of missionaries across

cultures, the continuing relationship of Christianity and Islam, the freedom of individuals to choose their religion, and the protection provided
citizens of a nation.

The twenty-first century will provide the Church and Islam, especially in the United States, the opportunity to explore these topics. As
Islam becomes a major religion in American society, being afforded all
the freedoms and liberties guaranteed by the constitution to all religions,
what will be its response to its relationships to politics, government,
laws, and guarantees? How will these responses be interpreted by
Qur'anic and/or Folk Islam? How will they be consistent or not consistent with worldwide Islam and its practices?

The forebears of the United States came to America to escape religious oppression. They framed the Constitution and the Bill of Rights to
protect citizens from oppression and to provide them with certain freedoms as long as they do not violate the rights of others. These include
freedom of worship and of religious expression. The plurality of religions is a feature of American society.

Christianity in its encounter with Islam must raise the issue of religious liberty. On one hand the Qur'an states, "Let there be no compulsion / In religion."[50] On the other hand it asserts, "If any one desires / A
religion other than / Islam (submission to Allah), / Never will it be
accepted / Of him, and in the Hereafter / He will be in the ranks / Of
those who have lost."[51] Within Islam can Christianity stand alongside
Islam and be granted the freedom of expression? Can a Muslim have the
right to change religion or is it apostasy punishable by death?

In Saudi Arabia only Muslims can worship openly. A death sentence
and bounty have been placed upon Salman Rushdie, author of *Satanic
Verses*, for criticizing something in Islam. Rushdie wrote the book in
England, and Ayatollah Khomeini issued the death sentence from Iran
with a reward to anyone who murdered him. A presidential decree is
necessary for a church to be built in Egypt. How does Islam respond to
the question of religious liberty?

The United States is founded upon the principles and practices of
democracy. Through elected officials, citizens are governed by representation. Governance is framed with reference to the Constitution and the
Bill of Rights. Laws are written, taxes are set and collected and spent, and
programs are developed and administered for the welfare of the people.

The separation of church and state is a basic concept within American
democracy. Islam claims there is no separation between the secular and
the religious, between Islam and the state. It also holds that the Qur'an
is the principal source of law and legislation. "We have sent down / To

thee the Book in truth, / That thou mightest judge / Between men, as guided / By Allah."[52] The Islamic worldview also holds that there is the world of Islam and the world of ignorance. The world of Islam must overtake and either convert or subsume the world of ignorance.

Christianity must encounter Islam in its view of relationship to governance and law in society. In multicultural and multireligious societies how does Islam respond to diversity and variety of religious worldviews and lifestyles?

In the United States there should be equality of citizens and therefore no discrimination based on race, color, gender, or religion. Christianity needs to engage Islam within a democratic society on Islam's perspectives on these matters within the public arena.

Christianity and Islam: Encounters of Change, Conversion, Contextualization

Christianity and Islam are missionary religions. Both the Bible and the Qur'an present mandates to their followers to be missionaries for their religions. History has demonstrated that Muslims have become Christians and that Christians have become Muslims. Christianity is tolerant of Christians joining Islam, if not pleased that a Christian would become a Muslim. Islam is not accepting nor tolerant of Muslims becoming Christians. As Christians and Muslims live beside each other, work together, send their children to the same schools, and engage in more social discourse, they will need to dialogue about change and conversion.

Each religion needs to consider what contextualization will mean for its religious expressions across cultural boundaries. Muslims who choose Christianity may desire to bring certain cultural attributes with them. They may want to continue their dietary customs, their postures in prayer, their month of fasting, and a certain vocabulary. Christians who convert to Islam may call their Friday class at the mosque "Sunday School" or move some of their Friday gatherings at the mosque to Sunday. Their ideas and feelings about Jesus may carry over into their Islamic understandings.

At first the commonalities between the two seem great: both are historical, monotheistic and ethical religions with similar religious stories of creation, prophets, angels, sacred books and a worldview of a heaven, a hell, and a judgment. Their religious lifestyles are similar, especially in the areas of the call for dedication and commitment to follow the divine will of God, a prayer life, a life of giving, and a missionary vision.

Upon closer examination, however, their dissimilarities soon surface. Islam criticizes and condemns Christianity's teaching about the divinity and crucifixion of Jesus as blasphemy. Thus, Islam denies the very foundation on which the Christian faith stands. It also considers the Christian teaching of the Trinity as the worst of errors about the nature and character of God.

On the other hand, Christianity for the most part has considered Islam as a Christian heresy. It does not consider Muhammad a prophet and often castigates the Qur'an's teachings on polygamy, the role of women, rules and regulations about inheritance, and punishments for crimes, and on its theocratic world vision.

As geography shrinks, as transportation and communication draw people closer together to speak and listen to one another, and as peoples of diversity increasingly mingle in the vocational, educational, and recreational areas of life, encounters between Muslims and Christians will continue. What the relationships will be and how they will be expressed will be the grist of future generations.

12

ISLAM:
REVIEW AND PREVIEW

REVIEW

I slam is a worldwide religion with a billion adherents. Muslims are united by a common monotheism and the practice of six fundamentals: prayer, fasting, giving, pilgrimage, jihad, and confession of one God and Prophet Muhammad as the last messenger. They have set times and positions of prayer, a common calendar of religious activities, and common pilgrimage site in the sacred city of Mecca. Universality has been demonstrated in the mission and mobility of Islam to cross cultures and take root in the lives of millions of people far away from its origins in the Arab society of the Arabian peninsula.

The ideal realization of Islam has revolved around a close association between form and function, and faith. Form and function were given in the Qur'an, were exercised and taught by the Prophet Muhammad, were included in the Sunnah or tradition of Muhammad, and were stipulated to Muslims to emulate.

From its early days, Islam provided a complete roadmap for life from birth to death and beyond. It furnished a pattern and an answer for religious, political, economic, and social expressions. Religion and state were not separated. Civil and religious matters were one. The Muslim community was mandated to express its collective and individual life upon the rules and teachings firstly of the Qur'an, secondly of the Sunnah, and thirdly of the Shari'a. The ideal community was that established and led by Prophet Muhammad in the city of Medina.

Yet schisms and factions have developed. Differences have not resulted from denial of or different practices from the major beliefs of one God, angels, prophets, sacred scripture, and judgment. Nor have there been deviations from the six solid practices. Most fragmentation within the Islamic community and most factions have resulted from politico-theological differences. Interpretations of the Qur'an and the Sunnah have resulted in various schools of theology and law with varying rulings on the economic, political, and social forms of life.

For example, there is little if any variation from what the Qur'an teaches and the Sunnah expresses in times to pray, requirements of the pilgrimage, and the observations of the fasting season. However, Muslims have differences of opinion on who was to succeed Prophet Muhammad, on what forms certain punishments for crime should take, and on the shape of government and the state. Muslims have also differed on the interpretation of jihad, when it should be applied, who should call for it, and against whom it should be called.

Thus, various groups have emerged within Islam with differences of politics and theology. The Sunnis and the Shi'ites have differed over the succession of leadership to Muhammad. The Muslim Brotherhood, Hamas, Hezbollah, and many other "parties" have begun over perceived and real threats to the integrity of Islam. Some of the groups have formed militias and waged warfare in the name of God. Other groups have worked for change within the political, economic, and religious structures.

Islam, like other religions, has its devoted and obedient adherents as well as its followers who are Muslims culturally but are detached from the praxis of the major pillars of Islam. They promote and wage jihad for Islam but are not especially practitioners of mosque prayer, fasting, and pilgrimage. Islam, too, has its Qur'anic Muslims who are fundamentalists and literalists, and it has its Folk Muslims who adapt other cultural traditions to overlay Islam. For example, there are Muslims who attend prayer services in the mosque led by a member of the ulama and visit a saint's tomb to voice prayer to the saint for assistance. Muslims may thus practice orthodox and Folk Islam simultaneously and may emphasize one over the other.

TEN MAJOR PATTERNS OF ISLAM

A review of Islam indicates the following:

1. Islam is a major world religion which began in seventh century Arabia during the lifetime of Muhammad (A.D. 572–632) and has become present in most nations with some one billion adherents.

2. Muslims point to the glory days of Islam as (a) the time of Muhammad when he established the Islamic community, the *umma*; (b) the Abbasid Caliphates (A.D 750–1250) with Islamic excellence in arts, architecture, science, medicine, and literature; and (c) the high days of the Ottoman Empire (1500–1924).

3. Pessimism characterized Islamic literature and public utterance during the nineteenth- and early twentieth-century decline of Islam. Islam pointed to the culprits of the imperialistic and colonialistic policies and intrusions of outsider forces, particularly Europe and later the United States.

4. Some Islamic countries received vast oil revenue after World War II. New wealth brought a fresh identity to Islam and to Muslims and a revivalism and resurgence. Monies were utilized for nation-building and renewal of Islamic culture and civilization as well as for extending the mission of Islam to other countries and cultures. Islam saw a new missionary movement during the latter half of the twentieth century, particularly in Africa, Europe, the United States, and Central Asia.

5. The establishment of the state of Israel in 1948 galvanized parts of the Islamic world against Zionism. Islamic states waged wars against Israel; Islamic groups were formed within and across Islamic states to wage jihad against Israel through raids, hijackings, and terrorist car bombings among civilian populations. The Palestine Liberation Organization (PLO) became a major force rallying support across Muslim nations to fight against Israel and Zionism.

6. The revolution in Iran brought Ayatollah Khomeini to power in 1979. He initiated the Islamic Republic of Iran, chased from the monarchy the westernizing Shah, and began a brand of Islamic fundamentalism that since has been exported to other countries and societies. Iran became a symbol of Islamic revival and resurgence which was to be emulated by other Muslim groups and some nations.

7. The demise of the USSR in the late 1980s freed former Soviet republics heavy with Islamic populations to become independent. Muslim nations, including Turkey, Saudi Arabia, and Iran, have focused attention on the new emerging republics with monies and personnel to influence their direction in nation-building as well as Islamic identity.

8. Europe and the United States now have significant Muslim populations. Muslims and Muslim organizations have become significant with presence and power in the political, economic, and social affairs.

9. With the rise of Islam after 1950, a debate has ensued about the "clash of civilizations" between that of Islam and that of the West and between Islam and Christianity. Various symposia, conferences, and dialogue meetings have been held in academia, held between Muslims and Christians, and held in the domain of world religionists.

10. Christians and Muslims have been brought together by the globalization of politics, economics, and cultures due to the technological revolution of transportation and communication. This is part of a larger movement that includes all world religions. The past has engendered much misunderstanding. The present has been seen as a time for knowledge and understanding.

RESPONDING TO THE TWENTY QUESTIONS

In chapter one, questions and challenges to understanding Islam were projected in twenty categories of concerns. These twenty questions are to be revisited. Some of these questions cannot be answered definitively, but this conclusion will at least provide directions and clues to all twenty questions.

Religion is a simple but complex phenomenon, and Islam is no exception. There is a Qur'anic Islam and a Folk Islam. Both overlap and are different. There is a public Islam and a private Islam. The two may have many similarities but also may have significant differences. There is an Islam embodied in a national polity and an Islam expressed in a family setting. One ayatollah or sheikh may interpret Islam differently from another. Often, Muslims make choices about Islam between and among various schools of interpretation, or related to what a political leader says, or according to one's own understanding and conscience.

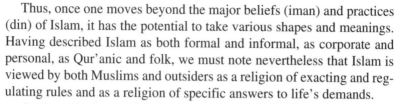

Thus, once one moves beyond the major beliefs (iman) and practices (din) of Islam, it has the potential to take various shapes and meanings. Having described Islam as both formal and informal, as corporate and personal, as Qur'anic and folk, we must note nevertheless that Islam is viewed by both Muslims and outsiders as a religion of exacting and regulating rules and as a religion of specific answers to life's demands.

In the early days of Islam perhaps Muslims would not argue or disagree over the set times of daily prayer or the fasting season or the contours of an Islamic ruled community or nation. In modern times Muslims perhaps would not argue or disagree over prayer or fasting, but might very well have different opinions over the nature and function of an Islamic state.

1. *What is the relationship of the worldview of the Prophet Muhammad to the Judaism and Christianity of his time?*

The worldview of the Prophet Muhammad was that presented in the Qur'an and in his teachings and practices. Its relationship to Judaism and Christianity was quite similar. All three religions saw a world in which one God created all matter and human beings. Humans were the epitome of creation. Prophets were sent as messengers to warn and to call back humans from their evil ways to follow the life and law which God originally gave.

Sacred scriptures contained the message of God as pronounced by the prophets. Human life was to be lived in a temporal and spatial dimension from the beginning—birth—to the ending—death—under the guidelines from God in the sacred scriptures. After death, there was a judgment based on rewards and punishments which resulted in a human's eternal condition in a paradise or a hell.

Therefore, the relationship of the Islamic worldview to that of Judaism and Christianity focused on monotheism, prophets, moral and ethical imperatives, societal structures for implementation of God's laws and commandments, a time to live and a time to die, and an eternal destiny.

To be sure, there were differences within the worldview between the three religions. Especially where Judaism anticipated a messiah, and where Christianity affirmed the messiah in Jesus Christ, Islam taught that Muhammad was the last prophet and that a Mahdi would likely come at the end of the world. Whereas Islam in its worldview taught that man was a viceregent to God and that there was no saving mediator between God and man, Christianity proclaimed that Jesus Christ was the mediator between God and man who brought salvation through his life, through his death by crucifixion, and through his resurrection.

Another major difference in worldview concerned the place of religion in society. Islam taught there was no separation between the religious order and the civil order. Islam presented a monolithic view of all of life as lived in the totality of Islam's ways. On the other hand, Christianity distinguished between religion and other features of life, accepted a separation of church and state, a difference between personal religion and corporate life. Thus, Islam's worldview sees itself as plurality and others as minorities who are dependent on Islam. Christianity's worldview sees itself as one religion among others who may or may not be majorities or minorities. However, both worldviews tend to be competitive in the marketplace of ideas and values, and both include missionizing aspects.

2. *Where did Muhammad gain his information about Abraham, Moses, Jesus, the Bible? Was it from Allah, angels, his travels, Jews and Christians of his time?*

This question is 1,400 years old. Devout Muslims believe that God revealed the truth about Abraham, Moses, Jesus, and other matters in the Bible through a series of revelations from the angel Gabriel to Muhammad which became codified in the Qur'an. Whatever the Qur'an says about these matters is the truth. If the Bible contradicts what is reported in the Qur'an, then the Bible is false or has been corrupted.

Scholars have not determined the extent to which Jewish and Christian presence was in the Arabian peninsula and particularly in the city of Mecca where Muhammad grew up. Although it is known from both the Qur'an and from the traditions of Muhammad that there were Christians and Jews in the societies on Arabian soil, it is still a question of how much Jews and Christians influenced Muhammad with knowledge of their teachings and beliefs. It is known that Muhammad traveled beyond the Arabian peninsula and likely may have engaged Jews and Christians in conversations along the trade routes.

Thus, devout Muslims believe that what Muhammad knows about Judaism and Christianity resides in the Qur'an and in his life experiences with those of his day in Mecca and Medina and possibly beyond the peninsula. Some scholars think that Muhammad's knowledge of Judaism and Christianity came from the forms of their expressions in particular Jews and Christians whom he met or about whom he heard.

3. *What are the grounds for the Muslim belief that Jesus did not die on a cross when history and historians confirm it?*

Muslims believe what the Qur'an says about the life and death of Jesus. Jesus is considered one among the prophets who came with the gospel (Injil) to the peoples of his time. The Qur'an indicates that it appeared that Jesus died on the cross. Muslim tradition says that some-one took his place on the cross.

Scholars have written that Muhammad was influenced by a certain early Christian theology of monophysitism or docetism which taught that Jesus did not really and physically die on the cross. Since Islam does not believe that Jesus died for the sins of humanity and does not have an atonement theology of Jesus' crucifixion, his death on the cross does not have to satisfy their theology. As far as history's validation of Jesus and the cross, Islam considers the Qur'an to have precedence in historical, scientific, and social facts.

4. *In the one hundred years after the death of Muhammad, how did Islam advance so rapidly and so far?*

Islam arose in the Arabian peninsula between the conflict of two empires, namely, the Byzantine empire of the West and the Persian empire to the East. As a new movement with a fresh vision and faith and with deeply committed warriors, it thrust itself beyond the peninsula to offer an alternative to peoples between and within the empires.

Some peoples willingly accepted Islam and became loyal followers. Others resisted and conflict ensued and deaths occurred. Jews and Christians who did not convert to Islam were given a special status of dhimmi with privileges for their appropriate worship and religious life but with restrictions not to proselytize and to pay a tax to the Islamic rulers.

Within one hundred years after the death of Muhammad in A.D. 632, Islam spread beyond the Arabian peninsula to the heartland of the Middle East, including Palestine and Jerusalem, across North Africa into Spain and on the edge of France, and eastward to Iraq, Persia, and into India and parts of Central Asia. Thus, Islam moved rapidly and established roots among millions of people in diverse locations and cultures. Hardly any other religious movement has done the same so quickly and widely.

Again, how did Islam accomplish this feat? There is no single factor. It was by force. Some call it jihad or holy warfare. It was by the capitulation of people to join Islam either by consent or by constraint. It was because some saw Islam as a liberating and stabilizing movement which offered direction and destiny to life. Like Judaism and Christianity, it was a movement which basically differed with their beliefs and practices but which offered them conditional religious and social life within the rule of Islam.

5. *During the Dark Ages of Christianized Europe, what was the greatness of Islamic civilization and why?*

Islamic civilization reached a zenith during the Middle Ages, especially during the Abbasid empire (750–1250) and to the edges of the Ottoman Empire around 1500. Crises in European cultures and in the Christian church were due in part to the barbarian invasions and to conflicts within the church.

Meanwhile, Islam had advanced to the heartland of the Middle East, North Africa, Spain, and Persia. The genius of Islam was in its attention to knowledge of the world of human societies, of sciences, of mathematics, of literature, and of art and architecture. It coopted and inspired its Persian and Indian and Arab and Spanish followers and converts to master these fields of knowledge. It preserved the writings and great thought of Western scholarship from its decay in Europe through translations.

The great cities of Damascus, Baghdad, Cairo, Isfahan, Samarkand, Bukara, Cordova, Fez, and Delhi became examples of Islamic resurgence and excellence in schools and research and writings and scientific and medical practices and architectural gems. The greatness of Islam was its capacity to inspire certain people with a highly focused worldview, with a disciplined and orderly life, and with a sense of responsibility and commitment to explore the world of knowledge and use it for the benefit and beauty of humankind in the humanities and arts and sciences.

6. *How have the Christian crusades influenced the Islamic world?*

Islam captured Jerusalem and Palestine in the seventh century as it advanced westward beyond the Arabian peninsula. Christian armies under the aegis of the Pope and European kings launched a series of wars against the Islamic peoples of Palestine and Jerusalem from A.D. 1099 into the thirteenth century. With few successes the Christians were defeated. The lands remained under the domination of Islam until the establishment of the state of Israel in 1948.

The influences of the Christian crusades upon the Islamic world are many. Muslims have viewed Christianity as a warring religion. They have believed that Christianity is a colonialistic, imperialistic, and political movement to dominate the world, including the lands of Islam. They have looked upon Europe and the United States as Christian entities whose governmental and foreign affairs have been improvised to dominate Muslim societies politically, economically, culturally, and religiously. They have seen Christian missionaries as agents of Western imperialistic societies.

Thus, the Christian crusades of the medieval period against Muslims have never been forgotten. Muslims are reminded of them in their primary and secondary school curricula. In sermons in the mosque the ulama preach about them and against them. Muslims speak of Napoleon's entry into Egypt in 1798 as a crusade, bringing the Western intrusion into Islamic society.

Muslims see the establishment of the state of Israel as a furtherance of the crusading mentality of the Western Christian nations. They view as colonialism the United States involvement in supporting the Shah of Iran during the 1960s and 1970s and his dependence on western aid and advice. This led to the Iranian revolution in which the United States was called "The Great Satan" and the epitome of a crusading nation. The crusades of the medieval ages launched centuries of distrust and disgust by Muslims toward Western nations, Western cultures, and Christianity.

7. Why have the words "terrorists" and "militants" been associated with Muslims in the mass media?

The mass media have used these words to refer particularly to various Islamic organizations who claim to be responsible for plane hijackings, car and bus bombings, explosions in buildings and among civilian populations, and the taking of hostages. The meaning of *terrorists* is stated differently by those perpetuating the destruction and by the media who describe them.

After this violence and destruction and loss of life have occurred, often the Islamic group which has perpetuated it claims responsibility through print or telephone call. Sometimes a video of the young Muslim is shown on television telling why he is about to become a martyr in his act of destruction in which he dies along with his intended victims. He does this in the name of Allah. He is identified with a Muslim organization like Hezbollah or Hamas or the Muslim Brotherhood or another of the many groups who train and exercise for this mission.

Does the Qur'an and Islamic tradition justify these acts? It depends on which Muslims one listens to, on which Qur'anic verses are recited, and on which Islamic tradition is followed. On one hand Islam is a religion of peace and justice. On the other hand Islam is a religion of jihad, both a personal struggle to obey God and a community struggle to establish the rule of Islam in the world where the straight path of God is implemented.

8. How does Islam perceive itself in relation to other religions when and where it is the dominant religion or when and where it is one among other religions in a religiously pluralistic society?

According to Islam the world is divided into two areas: the world of obedience to God and the world of disobedience. The word *Islam* means obedience. The motive and mission of Islam is to bring the world of disobedience under the rule of the Islamic world of obedience. In early Islam, Muhammad attempted to coopt the Jews to relate within the umma, the community of believers. The Jews refused. Warfare was declared against them.

As Islam spread to become dominant among other peoples and religions, it perceived itself as the superior straight path to God. Particularly in relation to Jews and Christians, it offered them a status of minority existence which included conditional freedoms in their worship and religious life as well as restrictions of proselytizing and also the requirement of paying taxes to the Islamic authorities.

Thus, where Islam has been dominant with power and control, it has generally allowed the conditional freedoms of other religions. However, patterns vary from one Islamic-dominated country to another. Saudi Arabia's rulers govern under an Islamic constitution which allows no freedom of worship among the few Christians and no construction of churches. No Jews or Christians may visit the Muslim holy sites of Mecca and Medina. In Indonesia, a predominantly Muslim-populated country, the government attempts to treat all religions with equity.

Where Islam has been a minority religion, it has had various relationships to other religions. In India because of politico-religious tensions with that Hindu-dominated society, Muslims advocated a new nation which resulted finally in Pakistan. In Lebanon Muslims have made accommodations with Christians in the governance of the nation although there has been warfare between the two.

Thus, the issues of religious liberty, religious freedom, and personal decision–making by a Muslim to join another religion are considered in a variety of ways by Islam. There is a debate over what is Qur'anic Islam, true Islam, practicing Islam, and Folk Islam over answers given to freedom, conscience, apostasy, and pluralism among religious communities.

History and literature are replete with examples of minority religious communities living under the restraints of a dominant Islam. While history gives little evidence of mass movements of Muslims to another religion, history tells of examples of Muslims who choose another religion, are declared apostates, are disowned by families and communities, and are sometimes killed. History has fewer examples of those who freely leave Islam and are given the freedom to do so.

9. *What is the meaning of political Islam and religious Islam and what are the differences between them if any? Is Islam a theocratic religion?*

Muslims consider true and correct Islam to be that practiced by Prophet Muhammad in accordance with the revelations given to him by God. During his lifetime all revelations were given to him for governance of the community in all matters political, economic, religious, and cultural. Muhammad was prophet, ruler, judge, 'pastor,' and exemplar of the community.

The revelations were codified in the Qur'an shortly after the death of Muhammad. Also, his sayings and actions became the handbook to complement and supplement the Qur'an. They became known as the Sunnah, the tradition of the Prophet. Later, schools of law and philosophy arose. But Muslims have believed that the order of priority is Qur'anic Islam, then Sunnah Islam, and then Shari'a Islam.

Ideally there is not a political Islam and a religious Islam. Islam is one. There is no church-state dichotomy. Islam is a theocracy. God has spoken through his last Prophet Muhammad and revealed the straight path. The ideal community is the umma founded by Muhammad in Medina during the period A.D. 622–632. The resurgence of Islam in the late twentieth century has beckoned Muslims to return to their Qur'anic roots and to the characteristics and values of Muhammad's life and teachings.

10. *Is one born a Muslim? How does this affect one's citizenship and one's religion and one's marriage? Is "one once a Muslim always a Muslim" true?*

The word *Muslim* means one who submits or obeys. The implication is one who submits to God and obeys. Islam means submission or obedience. It stands for a religion of revelation given to the last Prophet Muhammad which has been codified in the Qur'an.

In theory, anyone is a Muslim who obeys the God of the Qur'anic revelation. In practice, a Muslim is one born into a Muslim family in a Muslim community with an heritage and tradition rooted in Islam. Also, practically speaking, one is a Muslim who has converted from another religion to Islam or has adopted Islam of one's own free will.

In an Islamic society one is considered a Muslim by birth to Muslim parents and family. It is a given that one will grow up in Islam and be a Muslim for life. If one were to leave Islam, that would be a denial of one's birthright, of one's family, of one's community, and of the true religion. In Islam there is no reason for a Muslim to become a non-Muslim and/or to join another religion. There are serious religious, cultural, and political consequences. Apostates may be excommunicated from family and community and killed. Muslim identity may be associated with status and privilege in citizenship.

A Muslim woman may not marry a non-Muslim man. If a Muslim man marries a non-Muslim woman, any children should be brought up as Muslims. Thus, theoretically, once a Muslim always a Muslim. In an Islamic-governed nation, various rules are applied to the rights of non-Muslim citizens to serve in government or in the military.

11. *When a spokesman for Hezbollah (Party of God) speaks, what authority does he have in relation to Islam? Does he represent Allah? Islam? A few Muslims? An Islamic nation?*

Authority in Islam comes from a prioritizing order of sources. The written sources are the Qur'an, the Sunnah, and the Shari'a. Authoritative leaders in Islam achieve legitimacy through their knowledge of Islam, their leadership skills, and their acquisition of a significant following who believe in and trust them as leaders.

Leaders of Muslim communities are given titles such as ayatollah, sheikh, and mufti. A Muslim authority may give opinions on matters such as warfare. They may issue a fatwa, a ruling based on their interpretation of the Qur'an and/or Sunnah and/or Shari'a, which gives permission to a Muslim group to wage jihad against an enemy.

Hezbollah is led by a sheikh. He gives guidance to the followers of the movement on many matters, including who is the enemy and how the Party of God may relate to the enemy. It may be that other Muslim nations and groups of Muslims may give aid and comfort to the sheikh of Hezbollah in his leadership of dedicated Muslims who fight for Allah and who seek martyrdom on Allah's behalf. The name *Hezbollah* denotes Muslims who are devoted to the cause of Allah. The way they understand and implement their form of Islam may differ from that of other Muslim groups and nations. However, they proudly and profoundly fight for their cause with rulings and interpretations which they claim legitimize the living out of Islam in their lives.

12. *In a world of nation states, how does Islam address the issues of theocracy, separation of church and state, religion and politics, and freedom of religion?*

Islamic leaders, both the ulama who are cleric types and Muslim leaders of Islamic nations, have varying interpretations of the content and form of issues like theocracy, religion and politics, and freedom of religion. A general principle of Islam is that there is no separation between religion and other facets of life, both personal and corporate. Life is of one piece. God commands the personal life, the family life, the society's life, and the government's life. God rules. God rules through his vice-regents who follow the guidelines in the Qur'an with any needed assistance from tradition and law. Islam promotes a theocracy.

Among modern nation states in a closely related global network of communication and interdependence, Islamic nations give various answers and expressions to relationships to pluralism. Some have monarchies with or without parliaments. Some have presidents with various forms of socialistic and democratic assemblies. Some rely on Islamic jurists for counsel in shaping laws and programs. Others ignore the centralities of Islam.

The king of Saudi Arabia rules the nation based on forms of Shari'a law. There is little freedom of religion in the country. Iran established an Islamic Republic with the cleric class, members of the ulama, in power and reliance on Shari'a law. The Iranian government led an effort to cleanse the nation of the leadership of the Baha'i religion. The government of the Sudan has attempted to implement Shari'a law in its governance. Other Islamic nations have tended to rely on features and models of Western law and form for governance.

13. *What religious, political, and cultural meanings does Islam attach to the city of Jerusalem and to the land of Palestine? What is the meaning of Jerusalem compared to Mecca and Medina?*

Jerusalem has several significant meanings to Muslims. It is the city where the Dome of the Rock is located on the Jewish Temple Mount as well as al-Aqsa Mosque. The environs of the Dome of the Rock are associated with the patriarch Abraham, whom Muslims consider to be the first Muslim. The Dome is also associated with the night journey to heaven by Muhammad during his Meccan life.

Muslims consider Jerusalem the third sacred city. Mecca is the first city where the Prophet Muhammad was born and where the sacred Ka'ba is located, the place of pilgrimage. Medina is the second city, the city where the prophet founded the great community of Muslims, the umma, and where he is buried.

When Jerusalem was under the authority of the Hashemite kingdom of Jordan, prior to the state of Israel, Jews and Christians had freedom to worship in the holy city. Since 1948 with the establishment of Israel, there have been restrictions on certain Muslims from pilgrimage and worship at the Dome of the Rock and al-Aqsa mosque.

Islamic nations for the most part have supported the rights of the Palestinian peoples for a homeland in Palestine. Islam has viewed Zionism as a colonialistic impetus for the state of Israel and as an enemy of the Muslim people. Some Muslim nations and leaders from time to time have called for a jihad, a holy war, to recapture Jerusalem and Palestine. While non-Muslims are not allowed inside the cities of Mecca and Medina, Islamic leaders have called for peoples of all faiths to have access to Jerusalem.

14. *Jihad is a major belief and practice of Islam. What is it? Who can declare it? Against whom can it be declared? Why does one Muslim leader declare jihad against another Muslim leader?*

The basic meaning of jihad is to strive or to struggle to achieve one's basic responsibilities to God. The Islamic worldview divides the world into two areas: the world of Islam or obedience and the world of disobedience. Jihad means to work to enable the world of Islam to overcome the world of disobedience. Muslims interpret jihad in a personal way and a corporate way. Both the individual and the community are to be involved in struggle to establish the world of Islam over untruth, falsity, ignorance, and disobedience.

Both the Qur'an and the Sunnah establish criteria for jihad and who may declare it on behalf of the community. The individual employs jihad in firmly stating the beliefs of Islam and regularly practicing the pillars of Islam. A Muslim community expresses jihad in an apologetic of the Islamic faith against falsehoods and ignorance. It also employs jihad in warfare against attacks on the integrity of the Muslim community by outsiders. Jihad may take the form of war against declared enemies in which Muslim armies are sent against the foe.

A high Muslim authority and leader, relying on the Qur'an and Islamic jurisprudence, may issue a fatwa or ruling that jihad is necessary and appropriate against an enemy, whether the enemy be an individual, a group, a nation, or nations. Islamic communities and nations have made jihad against a non-Muslim people, but they have also declared jihad against another Muslim people. This means that an Islamic nation may be considered by another Islamic nation to be un-Islamic and worthy of warfare. Iran declared jihad against Iraq; both are Islamic nations. Often it is argued that the political leadership of a nation is corrupt and un-Islamic and deserves to be overthrown.

15. *What are Islamic views on sexuality, gender roles, and marriage and the family? Does Islam speak with one voice on these matters?*

Islam has a high view of the sanctity and importance of marriage and the family. The Qur'an and the Sunnah give specific roles to husbands and wives. Generally the husband has responsibility for the livelihood of the family, and the wife oversees the domestic affairs of the home.

Polygamy is allowed. A man may have up to four wives with certain regulations. Divorce is permissible although not encouraged. Homosexuality is condemned. Abortion is strictly regulated and basically disallowed after a specific time of fetus development. Suicide is forbidden.

In modern Islamic societies, various interpretations and forms are expressed in family and domestic matters. Many women work outside the home. Polygamy is not condoned or is frowned upon. Women's dress may include a veil or head covering or modern dress. Modern societies have moved from patriarchical family arrangements to the nuclear family. Thus, Islamic forms and values of the family and gender roles have been challenged in the modern world. Muslims have various interpretations over what the Qur'an and the Sunnah allow in these matters.

16. *What is appropriate in greeting Muslims? Handshake? Words?*

Etiquette among Muslims is specific and routine as it is among peoples worldwide. There are greetings and goodbyes usually flavored with religious language of the wishes of God's peace and health. Between men there may be a handshake or an embrace with kisses to both cheeks depending on familiarity. Between men and women there is usually not physical contact in greetings.

The left hand should not be used in greeting since it is utilized for hygiene purposes, and one does not point the bottom of one's feet or shoes to another's face while sitting or conversing.

Traditionally, business matters among Muslims are implemented upon one's word. The Qur'an expressly forbids the taking of usury or interest, for it is not good neighborliness and deprives the community of more mutual funds.

17. *What makes a Muslim group legitimate in terms of its correct Islam? How do various groups of Muslims relate to each other?*

God is said to be the final arbiter as to what is correct Islam and who is a true Muslim. The blueprint and roadmap for submission to God, which is the meaning of Islam, is first found in the Qur'an whose original or "first copy" is with God in heaven, secondly is complemented by the Sunnah, the sayings and actions of the Prophet Muhammad, and thirdly is explored as to meanings and applications in the Shari'a, the commentaries of law and jurisprudence.

There are various Islamic communities who both for theological and political reasons have differed with one another. In fact, some Muslim communities have battled each other not only with rhetoric but with armies. A Muslim community may look to the authority of an ayatollah or a mufti who may have a different interpretation and approach to a Qur'anic or Sunnah or Shari'a statement.

Islam generally claims and practices great unity and uniformity. However, Sunnis have fought Shi'ites over the successorship to the

Prophet Muhammad. Wahhabis interpret the Qur'an literally in administering the punishments of cutting off hands for certain crimes, while the Alawites differ in forms of punishment. The Ahmadiyya have been declared heretics by other Muslim authorities, as has the Nation of Islam.

Thus, legitimacy in Islam may vary according to one's interpretations of sources, one's following a Muslim authority represented in a leader and a particular school of jurisprudence, or one's attachment to a nation or group with a political ideology mixed with religious and cultural agendas. There is both unity and variety within Islam.

18. *Various leaders of Islamic nations or Muslim groups often speak in the name of Islam. Is one more legitimate or acceptable than the others?*

Heads of state, political leaders and religious leaders often speak as Muslims and in the name of Islam. Some are informed more by Islamic theology and law than others. Some intermesh political ideology with religious interpretations. Their legitimacy and acceptability depend on a mixture of their character, their knowledge, the numbers and loyalty of their following or members of their community or citizens of their nation, and the traditions of Islam out of which they come and on which they stand.

Many Muslim leaders accept President Saddam Hussein as a spokesman for Islam; he has declared jihad against others including the West and certain Muslim nations. King Fahd of Saudi Arabia rules over a people with a prevalent Wahhabi Islamic history and tradition and considers himself as the guardian of the holy sites of Mecca and Medina.

Ayatollah Khomeini of Iran was viewed as the arch "fundamentalist" who desired to establish in Iran the model umma (community), after that of the Prophet Muhammad in Medina. Yasser Arafat prays in the mosque and utters certain Islamic slogans in his appeal to the Islamic world to rally around the establishment of a homeland for the Palestinians.

Louis Farrakhan claims to be a Muslim as leader of the Nation of Islam in the United States, but he is ostracized by much of the orthodox Islamic world as a heretic. Wallace Deen Muhammad, a former member of the Nation of Islam, is seen by worldwide Islam as a bonafide Muslim to be trusted as one of the best emissaries of Islam in the United States.

19. *Why do Muslims come to America? What do Elijah Muhammad, Wallace D. Muhammad, Malcolm X, and Louis Farrakhan have in common and what are their differences?*

Muslims entered the United States with the slave trade. Waves of Muslim immigration have occurred especially since the turn of the twentieth century with trade and business and with students in colleges and universities. An indigenous Islamic population arose among African-Americans particularly with the establishment of the Nation of Islam in the 1930s.

Since World War II, Islam has grown in the United States to an estimated five million-plus Muslims. There are many Islamic organizations across the United States with emphases upon building mosques, printing literature, teaching and training Americans in Islam, and developing mission outreach to the American public.

Elijah Muhammad, Wallace D. Muhammad, Malcolm X, and Louis Farrakhan are all African-Americans. Elijah Muhammad served as their tutor and model as he founded the Nation of Islam and as they became leaders in it. The Nation of Islam was founded on a syncretism of bits and pieces of Islam, a racist ideology and platform, and many of Elijah Muhammad's personal views.

After Elijah's death in 1975, his son Wallace veered toward orthodox Islam. In the 1990s he became the titular head of the Islamic community in America with the recognition of orthodox Muslim countries as well as with the offering of an opening prayer in the United States Congress. Malcolm X was a loyal lieutenant to Elijah until he recognized orthodox Islam on his visit to the Middle East. Upon his return he exposed Elijah and the erroneous teachings of the Nation of Islam. He was murdered in 1965 by followers of the Nation.

Louis Farrakhan was also a loyal follower of Elijah, holding prominent positions in the Nation. Upon Elijah's death and upon Wallace's swing to orthodoxy, Farrakhan became head of the Nation of Islam and continued Elijah's main teachings and practices with some changes. Farrakhan has little recognition among the orthodox Islamic communities.

Islam in America has grown in numbers and organizations. With continuing growth rates and patterns, it is forecast that Muslims will exceed the numbers of Jews in the United States and become the second largest religion in the nation.

20. *What if any challenges do Muslims face in the United States? What are their strengths and weaknesses? How is Islam in America related to worldwide Islam?*

Islam is a world religion with some one billion followers. As with any religion, what its followers say and do in one part of the world may influence Muslims in other parts of the world as well as non-Muslims who view Islam. Worldwide Islamic organizations and governments contribute finances and personnel and material to Muslims and Islamic organizations in the United States. Muslims in America relate to worldwide Islam in many ways, including making the annual pilgrimage to Mecca and Medina in Saudi Arabia.

Muslims face several challenges in the United States. The diversity of Islam is evident and causes misunderstanding and uncertainty among many non-Muslims. There is great contrast between the Islam of Wallace D. Muhammad and that of Louis Farrakhan. As Islam grows in numbers and status, many question how they will fit into a democratic and pluralistic society. How will Muslims relate to a society in which Christianity is the dominant religion? Can Islam thrive as a minority religion? Also, how will Christianity and Judaism relate to a growing Islamic presence?

With expressions of militant Islam in other parts of the world and in the United States such as the bombing of the Trade Center in New York, American Muslims are asked their views on the nature and function of militant Islamic groups and their relationships if any to them. The primary challenge to Islam in America is to identify what Islam *is* and how it is to function in a democratic and pluralistic society. Another challenge is to deal with the stereotypes and biases of Americans toward Islam as it is presented in the mass media and in the actual events among Muslims worldwide and in the United States.

GLOSSARY

Abbasid
Caliphate at Baghdad from the eighth to thirteenth century; claiming descent from Abbas, uncle of Muhammad.

Abd
A slave or servant; used either literally or in the religious sense as a servant of God.

Ablution
A ritual washing before the prescribed daily prayers.

Abu Bakr
Early convert to Islam in Mecca; first Caliph in Medina.

Adab
Manners, etiquette.

Adhan
The Muslim call to prayer; performed by the muezzin from the minaret.

Ahl al-kitab
"People of the Book" or "People of Scripture"; Jews, Christians, Sabaens, and Zoroastrians who according to Islam received revelations through appropriate prophets and messengers; the revelations were later corrupted necessitating a new revelation through Muhammad.

Ahmadiyya Sect
Offshoot of Islam founded in India by Mirsa Ghulam Ahmad (died 1908); he is believed to be the Muslim Messiah; it is a missionary sect.

Ali
Son-in-law of the Prophet Muhammad; married the Prophet's daughter Fatima; first Imam of the Iranian Shi'ites; fourth caliph in Sunni tradition.

Allah
Arabic name for God; means "the God."

Allahu Akbar
"Greater is God."

American Muslim Mission
Founded by Wallace D. Muhammad after his father Elijah Muhammad's death; moved toward orthodox Islam.

Anno Hegira
Year of the hegira when Muhammad fled from Mecca to Medina; abbreviated A.H.; the Islamic calendar begins.

Ansar
"Helpers"; those early Muslims in Medina who received and assisted Muhammad after his flight (Hegira) from Mecca.

Ashura
Day of commemoration of the martyrdom of Imam Husein.

Asr
The third prayer; the afternoon prayer.

Ataturk
(1881-1938); Kemal Ataturk was founder and first president of secular Turkish state; he abolished Islamic law and caliphate at the demise of Ottoman Empire.

Awqaf	A religious endowments foundation; pious Muslims give to the institution to be used for stated purposes, which may include building and restoring mosques, education, propagation of Islam; singular is waqf.
Aya	A verse of the Qur'an; chapter is sura.
Ayatollah	Religious leader among the Shi'ites who is given high authority.
Baraka	Blessing; spiritual power inherent in a saint; more generally, inherent power.
Beautiful Names	Ninety-nine names that characterize Allah; most important are al-Rahman (the merciful) and al-Rahmin (the mercy giver).
Bilal	The first Muezzin (caller to prayer) appointed by Muhammad.
Bismalah	The general Islamic invocation of God; "In the name of the merciful Lord of mercy," which prefaces every Surah of the Qur'an except Surah 9.
Dar al-Harb	"House of War"; the areas of the world yet unsubdued by Islam.
Dar al-Islam	"House of Islam"; the geographical realm in which Islam is in full devotional, political, and legal actuality. In Muslim constitutional law, the world is divided into Dar al-Harb (territory not under the rule of Islam) and Dar al-Islam (territory under the rule of Islam); Dar al-Harb should be brought under Islam either by surrender or warfare.
Dawah	"Call"; missionary; organization for propagation of Islam.
Dervish	Member of a religious brotherhood like a Sufi order; a religious mendicant; a faqir; induce ecstacy by movement, dance, and the recitation of the names of God.
Dhimmi	A non-Muslim subject under Islamic rule in one of the tolerated minorities; subject to special taxes called jizya in place of zakat, which is required of Muslims.
Din	Religion in general; religious duties in particular.
Do'a	Non-ritual prayer; supplication in distinction to Salat prayer.
Faqih	Legal expert; jurisprudence.

Farrakhan	Lewis Farrakhan, close associate to Elijah Muhammad of Nation of Islam; after Elijah's death, Farrakhan continued the Nation of Islam as leader.
Fatwah	A legal opinion given by a high religious leader like an ayatollah or mufti in which the Shari'a is applied to cases or issues so that its authority may be upheld.
Fatima	Daughter of the Prophet Muhammad; wife of Ali.
Fiqh	Jurisprudence; the legal sytem of Islam adjudicated in courts and interpreted by the schools of law.
Five Pillars of Islam	Five duties of every Muslim; recitation of creed (Shahada); prayer (Salat); almsgiving (Zakat); month of fasting at Ramadan (Saum); pilgrimage to Mecca (Hajj).
Gabriel	The angel through whom Allah revealed the Qur'an to Muhammad.
al-Ghazali	(1058-1111); orthodox Muslim legal expert who became a Sufi; defended the teaching of the Qur'an and denied human deification.
Hadith	"Tradition"; reports of the words, actions, and attitudes of the Prophet Muhammad, constituting a body of literature second only to the Qur'an in authority for Muslims.
Hafiz	One who memorizes the total Qur'an.
Hajj	Pilgrimage to Mecca and its environs; one of the pillars (required practices) of Islam.
Hanafi	One of the four major Islamic schools of law (fiqh).
Hanbali	One of the four major Islamic schools of law (fiqh).
Hanif	"He who possesses the real and true religion"; a monotheist in pre-Islamic Arabia; used especially of Abraham as the first Muslim.
Haram	"That which is forbidden by the sacred law."
Hasan	Son of Ali; grandson of the Prophet Muhammad; second Imam of Shi'ites.
Hegira	The emigration of Muhammad and his community from Mecca to Medina in A.D. September 20, 622 from which the Islamic lunar calendar dates; Muslims use

	A.H. 1 (After the Hegira) to begin their official calendar.
Hira Cave	Cave outside Mecca where Muhammad received the first revelation of the Qur'an.
Hezbollah	Party of Allah.
Husein	Son of Ali; grandson of the Prophet Muhammad; third Imam of Shi'ites; Iranian Shi'ites revere him with the narrative and drama of his death.
Ibadat	Acts to be performed in religious ritual.
Iblis	Satan.
Id al-Fitr	The feast and celebrations of breaking the fasting season of Ramadan that is required of Muslims and is one of the basic pillars of Islam.
Id al-Adha	The feast that celebrates the conclusion of the pilgrimage to Mecca; a lamb or other animal is sacrificed by those in Mecca as well as all Muslims on this particular day.
Ijma	"Agreeing upon, consensus"; the consensus of the Muslim community as expressed by its mujtahids (those who have a right by virtue of their knowledge and position) to form a judgment of their own on a matter of interpretation of the Islamic law.
Ijtihad	The individual initiative of experts or leaders in the Islamic community whereby valid Ijma is generated with the community.
Ikhwan	Brotherhood.
Ilm	A term broadly meaning knowledge, especially religious knowledge.
Imam	(1) Leader of the congregational prayer (Salat) in the mosque; (2) among Sunnis, the Caliph; (3) among Shi'ites, one of the descendants of Ali recognized by Allah as supreme ruler of the world.
Iman	Faith, belief, and in particular the beliefs of religion in distinction to din, which refers to liturgical practices.
Injil	"Gospel"; revelation or book given to Jesus (Isa).
Inqilab	Revolution.

Insha'a Allah	God willing; "If Allah wills."
Islam	The faith, obedience, and practice of peoples who follow the teachings of Muhammad; the final, perfect religion of Allah; "submission to Allah."
Isma'ilis	A group of Shi'ite Muslims who believed the seventh Imam was the last Imam.
Isnad	The chain of authorities preceding a Hadith.
Ithna Ashariya	The "Twelvers"; the Shi'ites who believe that the Imamate passed through twelve descendants of Ali; the official Islam of Iran.
Jahiliya	The age of ignorance in pre-Islamic Arabia preceding Islam; the age of ignorance involves an element of unruliness or uncouthness.
Jama'a	Group.
Jihad	The concept of extraordinary effort in the belief and practice of Islam; often understood as a militancy in defending and/or extending the interests of Islam.
Jinn	Spiritual creatures of the Divine will and power.
Jizya	"Tribute, poll tax"; levied on the dhimmis by the Muslim rulers.
Ka'ba	"Cube"; the central sanctuary in the great house of pilgrimage at Mecca; made of grey stone and covered by a black curtain.
Kafir	Infidel; non-believer.
Kalam	"Speech"; the science of theology that sets forth the divine attributes according to the Islamic revelation.
Khadijah	First wife of the Prophet Muhammad; a wealthy widow and early follower of her husband's establishment of Islam.
Khatib	The mosque preacher; delivers the Friday sermon (Khutba).
Khalifa	"Successor, vice-regent"; politically the succession to the rule of Muhammad from the first caliph, Abu Bakr, down to 1924; (caliph is the anglicized form of khalifa, that is, the possessor of khalifa or caliphate); in the Qur'an the term means the status of humankind in the person of Adam as trustee for Allah in the world.

Kharijites	"Seceders"; fanatical moralistic sect of early Islam.
Khutba	Sermon delivered at the mosque at Friday noon prayer.
Khums	"1/5"; tax; 1/5 of annual income paid to religious authorities (Shi'ite).
La ilaha illa Allah	The first four words of the Muslim confession (Shahada); there is no god but God.
al-Lat	One of the three pagan "daughters of Allah" in pre-Islamic Arabia.
Madrasa	Institution where the Islamic subjects are taught; usually attached to a mosque and supported by endowments (Awqaf).
Mahdi	al-Mahdi; "the guided one"; the divinely guided one often associated with the Hidden and Twelfth Imam of the Shi'ites.
Malcolm X	Close associate of Elijah Muhammad in Nation of Islam; left the Nation of Islam; moved toward orthodox Islam; murdered in 1963 by members of the Nation.
Malikite	One of the major four schools of Islamic law (fiqh).
al-Manat	"Fate"; one of the three pagan "daughters of Allah."
Masjid	"Place of prostration"; a mosque, the building in which Muslims pray and gather for other religious and social occasions; its major features are the minaret, the mihrab, and the minbar.
Marja-i-taqlid	"Source of emulation"; supreme authority on Islamic law (Shi'ite).
Maulid	The Prophet's birthday; or a saint's birthday; festivities and celebrations.
Mecca	Holy city of Islam; birthplace of Muhammad; Muslims pray toward Mecca; take the pilgrimage to Mecca.
Medina	Second holiest city of Islam beside Mecca; Muhammad fled to Medina in A.D. 622; first established his religion there; location of his tomb.
Mihrab	The niche in the mosque which marks the Qiblah (direction) of Mecca; the recess into which the Imam (prayer leader) enters to pray.
Millat	"Community"; nation.

Minbar	The pulpit or raised platform, often with ascending steps, in the mosque from which the Friday sermon (Khutba) is given.
Minaret	The spiral column or columns of the mosque which houses stairs within and from whose top the prayer leader may call Muslims to prayer.
Miraj	Muhammad's ascent to heaven on his famous "Night Journey."
Mu'azzin	The person who calls Muslims to prayer; may ascend the minaret to utter the call or from inside the mosque or from a tape recording.
Mufti	A qualified Islamic religious leader who may issue a Fatwa (opinion) on a matter of law or of Islamic concern.
Muhajirun	Those followers of Muhammad who emigrated with him from Mecca to Medina in A.D. 622.
Muhammad	Prophet of Islam; (A.D. 570-632); born in Mecca; buried in Medina.
Muhammad, Elijah	Founder of Nation of Islam in the United States; syncretism of Islam with racist ideology.
Muhammad, Wallace D.	Son of Elijah Muhammad; Succeeded his father and founded American Muslim Mission; moved toward orthodox Islam. One of the months of the Islamic calendar.
Mujaddid	The renewer, the restorer, the reformer in Islam; one is to come in every century.
Mujahidun	Soldiers of Allah.
Muta	Temporary marriage.
Muslim	One who believes in, belongs to, and performs Islam; "one who submits."
Muslim Brotherhood	Egyptian puritanical organization founded in 1928 by Hasan Brotherhoodal-Banna.
Mu' tazilah	A school of theology in the ninth century A.D. which expressed speculative views toward the Qur'an and free will in distinction from orthodoxy.
Nabi	A prophet.

Nation of Islam	Founded by Elijah Muhammad in the United States in the 1930s; blended Islamic teachings with racist ideology; Louis Farrakhan became the leader of the Nation after Elijah's death.
Ottoman Empire	(A.D. 1453-1918); the empire of Ottoman Turks who were converted to Islam; empire stretched from Balkans through the Middle East; supported Sunni Islam; dismantled after World War II.
Qadi	A judge of Muslim law.
Qiblah	The direction of Mecca; a Muslim prays in this direction.
Qur'an	The holy book of Islam; contains revelations given from Allah to the angel Gabriel to the Prophet Muhammad; 114 chapters (suras).
Quraysh	Muhammad's tribe in Arabia.
Qiyas	Analogy; a provision whereby the law of Islam may be extended to cover matters analogous to but not explicitly in the Qur'an and Hadith.
Rabb	Lord; the most frequent title of Allah in the Qur'an.
Rahman	"Most merciful"; a divine attribute of Allah.
Rak'ah	Section of prayer.
Ramadan	The ninth month of the Muslim year; it is the month of obligatory fasting when one should not eat, drink, or participate in sexual intercourse; 27th of Ramadan is the day the fast is concluded.
Rasul	Messenger or apostle; title of Muhammad.
Salat	Ritual prayer; performed five times daily; one of the pillars of Islam.
Salat al Asr	Afternoon prayer.
Salat al Fajr	Dawn prayer.
Salat al Isha	Late evening prayer.
Salat al Maghrib	Evening prayer after sunset.
Salat al Zuhr	Midday prayer.
Salaam	"Peace"; a salutation, greeting, blessing.

Sawm	Fasting; an obligatory pillar of Islam; observed during the month of Ramadan.
Sayyid	A descendant of Husein, son of Ali and Fatima (daughter of Prophet Muhammad).
Shafite	One of the four major Islamic schools of law (fiqh).
Shahada	Witness or confession; first pillar of Islam; "there is no god but God, and Muhammad is the messenger of God."
Shahid	Martyr.
Shari'a	Sacred and canon law given in the Qur'an, Hadith, Qiyas, and Ijma; the path of duty both ritual and general for Muslims.
Sheikh	Title of respect; religious leader.
Shi'ite	"Partisan"; followers of branch of Islam, the Shi'ites, who accept Ali as the legitimate successor to Muhammad; believe the descendants of Muhammad should rule the Islamic community. Iran is the primary Shi'ite Muslim nation.
Shirk	"Association"; the act (sin) of regarding anything as equal to Allah; idolatry, polytheism, or attributing divinity to anyone.
Shukr	Gratitude or thanksgiving.
Siyam	Fasting.
Sufi	A Muslim mystic; Sufism is mysticism or tasawwuf. It has leaders called Sheikhs and followers called brotherhoods.
Sunnah	The path of tradition; orthodoxy; way of faith and conduct followed by the Sunni community of Islam.
Sunni	Term describing the larger branch of Islam which relies on the Qur'an and the Hadith; differs from the branch of Shi'ites who rely on the Imams.
Sura	A chapter of the Qur'an; a total of 114 suras.
Tafsir	Explanation or exegesis of the Qur'an.
Taqlid	The adoption of the utterances or actions of another as authoritative. Example: A Shit'ite Muslim may rely

completely on the interpretation and actions of the Ayatollah for one's faith and practice.

Tariqah   "Road, way, path"; the Sufi way of discipline and initiation into divine knowledge.

Tawhid   The doctrine of the divine unity of Allah.

Twelvers   The majority group of Shi'ite Muslims mainly in Iran; believe that the twelfth Imam will reappear as the Mahdi.

Ulama   Scholars of Islamic theology or law; plural of Alim.

Umayyad   First dynasty of caliphs A.D. 661-750 in Damascus.

Umma   The community of Islam; the solidarity of faith and prayer; the political incorporation of the Islamic faith.

al-Uzza   One of the three pagan "daughters of Allah" in pre-Islamic Arabia.

Wahhabi   Puritanial Islamic movement founded by al-Wahhab (A.D. 1703-92) of Arabia; accepts only the authority of Qur'an and Sunnah; dominant religious influence in Saudi Arabia.

Wahy   Inspiration; the state of receptivity in which Muhammad received and communicated the Qur'an.

Zakat   Almsgiving; an obligatory pillar of Islam.

Zuhr   Second prayer; noon prayer.

NOTES

Chapter 1

1. Please see Clifford Geertz, *Islam Observed* (Chicago: University of Chicago Press, 1968) and also Clifford Geertz, "Religion as a Cultural System," in *Anthropological Approaches to the Study of Religion*, ed. Michael Banton (London: Tavistock Publications, 1966).

2. Please see William Cantwell Smith, *The Meaning and End of Religion* (New York: New American Library, 1964), especially chapters 6 and 7.

Chapter 2

1. Please see George W. Braswell Jr., A *Mosaic of Mullahs and Mosques: Religion and Politics in Iranian Shi'ah Islam*, an unpublished Ph.D. dissertation, The University of North Carolina at Chapel Hill, 1975, for an anthropological and historical background of the development of Islam.

2. Please see W. Montgomery Watt, *Muhammad, Prophet and Statesman* (London: Oxford University Press, 1956) for his presentation on characteristics.

3. Please see W. Montgomery Watt, *Muhammad: Prophet and Statesman* (Oxford: Oxford University Press, 1956), especially chapters 1, 2, 3, for a historical overview of Mecca and its relation to Islam.

4. W. Montgomery Watt, *Muhammad at Mecca* (London: Oxford University Press, 1953), and W. Montgomery Watt, *Muhammad at Medina* (London: Oxford University Press, 1956).

5. A paper presented by a Muslim scholar, Akbar Muhammad, Ph.D., at a Baptist-Muslim dialogue, Pomona, California, May 16, 1981.

6. Please see Earle Waugh, "The Popular Muhammad Models in the Interpretation of an Islamic Paradigm," in Richard C. Martin, ed., *Approaches to Islam in Religious Studies* (Tucson: The University of Arizona Press, 1985), 41–58, for a critical study of writings about Muhammad.

7. Qur'an 53:1–18.

8. Qur'an 74:2.

9. Ibid.

10. Qur'an 96:1–5.

11. Muhammad Muhsin Khan, *The Translation of the Meanings of Sahih al-Bukhari,* Arabic-English vols. 1–9 (Beirut: Dar al Arabia [P.O. Box 6089], n.d.), Hadith 1:4; 1. 1. 3.

12. "The Satanic Verses" in the Qur'an deal with this subject.

13. Qur'an 72:1.

14. For the life of Muhammad, also please see Ibn Ishaq's *Sirat Rasul Allah*, translated by A. Guillaume (London: Oxford University Press, 1955); Muhammad Husayn Haykal, *The Life of Muhammad* (Indianapolis: American Trust Publications, 1976); W. Montgomery Watt and John Glubb, *The Life and Times of Muhammad* (New York: Stein and Day, 1970).

15. Mumtaz Ahmad, ed., *State Politics and Islam* (Indianapolis: American Trust Publications, 1986), 26ff. For a complete reading of the Constitution of Medina, please see Afzel Iqbal, *The Prophet's Diplomacy* (Cape Cod: Claude Stark & Co., 1975), 11–15.

16. Ibid.

17. Qur'an 2:159.

18. Gustave E. Von Grunebaum, *Medieval Islam* (Chicago: University of Chicago Press, 1961).

19. Please see Watt, *Muhammad* (1961).

20. Qur'an 8:65.

21. Qur'an 8:17.

22. Qur'an 33:37.

23. Iqbal, *Prophet's Diplomacy,* 37–38.

24. Ibid., 38.

25. Ibn Ishaq, *Sirat Rasul Allah.*

26. Khan, *Sahih al-Bukhari:* Hadith 4:173; 52. 165. 277.

27. Ibid., Hadith 4:487; 56. 22. 747.

28. Ibid., Hadith 5:526; 59. 8. 738.

29. Ibid., Hadith 1:199–200; 7. 1. 331.

30. Ibid., Hadith 8:257; 75. 45. 386.

31. Ibid., Hadith 8:213; 75. 3. 319.

32. Ibid., Hadith 5:183; 58. 45. 266.

33. Ibid., Hadith 2:238; 23.69.425.

Chapter 3

1. Kenneth Cragg and R. Marston Speight, *The House of Islam* (Belmont: Wadsworth Publishing Company, 1988), 88.

2. Ibid.

3. Ibid.

4. Ibid., 92.

5. Ibid., 89.

6. Ira G. Zepp Jr., *A Muslim Primer* (Westminster: Wakefield Editions, 1992), 196.

7. Ibid., 197.

8. Cragg, *House of Islam,* 90.

9. Zepp, *Muslim Primer,* 209.

10. Cragg, *House of Islam,* 93.
11. Ibid., 99.
12. Ibid., 104.
13. Ibid., 106
14. Charles A. Beckett, *Responses to Muslim Resurgence from Christians in the United States between 1979 and 1993* (Master's thesis, Hartford Seminary, 1993), 23.

Chapter 4

1. Please see Kenneth Cragg and R. Marston Speight, *The House of Islam,* 3rd ed. (Belmont: Wadsworth Publishing Company, 1988); and Nazar Mohammad, compiler, *Commandments by God in the Qur'an* (New York: The Message Publications, 1991) for data on Muslim world view and practice.
2. Qur'an 2:177.
3. Qur'an 2:177, 155; 59:21–14; 112:1–4; 1:1–5; 42:11.
4. Muhammad Husain Haykal, *Hayat Muhammad* (Indianapolis: North American Trust, 1976).
5. Please see Bernard Lewis, *The Arabs in History* (London: Hutchinson University Library, 1966) and DeLacy O'Leary, *Arabia Before Muhammad* (New York: Kegan Paul & Co., 1927).
6. Qur'an 53:19–23; 22:51.
7. A statement by a Muslim lecturer in my class on world religions, spring, 1994.
8. M. Amir Ali, Ph.D., *How to Present Islam: A Rational Approach* (Chicago: The Institute of Islamic Information & Education, 1994), 5.
9. Please see Sheikh Tosun Bayrak, *The Most Beautiful Names* (Vermont: Threshold Books, 1985) and Muhammad Iqbol Siddiqi, *Ninety-Nine Names of Allah* (Delhi, India: Adams Publishers & Distributers, 1990).
10. Qur'an 59:22–24.
11. Cragg and Speight, *House of Islam* (Belmont: Wadsworth Publishing Company, 1988), 11–12.
12. Qur'an 2:177, 285; 6:100; 15:27; 34:41; 46:29–32: 55:15; 72:1–28; 18:50; 114:6; 7:15–17; 15:39.
13. Qur'an 15:26–27.
14. Qur'an 2:34; 18:50; 38:71–77; 35:5; 4:120.
15. Qur'an 2:38, 177, 252, 285; 4:80, 164; 18:110; 33:40; 17:70; 7:26–27, 31, 35, 172; 17:70.
16. Qur'an 10:47; also please see 16:36; 40:15.
17. Qur'an 43:4; 13:39.
18. Qur'an 2:132, 136; 5:114.
19. Please see Geoffrey Parrinder, *Jesus in the Qur'an* (New York: Oxford University Press, 1977), for a comprehensive listing of Jesus' name in the Qur'an and implications of their meanings.
20. Qur'an 4:157–59; 3:55.
21. Ibid.
22. Qur'an 5:75.
23. Qur'an 2:4, 177, 285; 3:144; 5:67; 4:163; 15;19.
24. Qur'an 85:21–22; 43:3–4; 13:39.
25. Qur'an 15:9.
26. Kenneth Cragg, *Muhammad and the Christian* (Maryknoll: Orbis Books, 1984, 82–83).
27. Khan, *Sahih al-Bukhari,* Hadith 9:91–92; 87.1.111.
28. Ibid., Hadith 6:479; 61.3.510.
29. Richard C. Martin, ed., *Approaches to Islam in Religious Studies* (Tucson: The University of Arizona Press, 1985), 29.
30. Seyyed Hossein Nasr, *Ideals and Realities of Islam* (London: George Allen & Unwin LTD, 1966), 61.
31. Khan, *Sahih al-Bukhari,* Hadith 6:431–32; 60.332.459.
32. Qur'an 18:50; 114:6; 7:16–17; 15:39; 2:4, 177; 6:60; 7:34, 187; 10:49; 13:2; 18:8; 20:105–107; 22:1–2; 30:8; 31:29; 35:13; 39:5; 40:67; 46:3; 56:1–6; 99:1–5; 101:1–5; 6:2; 31:29; 103:1; 2:28, 284; 6:67; 6:95–97; 6:111; 6:149; 3:189–190; 10:99–100; 10:107; 25:2; 28:61.
33. Khan, *Sahih al-Bukhari,* Hadith 1:68; 3.22.81.
34. Ibid., Hadith 8:354; 75,47.539.
35. Ibid., Hadith 6:319; 60.254.338.
36. Qur'an 39:18; 46:33; 69:13–16.
37. Qur'an 16:89; 17:13–14; 18:49; 69:18–31; 37:18–21.
38. Qur'an 55; Also please see 37:43; 52:20; 56:22; 55:72; 44:54; 37:45–47; 52:24; 56:17; 74:19.
39. Ibid., Hadith 4:40; 52.4.48.
40. Ibid., Hadith 4:42; 52.6.53.
41. Ibid., Hadith 6:374; 60.294.402.
42. Qur'an; Please see Surah 44 and other references 4:45; 11:106; 14:16–17; 22:19–21; 25:12–13; 37:62–68; 67:7–8; 69:30–32.
43. Khan, *Sahih al-Bukhari,* Hadith 8:363; 76.51.555.
44. Ibid., Hadith 4:337; 54.15.535.
45. Isma'il R. al-Faruqi, *Islam* (Niles, Illinois: Argus Communications, 1984), 5.
46. Ali, *How to Present Islam,* 14.

Chapter 5

1. Qur'an 3:81; 5:83–84; 7:172; 3:144; 33:40; 48:29; 2:255; 3:18; 4:87; 64:8.
2. Qur'an 2:3, 177; 11:114; 17:78; 20:14, 130; 30:17–18.
3. Khan, *Sahih al-Bukhari,* Hadith 1:334–35; 11.1.578.

4. Ibid., Hadith 1:301; 10.6.506.
5. Ibid., Hadith 1:260; 8.61.436.
6. Cragg and Speight, *House of Islam,* 56–57.
7. Khan, *Sahih al-Bukhari,* Hadith 1:352; 10.30.620.
8. Ibid., Hadith 2:25; 13.29.51.
9. Please see George W. Braswell Jr., *To Ride a Magic Carpet* (Nashville: Broadman Press, 1977), 36–54, the chapter on "The Unveiling," to observe the Do'a prayers of women in homes and around tombs.
10. Qur'an 2:43, 83, 110, 177, 277; 9:60, 103; 24:56; 27:3; 57:7; 59:7; 98:5.
11. Khan, *Sahih al-Bukhari,* Hadith 2:325; 24.52.558.
12. Cragg and Speight, *House of Islam,* 45.
13. *Understanding Islam and Muslims,* a published pamphlet of The Islamic Affairs Department, Embassy of Saudi Arabia, Washington, D.C. (1989).
14. Phil Parshall, *Inside the Community: Understanding Muslims Through Their Traditions* (Grand Rapids: Baker Books, 1994), 95–96.
15. Khan, Sahih al-Bukhari, Hadith 2:299; 24.26.522.
16. Qur'an 2:183–185.
17. Ibid.
18. Khan, *Sahih al-Bukhari,* Hadith 3:82; 31.23.149.
19. Ibid., Hadith 3:72; 31.10.129.
20. Cragg and Speight, *House of Islam,* 61.
21. Khan, *Sahih al-Bukhari,* Hadith 9:434; 93.35.584.
22. Ibid., Hadith 3:88; 31.29.155.
23. Qur'an 2:196–201; 3:97; 22:26–29.
24. Qur'an 2:196.
25. Phil Parshall, *Inside the Community,* 84.
26. Khan, *Sahih al-Bukhari,* Hadith 2:390–91; 26:49.667.
27. Ali, *How to Present Islam,* 23.
28. Martin, *Approaches to Islam,* 85.
29. Khan, *Sahih al-Bukhari,* Hadith 3:38; 29.10.60.
30. Qur'an 2:244.
31. Qur'an 9:5.
32. Qur'an 47:4.
33. Qur'an 9:29.
34. E. Van Donzel, *Islamic Desk Reference* (New York: E. J. Brill, 1994), 136.
35. Ali, *How to Present Islam,* 35. Also, the author refers to the Qur'an references for jihad: Qur'an 2:218; 4:95; 8:72, 74–75; 9:16, 20, 24; 22:78; 61:11.
36. Qur'an 22:78.
37. Qur'an 49:15.
38. Khan, *Sahih al-Bukhari,* Hadith 1:300; 10.5.505.
39. Ibid., Hadith 4:50; 52.15.65.
40. Ibid., Hadith 2:274; 24.1.483.
41. Ibid., Hadith 5:309; 59.29.448.
42. Ibid., Hadith 4:254–55; 53.21.386.
43. Ibid., Hadith 9:45; 84.2.57.
44. Ibid., Hadith 9:213; 89.21.282.
45. Ibid., Hadith 4;62; 52.30.82.
46. Ibid., Hadith 9:413; 93.28.549.
47. Please see the writings of Robert Redfield for theories and descriptions of formal and informal, of orthodox and folk, and of great and little traditions in religions.
48. Please see Braswell, *Magic Carpet,* especially pages 36–54 for women's prayer meetings and meetings at tombs of saints.
49. Ibid., 43.
50. Please see Randal Gray and Dinah Hanlon, *Religions on File* (New York: The Diagram Group, 1990), 7:16 for chart of the Islamic calendar.
51. Qur'an 9:36–37.
52. Qur'an 17:1.
53. Braswell, *Magic Carpet,* 87–11.

Chapter 6

1. Qur'an 5:15–16.
2. Seyyed Hossein Nasr, "Sunna and Hadith," in *Islamic Spirituality: Foundations,* ed. Seyyed Hossein Nasr (New York: Crossroad, 1987), 104–105, as quoted in Parshall, *Inside the Community.*
3. Ram Swarup, *Understanding Islam Through Hadis* (Delhi: Voice of India, 1983), xv–xvi, as quoted in Parshall, Inside the Community.
4. Parshall, Ins*ide the Community,* 12–13. Please see Maurice Bucaille, *The Bible, the Qur'an and Science,* translated from the French by Alastair D. Pannell and the author (Indianapolis; North American Trust Publication, 1979).
5. Please see Reuben Levy, *The Social Structure of Islam* (Cambridge: At The University Press, 1962), 150–91 for a study of Islamic jurisprudence.
6. Please see Braswell, *Mosaic,* 56 ff. for data on the ulama.
7. George W. Braswell Jr., *The Ulama in Four Socio-Cultural Contexts* (master's thesis, University of North Carolina at Chapel HIll, 1973), 2.

8. Ayatollah Ruhollah Khomeini, *Islamic Government* (New York: Manor Books, Inc., 1979).

9. Levy, *Social Structures of Islam,* 297ff.

10. Levy, *Social Structures of Islam,* 141, 186, 203, 262, 349.

11. Please see Braswell, *Magic Carpet,* especially pages 114–116 for a description of how the Shah of Iran nationalized the Awqaf and thus got into trouble with the traditional religious leadership.

12. Please see Eerdman's *Handbook to the World's Religions* (Grand Rapids: Wm. B. Eerdmans Publishing Co., 1982), 330–31 for a succint description of the Sunni.

13. Please see Dwight M. Donaldson, *The Shi'ite Religion* (London: Luzon & Co., 1933) for a presentation of Shi'ite history and doctrines.

14. Shi'ite Islam in Iran may be viewed as a little tradition of religion within a great tradition, as an unorthodox expression of religion within orthodoxy, as a popular or folk expression of a religion. Refer to the writings of Robert Redfield for discussions of these meanings.

15. A Sofreh is a gathering around a table or tablecloth spread on the floor in a home to share food and the Husein story and to seek blessings from the imams. The food is often given to the poor. A Rowzeh is a meeting or series of meetings usually held during the month of Muharram in the home or mosque where a member of the ulama is present to recite and chant parts of the Husein narrative for the audience.

16. See Braswell, *Mosaic,* 40–41.

17. Ibid., 41–45.

18. Ibid. Please see pages 58–63 for a description of the ranks of the ulama and the meaning of the Twelfth Imam and a Marje' Taqlid.

19. Please see Muhammad Husayn Tabataba'i, *Shi'ite Islam* (Albany: State University of New York Press, 1975) for further discussions of Shi'ites.

20. Please see Von Grunebaum, *Medieval Islam,* for an overview of various types of theological thought within Islam.

21. Please see Idris Shah, *The Sufis* (Garden City: Doubleday & Company, Inc., 1971) for a full discussion of Sufism.

22. Qur'an 6:52.

23. Qur'an 50:16.

24. Qur'an 24:35.

25. John Alden Williams, ed., *Islam* (New York: George Braziller, 1962), especially pages 136–172 for the chapter "Sufism: The Interior Religion of the Commuity."

26. Ibid., 198.

27. Please see chapter 8 for a fuller presentation of the Nation of Islam within Islam in America.

Chapter 7

1. Please see an overview of morals and manners in Islamic life in Marwan Ibrahim al-Kayasi, *Morals and Manners in Islam* (New Delhi: Qazi Publishers, 1986).

2. Qur'an 4:43; 5:7.

3. Qur'an 2:173.

4. Qur'an 5:93–94.

5. Qur'an 2:168, 172; 5:90–91.

6. Qur'an 24:30–31.

7. Qur'an 7:32–33.

8. Please see Morroe Berger, *The Arab World Today* (New York: Anchor Books, 1964) for an overview of Arab personality and culture.

9. Qur'an 4:1; 7:107.

10. Qur'an 24:32.

11. Qur'an 2:228.

12. Qur'an 4:34.

13. Ibid.

14. Qur'an 2:223.

15. Qur'an 2:35–36; 7:19,27; 20:117–123.

16. Qur'an 58:1–4; 60:10–12.

17. Qur'an 2:178; 4:45.

18. Qur'an 16:57–59, 62; 42:47–50; 43:15–19; 53:21–23.

19. al-Kayasi, *Morals and Manners,* 84.

20. Zepp, *Muslim Primer,* 175.

21. Ibid., 176.

22. Ibid., 177.

23. Qur'an 4:3.

24. Qur'an 4:129.

25. Qur'an 33:50.

26. Hammudah Abdalati, *Islam in Focus* (Indianapolis: American Trust Publications, 1975), 174–79.

27. Khan, *Sahih al-Bukhari,* Hadith 5:371; 59.37.524.

28. Ibid., Hadith 1:165; 5.13.268.

29. Ibid., Hadith 7:50; 62.39.64.

30. Ibid., Hadith 4:411; 55.28.623.

31. Ibid., Hadith 3:455–56; 47.8.755.

32. Qur'an 3:102; also see 5:1–3.

33. Hammudah Abdalati, *Islam in Focus* (Indianapolis: American Trust Publications, 1975), 125–26.

34. Levy, *Social Structure of Islam,* 66.

35. Marwan Ibrahim al-Kayasi, *Morals and Manners in Islam* (New Delphi: Qazi Publishers, 1992), 150.

36. Ibid.

37. Qur'an 17:23–24.

38. Qur'an 17:26.

39. *Moral System of Islam*, a pamphlet published by The Institute of Islmaic Information and Education (P.O. Box 41129, Chicago, Ill. 60641–41129, n.d.).

40. Levy, *The Social Structure of Isalm*, 73–90.

41. D. S. Roberts, *Islam* (New York: Harper and Row, Publishers, 1982), 115.

42. Please see M. Umer Chapra, *Islam and Economic Development* (Islamabad: Islamic Research Institute Press, 1993), for a summary treatment.

43. Please see John L. Esposito, ed., *Voices of Resurgent Islam* (New York: Oxford University Press, 1983), especially the chapter by Khalid M. Ishaque, "The Islamic Approach to Economic Development" on Qur'anic principles of economic activity.

44. Qur'an 55:7–9.

45. Qur'an 83:1–6.

46. Roberts, *Islam*, 149.

47. Kenneth Cragg and Marston Speight, *Islam from Within* (Belmont: Wadsworth Publishing Company, 1980), 89.

48. Qur'an 2:274–276; also 3:130–31; 30:39; 2:278–79; 83:1–6.

49. Abdalati, *Islam In Focus*, 127.

50. Cragg, *Muhammad and the Christian*, 32.

51. Watt, *Muhammad at Medina*.

52. Ahmad, *State Politics and Islam*, 87–88.

53. Roberts, *Islam*, 78–79.

54. Qur'an 57:25.

55. Muhammad Hamidullah, *Introduction to Islam* (Paris: Centre Culturel Islamique, publication no. 1, 1969), 157f.

56. Ahmad, *State Politics and Islam*, 38–50.

57. Ibid., 9.

58. Qur'an 2:247; 5:2,8,105; 9:111; 7:72; 16:90; 39:9; 48:10; 49:13; 57:10; 68:10–15.

59. Ahmad, *State Politics and Islam*, 37.

60. Lewis, *The Arabs in History*, 19.

61. Ibid., 19–20.

62. Hassan al-Banna, *Bayna Al Ams Wal-Yom* (Between Yesterday and Today) as quoted in *Huna*, London, November 1983.

63. Ibid.

64. Al Nur, *The Islamic Center Quarterly*, 8, no. 3 (November, 1993): 9.

Chapter 8

1. Dr. Yusuf al-Qardawi, *The Lawful and the Prohibited in Islam*, 2nd ed. (Lahore, Pakistan: Islamic Publications LTD., February, 1991), 198.

2. Qur'an 17:31; 6:151.

3. Abul Fael Mohsin Ebrahim, *Abortion, Birth Control and Surrogate Parenting: An Islamic Perspective* (Indianapolis: American Trust Publications, 1989), 23.

4. Ibid., 24.

5. Ibid., 20.

6. Ibid., 33.

7. Ibid., 43.

8. Ibid., 37.

9. Qur'an 4:29; 54:32; 17:31–33; 81:8.

10. Qur'an 5:36.

11. Qur'an 24:2.

12. Qur'an 2:217.

13. Qur'an 21:178.

14. Ebrahim, *Abortion, Birth Control*, 70–72. Also, Qur'an 2:193.

15. Ibid., 73.

16. Qur'an 22:5.

17. al-Qardawi, *Lawful and Prohibited*, 201.

18. Ibid., 202.

19. Dr. Arafat El Ashi, "Islam and Abortion," *Muslim World League Series on Islam* no. 2.

20. Qur'an 7:80–81.

21. Qur'an 29:29.

22. Qur'an 7:82.

23. Sheikh Jaafar Idris, *Manar As-Sabeel* (Fairfax, VA.: Institute for Islamic and Arabic Sciences in America, May, 1993), 4–5.

24. Parshall, *Inside the Community*, 218–19.

25. Dr. Arafat El Ashi, "Islam and Homosexuals," *Muslim World League Series on Islam* no. 11.

26. Sheik N. Hassan, M.D., "AIDS—A Concern for Muslims," *Al Nur: The Islamic Center Quarterly* of Washington, D.C., 8, no. 3 (November, 1993): 17.

27. Ibid., 18.

28. Ibid., 19.

29. Albullah Muhammad Khouj, *The End of the Journey: An Islamic Perspective on Death and the Afterlife* (Washington, D.C.: The Islamic Center, 1988), 11–12.

30. Khan, *Sahih al-Bukhari*, Hadith 7:450–51; 71.56.670.

31. Ibid., Hadith 4:442–43; 55.45.669.

32. Khouj, *End of the Journey*, 12.

33. Translation made from a book by Dr. Mohammad Saeed Ramadan al-Butee, *Contemporary Issues in Islamic Law* (Damascus, Syria, 1991).

34. Marcel A. Boisard, *Jihad: A Commitment to Universal Peace* (Indianapolis: American Trust Publications, 1988), 23.

35. Ibid., 24.

36. John Kelsay, *Islam and War: A Study in Comparative Ethics, the Gulf War and Beyond* (Louisville: Westminster/John Knox Press, 1993), 1.

37. Ibid., 33. Please see Boisard, *Jihad*, 3–11, discussion on "The Division of the World."

38. Boisard, *Jihad*, 225.

39. Kelsay, *Islam and War*, 35–36.

40. Ibid., 44.

41. Boisard, *Jihad*, 23.

42. Ibid., 25–26.

43. Kelsay, *Islam and War*, 117.

44. Abdalati, *Islam in Focus*, 142.

45. Qur'an 2:216.

46. Abdalati, *Islam in Focus*, 142.

47. Qur'an 2:190–193.

48. Abdalati, *Islam in Focus*, 143.

49. Muhammad Hamidulah, *Introduction to Islam* (Paris: Centre Culturel Islamique, publication no. l, 1969), 156.

50. Abdalati, *Islam in Focus*, 148.

51. Ibid., 149.

52. Ibid., 150.

53. Ibid., 152.

54. Qur'an 6:137.

55. Qur'an 53:21–22.

56. Qur'an 53:27.

57. Qur'an 4:38.

58. Levy, *Social Structure of Islam*, 99.

59. Qur'an 33:50.

60. Levy, op.cit 99–103.

61. Qur'an 4:15.

62. Please see Sura 4 in the Qur'an for husband and wife relationships.

63. Qur'an 33:59.

64. Qur'an 24:30f.

65. Marwan Ibrahim al-Kayas:. *Morals and Manners in Islam*. New Delhi: Qazi: Publishers, 1992, 81–86.

66. Ibid.

67. David K. Wills, "The Practice of Islam," in *The Christian Science Monitor* (24 July 1984).

68. Ibid.

69. Hamidulah, *Introduction to Islam*, 134.

70. Ibid., 135–45.

71. Mary Ali and Anjum Ali, *Women's Liberation Through Islam*, a pamphet published by The Institute of Islamic Informatiion and Education, PO Box 41129, Chicago, Illinois 60641–0129, n.d.

72. Ibid.

73. Ibid.

74. Ibid.

75. Ibid.

76. Ibid.

77. Ibid.

78. Ibid.

79. *Human Rights in Islam*, a pamphlet published by The Institute of Islamic Information and Education, PO Box 41129, Chicago, Illinois 60641–0129, with permission of World Assembly of Muslim Youth, PO Box 10845, Riyadh 11443, Saudi Arabia, n.d.

80. Qur'an 5:44.

81. *Human Rights in Islam*.

82. Ibid.

83. Ibid.

84. Ibid.

85. Ibid.

86. *The Economist*, 4 April 1992, 47.

87. Bernard Lewis, "The Roots of Muslim Rage," in *The Atlantic Monthly* (September 1990), 49.

88. Ahmad Khomeini, in Kayhan, Teheran, 11 January 1992.

89. Bruce B. Lawrence, *Defenders of God: The Fundamentalist Revolt Against the Modern Age* (San Francisco: Harper & Row Publishers, 1989), 189.

90. Mohammad Mohaddessin, *Islamic Fundamentalism* (Washington: Seven Locks Press, 1993), 155–56.

91. *The Economist,* 2 April 1992, 11.
92. Lewis, "Roots of Muslim Rage," 56.
93. Ibid., 59f.
94. *The Economist,* 6 August 1994, 4–5.
95. Judith MIller, "Disenchanted Generation Turns to Two Islamic Fundamentalists," in *Foreign Affairs* (November-December 1994), as reported in *Raleigh (N.C.) News and Observer,* 27 November 1994.
96. Raleigh (N.C.) *News and Observer,* 27 November 1994, sec. A, p. 17.
97. Ibid., 17a and 22a.
98. Ibid., 22a.
99. Ibid.
100. Ibid.
101. Ibid, 23a.
102. Ibid.
103. Please see Martin E. Marty and R. Scott Appleby, *The Glory and the Power: The Fundamentalist Challenge to the Modern World* (Boston: Beacon Press, 1992), especially the chapter on "Remaking the World of Islam" for data on subjects like the Muslim Brotherhood and on Islamic movements in Egypt, Saudi Arabia, and Iran.
104. Eric Davis, "Ideology, Social Class and Islamic Radicalism in Modern Egypt," in *From Nationalism to Revolutionary Islam,* ed. Said Amir Arjomand (Albany: State University of New York Press, 1984), 10.

Chapter 9

1. *The Middle East and North Africa 1994,* 40th ed. (London: Europa Publications Limited, 1994), 14.
2. Please see Steven Emerson, *The American House of Saud* (New York: Franklin Watts, 1985) for coverage of the history of the Saud family and Arabia.
3. *Saudi Arabia: Islam,* a pamphlet published by the Royal Embassy of Saudi Arabia, Washington, D.C. (1989), 7–8.
4. Ibid. 9.
5. Gerald Sparrow, *Hussein of Jordan* (London: George G. Harrop Company, 1960), 16.
6. Stuart Mews, ed., *Religion in Politics: A World Guide* (Longman Group, UK Limited, 1989), 149–50.
7. Hassan Arfa, *Five Shahs* (New York: William Morrow & Company, 1965), 436.
8. Please see Braswell, Mosaic, for a description and analysis of the modernization attempts of the Shah versus the traditionalists' resistance of the ayatollahs and their followers.
9. Mews, *Religion in Politics,* Longman Group, UK, 108–15.
10. Braswell, *Mosiac,* for an overview of the conflict between the government and the traditionalists.
11. Please see Braswell, *Magic Carpet,* for a desciption of the author's years (1968–1974) in Iran, where he taught at the Muslim seminary of the University of Teheran.
12. Please see Khomeini, *Islamic Government,* for the theology and strategy of the Ayatollah.
13. *Religion in Politics* (Longman Group, UK), 116.
14. Ibid., 135–37.
15. *U.S. News & World Report* (14 March 1994): 35.
16. Stuart Mews, ed., *Religion in Politcs: A World Guide* (Chicago: St. James Press, 1989), 162–66).
17. Malcolm B. Russell, *The Middle East and South Asia 1994,* 28th ed. (Harpers Ferry: Stryker-Post Publications, 1994), 146–56.
18. Please see background articles on Assad in Arnaud de Borchgrave, "Interview with Assad," *Newsweek* (16 January 1978): 41–42; and David Pryce-Jones, "Assad the Terrible," *The New Republic* (30 January 1984): 20–25.
19. Ibid., 206.
20. Mews, *Religion in Politics* (St. James), 262–63.
21. Ibid., 269–70.
22. Please see *Middle East and North Africa* 1994, 88–97 for a history and description of the PLO.
23. George W. Braswell, *Understanding World Religions* (Nashville: Broadman Press, 1994), 142–51.
24. Please refer to a discussion of religion and politics in Mews *Religion in Politics* (Longman Group, UK), 62–66.
25. Ibid., 62.
26. Ibid.
27. Ibid., 169–71.
28. Ibid., 184.
29. Ibid., 268.
30. Mews, ed., *Religion in Politics* (St. James Press), 6.
31. Pierre Etienne Dostert, *Africa 1994* (Harpers Ferry: Stryker-Post Publications, 1994), 204–207.
32. Mews, *Religion in Politics* (St. James), 197–99.
33. Dostert, *Africa 1994,* 74–79.
34. Ibid., 254–58.
35. Dostert, *Africa 1994,* 200–203.
36. Patrick Johnstone, *Operation World* (Grand Rapids, Zondervan Publishing House, 1993), 511.
37. Patrick M. Mayerchak, *East Asia and the Western Pacific 1994,* 27th ed. in The World Today Series (Harpers Ferry: Stryker-Post Publications, 1994), 56.
38. Ibid., 57.
39. Mews, *Religion in Politics,* 107.
40. Mayerchak, *East Asia and the Western Pacific,* 58–61.
41. Ibid, 96.

42. Mews, *Religion in Politics* (St. James), 174–75.
43. Johnstone, *Operation World,* 366.
44. Please see Mews, *Religion in Politics* (St. James), 217–18 and Mayerchak, *East Asia and the Western Pacific,* 112ff. for a consideration of the Philippines.
45. Please see Mews, *Religion in Politics* (St. James), 30 and Mayerchak, *East Asia and the Western Pacific,* 16–19 for an overview of the politics and religions of Brunei.
46. Mews, *Religion in Politics* (St. James), 99–102.
47. Ibid., 1–5.
48. Ibid., 46.
49. *Eastern Europe and the Commonwealth of Independent States 1992,* 1st ed. (Europa Publications Limited), 440.
50. Ibid., 450–54.
51. Ibid., 464–68.
52. Ibid., 471–74.
53. Ibid., 506–09.
54. Ibid., 511–13.
55. Ibid., 525–28.
56. Mews, *Religion in Politics* (St. James), 5–6.
57. Ibid., 329.
58. Ibid., 77–78.
59. Ibid., 84.
60. Ibid., 291.

Chapter 10

1. Yvonne Y. Haddad, "A Century of Islam in America," in *The Muslim World Today,* Occasional Paper No. 4 (1986), 6.
2. *Raleigh (N.C) News and Observer,* 4 December 1993.
3. Newell S. Booth Jr., "Islam in America," in *Encyclopedia of the American Religious Experience,* ed. Charles H. Lippy and Peter W. Williams, vol. 2 (New York: Charles Scribner's Sons, 1988), 725.
4. Haddad, "Century of Islam," 2.
5. Booth, "Islam in America," 726.
6. Haddad, "Century of Islam," 3.
7. Booth, "Islam in America," 755.
8. J. Gordon Melton, *Religious Leaders of America* (Detroit: Gale Research Inc., 1991), 138.
9. C. Eric Lincoln, *The Black Muslims in America* (Grand Rapids: Eerdmans Publishing Co., 1994), 63.
10. Yvonne Haddad and Jane Smith, *Mission to America* (Gainesville: University Press of Florida, 1993), 67.
11. J. Gordon Melton, *The Encyclopedia of American Religions,* 4th ed., 892.
12. Please see Haddad and Smith, *Mission to America,* 170 ff for a discussion of United Submitters International.
13. Haddad and Smith, *Mission to America,* 137–38.
14. Ibid., 23 ff. and Melton, *Religious Leaders,* 901 for descriptions of the Druze.
15. Lincoln, *Black Muslims,* 17
16. A.B. Southwick, "Malcolm X: Charismatic Demagogue," in *Christian Century* (5 June 1963): 740–41.
17. Clifton Marsh, *From Black Muslims to Muslims: The Transition from Separation to Islam* (Meteushen: Scarecrow Press, Inc., 1984), 53.
18. A. Haley, *The Autobiography of Malcolm X* (New York: Grove Press, Inc.,1965), 310.
19. Ibid., 320.
20. Lincoln, *Black Muslims,* 432–33.
21. Haley, *Malcolm X,* 372.
22. A. Haley, "Epilogue," in *Malcolm X,* 423.
23. Lincoln, *Black Muslims,* 263.
24. Ibid., 118.
25. W. D. Muhammad, interview by Herbert Muhammad, Chicago, *Muhammad Speaks* (Chicago) 21 March 1975, 3.
26. W. D. Muhammad, *As the Light Shinest from the East* (Chicago: WDM Publishing Co., 1980). 113–119.
27. N. Sheppard, "Black Muslim Movement Divided in Dispute over Doctrinal Changes," *New York Times,* 7 March 1978, 18.
28. Steven T. Smith, *An Historical Account of the American Muslim Mission with Specific Reference to North Carolina* (Master of Theology thesis, Southeastern Baptist Theological Seminary, 1984).
29. A. A. Seifullah, "Human Revival Week Begins," in *Bilalian News* (Chicago) 9 March 1979, 4–5, 29.
30. Ibid., 29.
31. K. A. Alim, "Plots Exposed! Muslim Leader Challenges Followers," Chicago, *A.M. Journal* (Chicago) 18 June 1983, 8.
32. Chicago, *A.M. Journal* (Chicago), 1983, 1.
33. Haddad, "Century of Islam," 5.
34. Lincoln, *Black Muslims,* 265.
35. Melton, *Religious Leaders,* 147.

36. Lincoln, *Black Muslims,* 118.
37. J. Cummings, "Black Muslim Seeks to Change Movement," *New York Times,* 19 March 1978, 37.
38. W. D. Muhammad, 1978c, p. 3.
39. K. A. Alim, "Urge Support for Muslim Leadership," Chicago, *Bilalian News* (Chicago) 28 March 1980, 4.
40. M. A. Muharrar, "Minister Farrakhan and the Hoover Plan," *A.M. Journal* (Chicago) 29 April 1983, 2.
41. Smith, *Historical Account,* 152.
42. Lincoln, *Black Muslims,* 269.
43. Melton, *Religious Leaders,* 147.
44. Lincoln, *Black Muslims,* 272.
45. *Time* (28 February 1984): 21–22.
46. Ibid., 22.
47. *Time* (23 October 1995): 36.
48. *Time* (October 30, 1995): 35.
49. Ibid.
50. *U.S. News & World Report* (23 October 1995): 44.
51. *Time* (23 October 1995): 35–36.
52. *Newsweek* (30 October 1995, 36.
53. Ibid.
54. *Time* (30 October 1995): 52.
55. Alice Dembner, "Saudi Grant to Put Harvard at Fore of Islamic Studies," *Boston Globe,* 19 June 1993.
56. Braswell, *Understanding World Religions,* 118–223.
57. John Kelsay, *Islam and War: A Study in Comparative Ethics, the Gulf War and Beyond* (Louisville: Westminster/John Knox Press, 1993), 33.

Chapter 11

1. W. Montgomery Watt, *Muslim-Christian Encounters* (London: Routledge, 1991), 6.
2. Qur'an 2:62.
3. Qur'an 5:82.
4. Qur'an 57:27.
5. Qur'an 2:113.
6. Qur'an 5:14.
7. Qur'an 19:16–34.
8. Qur'an 3:45–53.
9. Qur'an 4:156–158.
10. Qur'an 3:55.
11. Qur'an 4:171.
12. Qur'an 5:72f.
13. Qur'an 5:116f.
14. Levy, *Social Structure of Islam,* 309–311.
15. Cragg and Speight, *House of Islam,* 82.
16. Watt, *Muslim-Christian Encounters,* 61.
17. Ibid, 62.
18. R. W. Southern, *Western Views of Islam in the Middle Ages* (Cambridge: Harvard University Press, 1962), 5–6.
19. Watt, *Muslim-Christian Encounters,* 66.
20. Ibid., 68.
21. Steven Runciman, *A History of the Crusades*, vol. 1 (London: Cambridge University Press, 1951), xi.
22. Watt, *Muslim-Christian Encounters,* 78.
23. Ibid., 81.
24. Ibid., 82.
25. Ibid., 83.
26. Charles Kimball, *Striving Together: A Way Forward in Christian-Muslim Relations* (Maryknoll: Orbis Books, 1991), 40–41.
27. Ibid., 84.
28. James Kritzeck, "Muslim-Christian Understandings in Medieval Times," *Comparative Studies in Society and History,* vol. 4 (1962), 395.
29. Ibid., 85–87.
30. Ruth A. Tucker, *From Jerusalem to Irian Jaya* (Grand Rapids: The Zondervan Corporation, 1993), 54.
31. Martin Luther, *On War Against the Turks*, trans. C. M. Jacobs and R. C. Schultz in *Luther's Works*, ed. by H.T. Lehmann (Philadelphia: Fortress Press, 1967), 170–77.
32. Watt. op. cit. 78.
33. Tucker, *From Jerusalem,* 276.
34. Ibid., 278–79.
35. William W. Stennett, *The Christian Missionary Confronts the Muslim* (a Master of Theology thesis, Southeastern Baptist Theological Seminary, April 1959), 35.
36. William Cantwell Smith, *On Understanding Islam* (The Hague: Mouton Publishers, 1981), 248–49.

37. *Nostra Aetate* quote from R. Marston Speight. *God Is One: The Way of Islam.* New York: Friendship Press, 1984, 101–102.

38. John L. Esposito, "Islamic Revivalism," in *The Muslim World Today,* Occasional Paper no. 3 (Washington, D.C.: American Institute for Islamic Affairs, 1985,) 1. Also see John J. Donohue and John L. Esposito, *Islam in Transition: Muslim Pespectives* (Oxford: Oxford University Press, 1982) for excellent articles by Muslim thinkers on politics, the modern state, social change, and economics.

39. Watt, *Muslim-Christian Encounters*, 126.

40. Ibid, 127.

41. Ibid.

42. Ibid., 128.

43. Kenneth Cragg, *Jesus and the Muslim* (London: George Allen and Unwin Ltd., 1985), 31.

44. Please see Abdullah Yusuf Ali, *The Meaning of The Holy Qur'an: New Edition with Revised Translation and Commentary* (4411 41st Street, Brentwood, Maryland 20722: Amana Corporation, 1989), Surah 4:171. Also see Surah 5:73 and Surah 5:116.

45. Zepp, *Muslim Primer,* 227.

46. Geoffrey Parrinder, *Jesus in the Qur'an* (London: Faber and Faber, 1965), 105–111.

47. W. C. Smith, "Is the Qur'an the Word of God?" in *Questions of Religious Truth* (New York: Charles Scribner's Sons, 1967), 49–50.

48. Please see Braswell, *Magic Carpet.* The chapter on "The Unveiling" (pp. 36–54) describes saints' tombs and folk religion.

49. Kelsay, *Islam and War,* 33–45.

50. Qur'an, 2:256.

51. Ibid., 3:85.

52. Ibid., 4:105.

BIBLIOGRAPHY

Abdalati, Hammudah. *Islam in Focus*. Indianapolis: American Trust Publications, 1975.

Ahmad, Mumtaz, ed. *State Politics and Islam*. Indianapolis, American Trust Publications, 1986.

Ali, Abdullah Yusuf. *The Meaning of The Holy Qur'an: New Edition with Revised Translation and Commentary*, Brentwood, Md.: Amana Corporation, 1989.

Ali, M. Amir. *How to Present Islam: A Rational Approach*. Chicago: The Institute of Islamic Information and Education, 1994.

Alim, K. A. "Plots Exposed! Muslim Leader Challenges Followers." *A. M. Journal*. (Chicago) 18 June 1983.

Al Nuri. The Islamic Center Quarterly. Washington, D.C., 1993.

Arfa, Hassan. *Five Shahs*. New York: William Morrow and Co., l965.

Bayrak, Sheikh Tosun. *The Most Beautiful Names*. Vermont: Threshold Books, l985.

Beckett, Charles A. *Responses to Muslim Resurgence from Christians in the United States between l979 and l993*. Master's thesis, Hartford Seminary, 1993.

Berger, Morroe. *The Arab World*. New York: Anchor Books, l964.

Boisard, Michael A. *Jihad: A Commitment to Universal Peace*. Indianapolis: American Trust Publications, l988.

Booth, Newell S. Jr. "Islam in America." in *Encyclopedia of the American Religious Experience*, edited by Charles H. Lippy and Peter W. Williams. New York: Charles Scribner's Sons, 1988.

Borchgrave, Arnaud de. "Interview with Assad." *Newsweek*, 16 January 1978.

Braswell, George W. Jr. *The Ulama in Four Socio-Cultural Contexts*. Master's thesis, The University of North Carolina at Chapel Hill, 1973.

————. *A Mosaic of Mullahs and Mosques: Religion and Politics in Iranian Shiah Islam*. Ph.D. diss., The University of North Carolina at Chapel Hill, 1975.

————. *To Ride a Magic Carpet*. Nashville: Broadman Press, 1977.

————. *Understanding Sectarian Groups in America*. Revised. Nashville: Broadman Press, l994.

————. *Understanding World Religions*. Rev. ed. Nashville: Broadman Press, l994.

Bucaille, Maurice. *The Bible, the Qur'an and Science*. Indianapolis: North American Trust Publication, 1979.

Butee Al, Mohammad Saeed. *Contemporary Issues in Islamic Law*. Damascus, Syria, 1991.

Chapra, Umer M. *Islam and Economic Development*. Islamabad: Islamic Research Institute Press, 1993.

Cragg, Kenneth. *The Call of the Minaret*. New York: Oxford University Press, l964.

————. *Muhammad and the Christian*. Maryknoll: Orbis Books, l984.

————. *Jesus and the Muslim*. London: George Allen and Unwin Ltd., l985.

Cragg, Kenneth, and R. Marston Speight. *The House of Islam*. Belmont: Wadsworth Publishing Company, 1988.

————, *Islam from Within*. Belmont: Wadsworth Publishing Co., l980.

Cummings, J. "Black Muslim Seeks to Change Movement." *New York Times*. March 19, l978.

Davis, Eric. "Ideology, Social Class and Islamic Radicalism," in *From Nationalism to Revolutionary Islam*, edited by Said Amir Arjomard. Albany: State University of New York Press, 1984.

Dembner, Alice. "Saudi Grant to Put Harvard at Fore of Islamic Studies." *Boston Globe*, 19 June l993.

Donaldson, Dwight M. *The Shi'ite Religion*. London: Luzon and Company, 1933.

Donohue, John J., and John L. Esposito. *Islam in Transition: Muslim Perspectives*. Oxford: Oxford University Press, 1982.

Donzel, E. Van. *Islamic Desk Reference*. New York: E. J. Brill, 1994.

Dostert, Pierre Etienne. ed. *Africa l994*, 29th ed. The World Today Series. Harpers Ferry: Stryker-Post Publications, 1994.

Faruqi, Isma'il R. *Islam*. Niles, Ill.: Argus Communications, l984.

Geertz, Clifford. "Religion as a Cultural System." In *Anthropological Approaches to the Study of Religion*, edited by Michael Banton. London: Tavistock Publications, l966.

————. *Islam Observed*. Chicago: The University of Chicago Press, l968.

Gibb, H. A. R. *Mohammedanism*. New York: The New American Library, l958.

Gray, Randall, and Dinah Hanlon. *Religions on File*. New York: The Diagram Group, l990.

Grunebaum, Gustave E. *Medieval Islam*. Chicago: University of Chicago Press, l961.

Eastern Europe and the Commonwealth of Independent States 1992. First ed. London: Europa Publications, 1992.

Ebrahim, Abul Fael Mohsin. *Abortion, Birth Control and Surrogate Parenting. An Islamic Perspective*. Indianapolis: American Trust Publications, 1989.

Eerdman's Handbook to the World's Religions. Grand Rapids: Wm. B. Eerdmans Publishing Co., 1982.

Emerson, Steven. *The American House of Saud*. New York: Franklin Watts, l985.

Esposito, John L. "Islamic Revivalism." *The Muslim World*. Occasional Paper No. 3, l985.

————, ed. *Voices of Resurgent Islam*. New York: Oxford University Press, 1993.

Haddad, Yvonne Y. "A Century of Islam in America." in *The Muslim World*. Occasional Paper No. 4, 1986.

Haddad, Yvonne Y., and Jane Smith. *Mission to America*. Gainesville: University Press of Florida, 1993.

Haley, A. *The Autobiography of Malcolm X*. New York: Grove Press, Inc., l965.

Hamidullah, Muhammad. *Introduction to Islam*. Paris: Centre Cultural Islamique, l969.

Haykal, Muhammad Husayn. *The Life of Muhammad*. Indianapolis: American Trust Publications, 1976.

Idris, Sheikh Jaafar. *Manar As-Sabeel*. Fairfax, Va.: Institute for Islamic and Arabic Sciences in America, 1993.

Iqbal, Afzel. *The Prophet's Diplomacy*. Cape Cod: Claude Stark and Co., l975.

Ishaq, Ibn. *Sirat Rasul Allah*. Translated by A. Guillaume. London: Oxford University Press, 1955.

Johnstone, Patrick. *Operation World*. Grand Rapids: Zondervan Publishing House, 1993.

Jones, David Pryce. "Assad the Terrible." *The New Republic*, 30 January 1984.

Kayas, al, Marwan Ibrahim. *Morals and Manners in Islam*. New Delhi: Qazi Publishers, 1986.

Kelsay, John. *Islam and War: A Study in Comparative Ethics, the Gulf War and Beyond*. Louisville: Westminster/John Knox Press, 1993.

Khan, Muhammad Muhsin. *The Translation of the Meanings of Sahih Al-Bukhari,* Arabic-English. Vols. 1–9. Beirut: Dar al Arabia (PO Box 6089), n.d.

Khomeini, Ayatollah Ruhollah. *Islamic Government*. New York: Manor Books, 1979.

Khouj, Albullah Muhammad. *The End of the Journey: An Islamic Perspective on Death and the Afterlife*. Washington, D.C.: The Islamic Center, 1988.

Kimball, Charles. *Striving Together: A Way Forward in Christian-Muslim Relations*. Maryknoll: Orbis Books, 1991.

Kritzeck, James. "Muslim-Christian Understandings in Medieval Times." in *Comparative Studies in Society and History*. Vol. 4, 1962.

Lawrence, Bruce B. *Defenders of God: The Fundamentalist Revolt Against the Modern Age*. San Francisco: Harper & Row Publishers, 1989.

Levy, Reuben. *The Social Structure of Islam*. Cambridge: At the University Press, 1962.

Lewis, Bernard. *The Arabs in History*. New York: Hutchinson University Library, 1966.

———. *Islam in History*. New York: The Library Press, 1973.

———. "The Roots of Muslim Rage." in *The Atlantic Monthly*, September 1990.

Lincoln, C. Eric. *The Black Muslims in America*. Grand Rapids: Eerdmans Publishing Co., 1994.

Luther, Martin. *On War Against the Turks*. Translated by C. M. Jacobs and R. C. Schultz. In *Luther's Works*, edited by H. T. Lehmann. Philadelphia, Pa.: Fortress Press, 1967.

Marsh, Clifton. *From Black Muslims to Muslims: The Transition from Separation to Islam*. Meteuschen: Scarecrow Press, Inc., 1984.

Marty, Martin E., and R. Scott Appleby. *The Glory and the Power: The Fundamentalist Challenge to the Modern World*. Boston: Beacon Press, 1992.

Mayerchak, Patrick M. *East Asia and the Western Pacific 1994,* 27th ed. in The World Today Series. Harpers Ferry: Stryker-Post Publications, 1994.

Melton, J. Gordon. *Religious Leaders of America*. Detroit: Gale Research Inc., 1991.

Mews, Stuart, ed. *Religion in Politics: A World Guide*. London: Longman Group, 1989.

Middle East and North Africa 1994. 40th ed. London: Europa Publications Limited, 1994.

Miller, Judith. "Disenchanted Generation Turns to Two Islamic Fundamentalists." *Foreign Affairs*, November-December, 1994.

Mohaddessin, Mohammad. *Islamic Fundamentalism*. Washington: Seven Locks Press, 1993.

Mohammad, Nazar, compiler. *Commandments by God in the Qur'an*. New York: The Message Publications, 1991.

Muhammad Speaks. (Chicago) 21 March 1975.

Nasr, Seyyed Hossein. *Ideals and Realities of Islam*. London: George Allen & Unwin Ltd., 1966.

———. ed. *Islamic Spirituality*. New York: Crossroad, 1987.

O'Leary, DeLacy. *Arabia Before Muhammad*. New York: Kegan Paul and Co., 1927.

Parrinder, Geoffrey. *Jesus in the Qur'an*. New York: Oxford University Press, 1977.

Parshall, Phil. *Inside the Community: Understanding Muslims Through Their Traditions*. Grand Rapids: Baker Books, 1994.

Qardaw Al, Yusuf. *The Lawful and the Prohibited in Islam* 2nd ed. Lahore: Islamic Publications Ltd., 1991.

Roberts, D. S. *Islam*. New York: Harper and Row, 1982.

Runciman, Steven. *A History of the Crusades*. 3 vols. London: Cambridge University Press, 1951.

Russell, Malcolm. *The Middle East and South Asia*, 28th ed. Harper's Ferry: Stryker-Post Publications, 1994.

Seifullah, A. A. "Human Revival Week Begins." *Bilalian News*, 9 March 1979.

Shah, Idris. *The Sufis*. Garden City: Doubleday and Co., 1971.

Sheppard, N. "Black Muslim Movement Divided in Dispute Over Doctrinal Changes." *New York Times*. 7 March 1978.

Siddiqi, Muhammad Iqbal. *Ninety-Nine Names of Allah*. Delhi, India: Adams Publishers and Distributors, 1990.

Smith, Steven T. *An Historical Account of the American Muslim Misson*. Master of Theology thesis, Southeastern Baptist Theological Seminary, 1984.

Smith, William Cantwell. *The Meaning and End of Religion*. New York: New American Library, 1964.

———. *Questions of Religious Truth*. New York: Charles Scribner's Sons, 1967.

———. *On Understanding Islam*. The Hague: Mouton Publishers, 1981.

Southern, R. W. *Western Views of Islam in the Middle Ages*. Cambridge: Harvard University Press, 1962.

Southwick, A. B. "Malcolm X: Charismatic Demagogue." *Christian Century*, 5 June 1963.

Sparrow, Gerald. *Hussein of Jordan*. London: George G. Harrop Co., 1960.

Stennett, William W. *The Christian Missionary Confronts the Muslim.* Master of Theology thesis, Southeastern Baptist Theological Seminary, 1959.

Swarup, Ram. *Understanding Islam through Hadis.* Delhi: Voice of India, 1983.

Tabataba'i, Muhammad Husayn. *Shi'ite Islam.* Albany: State University of New York Press, 1975.

Tucker, Ruth. *From Jerusalem to Irian Jaya.* Grand Rapids: The Zondervan Corporation, 1993.

Understanding Islam and Muslims, pamphlet of The Islamic Affairs Department of Embassy of Saudi Arabia, Washington, D.C., n.d.

Watt, W. Montgomery. *Muhammad at Mecca.* London: Oxford University Press, 1956.

———. *Muhammad at Medina.* Oxford: Clarendon Press, 1956.

———. *Muhammad, Prophet and Statesman.* London: Oxford University Press, 1961.

———. *Muslim-Christian Encounters.* London: Routledge, 1991.

Watt, W. Montgomery, and John Glubb. *The Life and Times of Muhammad.* New York: Stein and Day, 1970.

Waugh, Earle. "The Popular Muhammad Models in the Interpretation of an Islamic Paradigm." *Approaches to Islam in Religious Studies,* edited by Richard C. Martin. Tucson: The University of Arizona Press, 1985.

Webster's New International Dictionary. Unabridged. Springfield: Merriam-Webster, Inc., 1986.

Williams, John Alden, ed. *Islam.* New York: George Braziller, 1962.

Wills, David K. "The Practice of Islam." *The Christian Science Monitor,* November 10, 1984.

Zepp, Ira G. *A Muslim Primer.* Westminster: Wakefield Editions, 1992.

INDEX

A

A.M. Journal   231, 234
Abbasid Caliph   29, 32, 293
Abbasid empire   298
Abbasids   23, 29
Abdalati, Hammudah   106
abortion   136, 305
Abraham   14–15, 43, 49, 54,
   69, 80, 168, 217, 296, 303
Abu Bakr   13, 15, 18, 23, 90
Abu'l-a la Mawdudi   39
Adam   49, 54
Adhan   60
adornment   101–102
al-Afghani   34
Afghanistan   200
Africa   167, 207
Aga Khan   95
Ahmaddiya sect   95
Ahmadis   199
Ahmadiyya   306
Ahmadiyya Community of
   North America   216
AIDS   139
Akbar   34
Alawites   182, 306
Albania   205
alcohol   103
Algeria   164, 190
Algerian   276
Ali   13, 15, 23, 25, 27–28,
   75, 90, 118, 286
Ali, Ameer   264
Allah   45, 60
   beautiful names   47
al-Lat   10, 45
Alma-Ata Declaration   201
alms   245
Amal   180
American Druze Society   219
American Muslim
   Council   214
American Muslim
   Mission   99, 228, 231,
   234, 243
American Orthodoxy   219
animals   118
Ansar   15
Ansaru Allah   217
apostasy   73, 254, 262, 302
al-Aqsa mosque   79
Aquinas, Thomas   259
Arab   69, 177, 189

Arab culture   102
Arabian peninsula   297
Arafat, Yasser   6, 41, 180,
   183–184, 306
Argentina   167
Armenian Patriarch   261
Armenians   253
*As the Light Shineth from the
   East*   232
Ash'arites   258
al-Ashar University   95
al-Ashari   96
Asia   165, 207
al-Assad, Hafiz   6, 168, 182
Ataturk, Kemal   36, 152,
   174, 182, 262, 270
Averroes   29
ayatollah   142, 208
Azerbaijan   201–202
al-Azhar   33, 272
al-Azhur University   186

B

Ba'ath party   176
Babul   34
Baghdad   29, 31, 176, 298
Baha'i religion   303
Bangladesh   165
al-Banna   39, 129–130, 187
Baptist-Muslim dialogue   272
bargaining   124
Bashkortostan   201
Begin, President of Israel   187
belief *(iman)*   60
Berber   189
Bhutto   199
Bible   249, 268, 278, 296
Bilalian Muslims   230
Bilalian News   230
Bill of Rights   246, 287
birth control and
   contraception   134
black church   219
blood feud   104
Brazil   167
brotherhood of Islam   113
Brunei Darussalam   198
Bukara   298
Bukhara   33
al-Bukhari   33
al Buruni   31
business   121
   matters   305

transactions   124
Byzantine empire   297

C

Cairo   29, 32–33, 186, 265,
   272, 298
calendar   77, 246
caliph   23, 129
Caliph Mu'awiya's army   254
caliphate   48, 128, 182, 252
Camp David Peace
   Accords   187
Canada   167
Carey, William   263
Carlyle, Thomas   263
Carter, Jimmy, President of the
   United States   187
Central Asia   276
charms and amulets   117
Chavis, Benjamin   239
Chicago   221
Christianity   168, 185, 247–
   250, 295
Christianity and Islam
   Christianity's priority with
      Islam   277
   encounters of change, con-
      version,
      contextualization   288
   government and religious
      freedom   286
Christians   55, 114, 191,
   248, 251–254, 256, 258–
   259, 263, 300, 303
Chrysostom, John   35
church and state   129
Chuvashia   201
Civil Rights   155
civil war   180
cleanliness   101–102
clothing   101–102
commerce   121
   and trade   133
Committee to Remove All Images of the Divine
   (CRAID)   231
conduct of business   101
confession   59, 245
conscience   157
Constantinople   32, 35, 261
Constitution of Medina   15,
   125
contract   124

in business   123
Coptic Christians   185–186
Copts   253
Cordova   298
Council of Imams   230, 233
Council of the Masajid   213
Cragg, Kenneth   48, 66, 125,
   252, 268, 273–274
cross   296
crucifixion of Jesus (*see*
   Jesus)   250, 274, 282, 297
Crusades   5, 31–32, 256,
   298

D

Damascus   25–26, 91, 182,
   248, 254, 256, 298
Dante   258
dar al-Harb   71, 129, 143,
   246, 252
dar al-Islam   129, 246
Dark Ages   258, 298
David, king of Israel   168
decision making   104
Delhi   34, 298
destiny   57
Detroit   221
devotees of Islam   174
dhimmis   32, 252
diet   101–102
distance and touching   116
divorce   101, 106, 304
Do'a   65
docetism   297
Dome of the Rock   14, 26, 40,
   171, 303
Drew, Noble   214–215
Dubois. W. E. B.   220
Dutch East India
   Company   195

E

East India Company   263
Eastern Orthodox
   Christianity   261
economic life   101, 121
economic rights   155
Egypt   32, 39, 41, 130, 163,
   178, 185–187, 264, 287
empire of Mali   38
England   206
entertainment   103
equality   158
Ethiopia   38

etiquette   305
Europe   167, 204, 207, 272,
   294
euthanasia   141

F

face   104, 124
Fadlallah, Sheikh Muhammed
   Hussein   162
Fahd, King of Saudi Arabia   6,
   170, 306
family   101
Far East   194
Fard, W. D.   220, 286
Farrakhan, Louis   6, 99, 208–
   209, 219–220, 227–229,
   234–241, 306, 308
fasting   245
al-Fatah   180
Fatima   17, 75, 117–118
Fatimid dynasty   95, 186
fatwa   302, 304
Fedayeen-i-Islam   174
Federation of Islamic
   Associations   213
Fez, Morocco   298
The Final Call   237
folk Islam   74, 76
   and Christianity   285
four waves of
   immigration   212
France   174, 206
Francis of Assisi   259, 277
freedom   157
   of religion   179
Fruit of Islam   231, 240
Fulani   192
Fulani tribes   38

G

Gabriel, the angel   12, 14, 43,
   48, 66, 296
Gadhafi, Mu'ammar   188
Gadhafi, President of
   Libya   185, 257
Gairdner, W. H. Temple   264
gambling   103
Gandhi   198
Garvey, Marcus   220
Geertz, Clifford   3
Gengis Khan   260
Germany   206
ghaiba   95
al-Ghazali   135, 137, 255

Gibb, Sir Hamilton   264
Goldziher, Ignaz   264
Gospel   50, 249, 278
Gospel of Barnabas   265
Great Mosque of
   Damascus   26
Great Satan   40, 160, 271,
   299
Greek Orthodox Patriarch   261
Greeks   253

H

Hadith   11, 33, 56, 60, 74,
   81–84, 101, 120
al-Assad, Hafiz   182
Hajj   70, 80, 127
al-Hakim   32, 219
al-Hallaj   97
Hamaas Abdul Khaalis   218
Hamas   2, 40, 163, 178, 292,
   299
Hanafi   30, 218
   law school   150
Hanbali   30, 99
Hanbalite   84
harem   152
Harun al-Rashid   30
Hasan Banna   163
Hasan II, King   189
Hasan, King of Morocco   168,
   185
Hasan, son of Ali   28, 75, 91,
   118, 286
Hausa   191
Hausa kingdoms   38
heaven   56
Hegira   14, 77, 129
hell   56–57
heresy   259, 267
Herzl, Theodore   177, 183
Hezbollah   5, 40, 162–163,
   180, 292, 299, 302
Holy Sepulchre in
   Jerusalem   171, 256
holy war   146
homosexuality   138, 304
honor   104, 157
Hui   201
human rights   155–156
Husain, Ahmad   187
husband-wife
   relationship   105
Husein drama   93
Husein, Iman   93

Husein, son of Ali   27–28, 75, 91, 118, 286
Hussein, King of Jordan   2, 6, 168, 172
Hussein, M. Kamel   274
Hussein, Saddam, President of Iraq   6, 162, 168, 176–177, 208, 306

I

Ibn Khaldun   33, 122
Ibn Rushd   29
Ibn-Hazm   255
Ibo   191
Id al-Fitr   79
Id Fetr   67
idolatry   252, 257
ijma   82–83, 88
imamate   90–91
Immigrant Muslims   210
imprisonment   157
India   34, 39, 165, 194, 198, 216, 263
Indonesia   37, 165, 195, 207, 268, 286
intifada   178
Iran   39–40, 125, 163, 168, 173, 175, 202, 270, 272, 287, 294, 306
Iranian Shi'ite Muslims   276
Iraq   41, 168, 175, 270
Isa Muhammad   217
Isfahan   298
Ishmael   69, 80
Islam   43, 57, 120, 122, 165, 167–168, 185, 291, 293, 307
  among African-Americans   210
  revitalization and revival of   269
  ten major patterns of   293
al-islam   143
Islamic
  centers   209
  fundamentalism   158–160, 162–164
  state   252
Islamic Center of Raleigh   242
Islamic Center of Washington   242
Islamic Party of North America   218

Islamic Republic of Iran   85, 88, 163, 175, 270–271, 286, 293
Islamic Salvation Front   191
Islamic Society of North America   213
Isma'ilis   95
Israel   39, 41, 172, 177, 187, 269, 293, 299, 303
  issues   254
Istanbul   35, 261

J

Ja'fari   30
Jackson, Jesse   209, 239
Jacobites   255
al-Jahiliyya   71
Jenghiz Khan   33
Jerusalem   5, 8, 14–15, 23, 79, 169, 171, 177, 184, 207, 256, 298, 303
Jesus   14, 43, 49, 54, 168, 247, 249, 251, 255, 265, 278, 296
  a prophet among prophets   284
  and suffering   274
  as messiah   55
  his holiness and purity   279
  miracles of   279
  resurrection of   283
  similarities and differences in the Qur'an and the Bible   278
  virgin birth   278
Jewish tribes   125, 248
Jews   15, 55, 114, 125, 177, 249, 251–252, 300, 303, 307
al-Jihad   188
jihad   4–5, 23, 40, 71–72, 74, 127, 129, 133, 142–144, 164, 168, 177, 187, 207, 245, 252, 257, 293, 299, 304
Jinn   48
John of Damascus   27, 254
Jones, E. Stanley   267
Jordan   41, 171
Judaism   168, 295
judgment: heaven and hell   53

K

Ka'ba   8, 10, 14, 18, 68
Kairanawi, Maulana Rahmat Allah   263
Kashmir   199
Kazakhstan   201–202
Kelsay, John   143, 246, 286
Kenya   38
Kerbala   28, 76, 91, 93–94
Khadija   12–13, 247
khalifa   88
Khomeini, Ayatollah of Iran   2, 5–6, 40, 56, 74, 85, 88, 95, 130, 159, 163, 173–175, 270–271, 287, 293, 306
King, Martin Luther Jr.   225, 232
Kraemer, Hendrik   267
Kufa, Iraq   91, 168
Kurds   183
Kyrgyzstan   201, 203

L

Lebanon   162, 168, 179, 268, 286, 300
Libya   185, 188
Lull, Raymond   259, 265, 277
Luther, Martin   259, 261

M

al-Ma'mun   30–31
mahr   148, 150
Malaysia   194–196, 276
Malcolm X   70, 208, 219–220, 222, 226, 241, 306–307
Maliki   30
Malikite   84
Mamluk Turks   32–33
al-Manat   10, 45, 148
Manichaeans   258
manners   101
al-Mansur   30
Marco Polo   37
Marje' Taqlid   95
Maronites   253
marriage   101, 105
Martel, Charles   26, 256
Martyn, Henry   263
martyr   92

martyrdom 56, 74
Mary, mother of Jesus 249, 251
mass media 299, 308
Massignon, Louis 265
Mecca 5, 7–8, 14, 17–18, 44, 53, 63, 68–69, 76–77, 79–80, 114, 125, 168, 207, 213, 221, 248, 303, 306, 308
Medina 5, 7–8, 14, 16–17, 44, 53, 62, 68–69, 77, 114, 125, 168–169, 207, 248, 292, 301, 303, 306, 308
Medina, Constitution of 5
Mehmet II 261
Melchites 255
Meshed 37, 94
Middle East 167–168, 207, 235
millet 253
millets 253
Million Man March 239–241
Mirza Ghulam Ahmad 199, 216
Monophysite 253
Monophysite Copts 261
monophysitism 297
morals 101
Morocco 41, 185, 189
Moses 14, 43, 49, 54, 168, 278, 296
mosque (Masjid) 85
mosques 63, 85, 209, 242
Mozambique 38
Mu'awiya 25, 91
Mu'tazilites 258
Mubarak, Muhammad Hosni, President of Egypt 6, 168, 188
Mughal Empire 34
Mughals 34
Muhajirun 15, 114
Muhammad Abdul 163
Muhammad Ahmed ibn Abd'ullah 217
Muhammad Ali Jinnah 198
Muhammad Speaks 224, 226–228, 230
Muhammad, Elijah 99, 209, 219–222, 227, 232, 237, 306–307
Muhammad, prophet of Islam 8, 10–11, 15–16, 18–19, 27, 43, 48–49, 54, 60, 62, 66, 68, 71, 75, 77–78, 83–84, 90, 110–111,

114, 117–118, 122, 125, 134, 137, 168, 248, 257, 259, 286, 292, 295–297, 301
Muhammad, Wallace 6, 99, 209, 219–220, 228–229, 232, 234–236, 243, 306–308
Muharram 28, 75, 78, 91
Muir, Sir William 263
Mujahadin-i-Islam 174
Mujahidin 2
Muslim 191, 301
  brothers 188
  chaplain 209, 275
  missionaries 270
  oil-rich nations 270
  organizations 213
  state 128
  student association 213
The Muslim World 266
Muslim Brotherhood 162–163, 182, 189, 193, 292, 299
Muslim Mosque, Inc 225
Muslim Student Associations 243
Muslim World League 170, 213
Muslim-Christian relationships 274
Muslims
  in England 276
mut'a 150
Mutazilites 96

names 117
Napoleon 36, 185–186
Nasr 82
Nasser 187
Nation of Islam 1, 99, 209, 218, 220–221, 223–224, 228, 230, 235, 237, 241, 306–307
National Pact 179
Nejaf 94
Nestorian patriarch 258
Nestorians 255
New Testament 255
Nicholas of Cusa 260
Nigeria 191
Noah 49, 54
North Africa 184–185
North America 207

Nubian Islamic Hebrews 217

oil 160, 175, 269, 293
  embargo 40
Organization of Islamic Conference 170
Orthodox Islam in America 241
orthodoxy 307
Ottoman Empire 32, 35–36, 90, 125, 127, 152, 182, 186, 253, 262, 293, 298
Ottoman Turks 33, 260

Pahlavi kings 174
Pakistan 136, 152, 161, 165, 194, 199, 269, 271, 300
Palestine 5, 171, 262, 298, 303
Palestine Liberation Organization 41, 172, 178, 180, 183, 185, 190, 293
Palestinian refugees 172
Palestinians 164, 169, 171, 178
Panama 167
pan-Arabism 187
paradise 47, 55–56, 74
parents and the elderly 118
Parshall, Phil 66, 68, 83
people of the Book 50, 114, 252, 278
People's Republic of China 201
Persia 25, 36
Persian empire 297
Persian Gulf War 171, 176, 178
personal decision making 300
personal relations 104
Peter the Venerable 258
Pfander, Carl Gottlieb 263
Philippines 197
Pilgrimage *(Hajj)* 68, 245
political life 101, 125
Political Rights 155
poll tax (jizya) 114
polygamy 109, 112, 150, 153, 304
Pope Urban II 256
practice *(din)* 60

prayer   60, 245
Prayer and Al-Islam   232
predestination   57
private life   157
property   156
Prophet's mosque in
   Medina   171
Protestant Reformers   261
Psalms   50
public appearance   104
purity   101–102

Q

Qiyas   84
Qum   37, 85, 94
Qur'an   12, 16, 47–50, 52–
   53, 56, 60, 66, 71, 74, 81–
   82, 101, 120, 138, 145,
   248, 258, 268, 292, 302
Qur'anic Islam and
   Christianity   277
Quraysh   44

R

Rafsanjani, President of Iran   6
raids   125
Ramadan   15, 67, 79, 231,
   276
Rashad Khalifa   218
al-Rashid   152
al-Razi   33
religious endowments   88
religious freedom   171, 300
religious liberty   5, 300
revenge   104
Roman Catholic Church   268
Rowzehs   93
rulers   158
Rumi   98
Rushdie, Salman   74, 161,
   287
Russia   204
   Commonwealth of Indepen-
      dent States   201

S

Sabians   114
Sadat   187
Sadat, Anwar   2, 130, 178,
   187
Safavid dynasty   32, 36
Saint Sophia Cathedral   35

Saladin   256
salam alekum   115
Samarkand   33, 298
Satanic Verses   45, 74, 161,
   271, 287
Saudi Arabia   40–41, 69, 98,
   125, 152, 163, 168, 170,
   202, 213, 242–243, 270,
   272, 276, 287, 294, 300,
   303, 308
SAVAK   174
sawm   66
Sayid Qutb   39, 187
Schacht, Joseph   264
Senegal   38
sex   111
Shafi'i   30
Shafite   84
Shah   40, 85, 88, 173, 293
Shah Abbas   36
shahada   59
Shari'a   23, 30, 81–82, 90,
   120, 124, 128, 252, 254,
   292, 302, 305
sheikh   98, 302
Shi'ite imams, the twelve   37
Shi'ite Muslim   274
Shi'ites   25, 27, 37, 41, 75–
   76, 78, 90–91, 93–94, 173,
   179, 208, 292, 305
shirk   45
shrines   87, 285
Simpson, O. J.   241
Sister Clara Muhammad
   Elementary   231
slavery   113, 119–120, 151,
   219
   slave trade   307
Smith, William Cantwell   3,
   267
social rights   155
Sofrehs   93
South Asia   194
South of the Sahara   38
Southern Baptist
   Convention   267
   leaders   272
Soviet Union   40
Spain   256
sports   103
state   158
status   104
status of women   106
stereotypes   1, 208, 308
Sub-Sahara Africa   184–185
Sudan   38, 162, 192, 303
Sufi   39

Sufism   32–33, 75, 97–98
suicide   141, 305
Suleyman the Magnificent   35
Sunnah   81, 120, 292, 302
Sunni   25, 41, 88, 92, 130,
   179, 292, 305
surahs   53
Syria   32, 41, 181
Syriac Christians   253
   (Jacobites)   254

T

Taj Mahal   35
Tajikistan   201, 203
Tanzania   38
Tartarstan   201
Tashkent   33
tawhid   45
taziyahs   92
Temple Mount   171
terrorists   5, 299
*The Thousand and One
   Nights*   31
Timur   33–34
Torah   50, 249, 278
trade   121
Trinity   251, 254
Tunisia   25, 190
Turabi   162
al-Turabi   162
Turkey   36, 182, 294
Turkish tribes   260
Turkmenistan   201, 203
twelfth imam   91, 95
twentieth-century islam   39
twenty questions   4, 294
tyranny   157

U

U. S. Congress   243
U. S. Constitution   246, 287
U. S. Senate   209, 275
Uganda   38
ulama   84, 136, 271, 302
Umar   23, 25, 90, 253
Umayyad Caliphate   25, 256
Umayyad dynasty   254
Umayyads   23, 29, 34
umma   16, 18, 25, 113–114,
   127–128, 159, 252, 293
United States   40, 160–161,
   167, 175, 188, 200, 209,
   212–213, 217, 231, 271–

272, 276, 287, 294, 299, 307

United Submitters International   218

University of Al Azhar in Cairo   31

University of Islam   231

USSR   271, 294

usury   17, 123

Uthman   23, 25, 90

Uygurs   201

Uzbekistan   201, 204

al-Uzza   10, 44–45, 148

V

Vatican Council in 1964   268

veil   108, 151–152

virtues and vices   120

W

al-Wahhab   169

Wahhabis   306

Wahhabism   98

war   146
  and peace   142

Webb, Alexander Russell (Muhammad)   266

West   160–161

West Bank   171, 178

White Revolution   174, 270

wife
  duties of   156
  plurality of   17
  rights of   155

women   148

World Community of Islam in the West   230

World Council of Churches   267

World Muslim News   231

World Parliament of Religions   266

World War II   160

Y

Yacub   237

Yacub's History   221, 224

Yazid   254

Yoruba   191

Yugoslavia   205

Z

zakat   65–66, 127

Zepp, Ira   108

Zeroual, Brig. Gen.   191

Zionism   164, 293

Zionist   169, 177, 183

Zoroastrians   114

Zwemer Institute of Muslim Studies   266

Zwemer, Samuel   265, 277